To Rob,

My very best regards

Art Buchwald

2/27/87

Cognitive Therapy with Couples and Groups

Cognitive Therapy with Couples and Groups

Edited by
Arthur Freeman
Center for Cognitive Therapy
Philadelphia, Pennsylvania

Plenum Press • *New York and London*

Library of Congress Cataloging in Publication Data

Main entry under title:

Cognitive therapy with couples and groups.

Includes bibliographical references and index.
1. Cognitive therapy. 2. Marital psychotherapy. 3. Group psychotherapy. I. Freeman, Arthur M. [DNLM: 1. Behavior therapy. 2. Cognition. 3. Psychotherapy, Group. WM 425 C6765]
RC489.C63C65 1983   616.89′15   83-13210
ISBN 0-306-41149-0

© 1983 Plenum Press, New York
A Division of Plenum Publishing Corporation
233 Spring Street, New York, N.Y. 10013

Printed in the United States of America

To
Abe Freeman (1907–1951)
and to my sons,
Andrew, Russell, and Aaron,
with love

Contributors

JANIS LIEFF ABRAHMS, Department of Psychology, Yale University, New Haven, Connecticut

AARON T. BECK, Department of Psychiatry, School of Medicine, University of Pennsylvania, Philadelphia, Pennsylvania

RICHARD C. BEDROSIAN, Massachusetts Center for Cognitive Therapy, Westborough, Massachusetts

DAVID D. BURNS, Department of Psychiatry, School of Medicine, University of Pennsylvania, Philadelphia, Pennsylvania

ANNA ROSE CHILDRESS, Department of Psychiatry, School of Medicine, University of Pennsylvania, Philadelphia, Pennsylvania

NORMAN EPSTEIN, Center for Cognitive Therapy, 133 South 36th Street, University of Pennsylvania, Philadelphia, Pennsylvania

MARK D. EVANS, Department of Psychology, University of Minnesota, Minneapolis, Minnesota and Department of Psychiatry, St. Paul–Ramsey Medical Center, St. Paul, Minnesota

ARTHUR FREEMAN, Center for Cognitive Therapy, 133 South 36th Street, University of Pennsylvania, Philadelphia, Pennsylvania

MEYER D. GLANTZ, National Institute on Drug Abuse, Division of Clinical Research, 5600 Fishers Lane, Rockville, Maryland

VINCENT B. GREENWOOD, Center for Cognitive-Behavioral Therapy, 5225 Connecticut Avenue, N.W., Washington, D.C.

STEVEN D. HOLLON, Department of Psychology, University of Minnesota, Minneapolis, Minnesota and Department of Psychiatry, St. Paul–Ramsey Medical Center, St. Paul, Minnesota

Susan Jasin, California School of Professional Psychology, 3974 Sorrento Valley Boulevard, San Diego, California

William McCourt, Southwood Hospital, Norfolk, Massachusetts

Stirling Moorey, The Maudsley Hospital, Denmark Hill, London SE5, England

Michael W. O'Hara, Department of Psychology, University of Iowa, Iowa City, Iowa

Laura Primakoff, Center for Cognitive Therapy, Department of Psychiatry, 133 South 36th Street, University of Pennsylvania, Philadelphia, Pennsylvania

Lynn P. Rehm, Department of Psychology, University of Houston, Houston, Texas

Susan R. Walen, Department of Psychology, Towson State University, Towson, Maryland

Richard L. Wessler, Department of Psychology, Pace University, Pleasantville, New York

Janet L. Wolfe, Institute for Rational Living, 45 East 65th Street, New York, New York

Foreword

It is with great pride and satisfaction that I welcome the publication of *Cognitive Therapy with Couples and Groups.*

For several years, Arthur Freeman, Director of Clinical Services at the Center for Cognitive Therapy, has been a leader in attempting to extend a cognitive approach to new problems and new populations and to expand the approaches for treating the depressed outpatients for whom this approach was first developed. Dr. Freeman brought to the Center the full range and depth of a diverse clinical background which had and continues to broaden and enrich his work both as a therapist and as a teacher. I believe he has applied these dimensions of his experience fully in developing and editing this volume.

The chapters in this book clearly reflect those clinical problems that have attracted the keenest interest on the part of practicing cognitive therapist, which are encountered so frequently in the course of treating depression. The utilization of cognitive therapy with couples, families, groups, and in training is a clear example of this process, an intriguing topic in its own right. Conversely, coping with special clinical phenomena such as loneliness is a familiar problem to therapists of depressed patients. Laura Primakoff demonstrates her creativity and experience in her treatment of this subject. Similarly, the chapters on alcoholism and agoraphobia are timely elaborations of the original cognitive model for the individual treatment of depression. Vincent Greenwood's chapter on the young adult chronic patient will, I believe, be recognized as an innovative contribution to an area of particular clinical difficulty.

Another notable aspect of this volume is the interweaving of elements from different cognitive therapy traditions. The chapter by Michael O'Hara and Lynn Rehm extends Rehm's self-control model for the treatment of depression to a group format. The lucid chapters by Richard Wessler and Susan Walen and Janet Wolfe present cognitive approaches from the framework of the rational-emotive therapists.

Other contributors, trained primarily at the Philadelphia Center or by former staff of the Center, show the influence of cognitive therapy developed at the University of Pennsylvania. Janice Abrahms and Norman Epstein offer two cognitively based views of theory and strategies of working with distressed couples; Richard Bedrosian has integrated his family therapy training and experience into an understanding of cognitive therapy utilized within a family system. Steven Hollon, an early co-worker of mine, offers a basic introduction to cognitive therapy of depression utilizing the group format. His co-author, Mark Evans, trained by Hollon, represents the next generation of cognitive therapists.

Given his long experience in training and supervision, Dr. Freeman closes his book appropriately with two chapters on cognitive approaches to training. Not coincidentally, both are co-authored by David Burns who has done much to enliven and diversify the time-honored procedures of individual supervision.

Cognitive Therapy with Couples and Groups should reward the clinician with a stimulating view of a recent development in cognitive therapy—its application to groups. I hope ths book will, at the same time, whet the appetite for further exploration and experimentation in these areas.

AARON T. BECK

Department of Psychiatry
School of Medicine
University of Pennsylvania
Philadelphia, Pennsylvania

Preface

For virtually every model of individual psychotherapy that has been developed a group model also has been developed, utilizing the same basic theoretical format but applying it to dyads or larger groups. The rationale for utilization of groups in therapy is based upon a broad range of theory, philosophy, economics, and practicality. Given the efficacy of the cognitive-behavioral model, it is not surprising that cognitive therapy has been applied and utilized in a broad range of group therapeutic treatments. The purpose of this book is to offer clinicians theoretical, conceptual, and practical models for the application of the cognitive psychotherapy in a group format. The contributors are all experienced clinicians who represent variations of the cognitive therapy model from Beck's cognitive therapy to Ellis's rational-emotive therapy. What we all have in common is the idea that behavior, emotion, and cognition are related and that by modifying beliefs, attitudes, ideas, and images, we can alter affect and behavior.

The present volume emerged as the natural consequence of a number of colleagues sharing with me ideas relative to their ongoing group work. As we discussed group work, it became clear that cognitive therapy was being applied in a number of situations far beyond treating depression. We all felt that it would be helpful to develop a vehicle to share with other clinicians the ideas, conceptualizations, and treatment strategies that had been developed. Over the last year and a half I have had the opportunity to meet cognitive therapists at a number of international conferences and meetings. They were applying cognition therapy with groups and were interested in sharing their therapeutic experience with others. The book therefore has grown markedly, both in size and quality, from its original conception. What follows is not the last word on group treatment. Even as the final manuscript was being typed, I had become aware of clinicians working with groups whose ideas and practice would have fit well within the context of the present volume. The work of these clinical researchers may be reported in a later volume.

It is traditional and customary for authors to thank all of those who have contributed to the life and growth of a book. Being a traditionalist by nature, I would like to thank all of the contributors without whom an edited volume could not exist. All are colleagues, some personal friends. All have earned, by their work, my highest regard. Emmanual F. Hammer, an early teacher and colleague, first introduced me to the theory and practice of group psychotherapy. Although our theoretical paths have diverged, Manny has taught me more about being a good therapist than anyone else. Aaron T. Beck has been my major teacher in cognitive therapy. Through my contacts and work with him, I have grown immeasurably. His high standards and ideals have been an inspiration. Albert Ellis, an early teacher and therapist, introduced me to cognitive therapy as a problem-solving approach to life issues.

Special thanks go to Tina Inforzato who has taken my verbal ramblings and converted them to orderly typescript. Without her, this book would not exist.

Dr. Karen M. Simon shares my life and my work. She is an enthusiastic supporter, gentle critic, and willing helper in moving this and other projects from idea to completion. Finally, I want to thank my father, Abe Freeman. Although he has been dead for many years, he introduced me to books and encouraged me to read and to get the college education that he never had. I had promised myself that if I ever wrote or edited a book, I would dedicate it to his memory.

ARTHUR FREEMAN

Contents

Cognitive Therapy
An Overview

Arthur Freeman

In the past several years, cognitive therapy has emerged as one of the more powerful models of psychotherapy (Smith, 1982). There are two interactive reasons for its emergence and popularity. First, cognitive therapy has been demonstrated to be an efficacious model of treatment. Second, a number of practitioners, impressed by the available outcome studies, have learned more about cognitive therapy and have been impressed by the results in their own practice.

Cognitive therapy generally has come to mean the work of Aaron T. Beck (1976), but there are several cognitive therapies, including Albert Ellis's (1962, 1973, 1977) rational-emotive therapy, Arnold Lazarus's (1976, 1981) multimodal therapy, Donald Meichenbaum's (1977) cognitive-behavior modification, and Maxie Maultsby's (1975) rational behavior therapy. The issue of cognition as a central focus of psychotherapy has also been proposed by psychoanalysts (Arieti, 1980; Bieber, 1981; Crowley, in press; Frankl, in press). In discussing cognitive therapy in this overview, I will offer a generic cognitive therapy under which all of the models proposed in this text can be subsumed.

History

The historical roots of cognitive-behavior therapy are mixed. Kelley and Dowd (1980) see cognitive therapy as growing out of the behavior modification model, with the work of Bandura (1977a, 1977b) being an important milestone. Beck and Ellis, however, credit their early training

Arthur Freeman • Center for Cognitive Therapy, 133 South 36th Street, University of Pennsylvania, Philadelphia, Pennsylvania 19104.

in Adlerian and Horneyan models as central to their formation of a cognitive model of psychotherapy.

Rather than becoming embroiled in the argument of the origin of cognitive-behavior therapy (a much more psychoanalytic focus), it may be more appropriate to describe where we are, which offers a mix of the behavioral and dynamic models. We borrow from our behavioral colleagues the scientific method, a focus on behavioral change, and a variety of behavioral techniques and strategies (i.e., graded task assignments, scheduling, behavior rehearsal, and role playing). From our dynamically-oriented colleagues we have taken the notion of the importance of understanding the internal dialogue and process. Although avoiding the pitfalls of accepting the construct of the unconscious, the cognitive therapist, nevertheless, works to make the unspoken spoken and to help patients redirect their thinking, attitudes, and behavior.

DEFINITION OF COGNITIVE THERAPY

Cognitive therapy is a relatively short-term form of psychotherapy which is active, directive, and in which the therapist and patient work collaboratively. The goal of therapy is to help patients uncover their dysfunctional and irrational thinking, reality test their thinking and behavior, and build more adaptive and functional techniques for responding both inter- and intrapersonally. Specifically, cognitive therapists work directly with their patients proposing hypotheses, strategies for testing them, and opinions. With the severely depressed individual, the therapist's activity level must be high enough to supply the initial energy to complete the therapy work. He would not then rely on restatement but rather on restructuring, on interaction rather than interpretation, on direction rather than nondirection, and on collaboration rather than confrontation.

Cognitive therapy is a coping model of psychotherapy as opposed to a mastery model. The goal of cognitive therapy is not to "cure" but rather to help the patient to develop better coping strategies to deal with his or her life and work. By helping the patient uncover his or her dysfunctional and irrational belief systems, the cognitive therapist sets the model for patients to continue this process on their own.

THE MYTH OF SIMPLICITY

One of the myths about cognitive therapy is its total and absolute simplicity. For many professionals initially seeing the cognitive model demonstrated by major practitioners or by their students (many of the authors represented in this volume), their first reaction is, "Oh, it's easy. All I have to do is tell them what they are doing wrong," or "I just have to get them to say more positive things." Although that may be more reflective of the works of Norman Vincent Peale (1978), Dale Carnegie (1982), and Fulton J. Sheen (1978), it is not what cognitive therapy is. Cognitive therapy is not a collection of techniques, gimmicks, or strategies to fool the patient. It is not a system whereby the therapist tries to outargue, outreason, or outsmart the patient. Cognitive therapy is not a superficial "Band-Aid" model of psychotherapy. It cannot be learned in a single hour or a single week, but takes one to two years of intensive training, which has been found demonstrated both at the Institute for Rational Living in New York and at the Center for Cognitive Therapy in Philadelphia. These institutions have shown that the most effective training model is one including both *didactic presentation* and *demonstration* of competence in supervised psychotherapy on an inhouse basis. Cognitive therapy is no simpler to learn or practice than any other model of therapy. It would be astounding for someone to observe *in vivo* or videotaped psychoanalytic sessions in which the psychoanalyst said virtually nothing and the patient free associated. The budding therapist seeing this could say, "Yes, I could do that; I could sit there and say 'ah-huh,'" or to observe classical Rogerian therapy where the "ah-huh" is added to a restatement of the patient's statement. Cognitive therapy is not as simple as ABC, that is, simply helping the patient to identify his or her irrational or dysfunctional belief systems. The danger in utilizing the apparent ease of cognitive therapy as a reason for practicing it can cause a number of difficulties. With the patient for whom ABC is as simple as ABC then no problem exists at that moment. However, the problems the majority of patients present are not that simple, but rather require the therapist to develop a conceptualization of the case within a cognitive frame and then decide which therapeutic strategies best can be utilized to achieve the maximum therapeutic effect.

All humans appear to have a capacity to distort reality in a number of significant ways. If the distortion is severe enough, the individual may lose touch with reality and be labeled psychotic. However, the neurotic distorts reality in particular significant and dysfunctional ways. Beck (1976; Beck, Rush, Shaw, & Emery, 1979) and Burns (1980a,b) have classified particular types of distortions that are seen more commonly. These distortions are fueled by the basic life schemata or underlying assumptions (similar to Ellis's rational and irrational beliefs). These irrational belief systems or rules for living become a substrate, a wellspring from which the basic cognitive distortions emerge. These schemata can be established early in childhood. When an external event stimulates a particular schema, it generates specific distortions or more general styles of distortion. Examples of these distortions include:

All-or-nothing thinking.[1] This refers to the tendency to evaluate your performance or personal qualities in extremist, black-and-white categories. For example, a prominent politician told me: "Because I lost the race for governor, I'm a zero." A straight-A student who received a B on an exam concluded: "Now I'm a total failure." All-or-nothing thinking clearly is illogical because things are not completely one way or the other. For example, no one is either completely attractive or totally ugly. Similarly, people are neither "absolutely brilliant" nor "hopelessly stupid." All-or-nothing thinking forms the basis for perfectionism. It causes you to fear any mistake or imperfection because you then will see yourself as a complete zero and feel inferior, worthless, and depressed.

Overgeneralization. You arbitrarily conclude that a single negative event will happen over and over again. For example, a shy young man mustered up his courage to ask a girl for a date. When she declined he thought: "I'm *never* going to get a date. Girls are *always* turning me down." A depressed salesman noticed bird dung on his car and thought: "Just my luck! The birds are *always* crapping on my front window." When I questioned him about this he admitted that in his 20 years of driving he could not remember another instance when he noticed bird dung on his car!

Selective negative focus. You pick out the negative details in any situation and dwell on them exclusively, thus concluding that the whole situation is negative. For example, a severely depressed college student heard some premed students making fun of her roommate. She became furious because of her thought: "That's what the human race is like— cruel and insensitive!" She was overlooking the fact that in the previous months few people, if any, had been cruel or insensitive to her. On another occasion when she completed her first midterm exam she decided to commit suicide because she thought only about the 17 questions she felt certain she had missed and concluded she could not succeed as a college student. When she got the exam back there was a note attached which read: "You got 83 out of 100 correct. This was by far the highest grade of any student this year—A+."

Disqualifying the positive. This is to me one of the most amazing and magical of all the thinking errors. When a depressed individual is confronted with data that clearly contradicts his or her negative self-image and pessimistic attitudes, he or she quickly and cleverly finds some way to discount this. For example, a young woman hospitalized for chronic

---

[1]This list and descriptions was developed by David Burns (1980).

intractable depression told me: "No one could possibly care about me because I'm such an awful person." When she was discharged from the hospital, many patients and staff members paid her a warm tribute and expressed fondness for her. Her immediate reaction was: "They don't count because they're psychiatric patients or staff. A real person outside a hospital could never care about me." When I then asked her how she reconciled this with the fact that she had numerous friends and family who did *seem* to care about her she stated: "They don't count because they don't know the real me." By disqualifying positive experiences in this manner, the depressed individual can maintain negative beliefs that are clearly unrealistic and inconsistent with everyday experiences.

Arbitrary inference. You jump to an arbitrary, negative conclusion that is not justified by the facts or the situation. Two types of arbitrary inference are *mind reading* and *negative prediction*.

1. *Mind reading.* You make the assumption that other people are looking down on you and you feel so convinced about this that you do not bother to check it out. You then may respond to this imagined rejection by withdrawal or counterattack. These self-defeating behavior patterns may act as self-fulfilling prophecies and set up a negative interaction when none originally existed.

2. *Negative prediction.* You imagine that something bad is about to happen and you take this prediction as a *fact* even though it may be quite unrealistic. For example, during anxiety attacks a high school librarian repeatedly told herself: "I'm going to pass out or go crazy." These predictions were highly unrealistic because she had never passed out in her entire life and had no symptoms to suggest impending insanity. During a therapy session, an acutely depressed physician explained why he wanted to commit suicide: "I realize I'll be depressed forever. As I look into the future, I can see this suffering will go on and on, and I'm absolutely convinced that all treatments will be doomed to failure." Thus, his sense of hopelessness was caused by his negative prediction about his prognosis. His recovery soon after initiating therapy indicated just how off-base his negative prediction had been.

Magnification or minimization. I call this the "binocular trick" because you are either blowing things up out of proportion or shrinking them. For example, when you look at your mistakes or at the other fellow's talents, you probably look through the end of the binoculars that makes things seem bigger than they really are. In contrast, when you look at your own strengths, or the other guys imperfections, you probably look through the opposite end of the binoculars that makes things seem small and distant. Because you magnify your imperfections and minimize your good points, you end up feeling inadequate and inferior to other people.

Emotional reasoning. You take your emotions as evidence for the way things really are. Your logic is: "I *feel*, therefore I *am*." Examples of emotional reasoning include: "I feel guilty. Therefore I must be a bad person." "I feel overwhelmed and hopeless. Therefore my problems must be impossible to solve." "I feel inadequate. Therefore I must be a worthless person." "I feel very nervous around elevators. Therefore elevators must be very dangerous." Such reasoning is erroneous because your feelings simply reflect your thoughts and beliefs.

Should statements. You try to motivate yourself to increased activity by saying, "I *should* do this" or "I *must* do that." These statements cause you to feel guilty, pressured, and resentful. Paradoxically, you end up feeling apathetic and unmotivated. Albert Ellis calls this "*must*urbation."

When you direct "should" statements toward others, you probably feel frustrated, angry, or indignant. When I was five minutes late for a session, an irate patient had the thought: "He *shouldn't* be so self-centered and thoughtless. He *ought to be* more prompt."

Labeling and mislabeling. Personal labeling involves creating a negative identity for yourself that is based on your errors and imperfections as if these revealed your true self. Labeling is an extreme form of overgeneralization. The philosophy behind this tendency is: "The measure of a man is the mistakes he makes." There is a good chance you are involved in self-labeling whenever you describe yourself with sentences beginning with "*I am.* "For example, when you goof up in some way, you might say, "I'm a loser" instead of "I lost out on this," or you might think "I'm a failure" instead of "I made a mistake."

Mislabeling involves describing an event with words that are inaccurate and heavily loaded emotionally. For example, a physician on a diet ate a dish of ice cream and thought: "How *disgusting* and *repulsive* of me. I'm a *pig.* "These thoughts made him so upset that he ate the whole quart of ice cream.

Personalization. You relate a negative event to yourself when there is no basis for doing so. You arbitrarily conclude that the negative event is your fault, even when you are not responsible for the event and did not cause it. For example, when a patient failed to do a self-help assignment that a psychiatrist suggested, the doctor thought: "I must be a lousy therapist, or else he would have done what I recommended. "Similarly, when a mother saw her child's report card, there was a note that her child was not working effectively. She immediately concluded, "I must be a bad mother. This shows how *I'm* goofing up."

Although all of the preceding distortions are negative and can lead to dysfunctional behavior, it should be noted that at some point each of them most likely would have had a functional use. The ability to monitor and assess our behavior and experience is an important part of this function. When this is taken to an extreme, however, it becomes dysfunctional. It is important for individuals to learn to monitor nonverbal cues, but when they monitor them and make inferences about behavior (arbitrary inference) it may be dysfunctional. Striving for success is an important part of the American ideal but, taken to the extreme of all or nothing, it becomes a perfectionism that leads to dysfunction.

Another possible distortion that lends itself to improved productivity or greater risk taking may be termed *positive distortion*. Here the individual acts as a personal cheerleader, telling him or herself that he or she can do it and that the attempt would be worthwhile even though some objective measure might indicate that he or she would not have the necessary skills for successfully attempting or completing a particular task. However, the experience gained in the attempt may serve to make the individual better able to be successful later.

Underlying Assumptions and Irrational Beliefs

The source of the distortions are the irrational belief systems. They are of various strengths and include *social learning*—please and thank you; *religious learning*—the shalt and shalt nots; and *internalization of legal codes*—walk/do not walk. The individual's degree of belief in these underlying assumptions or rules of living will determine his or her strength as a wellspring of distortions.

An example of this connection can be seen in the following reconstruction. A child of elementary school age comes home from school with a 98 on a math test. The parents either overtly or covertly inquire about the other two points with statements such as, "I thought you knew that work?" or "What happened to the other two points?" When the child came home with a perfect exam paper, the child was greeted with smiles, hugs, and kisses (a 98 only warranted a pat on the back and better luck next time). A basic rule of life developed in this way would be: To be accepted and/or loved, I must/should/ought to be perfect. With this as a basic underlying belief, the individual dichotomizes experiences as success (100%) or failure (99.9% or below).

Treatment

In terms of treatment, the first issue looked at would be the distortion, using the style, type, and content of the distortion to point to the underlying assumptions. A patient often will terminate therapy having learned to cope successfully with his or her distortions but leaving the underlying assumptions untouched. The more elegant solution, however, would be to have the individual cope not only with the distortions but with the assumptions.

SPECIFICITY

The cognitive therapist makes up problem lists and specifies the problems to be worked on. Patients coming into treatment to work on depression or communication or, the most ambiguous of all, "to get their head together," do not present symptoms that can be worked on or problems that can be ameliorated. The cognitive therapist first needs to assess the problems and then prioritize them. Lazarus (1981) spells out the need for specificity in his BASIC ID model where the clinician evaluates problems in terms of *B*ehavior, *A*ffect, *S*ensation, *I*magery, *C*ognition, *I*nterpersonal relationships, and *D*rugs/*D*iet (physiologicalissues).

COGNITIVE AND BEHAVIORAL STRATEGIES

A number of cognitive strategies are utilized to help patients test the reality of their cognitions:

1. Questioning the evidence
2. Reattribution
3. Fantasizing consequences
4. Understanding idiosyncratic meaning
5. Developing options and alternatives
6. Decatastrophizing

Behavioral strategies include:

1. Graded task assignments
2. Activity scheduling for mastery and pleasure
3. *In vivo* work
4. Collecting evidence

HOMEWORK

An important part of cognitive therapy is the idea that therapy does not happen an hour or two hours a week but needs to be a process that is constantly lived. The cognitive therapy patient is not being therapized so much as collaborating with the therapist. An important part of the collaboration is doing self-help work at home. Our clinical experience has indicated that the patients who do more self-help work move along more quickly in therapy and are able to meet their stated therapy goals more quickly.

The contributors to this volume have taken the basic cognitive model and extended it to new populations and problems utilizing the group context. The reader is encouraged to be familiar with the basic model before attempting to utilize the application described here.

REFERENCES

Arieti, S. Cognition in psychoanalysis. *Journal of the American Academy of Psychoanalysis.* 1980, *8,* 3–23.

Bandura, A. Self-efficacy: Towards a unifying theory of behavior change. *Psychological Review,* 1977, *84,* 191–215.(a)

Bandura, A. *Social learning theory.* Englewood Cliffs, N.J.: Prentice-Hall, 1977.(b)

Beck, A. T. *Cognitive therapy and the emotional disorders.* New York:International Universities Press, 1976.

Beck, A. T., Rush, A. J., Shaw, B. F., & Emery, G. *Cognitive therapy of depression.* New York: Guilford, 1979.

Bieber, I. *Cognitive psychoanalysis.* New York: Aronson, 1981.

Burns, D. D. *Definitions of cognitive distortions.* Unpublished manuscript,1980.(a)

Burns, D. D. *Feeling good.* New York: Morrow, 1980.(b)

Carnegie, D. *How to win friends and influence people.* New York: Pocket Books, 1982.

Crowley, R. Cognitive elements in the work of Harry Stack Sullivan. In M. Mahoney & A. Freeman, *Cognition and psychotherapy.* New York: Plenum Press, in press.

Ellis, A. *Reason and emotion in psychotherapy.* New York: Lyle Stuart, 1962.

Ellis, A. *Humanistic psychotherapy: The rational-emotive approach.* New York: Julian, 1973.

Ellis, A. The basic clinical theory of rational-emotive therapy. In A. Ellis & R. Grieger (Eds.), *Handbook of rational-emotive therapy.* New York: Springer, 1977.

Frakl, V. Cognition and logotherapy. In M. Mahoney & A. Freeman, *Cognition and psychotherapy.* New York: Plenum Press, in press.

Kelley, F. D., & Dowd, E. T. Adlerian psychology and cognitive behavior therapy: Convergences. *Journal of Individual Psychology,* 1980, *36,* 119–135.

Lazarus, A. (Ed.) *Multi modal behavior therapy.* New York: Springer, 1976.

Lazarus, A. A. *The practice of multi modal therapy.* New York: McGraw-Hill, 1981.

Mahoney, M. J. *Cognition and behavior modification.* Cambridge, Mass.: Ballinger, 1974.

Maultsby, M. *Help yourself to happiness.* New York: Institute for Rational Emotive Therapy, 1975.

Meichenbaum, D. *Cognitive-behavior modification.* New York; Plenum Press, 1977.

Peale, N. V. *Power of positive thinking.* New York, Fawcett, 1978.

Sheen, F. J. *Life is worth living.* New York: Doubleday, 1978.

Smith, D. Trends in counseling and psychotherapy. *American Psychologist,* 1982, *37(7),* 802–809.

Wachtel, P. *Psychoanalysis and behavior therapy: Toward an integration.* New York: Basic Books, 1977.

2

Cognitive Therapy for Depression in a Group Format

STEVEN D. HOLLON AND MARK D. EVANS

INTRODUCTION

Can depressed patients be treated with cognitive therapy in a group format? We think that they can. Cognitive therapy, the systematic attempt to identify and alter dysfunctional, depressogenic cognitions, appears to be a powerful intervention for depressed clients. A group treatment format allows the clinician to treat more people in the same amount of therapy time. In addition, a group format may offer certain advantages not available in an individual treatment context.

In this chapter, we focus on the steps involved in practicing group cognitive therapy with depressed clients. Our primary interest is in actual therapy procedures. What steps need to be taken and what maneuvers are likely to prove effective? In an effort to highlight clinical material, we have relied heavily on vignettes drawn from actual group clinical sessions. The reader interested in a more theoretical discussion should consult Hollon and Shaw (1979).

THE EFFICACY OF GROUP APPROACHES

Depressed and suicidal clients traditionally have been considered poor candidates for group therapy (Christie, 1970). Concerns have in-

STEVEN D. HOLLON AND MARK D. EVANS • Department of Psychology, University of Minnesota, Minneapolis, Minnesota 55455 and Department of Psychiatry, St. Paul–Ramsey Medical Center, St. Paul, Minnesota 55101. Preparation of this chapter was supported in part by a grant from the National Institute of Mental Health (RO1–MH33209) to the Department of Psychology, University of Minnesota, and the St. Paul–Ramsey Medical Education and Research Foundation (No. 6287).

volved both fears for the depressed patient and fears for the welfare of the group. With regard to the patient's welfare, it often is stated that the particular needs of such patients are so intense, but their performance capacities so impaired, that they are unlikely to benefit from group process. With regard to the group's welfare, the pervasive pessimism, self-absorption, and rejection of others' suggestions are seen as impediments to the developments of the group process.

Yalom (1970) has suggested that these considerations may be less of a constraint on including depressed patients in groups than on including depressed patients in groups with other types of patients. Such mixed groups typically have been referred to as *heterogeneous* groups. We tend to concur with Yalom in not wanting to mix depressed clients with other types of patients in a traditional group format. The bulk of our experience with such patients has involved groups *homogeneous* with regard to diagnostic composition. However, we do not want to rule out the possibility that it is the type of *therapy*, not the type of *group*, that is critical.

A brief review of the therapy outcome literature with respect to depressed patients should suffice to document this point. Efforts to treat homogeneously depressed patients with traditional psychotherapy generally have proven unsatisfying, regardless of whether that treatment was provided individually (Daneman, 1961; Friedman, 1975; Klerman, DiMascio, Weissman, Prusoff, & Paykel, 1974) or in groups (Covi, Lipman, Derogatis, Smith, & Pattison, 1974). Cognitive therapy, on the other hand, has proven consistently effective in treating such patients, whether provided in an individual format (e.g., Hollon, Bedrosian, & Beck, 1979; Rush, Beck, Kovacs, & Hollon, 1977; Taylor & Marshall, 1977) or a group format (e.g., Gioe, 1975; Morris, 1975; Rush & Watkins, 1981; Shaw, 1977; Shaw & Hollon, 1978). The interested reader would do well to consult these articles or recent major reviews (e.g., Blaney, 1981; Craighead, 1981; Hollon, 1981; Hollon & Beck, 1979; Rehm & Kornblith, 1979; Shaw & Beck, 1977; Weissman, 1979) for more in-depth discussions of this literature. None of these studies has yet contrasted diagnostically homogeneous with diagnostically heterogeneous groups. Although we can be reasonably comfortable in suggesting that group cognitive therapy appears viable with homogeneously depressed patients, it would be premature, at this time, to rule out diagnostically heterogeneous groups, so long as the basic approach were cognitive. The basic failure of traditional approaches to assist depressed clients in heterogeneous groups may be attributable more to the nonviability of the process–orientation of such groups for depressed clients than to the heterogeneous composition.

The available evidence favors a structured, time-limited, problem-focused approach such as cognitive therapy over other alternative group approaches for working with depressed clients. Cognitive therapy, despite its name, is not limited in focus solely to cognitive phenomena. Rather, a broadly based range of cognitive, behavioral, and affective change strategies are brought to bear in an integrated fashion on the beliefs and actions of the depressed individuals (see Beck, Rush, Shaw, & Emery, 1979; Emery, Hollon, & Bedrosian, 1981; Hollon & Beck, 1979; or Shaw & Beck, 1977 for extended discussions of therapeutic rationale and procedures). How can these procedures best be adapted for group work with depressed clients? In the sections that follow, we focus on those steps we believe necessary actually to implement cognitive therapy with depressed clients.

STRUCTURAL CONSIDERATIONS

As in individual cognitive therapy, the fundamental goals of group cognitive therapy include an identification and modification of depressed patients' maladaptive belief systems and dysfunctional forms of information processing. Basic techniques include behavioral assignments; systematic self-monitoring of activities, affects, and cognitions; and training in strategies designed to identify and change distorted cognitive systems. Much of the work goes on between sessions, with the client making extensive use of a variety of structured homework assignments. These include activity schedules, records of cognitions, and dysfunctional thought records as bases for efforts to change these cognitions. Patients and therapists frequently collaborate with one another in the design of "experiments" to test views held by those clients.

Other group members frequently can play a major role in identifying, examining, and testing one another's belief systems. This capacity to assume a therapeutic stance toward one another has, we believe, several useful functions. Taking such a role (1) provides practice in identifying and critically examining beliefs, (2) minimizes "distance" between "helper" and "helpee," (3) increases the probability that someone in the room will think of something, and (4) demonstrates to patients that they can, indeed, think quite rationally.

As in individual cognitive therapy, group sessions are structured, problem-oriented, and focused. Therapists typically take an active role in terms of questioning, challenging, exploring, and instructing. Incorporating such procedures in a group format can present a host of special problems in terms both of the focus of the sessions and in a number of practical problems that may arise in a group context. In the following section, we illustrate several of these issues.

Problem-Oriented versus Process-Oriented Groups

Cognitive therapy is, in essence, a problem-oriented approach to treatment. Process is dictated by the therapeutic strategy; early sessions generally focus on behavior change and training in self-monitoring, with the therapist carrying the bulk of the responsibility for presenting and demonstrating the use of cognitive restructuring procedures. In later sessions, the clients take an increasingly greater role in the cognitive testing process. The key point is that therapeutic change is not seen as being the result of insights growing out of group interaction. Rather, it is considered the result of the application of specific change strategies taught by the therapist but utilized by the patients. The goal of the group is not to discover a strategy for change, but to teach a methodology for change. Nonetheless, psychological problems related to the group process occasionally may arise. Often, they can serve as "grist for the therapeutic mill," rather than simply being nuisances or distractions. The vignette that follows illustrates this point. One group member, Erik, had joined a group about three weeks after it had started but, despite being quite depressed, had shown rapid change. A second member, the other male, Craig, who had started therapy several weeks earlier and initially had shown good progress, became increasingly critical of himself and appeared to be losing ground therapeutically. The following vignette is adapted from audio tapes of the exchange that followed:

THERAPIST 1: Craig, how about for you? How have things been going?
CRAIG: All right I guess . . . not real good, but all right.
THERAPIST 1: Anything for the agenda?
CRAIG: Not really . . . well, I just wonder how much I'm getting out of the group . . . I wonder if I should really continue.
THERAPIST 1: What leads you to wonder about that?
CRAIG: Well, I just don't seem to be doing too well lately.
THERAPIST 2: You've not been as active in group and today's the first session in weeks that you haven't done any "triple-columns." Have your Beck scores (Beck Depression Inventory: Beck, Ward, Mendelson, Mock, & Erbaugh, 1961) changed at all?
CRAIG: Well, I've been feeling worse . . . (looks through folder). . . Yeah, I'm at a 27 today, I was a 25 last week . . . I was down in the 10–15 range a couple of weeks back.

THERAPIST 2: Well let's put that on our agenda and come back to it. It sounds like something important is going on.

Later in the session

THERAPIST 1: Well, Craig, maybe we had better come back to your concerns about staying in group. What do you think might be going on?

CRAIG: I don't know . . . I just don't feel as comfortable, I don't feel like I can keep up, or something.

THERAPIST 2: Don't feel you can keep up? What do you mean by that?

CRAIG: Well, like maybe I don't understand, like maybe I'm not smart enough.

THERAPIST 2: If you can't keep up, and if that's because you're not smart enough, where does that leave you?

CRAIG: Well, it doesn't make a whole lot of sense for me to continue in group.

THERAPIST 2: I see, I think. If you believe that you aren't smart enough to follow what's going, then you can't keep up well, and there's little reason for you to continue. Is that what you've been thinking?

CRAIG: Yeah, that's a lot of it.

THERAPIST 2: Want to test those beliefs?

CRAIG: Yeah, I guess so. Let's see. First I ask myself what my evidence is . . . I don't know, I guess my evidence is that I haven't been keeping up.

THERAPIST 1: Specifically?

CRAIG: Well, I don't seem to be following things as well in the sessions, and I haven't been doing much between sessions.

THERAPIST 1: You seem to think that's because you are too stupid. Any other possible explanations?

CRAIG: Like what?

MARY: Like maybe you're sitting there so preoccupied with being stupid that you haven't been listening?

CRAIG: (*Laughs*) Yeah, maybe, I have been doing a lot of that . . . But seriously, look at Erik. He started so much later, and look at how fast he's been learning this.

THERAPIST 1: Oh, so you've been comparing yourself to Erik. Is that what's started this all off?

CRAIG: Well, a lot of it. He just seems so much smarter than me.

ERIK: (*Laughs*) I don't feel that way; actually, I've been feeling kind of guilty about taking up so much of the time; I've been feeling like I could never catch up with the rest of you all.

THERAPIST 2: Let's take a very careful look at that notion of yours Craig about being "stupid" and not being good enough. Let's go back again and look at the evidence for and against that belief.

Dealing with such ongoing cognitions arising in group can provide a powerful learning model. In all cases, the process is secondary to the procedure, and is used as a means to help teach cognitive therapy techniques, not to supplant them.

Open versus Closed Groups

In the vignette above, a new member had been added to an existing group. Such a group is said to be an *open* group. Groups in which all clients start at a given time are considered *closed*. We have run cognitive therapy groups of both types and find that each has its advantages, each its liabilities. Open groups are somewhat more flexible and often fit ongoing clinical practices more adequately. When advanced group members are encouraged to take a tutorial role with newer members, the introduction of new members can provide an opportunity to teach what has been learned. (We are struck by how closely our practice has followed the old medical school dictum, "Watch one, do one, teach one.")

Closed groups, meanwhile, permit moving numerous individuals along at a similar pace. This may prove to be a more economical procedure with regard to the way group time is spent. At this time, neither practice can be said to be clearly superior to the other.

Role of Co-therapists

We prefer the use of co-therapists or multiple therapists. Working with depressed clients can be particularly demanding. Such patients often are doing the worst when they are saying the least. Use of co-therapist allows at least one therapist continually to monitor group numbers not actively involved at any given moment.Similarly, the large amount of written material generated by patients between sessions often is best reviewed by one therapist as the other gets the session started. Nothing is so likely to undermine patients' activity between sessions as lack of therapeutic attention to their products during the subsequent session. Use of co-therapist, with appropriate role division (and, perhaps, role switching) appears to maximize therapeutic impact.

Group Composition

We already have discussed at some length the issue of heterogeneous versus homogeneous group composition. As noted, it is not clear that heterogeneous groups will not prove feasible, but most of the work, to date, has been done with homogeneous groups.

Few guidelines exist with regard to type of depression. Our previous work suggests that, if anything, *greater endogenicity* and *lessor chronicity* are better prediction of outcome (Rush, Hollon, Beck, & Kovacs, 1978). It is important to keepin mind, however, that efforts at selection based on such evidence tend to make therapists feel better than patients. From the potential patient's point of view, the question of interest is not "Will I do as well in this therapy as someone who is more endogenously or less chronically depressed?" Rather, it is "Given that I am not very endogenous and my depression has been long-lasting, will I do better in this type of treatment than in some other approach?" Stated in this fashion, it becomes clear that selection really should be keyed to differential outcome studies. Although we are beginning to get a sense for patients more likely to improve than others, for example, endogenously depressed middle-aged maleswith acute onset, we suspect these are general prognostic factors. As such, they are not likely to be helpful in selecting group patients.

Frequency and Duration of Session

There appear to be no firm guidelines as to the frequency and duration of sessions. Shaw and Hollon (1978) utilized two-hour sessions held once a week for 12 weeks; Rush & Watkins (1981) held shorter meetings twice weekly. Future studies might well address this issue.

For the present, our experience suggests that sessions lasting from one and one-half to two hours provide an optimal time frame for comprehensiveness without fatigue. Weekly contacts appear to represent minimum frequency.

Conducting Group C/B

Preparatory Interviews

Upon entrance into a therapy group, a depressed patient may feel particularly threatened. This apprehension could be reflected in thoughts such as, "I couldn't possibly talk about my problems in front of all those people," "I get uncomfortable in groups," "I must be an uninteresting patient," or "I must be too sick (or not depressed enough) to benefit from individual therapy." Preparatory interviews scheduled for discussing these or related concerns are helpful.

Conducting Sessions

Assessing Depression

We prefer to begin cognitive group therapy (see Table 1) with one or more structured assessments of target problems. The Beck Depression Inventory (BDI; Beck, Ward, Mendelson, Mock, & Erbaugh, 1961) provides a brief, well validated self-report measure of syndrome depression. The initial interview, the first group therapy session, and all subsequent group sessions routinely begin with an administration of the BDI. Patients who have completed the BDI several times may be given a supply to keep at home and may fill out the scale either just before coming or while waiting for the group session to begin.

Such attention to the BDI permits a close monitoring of depression levels, signals any important shifts in discrete symptomatology (such as suicidal ruminations), and clearly keeps the focus on the production of change within the time-limited contract. Although depression generally is the major phenomenon of interest, we have at times monitored other relevant processes, such as anxiety, on a regular basis. An additional measure recently developed by Hollon and Kendall (1980), the Automatic Thoughts Questionnaire provides a useful assessment of negative beliefs, cognitions, and self-statements often experienced by depressed persons.

Setting Agendas

At the beginning of each session, it generally is desirable to set a flexible agenda that will allow patients and therapist(s) to target specific areas for discussion. It frequently is useful to poll each participant for suggestions so that everyone may begin the group session with some kind of active participation. This enables group participants to comment on major events or changes in sympotomatology over the preceding week. It also decreases the chance that a participant will spring a "hot" topic on the group in the midst of a session, either disrupting an ongoing discussion or coming so late in the session that there is not adequate time to discuss it. The therapist(s) adds topics that he or she wants to be sure are covered (e.g., homework or didactic material) and takes the lead in prioritizing agenda items so that the most important items are sure to be covered. Generally, itis preferable to specify a topic, then continue to complete the construction of the agenda and return to that topic later, rather than risk dwelling too long on any given subject at the beginning of the session.

TABLE 1
Schedule for Group Cognitive Therapy[a]

Week		Session objectives and methods
0	Diagnostic and/or preparatory session	1. Assess appropriateness for group
		2. Assess and discuss expectations
		3. Distribute *Coping with Depression*
1	Initial session	1. Measure depression (give BDI)
		2. Introduce new members
		3. Set agenda
		4. Establish ground rules
		5. Discuss expectations and review treatment goals
		6. Elicit initial statements of individual problems
		7. Introduce cognitive theory and technique
		9. Focus on training self-monitoring skills and/or behavioral experiments
		10. Homework assignments
		11. Assess reactions to session
2–10	Subsequent sessions	1. Measure depression (give BDI)
		2. Set agenda
		3. Review status since last session
		4. Discuss reactions to previous sessions
		5. Review homework from last session
		6. Introduce new topics and relate material to basic cognitive theory
		7. Homework assignments
		8. Assess reaction to session
		9. Summarize session
11–12	Termination sessions	1. Measure depression (give BDI)
		2. Set agenda
		3. Review status since last session
		4. Discuss progress to date
		5. Discuss expectations regarding termination
		6. Assess reactions to session(s)
		7. Summarize sessions

[a]Adapted from Hollon and Shaw (1979).

This approach provides an explicit, formal structure within which the group can function at maximal efficiency. When a therapist is working with depressed patients, it is important that he or she has such a structure planned in advance and available at all times. Such a strong organizational aid also serves as a precaution against the deadly effects of depressive inertia and pessimism that so readily appear during unfocused moments. Far from inhibiting spontaneity during the group session, an predetermined agenda appears to facilitate spontaneity and involvement on the part of the patients. It seems likely that the apparent poor prognosis for depressed patients in less highly structured groups or in process-oriented group settings may be attributed to the failure of such unstructured groups to offset adequately the operation of negative cognitive sets. These negative sets seem to dominate in situations where the lack of structure permits ambiguity, thereby creating a meaning vacuum that are filled by the patients' depressive interpretations.

When a new group is starting and before individual patients' concerns are taken up, it is useful to indicate clearly those areas that must be discussed at the first session (e.g., the general structure for sessions, group ground rules, individual goals and expectations, and a general discussion of cognitive therapy). If a new member is being added to an existing group, the therapist typically will use this time to make introductions and to indicate that some time will be set aside for exploring the new member's goals, problems, and current situation.

Establishing Ground Rules

In the initial session, it is useful to discuss basic ground rules, eliciting agreement from all participants. Confidentiality presents special problems in a group setting. We typically approach the issue directly, requesting that each patient agrees to respect the other patients' rights to privacy. A general guideline is that all patients are free to discuss their own specific goals, progress, and the procedures they are learning with whomever they choose, but that no other member is ever identified nor their problem talked about.

The second major ground rule that is useful is the notion of "going around." This means that the group agrees to structure its time in such a way that each member might have an opportunity to bring up one or more of his or her concerns for discussion and that the group will stay with that topic long enough to reach some kind of resolution. Input is actively sought from each patient who has not already volunteered comments. This procedure prevents the flow of the discussion from becoming too diffused, while also ensuring that no patient gets neglected. Early in any given session and during the first several sessions, it usually is advisable for the therapist to be somewhat more formal in soliciting comments from each member in turn, just as was done in setting the agenda.

Depressed clients typically start therapy identifying with one another's negative perceptions. Initially, comments from other group members often take the form of agreement with the pessimistic view, followed by recounting of idiosyncratic experiences or inferences from the commenting member about his or her own situation. These comments have the effect of diverting attention from the initial problem and the initial speaker. It is unlikely that this process reflects anything more than a spontaneous desire to empathize and/or identify with the first speaker. The therapist generally can redirect the discussion to the initial topic and the initial speaker, then proceed to examine and work through the initial problem raised.

Assessing Expectations and Eliciting Reactions to Previous Sessions

Early in the initial session, the therapist might find it useful to ask each patient what he or she expects therapy to be like and what his or her personal goals and expectations are for participation in the group. The answers to these questions may provide useful indications of unrealistic expectations (generally negative) and may alert the therapist(s) to expectations and assumptions that may not be met during the typical course of cognitive therapy.

THERAPIST 1: (*After explaining the ground rules*) Maybe we can start off by going over each individual's reasons for being here. One of the things I've found over and over is that people do not have common reasons for coming into agroup and it's important that we all understand what our particular goals are. If someone is willing to start we can then go around the group and find out from each of you what you hope to have happen as a result of being in this group and how you think being in the group might help you to attain those goals.

MARY: I've been married 35 years and have three grown sons. My husband is a traveling businessman and I'm left alone quite a bit. I depend on my husband a great deal and I do not like it that he is gone so much of the time. I woke up one morning and felt that everything was closing in on me, and I took a bottle of sleeping pills. I wanted to die because the future doesn't hold anything good for me because my husband will always be traveling.

THERAPIST 1: So what goals do you want to be working on?

MARY: I'd like to know what to do with my life, yet I have no real desire to do anything with it. I don't know how to get started. . . . I've always wanted to do volunteer work, but I did do volunteer work before and you have to be in at a certain time. I just can't get out of bed early enough so that I could do that.

THERAPIST 1: Okay, so one of the things you're saying is a problem with motivation.

MARY: Motivation and I have been depressed practically all of my life and I think that is because of my family situation.

THERAPIST 1: One of the things we will be talking about later is the cause of depression but for now why don't we just say that you have some ideas about what might be causing the depression and we'll take that a little further later. Are there any other goals that you have?

MARY: I want to get out of depression and I want to do something but I don't have that motivation like you said.

THERAPIST 1: How about you, Irene?

IRENE: Why I came here? Because you asked me to.

THERAPIST 1: What are your goals?

IRENE: Well, I'd like to be able to feel like I can get up and go to work and deal with everyday situations.

THERAPIST 1: So it sounds like, similar to Mary, getting the motivation to go out every day and having more self-confidence. Is there anything else?

IRENE: No.

THERAPIST 1: June?

JUNE: I guess I just want to stop being unhappy. The unhappiness has been extreme for a while and though I have been receiving treatment I feel that my symptoms have remained extreme and I came here as a result of looking for other help. I want to stop being tired, I want to stop being unhappy, I want to stop feeling discouraged.

THERAPIST 1: Okay. Bonnie, what are your goals?

BONNIE: I guess learning how to cope with depression without completely going to pieces. You know, I realize that everyone at certain times of their lives get depressed but some people know how to handle it better, you know, without sitting around crying and going to bed. I think by talking to other people this might help me to get a clearer view and understand it better.

THERAPIST 1: I have some goals as well and one of the major goals is to see each and every one of you learn a little bit about yourself and also learn how to cope with depression. Every group I have participated in I have found something that helps me personally and professionally and I'm looking forward to that as well.

Patients frequently come into a therapy situation with some notion of how well they will fare in treatment and of how treatment is likely to progress. With depressed patients such expectations typically are pessimistic, so eliciting an expression of these from each patient often demonstrates how negative self-appraisals operate. For example, near the end of the first session for a new therapy group, one of the authors asked each participant separately to rank all group members, including themselves, in terms of whom they thought would benefit the most from the group. All participants put themselves at the bottom of their own list. In the discussion that followed, it became clear that some very striking similarities existed in terms of how participants tended to view themselves vis-à-vis the others. Such thoughts as "Nobody else is as depressed (or as hopeless) as I am," "Everyone else seems so normal; I'm really messed up," and "This approach may work for some of the others, but my depression is caused by my husband (or my job, being out of work, my illness, etc.); the way I think has nothing to do with it," were typical. Pointing out the real similarity in the ways they thought about themselves and their situations facilitated the identification of their negative cognitive distortions.

Depressed people often are surprised when they see that other depressed people experience similar situations and think about themselves in similar ways. Group settings often are an excellent opportunity for participants to begin to view the situations they find themselves in and the thoughts they have about themselves as common to depressed persons. This knowledge may be helpful to them in learning to identify their negative cognitive distortions and subsequently treat them as symptoms of depression that they can work to alleviate.

In subsequent sessions this time may be used profitably as an opportunity for participants to react to the previous week's session and report any thoughts they may have had about something that was said or happened during that session. This allows the therapist(s) to monitor how group participants are reacting to what is happening in the sessions. Depressed persons often construe experiences in idiosyncratic and negative ways. If the therapist is able to identify examples of this process from the group session, the group then can explore discrepancies among participants in how that incident was interpreted. This offers an excellent example of how different meanings may be attached to the same stimuli and how a negative construction may not be as accurate or widely shared as a depressed person initially might think.

Initial Statements of Individual Problems

After assessing expectations it often is interesting and helpful to go around the group again asking participants to share what they believe to be the precipitating and/or contributing factors to their depressions. Depressed clients often have some ideas about what might be causing their depression and it is useful to give clients an opportunity to share their explanations before introducing a cognitive explanation for depression. Once the therapist has listened to a client's explanation, the client might be less resistant to considering an alternative explanation for his or her depression. In addition the therapist may be given enough information about an individual's circumstances in order that he or she can draw on examples from these statements to present a plausible alternative explanation for that person's depression.

THERAPIST: What I'd like to go over now is exactly what you feel is contributing to your feeling of depression and lack of self-confidence, fatigue, or whatever you are experiencing. This will help give us some understanding of things that are going on in your life as an individual that may be contributing to your depression.

MARY: I've been to a psychiatrist for many years and have tried to be honest with him. You want to know what the cause of my depression is, is that what it is?

THERAPIST: As you see it.

MARY: Well, the biggest reason for my depression is my husband traveling and he can't give it up. I am left along from Tuesday until Saturday morning. I have no friends and I don't want to burden myself onto my neighbors or my children and I cannot have my husband stop traveling cause that's our bread and butter. I think that's my biggest reason for my depression. When he is home, even though he is working in his office which is in our house, I don't like it but I'm satisfied just to have have him there so I can walk in and see him. Basically, I have wrapped my life around him and that's what my private psychiatrist said, that I have to let go. But I don't want to let go because I love my husband and I want to spend as much time with him as I can. Although I know he can't be with me during the day, at night I miss him tremendously and I don't sleep well when he's away. . .

THERAPIST: Do you think that the sleeping problem can be tied up with depression?

MARY: Well, you see when I go to bed at night I think that I'm sleeping in my bed and my husband is sleeping alone in a hotel room and I say why can't we be together, why me? I just can't cope with things like I used to when my children were little . . . those days I was able to tackle anything. I was a real fighter and as I'm getting older I'm not the fighter I used to be. You see, I have a heredity for mental illness. My mother was put in a mental institution when I was 17. And I see I'm falling into the same pattern in my life. I don't want to and I'm trying to fight it but I don't have that fight that I had when my children were little. I'm afraid of the future, I'm afraid of being left alone.

THERAPIST: There are a number of things you bring up that I think we will be able to get into and maybe clarify further. Irene, do you have any ideas about what is causing your depression?

IRENE: My father was like that, he had a breakdown when I was 20 years old and I feel like I'm a lot like him. He jumps at little things and then he's real cool. I guess I'm the same way.

JUNE: My mother is very ill. She is in her 80s and has been in and out of homes and hospitals . . . and she is getting worse everyday. All of that is very depressing and I think everyone has a perfect right to be depressed about those things. . . . I don't have a lot of hobbies and my husband's job is not the best, but I don't think that any of those things by themselves are enough to make you give in. Somehow maybe you don't have to give in and that's what I'd like to find. I hope that I can . . . there will always be problems but only recently have they seemed to close in on me and I can't even get out of bed in the morning. My only hope is to believe that there is a way out and that I will find it.

BONNIE: Well, it seems to me that everyone has given reasons for why they're depressed and I really have no reasons. My mother or father was never depressed; my family life is fine. There's no real reason for me to feel that way or get really down. You know, like it's amazing you wonder why is this happening you know, your life is perfectly fine . . . there is really nothing that I can point to, it just seemed to creep up on me.

THERAPIST: Nothing you've found yet.

BONNIE: No.

Presenting Cognitive Theory and Technique

Cognitive therapy makes several explicit statements about the nature of the relationship between events, ideation, and subsequent affect and behavior. Once group participants have been given a chance to identify their problems the therapist(s) introduce an alternative way of viewing their depression. He or she encourages them to begin examining the way they look at things and helps them to recognize the role of how they view things in making them depressed.

THERAPIST: Let me tell you about an idea that many people who treat depressed people, including myself, believe very strongly. That is that you don't necessarily have to have an external thing happen to you to make you depressed. One of the things that we've found over and over again is that the way a person thinks is the closest thing that causes his or her depression and one of the things we're going to be asking you to do is to keep a record of things that you think are associated with any sort of feelings of depression or any other negative thoughts that you might have. So what I'd like you to think about is perhaps it isn't necessarily things that are happening outside of you that make you depressed but things you think that make you depressed.

BONNIE: The way we perceive them.

THERAPIST: Okay, the way we perceive them and maybe, June, I can use your example. I think what you're saying is that there can be all sorts of events that go on and that maybe happened 5 years ago, 2 months ago, or 20 years ago. It may be that you're best in forgetting those particular events or things that have gone on that are unpleasant or that you had difficulty coping with. But what I maintain is that until you change the way that you perceive things and the way that you think about situations then the chances are that what you are facing now you are going to be facing over and over and over again. No matter what the stress is at the time, whether it is the loss of a parent or a problem in a relationship or losing a job or whatever, all of these things can be depressing but they don't necessarily lead to the depression that some of you have been experiencing. There has to be a key in there and what we refer to this as is the ABC's of depression. A being the event that is outside of you, the situation; the C being the feeling that you have, the depression, the unhappiness, the sadness; and the B being the ideas, the way you perceive things, and the way you think about things.

It is useful to present a statement of the cognitive model as in the above vignette and whenever possible tie the concepts to examples arising from the patients' presentation of problems. For instance, in this case, the therapist would have done well to draw from the rich clinical material provided by Mary. In fact, in her presentation she even reported the cognitions she had when lying in bed at night. Thus the therapist might have outlined for the group the ABC's of what occurs for Mary when she goes to bed alone. For instance, the exchange might have gone like this:

THERAPIST: Mary, when you were telling us about what you perceive to be the factors precipitating your depression you mentioned what I thought was a particularly good example of the way the ABC model works. I wonder if we might go back to the example of what happens on nights when your husband is on the road and try to outline that in ABC terms.

MARY: Well, like I was telling you, my husband is gone from Tuesday until Saturday morning and at night I miss him tremendously and I feel so lonely because none of my children are still at home and my husband is all I have.

THERAPIST: Let me interrupt you to note that it is usually feeling states, like loneliness, or sadness, or feeling like we want to cry that alerts us that an ABC chain of situation, cognitions, and emotions is occurring. Since we are usually most aware of our emotions, we can use these as a cue to kick into the process of investigating the situation we are in and the thoughts we are having in order to discover why we are feeling the way we are. So, if we were to draw three columns on the chalkboard for our A's (situation), B's (cognitions), and C's (emotions) we can begin by filling "lonely" into Column C, the feelings column. What other feelings did you have, Mary?

MARY: Well, like I said, I miss him tremendously.

THERAPIST: When we say we miss somebody sometimes that is more of a clue to the kinds of thoughts we are having than an actual emotion. A good clue to whether something belongs in Column C as an emotion is if we can say "I feel _____," such as I feel lonely or I feel sad or I feel happy. Did you have any other feelings the last time this situation occurred?

MARY: I felt sad and I guess I felt hopeless cause I know that my husband will always be traveling and I will always be left alone.

THERAPIST: It sounds like there are some cognitions creeping in there but let's hold off on those for a minute. We'll add *sad* and *hopeless* to the emotions column and then let's switch over to Column A and fill in the situation. Can you tell us where you were when these feelings occurred?

MARY: It always happens on nights when my husband is on the road and I'm home alone.

THERAPIST: Okay, good. Now tell me again when it is that you begin feeling especially lonely.

MARY: After I have gotten ready for bed and I lay down and I'm just lying there because I can't go to sleep.

THERAPIST: (*Writing this under* A, *situation, on the board*) Okay, now we have a good reconstruction of what the situation was and we put that inthe A column. When you were telling us earlier you mentioned some specific thoughts that went through your mind as you were lying there. Can you tell us again what those were?

MARY: I think about my husband sleeping alone in some hotel room and I'm sleeping alone in my bed and I wonder why we can't be together, why me?

THERAPIST: (*Writing these cognitions on the board under* A) You've given us a good string of cognitions there and I'm interested in the last one you mentioned, "Why me?" Can you tell us more about that?

MARY: Well, I feel as though it's not fair because I've wrapped my life around my husband and now that my children are gone, I just can't cope like I used to.

THERAPIST: And what does that mean to you?

MARY: I'm not the fighter I used to be and I'm afraid of the future, I'm afraid of being left alone.

THERAPIST: Okay, let's stop there and review the string of cognitions. We refer to these as automatic thoughts because of the way they occur in a rapid, automatic fashion, seemingly without our having much control over them.

At this point the therapist might go through the string of cognitions with the group and point out how they become increasingly global and ominous in their implications. It also might be useful to poll group members to see how many would experience similar emotions and be unable to fall asleep if they were to lie in bed thinking those same thoughts. The therapist can comment on how quickly this whole process usually occurs and how it will take a special effort initially to be able to reconstruct the situation and cognitions leading to a feeling state. But, he or she can point out, expending the time and effort necessary to do so will facilitate greatly the process of learning how to intervene in the process, the goal being to short-circuit the run of automatic thoughts and avoid subsequent negative feeling states. The main point is that the therapist is likely to get a lot of mileage out of one or more good examples, especially if they arise from the group and the therapist can use the example(s) to involve participants in a discussion of the ABC model.

Trying the Cognitive Model on for Size

Once the therapist has had the opportunity to make an initial presentation of the cognitive model, it is useful to turn the floor over to the group participants to react to aspects of the cognitive model that they perceive to be particularly applicable to their personal lives. We recommend giving patients a copy of the pamphlet *Coping with Depression* (Beck & Greenberg, 1974) to read before they come to the first group session. This pamphlet does a nice job of introducing the cognitive model and providing examples of typical ways in which depressed people think about things that help maintain their depressions. This time serves as a good opportunity to elicit group participants' reactions to this material as well.

THERAPIST: I hope you've all had a chance to read *Coping with Depression*. I'd like to spend some time now to talk about the parts of *Coping with Depression* and the ABCs that we've talked about here today that you think might apply to you and the parts that don't apply to you. What parts do you find apply to you?

MARY: Everything. Every part of the book applies to me and my husband took me to see a movie. . .

THERAPIST 2: (*At the first chance*) To focus back on the pamphlet for a moment, given that everything was right down main line center for you, what things in it would you have particularly keyed on, what things particularly applied?

MARY: Well, the tiredness, the fatigue, the motivation, um . . . I can't . . . if I had the book in front of me I could . . . I read it twice and itseemed like it was witten for me.

THERAPIST 1: How about the thinking aspect, one of the things the pamphlet talks about is the way people interpret things in a negative way sometimes and tend to exaggerate things.

MARY: Yes, I do. I make it worse than it really is or I exaggerate, and I have this fear of going out at night which stems, I think, to my childhood. . . . I have tried, I have gotten dressed and gone to the garage door and I turn around and go back because I think I will be raped or robbed or somebody will grab me and that would set me mentally out of my mind. . . . I'm a prisoner in my own home; I don't know how to overcome this and I'd like to overcome it just like I'd like to overcome my depression.

THERAPIST: The pamphlet talks about the association between situations and the thoughts that we have in those situations. Do you see how that applies to your experience, such as in the example you just gave?

MARY: Yes, like I have a cousin that just had a finger taken off because she has cancer and that just sent me mentally wild.

THERAPIST: How about you, Irene, does that idea of the association between thinking and depression have any meaning for you? Do you understand that?

IRENE: Yeah. As soon as you read parts of the book you recognize situations you've been in and your reactions to them.

THERAPIST: Can you describe one of those situations for us?

IRENE: Yeah, a really indicative thing happened to me the other day. My little girl (she's 10 years old) and I were sitting down on New Year's Day to write dates and appointments on the new calendar. We were doing the family dates and I was making up the one that I keep for the family and there was a lot of cross referencing. Although I often feel like I can't do things, I guess I am pretty efficient over the long haul and my husband even remarks that he rarely misses any important dates because I'm so organized. Even while I was doing this I was thinking I'm getting a lot done and I was feeling good about that. Anyway, at one point I had to check a date and my daughter laughed and she said "Oh, mommy, you're so inefficient." For just an instant I almost went into a terrible fury and I thought "She doesn't appreciate anything I do" and blah, blah, blah and I had to get up and I walked out into the kitchen and all I could think was this was one of the bad times and I have to keep the lid on. It wasn't real good, but I did. My daughter didn't mean anything by her remark, she's a child and she's at the age where she wants to joke and laugh the way adults do and she didn't mean it. It was me. I was convinced that I had to defend myself; that I have to prove that I'm useful; that I'm doing worthwhile things. I can analyze it now but I couldn't then. All I knew at the time was that I was flying into this unreasonable rage and I wanted to stop and I was able to by telling myself over and over this is one of the bad times, but I ended up feeling miserable for a while.

THERAPIST 2: That's a very nice example. It sounds like you really got into what you were thinking.

IRENE: Well, I didn't get the analysis until we sat here talking now.

THERAPIST 2: Can you apply the ABC way of looking at things to that situation?

IRENE: All right, the event is what she said, which seemed to me to be belittling or it wasn't so much that she was belittling as it seems to me she really pointed to something that's true, that I'm really not efficient . . . and all I knew is that I could feel this terrible rage coming on and I could not analyze any of these thoughts at the time.

THERAPIST 2: So then, in terms of the ABC's. . .

IRENE: Well, A was what she said and it was my reaction to it that she thinks I really am inefficient and confused and I have to defend myself to prove that I'm not.

THERAPIST 2: Okay, so A was what she said and C was your rage reactions, but the B was "I really am efficient" and "I am going to have to prove. . ."

IRENE: Yes! That's really what it was, yes.

THERAPIST 2: That's a very nice example of how that process works.

THERAPIST 1: Right, it's that whole idea that thinking and depression are really tied together and it might not necessarily be exterior things that arecausing the depression. It's what you think.

In this vignette both Mary and Irene came up with good examples. In Irene's case the therapist was able to encourage her to think back to that situation and outline the cognitions that intervened between the situation and her subsequent emotional reaction. As we can see from this example, it initially can be very difficult for persons to reconstruct situations in terms of the ABC model. Therapist(s) need to take a very active role early on to help group participants do this.

A similar technique involves asking participants to recall a specific recent situation in which they became upset or depressed. The participant is then asked to try to recall the cognitions that he or she was having in that situation and to make an association between the thoughts and the affect he or she experienced as per the ABC model.

Clients often can recall situations in which they reacted emotionally but cannot identify the cognition they were having in the situation. It is usually helpful to ask them to reconstruct the situation as carefully as they can and try to put themselves back into the situation as if they were living it over. This often will make it easier for them to recall thoughts that were triggered in response to specific environmental stimuli. If a participant still is unable to come up with the thoughts that were occurring, the therapist can call upon the group to generate a list of cognitions that possibly might have occurred in the situation. If that original participant provides situation and background information, other group members may be good at helping to identify possible cognitions. One or more might then be recognized by the client, who initially was unable to come up with them on his or her own.

As an example, there was a woman in one of the author's previous groups who was attending night classes to become a disc jockey. She reported in a group session that she had missed her last class session and had felt badly about that. When asked why she had missed class she said she had decided at the last minute not to go because she had not completed her homework for that week. Instead she sat at home that evening and felt depressed. She was unable to identify what her cognitions were that might have kept her from going to class or that were associated with her subsequent depressed mood. She was able to provide some additional information, however, that was useful in helping other group members speculate what her cognitions might have been. It turned out that the class was being taught by some very prominent local disc jockeys. She felt that she could not make a fool of herself in front of people whom she admired and she imagined she would do just that by going to class without having completed her homework. In addition, she apparently had been doing well and several of the instructors had mentioned to her that she was one of their best students. This made it even more difficult for her to go to class unprepared because she thought they would find out that she was not as good a student as they originally had thought. Not surprisingly, the cognitions associated with her feeling depressed while sitting at home were centered around her chastizing herself for not having done her homework, thereby causing herself to miss an important class session. In addition, she allowed herself to believe that she would fall into disfavor for missing class, she would not continue to do well in the course because she had fallen behind, and that this was another example of a failure in her life.

We have found that it is often is easier for people to identify and work with other people's automatic thoughts and distorted beliefs than it is to deal with their own. Creating a situation in which participants can help other participants deal with their cognitions serves as a "power test" to find out what their capabilities are. Clients may be surprised that they are able to act as therapists with others' cognitions although they are less successful at working with their own. Such an observation can provide for an interesting discussion of the factors involved that might explain such a discrepancy and which, if intentionally manipulated, might improve one's own typical performance. A participant may learn, for instance, to avoid competing negative cognitions that interfere with his or her ability to stay as task focused when attending to his or her own cognitions as when helping others.

In summary, it is useful to get participants involved early in attempting to relate cognitive formulations to their personal experience. In a group setting the possible therapeutic interactions are multiplied. The therapist(s) only need remain alert to opportunities to involve actively one or more group members in a learning or teaching role.

Identifying and Testing Dysfunctional Beliefs

In the preceding section, we gave some examples of identifying automatic thoughts. We mentioned that it is useful to focus on occasions in which the client experienced an unpleasant emotion and then try to reconstruct the situation. Once the situation is clearly in mind (which may require that the client actively imagine himself or herself in it) the therapist asks the client to attempt to recapture the thoughts that were occurring. The therapist attempts to draw the client out in reporting those thoughts because the most upsetting thoughts often occur later in the chain. Those latter cognitions usually take the form of dysfunctional beliefs that are implied by the automatic thoughts that precede them in the chain.

The first session or two may be devoted largely to teaching participants to identify and report their automatic thoughts. Once they have become familiar with this process the notion of evaluating those thoughts can be introduced. The therapist(s) might choose to introduce the rationale for the cognitive technique of evaluating one's own thoughts and beliefs by first asking group participants what has helped in the past to bring them out of a depressed mood. Depressed persons often will report that it is helpful to have someone talk to them, especially in a reassuring or supportive way, even if it only provides a distraction from their own thoughts.

In the latter case the therapist(s) can point to the benefit of distracting oneself as further evidence of the important role cognitions play in contributing to depressed affect. The therapist also can acknowledge that it is often helpful for a client to talk with someone about the things that are bothering him. Often this is because the reassurance and support given the client help relieve his concerns that he is a failure, unlovable, worthless, and so forth. This relief is short-lived, however, and depressed persons find themselves seeking constant reassurance and support from others. In addition to being difficult for the depressed person's family and friends, such continuing requests for support and reassurance often result in the depressed person feeling guilty and more depressed. However, depressed people can learn to do for themselves what others have been only partially successful at doing for them in the past. Just as they think things that make them depressed, they can learn to think and view situations in ways that will help them feel better.

As with all cognitive techniques there are many ways in which they can be presented to produce the desired effect. The following vignette illustrates one way in which the therapist might introduce belief testing.

THERAPIST 1: Up until now we have largely focused on recognizing the negative thoughts that we have in situations. We have even had you recording some of those thoughts when they occur. Earlier we mentioned that depressed persons could learn to examine their beliefs in ways which would help them become less depressed. I'd like to focus now on techniques that you can use when you catch yourself thinking automatic thoughts. The first thing we must learn to do is to take the role of a skeptical observer in looking at our thoughts. You'll find that if you first step back and attempt to *distance* yourself from the thoughts it will be easier to look at them more objectively. Some people pretend that the thoughts they are having are those of a friend who is coming to them for help. Distancing ourselves in this way helps us to avoid taking our negative thoughts at face value.

If a friend were to tell you that she was worthless and not liked, you probably would not accept that. You would want her to give you good reasons why she believed that to be true. Yet, when you think those thoughts about yourself, if you are like most depressed people, you don't demand the same kind of proof that you would demand of a friend before you'd believe their negative thoughts and beliefs. So, the first thing you need to do when you catch yourself thinking automatic thoughts is to stop and say something like,

"That's something I believe but it is not an established fact." Another thing you might tell yourself when you are thinking about something that might or might not happen in the future is "That's a prediction I am making about the future but I do not know that it will turn out that way." In both cases the idea is that we need to recognize that our thoughts are not necessarily true or valid and we need to evaluate them before we accept them. I think it would be helpful if we could tie some of what I'm saying into an example from one of your experiences. Bonnie, when we were setting our agenda for today, you mentioned that one of the things you wanted to talk about is your concerns about being elected president of your women's club. Can you tell us what some of those concerns are?

BONNIE: Well, I guess basically I don't believe that I'll be able to do it.

THERAPIST 1: What is it that you don't think you will be able to do?

BONNIE: I don't think I will be a good president.

THERAPIST 1: Okay, so your biggest concern is that you will not do a good job as president of the women's club, is that right?

BONNIE: Yes.

THERAPIST 1: That is a good example of a prediction that you are making. If you believe that to be a forgone conclusion rather than a prediction on which you will have to wait and see, I would imagine that might be pretty upsetting.

BONNIE: It is whenever I think about it.

THERAPIST 1: It is a difficult belief to evaluate as it stands, however, because just saying you're concerned about being president doesn't tell us what in particular you are concerned about. I'm wondering if it is some of the things that are expected of you as president rather than just being president that has you concerned. What I'm suggesting is that we often need to break down our beliefs into specifics if we are to be able to really understand them and evaluate their validity. What is there about being president that particularly concerns you?

BONNIE: As president I'm in charge of coming up with programs for our monthly meetings and that's what worries me the most.

THERAPIST 1: What does that involve?

BONNIE: I have to come up with ideas for topics and arrange for speakers.

THERAPIST 1: What about having to do that concerns you?

BONNIE: I don't think I will be able to come up with any good ideas.

THERAPIST 1: Okay, that's a good example of a negative prediction that is defined well enough that we can evaluate it to see if that's a reasonable thing for you to believe. Before we do that I'd like to write on the board three questions that often are useful to ask in evaluating a negative thought or belief. They are: (*Writes on board*)

1. What's my evidence?
2. Is there any other way of looking at that?
3. Even if it is true, is it as bad as it seems?

There are times when you may need to ask additional kinds of questions and times you may not need to ask all of these but these three offer a good general approach to evaluating our negative beliefs. The first "What's my evidence?" is usually a good one to start off asking yourself. Bonnie, what is your evidence for your belief that you won't have any good ideas; what makes you believe that will be the case?

BONNIE: Well, I was made president-elect last month and I haven't had any ideas yet. In fact, every time I think about it I just get anxious about not having done anything yet.

THERAPIST 1: It sounds like part of why you believe you won't be able to come up with any good ideas is that you haven't thus far. I have found this to be a common reason that depressed people give for why they believe they won't be able to do something.

THERAPIST 2: It is an interesting notion that past performance perfectly predicts future performances. Can anyone in the group think of an occasion on which they initially had difficulty learning how to do something that they eventually mastered.

JUNE: Like learning how to ride a bike?

THERAPIST 2: That's a good example. Most people I know of didn't learn how to ride a bike the first day they tried.

JUNE: I know I didn't.

THERAPIST 2: If you were to have predicted whether you would be able to ride a bike successfully on the basis of your first try what would you have predicted?

JUNE: That I wouldn't be able to.

THERAPIST 2: Bonnie, how would learning how to ride a bike be similar to your situation involving coming up with good ideas?

BONNIE: Well, maybe since I wasn't able to come up with any ideas the first time, I think I won't be able to.

THERAPIST 2: Does it seem reasonable to you that you would feel anxious if you were predicting that you would not be able to come up with any good ideas?

BONNIE: Yes, I can see how that would make me feel anxious.

THERAPIST 2: When you consider the analogy of riding a bike, how reasonable is it for you to believe that you won't be able to come up with any good ideas on the basis of not having been able to when you first tried?

BONNIE: Well, I suppose that would be kind of dumb but it seems like whenever I think about it I don't have any ideas.

THERAPIST 2: Uh uh. What happens when you think about it.

BONNIE: I get anxious.

THERAPIST 2: Do you get anxious right away or only after you've thought about it for a while?

BONNIE: At first I would get anxious only after I thought I about it a while, but now I get anxious right away.

THERAPIST 2: To relate that back to riding a bike, how many times would you say you actually got on the bike and tried to ride it and how many times did you just get so anxious you didn't even get on the bike?

BONNIE: You mean how many times did I actually think about who I might get for speakers? I suppose twice. The other times I just got so anxious I couldn't think about it.

THERAPIST 2: Altogether, how many minutes do you think you have spent actually thinking about what would be interesting topics or who would be good speakers?

BONNIE: I suppose about 15 minutes, 10 the first time and 5 the second.

THERAPIST 2: It sounds like your belief that you can't come up with any ideas is based on the fact that you haven't thus far. Perhaps this is a good opportunity to ask the second of the three questions that we introduced earlier. (*Points to board*) Is there another way of explaining why you haven't come up with any good ideas other than that you can't? I wonder if you have been so focused on your inability to come up with any ideas and have become so anxious whenever you think about it that you have not been able to focus on the task.

BONNIE: Yeah, you could be right.

THERAPIST 2: If you look at it in that way, does it mean that you don't have the ability to come up with good ideas or is it more likely that the negative predictions you have been making and the anxiety you've been feeling have prevented you from being able to concentrate on the task?

BONNIE: I think I haven't given myself much of a chance.

THERAPIST 2: I think you're right.

THERAPIST 1: The third question we could focus on is what the implications would be if it were the case that you couldn't come up with any good ideas. Depressed people often don't ask themselves this question because they assume the consequences would be so bad that they don't even want to think about it. What do you think would happen, Bonnie, if you weren't able to come up with any good ideas for topics or speakers?

We will leave our vignette here, but it should be noted that it usually is not difficult to address all three questions and it often is helpful to do so. More or less time may be spent on any one, however, as the situation dictates. After the group becomes more familiar with this process it can be beneficial to enlist other group participants as co-therapists. So as to make that less threatening it can be introduced as a well established fact that people usually are better at detecting the unfounded inferences that others are making and evaluating others' thoughts and beliefs than they are their own. That is why it is helpful to have others assist us by pointing out when we overlook something or when we encounter a blind spot. Of course, in addition to helping one another overcome past obstacles, it is a useful experience to view objectively and help correct the kinds of errors in thinking that we all are prone to.

Assigning Homework

By the end of a session, each member of the group should have been assigned at least one explicitly planned activity to execute before the next session. Initially, the assignment typically will involve some sort of self-monitoring in which clients record their activities and their mood each hour of the day. This kind of record can provide some interesting information about what clients are doing with their time, which activities are associated with increased moods, and which times are their worst.

There is some evidence to suggest that it is very important that self-monitoring be done on an hourly rather than daily basis (Evans & Hollon, 1979). When depressed people report their mood retrospectively, for instance at the end of the day, their report may be negatively biased, inaccurately reflecting lower moods than actually were experienced. Depressed people often report in session that they experienced pervasive low moods or that they do not find any activities enjoyable, even ones that used to give them pleasure. These statements often are not supported by the mood ratings they make. When possible, portions of a self-monitoring record might be displayed to the group to assess whether they would agree to such a statement based on the ratings.

With severely depressed patients it may be necessary to plan an activity schedule with them that they can follow through the week. Sometimes less severe patients have particular difficulties only at certain times of the day or week. For them it may be helpful to schedule activities selectively during those periods.

A useful cognitive-behavioral technique involves the planning of "experiments" for clients to carry out between sessions. The purpose of these is usually to test out beliefs that require the client to gather more evidence outside of the group. After a session or two, greater emphasis is placed on regularly monitoring cognitions that are associated with negative affect. Once clients become adept at recognizing these situations and identifying their automatic thoughts and dysfunctional beliefs, they are encouraged to evaluate those beliefs and attempt to respond rationally to them. One of the main goals of cognitive-behavioral therapy is to enable clients to intervene successfully with their negative thoughts when they occur. Incorporating techniques such as the triple-column record in evaluating beliefs hopefully increases the likelihood that these skills will be learned, maintained, and employed when they would be useful.

It is good practice to assign new homework only as previous assignments are mastered. In addition, even a homework failure can be turned to therapeutic advantage if the time is devoted to discussing the reasons for the failure. We like to convey homework as a no-loss proposition from which the patient is likely to learn something no matter what happens. Also, it is very important that the therapist actively attend to assignments at the next session. Reviewing homework is an item that the therapist always adds to the agenda. As we noted earlier, failure to do so undermines the motivation to continue utilizing various techniques between sessions.

Summarizing Session and Eliciting Feedback

Summarizing the main points of the session is a particularly good way of increasing the probability that group members will apply cognitive ways of looking at their thoughts and experiences outside the sessions. Whenever possible, it is desirable to have participants do the summarizing. In addition to increasing their active involvement in the session, it gives the therapist an opportunity to assess how well participants are assimilating points made in the session. The therapist also may rephrase or amplify clients' statements about the material covered. Summarizing also may be employed profitably in the midst of sessions, especially before moving on to a new topic.

Finally, it is important to give participants a chance to express any reactions they may have had to things that were said or done in the session. Given the potential for depressed patients to misinterpret or react negatively to the actions of others, remarks made to them, and so forth, it is important to attend to their occurrence and use it to demonstrate cognitive evaluative processes.

Subsequent Sessions

Much of the structure adopted in the initial session is carried over into subsequent sessions. We routinely begin each session by assessing level of depression, asking for copies of all homework, and setting a working agenda, usually utilizing that sequential inquiry of each patient described previously. The bulk of the session often is devoted to selecting one or more agenda items from each patient and demonstrating the application of cognitive change procedures. Particular care is given to reviewing homework generated or experiments attempted between sessions.

In early sessions, for closed groups, or whenever a new client is added for open groups, the initial emphasis typically is on obtaining behavioral change. Clients are encouraged to try things that they do not anticipate working, generally presented as "an experiment," with an eye to generating concrete evidence to counter dysfunctional beliefs.

After one or two such sessions, the focus typically shifts to a greater emphasis on more purely cognitive procedures. Particularly useful is the Dysfunctional Thoughts Record (DTR), a no-carbon-required tablet (NCR tablets automatically reproduce multiple copies of written materials without requiring the insertion of carbon paper) printed to provide columns for situations, feelings, thoughts, rational restructuring, and subsequent feelings (see Beck *et al.*, 1979; Hollon & Beck, 1979). This does not mean that behavior change is ignored. Rather, attention to specific acts or concrete counts is heavily relied on in the hypothesis testing proceeds.

Generally, after about six to eight sessions group members are becoming fairly adept at using self-monitoring, behavioral, and cognitive change techniques. They also should be showing at least initial signs of symptom relief.[1]

During these later sessions, we begin to pull for the clients underlying assumptions, world views that, in and of themselves, do not produce depressions but which, when stimulated by events, seem to make the individual susceptible to becoming depressed. Such assumptions often must be extrapolated from repetitious automatic thoughts. In our experience, it is rare for a client to be able to formulate an underlying assumption. This is the point when historical reconstruction can prove helpful; for example, "Can you remember when you first felt that way? What was going on for you? What were you thinking?" As before, this stage does not represent a clean break in the sense that behavioral and earlier cognitive change techniques are discontinued. Rather, efforts to identify more generalized assumptions are integrated into those ongoing endeavors.

Specific Management Problems

Any of a variety of specific managements problems that are not typically encountered in individual sessions can arise readily in group contexts. Examples include efforts to monopolize group time by one or more members, lapsing into small talk, personal attacks by one member on another, the development of subgroups, and the development of different improvement rates. In general, these problems can be handled

---

[1]Our experience suggests that even the most depressed patients typically can learn and utilize these procedures. We are less likely to be concerned about someone who is not attempting and/or not using these techniques than the occasional patient who works hard and diligently but seems to receive no relief. For the former patient we examine our teaching styles or look for idiosyncratic blocks to learning. For the latter patient, we look to other types of therapy.

readily if the therapist is willing to take the initiative and keep the group focused on productive material.

SUMMARY

Overall, group cognitive therapy appears to be a viable option, even at this relatively early stage of its development. The approach certainly already has generated more evidence of specific efficacy than have many other approaches in more widespread clinical use.Group cognitive therapy for depression, like individual cognitive therapy for depression, is problem focused and heavily structured. Great attention is paid to identifying and testing dysfunctional beliefs. The basis therapeutic stance is educative; the therapists have a discrete body of theory and technique that they wish to impact. Based on early returns, it appears that such efforts are likely to meet with clinically meaningful success.In this chapter, we have attempted to outline what we have seen done in the past and have speculated as to why it appears to work. Much more clinical and experimental work remains to be done before we can feel comfortable with our level of understanding. Even now, however, it appears that the types of approaches described can provide a powerful means of combating depression in a group format.

ACKNOWLEDGMENTS

The authors wish to express their appreciation to V. B. Tuason, Head, Department of Psychiatry, St. Paul–Ramsey Medical Center, for his support; to Robert J. DeRubeis for his comments on an earlier version of this chapter; and to Mary Jones for typing it.

REFERENCES

Beck, A. T., & Greenberg, R. L. Coping with depression. New York: Institute for Rational Living, 1974. (Pamphlet)

Beck, A. T., & Shaw, B. F. Cognitive approaches to depression. In A. Ellis & R. Grieger (Eds.), Handbook of rational-emotive therapy. New York: Springer,1977.

Beck, A. T., Rush, A. J., Shaw, B. F., & Emery, G. Cognitive therapy for depression: A treatment manual. New York: Guilford, 1979.

Beck, A. T., Ward, C. H., Mendelson, M., Mock, J. E., & Erbaugh, J. K. An inventory for measuring depression. Archives of General Psychiatry, 1961, 4,561–571.

Blaney, P. H. The effectiveness of cognitive and behavioral therapies. In L. P. Rehm (Ed.), Behavior therapy for depression: Present status and future directions. New York: Academic Press, 1981.

Christie, G. L. Group psychotherapy in private practice. *Australian and New Zealand Journal of Psychiatry*, 1970, *43*, 43–48.

Covi, L., Lipman, R. S., Derogatis, L. R., Smith, J. E., & Pattison, J. H. Drugs and group psychotherapy in neurotic depression. *American Journal of Psychiatry*, 1974, *131*, 192–198.

Craighead, W. E. Issues resulting from treatment studies. In L. P. Rehm (Ed.), *Behavior therapy for depression: Present status and future directions*. New York: Academic Press, 1981.

Daneman, E. A. Imipramine in office management of depressive reactions (a double-blind study). *Diseases of the Nervous System*, 1961, *22*, 213–217.

Emery, G., Hollon, S. D., & Bedrosian, R. C. *New directions in cognitive therapy: A casebook*. New York: Guilford Press, 1981.

Evans, M. D., & Hollon, S. D. *Immediate versus delayed mood self-monitoringin depression*. Paper presented at the Annual Meeting of the Association for the Advancement of Behavior Therapy, San Francisco, December, 1979.

Friedman, A. S. Interaction of drug therapy with marital therapy in depressed patients. *Archives of General Psychiatry*, 1975, *32*, 619–637.

Gioe, V. J. Cognitive modification and positive group experience as a treatment for treatment depression. (Doctoral dissertation, Temple University, 1975).

Dissertation Abstracts International, 1975, *36*, 3039B–3040B. (University MicroFilms No. 75–28, 219)

Hollon, S. D. Comparisons and combinations with alternative approaches. In L. P. Rehm (Ed.), *Behavior therapy for depression: Present status and future directions*. New York: Academic, 1981.

Hollon, S. D., & Beck, A. T. Cognitive therapy for depression. In P. C. Kendall & S. D. Hollon (Eds.), *Cognitive-behavioral interventions: Theory, research, and procedures*. New York: Academic, 1979.

Hollon, S. D., Bedrosian, R. C., & Beck, A. T. *Combined cognitive-pharmaco-therapy versus cognitive therapy in the treatment of depression*. Paper presented at the Annual Meeting of the Society for Psychotherapy Research, Oxford, England, July 1979.

Hollon, S. D., & Kendall, P. C. Cognitive self-statements in depression: Development of an automatic thoughts questionnaire. *Cognitive Therapy and Research*, 1980, *4*, 383–396.

Hollon, S. D., & Shaw, B. F. Group cognitive therapy for depressed patients. In A. T. Beck, A. J. Rush, B. F. Shaw, & G. Emery (Eds.), *Cognitive therapy for depression: A treatment manual*. New York: Guilford, 1979.

Klerman, G. L., DiMascio, A., Weissman, M., Prusoff, B., Paykel, E. S. Treatment of depression by drugs and psychotherapy. *American Journal of Psychiatry*, 1974,*131*, 186–191.

Morris, N. E. A group self-instruction method for the treatment of depressed outpatients. Unpublished doctoral dissertation, University of Toronto, 1975.

Rehm, L. P., & Kornblith, S. J. Behavior therapy for depression: A review ofrecent developments. In M. Hersen, R. M. Eisler, & P. M. Miller (Eds.), *Progress in behavior modification* (Vol. 7). New York: Academic, 1979.

Rush, A. J., & Watkins, J. T. Group versus individual cognitive therapy: A pilot study. *Cognitive Therapy and Research*, 1981, *5*, 95–104.

Rush, A. J., Beck, A. T., Kovacs, M., & Hollon, S. D. Comparative efficacy of cognitive therapy and imipramine in the treatment of depressed outpatients. *Cognitive Therapy and Research*, 1977, *1*, 17–37.

Rush, A. J., Hollon, S. D., Beck, A. T., & Kovacs, M. Depression: Must pharmacotherapy fail for cognitive therapy to succeed? *Cognitive Therapy and Research,*1978, *2*, 199–206.

Shaw, B. F. Comparison of cognitive therapy and behavior therapy in the treatment of depression. *Journal of Consulting and Clinical Psychology*, 1977, *45*,543–551.

Shaw, B. F., & Beck, A. T. The treatment of depression with cognitive therapy. In A. Ellis & R. Grieger (Eds.), *Handbook of rational-emotive theory and practice*. New York: Springer, 1977.

Shaw, B. F., & Hollon, S. D. *Cognitive therapy in a group format with depressed outpatients.* Unpublished manuscript, University of Western Ontario,1978.

Taylor, F. G., & Marshall, W. L. Experimental analysis of a cognitive behavioral therapy for depression. *Cognitive Therapy and Research*, 1977, *1*, 59–72,1977.

Weissman, M. M. The psychological treatment of depression. *Archives of General Psychiatry*, 1979, *36*, 1261–1269.

Yalom, I. D. *The theory and practice of group psychotherapy.* New York: Basic, 1970.

3

Rational-Emotive Therapy in Groups

RICHARD L. WESSLER

Rational-emotive therapy (RET) as group psychotherapy began almost as early as individual RET. In 1955, Albert Ellis, who had been trained as a psychoanalyst and who already was well known as a sex and marriage counselor, became dissatisfied with the results he obtained from employing psychoanalytic principles. Therefore, he (Ellis, 1962) took the bold step of directly confronting patients with their self-defeating philosophies, of actively arguing against their ideas, and of assigning behavioral and cognitive homework for them to practice their newly adopted ways of thinking and acting.

The goals of RET, whether done in groups or individually, are to teach clients how to change their disordered emotionality and behavior and to cope with almost any unfortunate event that may arise in their lives. RET holds that humans can employ their conscious thought processes to their own benefit by solving their problems and rethinking the self-defeating assumptions about their own and other people's presumed perfectability.

The ideal outcome of RET would be for the individual to adopt an attitude of self-acceptance rather than of self-judgment; to accept life's realities, including grim realities, by acknowledging their existence and not attempting to avoid or prevent them with magical thinking and superstitious maneuvers. It would involve refraining from judging other people in a global manner and especially from damning them for their shortcomings and transgressions. It would mean independently thinking out for oneself an ethical philosophy rather than childishly depending upon other people or on religion for absolute rules about right and

RICHARD L. WESSLER • Department of Psychology, Pace University, Pleasantville, New York 10570.

wrong; unashamedly pursuing pleasure in both long-term and short-term interests, rather than unpleasurably conforming to rigid rules, or shortsightedly indulging oneself with no heed for the future.

RET seeks to help people reduce or eliminate strong negative emotions (e.g., anxiety, depression, and hostility) so they can live more personally satisfying lives. To accomplish this goal, RET seeks to help people identify the beliefs that produce and sustain dysfunctional emotional experiences and maladaptive behaviors and to change them to beliefs that promote rather than thwart their personal objectives.

The goal of change, in other words, is an elegant philosophical restructuring to enable the individual to pursue more efficiently the common human goals of survival and happiness.

Basic Concepts

The label *Rational-Emotive Therapy* refers to two different activities of psychological therapists. First, the label stands for classical RET, characterized by the extensive writings of Albert Ellis. In this form of RET, neurotic disturbance is postulated to be caused by irrational thinking, and the client is taught to identify his or her irrational thinking. The process is highly directive, confrontive, and educative. It has been illustrated amply by Ellis in transcripts of therapy sessions (viz., Ellis, 1971) and in tape recordings issued by the Institute for Rational Living in New York City and in films and video tapes.

The second meaning of the label *RET* is co-extensive with the cognitive-learning approaches to therapy. It has been called comprehensive RET (Walen, DiGiuseppe, & Wessler, 1980) to distinguish it from classical RET. In this form of RET, neurotic disturbance is postulated to be caused by irrational thinking as well as by faulty perceptions, muddled inferences, arbitrary definitions, and illogical reasoning.

The classical version is highly philosophical in the sense that it focuses explicitly on human values, on issues of right and wrong (i.e., morality), and a philosophy of living that includes tolerance for one's imperfections, other people's transgressions, and the world's ample supply of frustration.

Like classical RET, comprehensive RET is highly directive, confrontive, and educative; but it is in addition, persuasive and makes use of techniques and procedures developed by cognitive learning and other forms of treatment. It tends to be a good deal more eclectic, but without losing the philosophic core that distinguishes RET from its allied approaches. Unfortunately, there are fewer examples of comprehensive

RET available for reading, listening, and viewing. However, comprehensive RET is what most RET practitioners, including Albert Ellis, do, especially in group therapy.

Therapy

Theory

The theory of RET as a treatment of disturbance is quite simple: If a person changes his or her irrational beliefs to rational beliefs, he or she will suffer less and enjoy life more. The evaluation of self, of other people, and of the world in general are the major targets of change.

RET treatment is based on an educational and persuasive model. Clients are taught to identify how they are disturbing themselves by uncovering their irrational beliefs, then they are informed about why their beliefs are irrational and how to change them. If they change their philosophical rules of living and then live according to those changes, they will lead more satisfying and enjoyable lives. There is no assumption that some deep or mysterious forces keep them from changing their philosophy of living. People are postulated to have innate tendencies to retain or readopt their irrational beliefs (Ellis, 1976), and because there is widespread social approval for some of them, to readily retain those.

Since people often resist change or fail to change when new information is presented to them, persuasive attempts other than information giving are typical of RET sessions (Wessler & Ellis, 1980). These persuasive attempts are better labeled *dissuasive methods* because their aim is to help people give up their dysfunctionl ones (Wessler & Wessler, 1980).

Dissuasive methods are based on theories of attitude formation and change. The evaluative component of attitudes is the particular target of change because in RET the belief system consists of evaluations. Information giving is directed at the knowledge component of an attitude, but because many attitudes are not based upon knowledge, information giving has its limitations.

Attitudes often are represented as having three components (knowledge, evaluation, and action) in interdependent relationship. A change in one may result in a change in the other two. A major theory of attitude change, cognitive dissonance (Festinger, 1957), proposes that changes in evaluations will follow changes in knowledge or action or both. The RET theory of treatment makes use of this principle by offering arguments against rigidly held absolutistic beliefs and assigning homework between therapy sessions. Homework usually consists of the client's doing something that is inconsistent with his or her beliefs and thus inducing dissonance. As Festinger pointed out, it is difficult to deny that you did something against your evaluative beliefs, especially if there are witnesses. People tend to adjust their evaluative beliefs to fit what they have done, or to fit what they have learned, or both.

Many other dissuasive maneuvers will be presented later in this chapter. All can be understood as attempts to change attitudes. RET does not depend upon rational discussion alone to produce therapeutic change. In the broadest sense of RET, anything within the bounds of professional ethics that helps people change their minds in favor of a more personally satisfying philosophy of living is a legitimate part of RET. RET assumes that the individual changes his or her own mind and can choose to do so. It is not the therapist's responsibility to force change.

Therapy Process

In broad outline, RET proceeds as follows: The individual identifies explicitly or implicitly that he or she wants certain changes or goals. The therapist shows the client that the goals of personal change can be attained by cognitive change. The therapist goes on to show what the client's maladaptive beliefs are and how they can be changed. The client then can choose to work to change his or her thinking.

This simply stated process can occur over one session or many. Some people never change much despite genuine efforts. (Why their thinking is so difficult to change is not known, but Ellis suspects biological diathesis.)

There is no assumption that any special relationship must be established with the therapist before change can occur. The therapist exhibits nondamning acceptance of the client, though he or she may express judgments about some of the client's actions.

The therapist probably has to be seen in certain ways by the client in order to be effective. The literature on attitude change and persuasion (Karlins & Abelson, 1970; McGuire, 1969; Zimbardo & Ebbesen, 1969) suggests some perceptions of the therapist that promote effective RET.

The therapist probably is more effective if seen as credible by the client. A perception of credibility can be promoted by showing expertise and trustworthiness. A confident manner and a belief in what he or she says tend to communicate such expertise (cf. Frank, 1978), as do educational degrees and professional reputation. Trustworthiness may occur when clients see therapists as genuinely interested in helping them and not working for the therapist's sole benefit. The beginning of trustworthiness is to have genuine concern for the client's improvement and welfare. The list of characteristics includes warmth, empathic ability, and so forth.

The relationship with the client is important for another reason that is unrelated to any presumed curative aspects. Therapist characteristics that are irrelevant to the client's belief system probably influence acceptance of rational thinking. In other words, clients may change their minds for reasons unrelated to logic and evidence presented to them. Just as college students say they like a course or expect to do well because they like the professor, clients may believe a therapist because they like him or her or reject a therapeutic message because they do not. In group therapy the same concerns are multiplied. If the individual does not like, respect, or believe the group members and the therapist, the chances of his or her being helped are reduced greatly.

An issue in any group is its dynamics. Since the individual is the focus of change in RET groups, dynamics are important insofar as they affect the individual's thinking, feelings, and behaving. The norms of the group, its communication patterns, and emerging leadership roles can be used therapeutically or, if they encourage continued irrational thinking, can function iatrogenically. Thus, in an RET group, cohesiveness is allowed, promoted, or discouraged, depending on whether the therapeutic aims of the individuals in the group are helped or hindered by group cohesiveness.

Group therapy provides opportunities for observing a client's interactions and making comments about them. At times the teaching of interpersonal skills is the chief concern of an RET group. This, however, usually occurs in conjunction with or after attention has been given to the client's belief system. For example, the teaching of assertive communication skills may aid a person in his or her everyday life, but by itself it is a palliative. Assertive skills may help increase the chance for getting what one wants, but that does not reduce exaggerating the unfairness of not getting what one wants. Similarly, the improvement of communications skills between couples, so often cited by couples and counselors as a serious difficulty, is a secondary aim in RET. The primary aim is to reduce personal disturbance; then the couple can be shown how to improve communications.

Treatment Tactics

The initial considerations in the process of RET in groups are the same as with individuals. The individual is the focus of change and, therefore, an assessment of the individual's problems is necessary. Assessment here means understanding the cognitive dynamics—the person's main rational and irrational beliefs and their resulting emotional and behavioral consequences. Facts about the individual's social status, marital status, birth-order, height, weight, and age are of little or no importance in RET. To an extent, even the practical problems in a person's life (the A's in the ABC model) are of little importance at least initially. Later, after dealing with the belief system, the practical problems may be taken up.

The therapist who leads the group is in a better position than group members to make an assessment of problem diagnosis in terms of the ABC model. However, group members, as they learn the ABC model, often become adept at spotting each others' irrational beliefs and defenses. There is the risk that group members may tacitly agree not to confront each other or to offer only practical problem-solving suggestions, but an experienced leader-therapist will recognize such actions, comment on them, and try to prevent their recurrence.

In order to make an assessment or problem diagnosis, the therapist and group members actively ask questions, probe answers, offer comments, and test hypotheses inferred from a focal client's in-group behavior and self-reports of thoughts, feelings, and actions. The general strategy is to follow the *ABC* model. The focal client, in presenting a personal problem, usually starts with the *A* or activating experience. Then the *C* or emotional consequences are sought and clarified. Sometimes both *A* and *C* are revealed in the initial presentation of a specific problem, for example, "I got very angry at my boss when he asked me to work overtime last night!" In this illustration the individual identifies the *A* (the boss's asking the person to work overtime) and *C* (hostility). The group members, led by the therapist, then may ask questions about both *A* and *C*, for example, "What reasons did the boss give?" (an *A* probe); "Did you have something else to do?" (another *A* probe); "Has this happened very often?" (yet another *A* probe).

And, "Did you let him know you were angry?" (*C* probe); "How did you know it was anger that you experienced?" (another *C* probe). These questions clarify and add richness to the report and are especially helpful if the client has difficulty recognizing and reporting emotional experiences, as is sometimes the case.

The therapist then leads the group in focusing on the belief system. Using the model of anger presented earlier in this chapter, the therapist asks questions about the demands the client placed upon the boss's behavior ("He must not ask me to work overtime"), blame ("and he's a rotten bastard for making such a request"), intolerance ("he shouldn't have a responsible position if he's going to make such requests"), and grandiosity ("he has no right to ask me to work overtime"). One by one the client's evaluative thinking about the situation would be uncovered. He or she might be asked to challenge the truth of the self-statements or the group members might offer reasons why the self-statements were untrue.

In addition to the approach of presenting personal problems, RET groups also may be experiential. Group exercises adopted from many sources may be used to "produce" emotional consequences. The following exercise easily might be used with a new group; its purpose is to "produce" emotional consequences (usually anxiety); to expose defenses; to introduce the notion that thinking, especially evaluative thinking, largely determines emotional experiences; and that a great deal of such thinking is automatically done without much awareness. The therapist addresses the group:

> I'm going to ask you to think of some secret, something about yourself that you normally would not tell anyone else. It might be something you have done in the past, something you're doing now in the present. Some secret habit or physical characteristic. (*Pause*) Are you thinking about it? (*Pause*) Good. Now I'm going to ask someone to tell the group what they have thought of . . . to describe it in some detail. (*Short pause*) But since I know everyone would want to do this, and we don't have enough time to get everyone in, I'll select someone. (*Pause—looking around the group*) Yes, I think I have someone in mind. (*Pause*) But before I call on that person, let me ask what are you experiencing right now?

Answers such as tense, anxious, and nervous are commonly mentioned. Ideas such as "I hope you don't call on me!" are expressed. At this point the therapist shows the group that it is the *thought* of doing something, not the doing itself, that leads to their feelings. The therapist then asks questions about what kinds of thoughts led to these feelings. Typical responses are: "If they would find out something about me I wouldn't want them to know, that would be awful!" Once the discussion has begun, it often picks up momentum as people realize that their strongly evaluative thinking about what might happen led to their anxious reactions. As the discussion progresses, the therapist can show the group members that they may be demanding that they follow social norms implicit in the situation, for example, "I must do what the leader says." The anxiety-producing conclusions are obvious: "And if I don't do what he says, he and the others will think that I've copped out or can't take it or have some other weakness. That would be awful and prove what a worthless person I truly am!"

Further discussion may show people their defensiveness and self-protectiveness. For example, some people will admit that they would not have revealed anything too embarassing, just something that sounds risky but really is "safe." Others will admit that they thought of leaving the room. Such responses often are generalized to other situations as well and can be uncovered by asking, "Is your reaction typical of the way you usually act when put on the spot?"

An imaginative RET group leader can incorporate almost any exercise into the process. The "secret" is how the experience is processed, not how it is conducted. Any experience or exercise intended to generate "here-and-now" feelings can be processed using the ABC model. And, of course, awareness of one's belief system or insights into one's behavior is not the end of the processing of an experience. Dissuasion—helping the person change dysfunctional evaluative thinking—is the crucial activity.

Nardi (1979) has combined elements of psychodrama with RET. For example, a group member playing another member's parent shouts irrational beliefs and hits the focal person with a foam rubber bat; then the focal client takes the bat and hits him or herself while shouting the same beliefs. Although this exercise overstates the importance of early socializing agents in acquiring of irrational beliefs, it is an effective demonstration of what the client does *today* to create his or her own misery. In another psychodrama-inspired exercise, group members acting as alter egos speak the irrational beliefs of the main characters in a psychodrama; this exercise gives members opportunities to clarify what irrational thinking is and how it affects behavior.

Didactic exercises can teach RET principles, such as the following demonstration created by the author to teach the notion of human complexity and the illegitimacy of self-evaluation. It is most conveniently introduced after a client's saying some self-deprecating remark. The therapist says, "Before we respond to John's remark, I'd like to ask everybody to do something for me. Do you see this table? I'd like someone to measure it for me." If no one responds, he asks someone, especially John, to attempt the task. Ambitious group members will report the table's length, width, height, or weight. None of this is accepted by the therapist. It is not the length, width, height, or weight that is of interest, but the table itself. Of course, there is no way to measure the table itself; *partis por toto,* the part–whole error in self-evaluation can then be discussed: to measure one's whole worth on the basis of a few dimensions is illegitimate, a form of self-prejudice. Humans, of course, are considerably more complex than tables.

Cognitive and behavioral rehearsal, especially in the form of role playing, readily may be used in an RET group. The group often provides a "safe" environment in which to try out new behaviors acquired through skill training and to reinforce new rational ways of thinking. When a client's problems involves a good deal of interpersonal anxiety, the group provides a forum to try out interpersonal skills; more importantly, it provides a forum for attacking the shame that in RET theory is at the heart of interpersonal anxiety. Shame is hypothesized to occur as one fearfully anticipates or experiences real or attributed criticism by other people of one's weaknesses. In the group one can learn not to feel shame about any of his or her characteristics and can work at improving those characteristics that can be modified.

To summarize, the initial activity in the rational–emotive therapy process is assessment of the individual's problem. To do this, questions are framed in a way that yields information to support or refute the hypotheses about the individual's cognitive dynamics as formulated by the therapist and group members. The next step is to make the individual aware of how he or she is creating self-sabotaging emotional and behavioral consequences. The next step is dissuasion, any activity intended to help the individual change his or her maladaptive, unrealistic, irrational beliefs to ones that promote individual survival and happiness. The two most common approaches are (1) educational and (2) direct and indirect methods of influence. The principle direct methods are Socratic dialog and logical disputation. When direct methods do not seem to be effective, indirect methods may be used.

Homework has been a characteristic part of RET since its inception. Its use in groups differs little from its use with individuals. The client agrees to do some activity during the time between sessions. The activity might be reading RET literature (bibliotherapy), writing out challenges to his or her irrational thinking (written homework), or some shame-attacking or risk-taking experiential assignment.

To aid in getting rid of irrational ideas that lead to shame (interpersonal anxiety over real or fictitious inadequacy), the client is asked to do something foolish in public. The violation of social norms is an effective shame-attacking exercise. For example, most people seem unaware that they conform to custom when riding elevators and almost always face the front of the elevator, even though they are not sure whether it is illegal not to do so. A shame-attacking exercise, then, would consist of asking someone who says he or she would feel anxious riding in elevators while facing the back instead of the front, to do so. Anticipation can be probed; people may have images of the other passengers giving them strange looks or thinking that the deviant was crazy or stupid. The therapist can show that looks or thoughts cannot directly affect anyone, and even spoken words are ineffective unless taken seriously.

The RET practitioner urges shame-attacking experiences for yet another reason. Even if the client has correctly interpreted the meaning of people's glances or read their minds accurately, it is the *B* or belief system that leads most directly to the anxiety. Thus, one's evaluative philosophy about harmlessly breaking social rules and receiving criticism for so doing is the main concern of this exercise. RET teaches self-acceptance—to follow one's own conscience despite others' disapproval. Thus, the shame-attacking exercise is aimed at increasing self-acceptance and mature responsibility, not simply at achieving comfort while doing a specific zany activity. Although these exercises often are humorous because they involve harmless social rule breaking, they have a serious purpose. Shame-attacking exercises can be done not only within the group but also as an assignment to all group members to perform outside the group and to report during the next group meeting.

The risk-taking exercise is any activity that the individual defines as "a risk." Since the risk referred to is psychological, what is risky is both idiosyncratic and objectively nondangerous. Thus, in the final analysis, it is not truly a risk, but the discovery of this fact is a main purpose of risk-taking exercises. A man who fears striking up conversations with women may be asked to do so. A person who "must" do everything perfectly is asked to make mistakes. Through their experience, if they carry out the activity, they learn that their dire prophecies do not come to pass, that the anticipation is worse than the doing, and that what they have done once they can do again, thus building confidence.

These activities are assigned with the person's consent. The group often can exert influence on the individual to do the assignment and can provide a forum for rehearsal and practice. It is important to note that the group may misunderstand the shame-attacking and risk-taking homework assignments. The point is not to do them well nor to overcome uncomfortable situations by gaining mastery over them. The point is to gain mastery over oneself by actively confronting self-limiting philosophies of living. Thus, the woman who refuses to initiate contacts with men because she would feel worthless if she were rejected is encouraged to approach men *not* because she can become better at it with time and thereby escape rejection, but to accept herself *even if* she receives rejections. In fact, were she to approach men and not receive rejections, an experienced RET therapist might comment, "That's too bad. Try again!" These exercises are deliberately couterphobic because it is one of the best ways to overcome irrational thinking about life's "horrors."

Consistent with the aim of risk taking, the RET group leader does not try to create a climate of support in which people are reinforced for their neurotic "need" for love and approval. Group members are encouraged to adopt and express nonjudgmental attitudes toward each other, to practice what Ellis calls nondamning acceptance. This is somewhat different from positive regard and is closer to affective neutrality. Given time and the freedom to communicate with each other, group members often develop warm feelings and cohesiveness even though these sentiments have not been promoted by the leader. So, although some initial attempts to encourage people to reveal personal facts and to "trust" each other are desirable to get the group started, their continued use is seldom necessary.

The whole issue of *trust*, which some group members (and some therapists, too) overemphasize, requires reassessment. Trust means several things. First, that I can trust you with information about myself and that you will not practically disadvantage me because of your privileged communication. This is essentially an ethical issue having to do with confidentiality. Second, most clients worry about the *psychological* harm they might suffer at the hands (or is it mouth?) of another person. Since psychological reactions are of our own making, however, and based upon our belief systems, there is in fact nothing to "trust" another person with. Trust also means that I can trust you to help me. But this issue, which is by far the more realistically important one, seldom is mentioned in therapy groups.

Uncomfortable with strangers is another phrase that group members use to justify remaining silent when actively working on their problems would be better for their purposes. Some people have a life philosophy that says, "I must never feel uncomfortable," known in RET jargon as low frustration tolerance of LFT. Both trust and uncomfortable are socially respectable ways of labeling shame. They are better dealt with as B's to be changed than as conditions the group has to fulfill. In other words, speaking up about oneself is both a shame-attacking and risk-taking experience. Clients are done a disservice when allowed to avoid anxiety-provoking situations either within or outside the group.

PRACTICE

Problems

Almost all neurotic problems can be treated in an RET group. Psychosis, whether of organic or of unknown origin, cannot be treated in an RET group, but its sufferers frequently can benefit from working on their neurotic problems or, more simply, on their problems of living.

It is better, then, to specify what cannot be treated in an RET group. Psychosis itself, cannot be, but some of its symptoms, for example, egocentric thinking can be by a vigorous leader and group members who feel free to point out the self-centeredness. Disorders in which the individual does not seek change are not appropriate for an RET group. Some involuntary referrals can be "hooked" into therapy by showing that RET can help them achieve some goals, but many cannot. Criminals are not necessarily imprisoned because of neurosis. Although they stupidly may think they can get away with crime in the long run, they hardly are driven to commit it by anxiety, depression, or hostility. The latter factors might be a reason in some cases, and the skillful therapist might show how the criminal's life would be better without enraged hostility; such persuasion would be a first step in eventually doing RET with the law breaker.

Other involuntary referrals can be treated similarly: First, "motivate" the client by showing that he or she can benefit in some way from taking RET seriously. RET or any therapy is a means to an end; if the end therapy can serve as one that is important to the person, he or she will tend to see therapy as somewhat valuable. In involuntary referrals, the therapist might be seen as the agent of society, and in fact may so act to try to get the person to become the "standard" socially acceptable model of a human. In this writer's opinion it is unethical to use therapy in this way. It is the client's goals that we can work on, not society's. In fact, RET often goes *against* societal norms and explicitly asks people to decide for themselves what is right and wrong rather than passively accepting "society's" (or someone's version of "society's") rules. Oversocialization creates neurosis. Undersocialization creates sociopathy, but that, strictly speaking, falls outside the scope of RET.

Assessment

Precise differential diagnosis usually is not done in RET. Rough categorization based on an initial individual interview is enough to screen out persons who are blatantly psychotic, overly egocentered, withdrawn to the point of perpetual silence, or talkative to the point of compulsiveness. A psychotic individual would not be excluded because of the psychosis, but because he or she might be too withdrawn or otherwise unable to interact with other group members.

Evaluation of a different kind is done as the leader sorts through the client's reports and actual behavior to discover the main irrational philosophies he or she lives by. This is more discriminating than simply asking a person about his or her troubles. If clients could report all of their beliefs when asked, there would be little for therapists to do. But a person with an anger problem over his or her boss's behavior may have several problems, for example, putting him or herself down when the boss treats him or her unfairly or taking the boss's unreasonable request as a lack of respect and then "awfulizing" about that. We often get angry at others because they say or do things that "cause" us to feel ashamed or anxious. Within a few sessions, the RET leader can give fairly complete accounts of each person's main life difficulties, belief system, main symptoms, and how hard he or she works to change.

This last point, how hard the client works at change, is particularly important. Most people can uncover or recognize their beliefs and can understand how those beliefs are leading to upset and goal-defeating behaviors. Som people, however, find it exceptionally difficult to overcome their irrational thinking or to do what would help them effect significant changes. It is one thing when an individual does not change thought habits of a lifetime; this takes time and practice. It is quite another when the person does not attempt to carry out behavior-experiential homework assignments. The reason may be LFT or discomfort anxiety.

When a person claims that something is too difficult or too inconvenient, he or she is expressing a philosophy of low frustration tolerance—that life should not be so hard. Most people want to change easily and comfortably. Others fear the discomfort they might experience in doing, say, a risk-taking assignment. They want to feel better *before* changing, instead of changing to feel better.

One of the important evaluation tasks of the therapist is to discover what the person fears and to help reduce the fear before they attempt to make significant behavioral changes. To accomplish this, imagery and time projection can be employed: imagery to discover exactly what the person fears and time projection to help him or her develop some confidence to cope.

In one example, a young woman who refused to dance in public despite the repeated requests from her husband to go to a disco reported that she imagined everyone would laugh at her. Rather than reassure her that this would not happen, the therapist asked her to imagine the details: How many people would be there? Would they all laugh? Would they laugh simultaneously or consecutively? How long would each laugh? The therapist then deliberately exaggerated the scene and asked her to imagine all 30 patrons consecutively laughing for 10 seconds. To illustrate the length of a 10-second laugh, the therapist laughed for 10 seconds and was joined by the client in laughter during the last 3 seconds. She was then asked if she could stand this "horrible torture" for 300 seconds and to imagine what it would be like. She decided that she could stand it for 5 minutes even though she previously had been convinced that she could not stand it at all. Armed with this cognitive rehearsal she successfully carried out her homework assignment of dancing in public and later used the same approach to overcome other social phobias without the help of the therapist.

If it is apparent after a group has begun that one or more members do not participate and seem unlikely to, they may be excused from the group and referred for individual treatment. Each is there for help; if they are neither giving nor getting help they would best be excused from the group.

Treatment

The process and mechanisms of treatment have been described in the previous section. In this section the beginning of a group will be illustrated. Assume that the group members are unknown to each other but have had an initial screening interview with the therapist.

The initial task is to get the group members acquainted with each other. This can be accomplished by each person's simply saying his or her name and mentioning a little about him or herself, or it can be the focus of an exercise in which pairs get acquainted with each other, then form larger groups.

An early issue is the trust one. It can be handled by the leader's discussion of the issue or by an experiential exercise such as the one of asking for "secrets." The "secrets exercise" also can be used to introduce the ABC model.

Another introduction to the ABC model is one developed by this writer and labeled the *emotional dictionary*. It is especially useful with groups that are not accustomed to talking about their emotional experiences. A chalkboard or other large writing surface is required. Group members are asked to name common English words that stand for emotions, which are listed on the board. If any controversies arise from the choice of a word, they are discussed to discover common meanings (one of the points of the exercise).

The group then is asked to vote on whether each word stands for a negative or positive emotional experience (not whether it can have positive or negative outcomes). In case of doubt, the leader can ask, "Would you look forward to experiencing (say) anxiety?" A plus or minus sign is placed next to each word.

Then the group is asked to indicate whether the word stands for an experience that is usually extreme and dysfunctional, or mild-to-moderate, or perhaps even motivating. Again a vote is taken and disagreements discussed. A 2 or 1 respectively is placed next to the algebraic sign of each word. Then, the leader tells the group that in RET we make the assumption that -2 emotions are due to iBs, and that -1 emotions are due to rBs. Although this is something of an oversimplification, it presents the idea of discriminating rational from irrational beliefs and motivating but negative emotions from goal-defeating ones.

The processing of additional exercises or personal problem solving using the ABC model can be done with greater awareness on the part of the group members. In all of RET there is an emphasis on the non-mysterious: therapy and counseling are seen as educational and dissuasive processes without intentions or "insights" that must be concealed from the cliend or carefully timed. If an individual client or group member asks a question about theory, philosophy, or procedure, it is answered unless the question is an obvious attempt to sidetrack the discussion; even then, it might be answered and the discussion refocused on the topic.

Treatment may be either time limited or open ended. Ellis's therapy groups at the Institute for Rational-Emotive Therapy have been in existence for many years, with several complete turnovers of membership. New members are incorporated rather easily into the group, partly because the leader discourages a "we-are-special" attitude among group members, and partly because established group members seem eager to work with new people.

Termination, as mentioned above, is a matter of individual decision, although both therapist and group members may comment on the decision and even try to dissuade the individual from his or her choice if further treatment seems warranted. Good questions for the therapist to ask are: What are you not doing that you would like to do? And what are you doing that you would like to stop? These concrete questions can assist an individual in reviewing his or her own desire for further treatment. Some clients remain in group long after they have ceased to create significant problems in their lives, usually because they enjoy the group experience and it helps them to keep their own thinking clear. When obvious dependence on the group is detected, the therapist will move to encourage greater independence, perhaps insisting that the person leave the group. Termination in time-limited groups is not an issue in RET.

Therapist's Tasks

The leader of an RET group is a therapist not a facilitator. The term *facilitator* implies that the leader merely creates conditions for positive growth potentials to become fulfilled. Since no positive growth potentials thwarted by society or other people are assumed in RET theory, the notion of facilitator is inappropriate.

Nor is the leader first among equals. His or her job is to provide structure for group experience or problem-solving attempts. The clients, of course, furnish the specific content.

The communication pattern in problem solving within groups is one of therapist to focal client, with other group members either observing if the therapist is especially active or directing their messages to the therapist or to the focal client. There is little interaction among nonfocal clients in this situation.

Another communication pattern emerges when the therapist teaches inductively; most of the messages are exchanged between the therapist and the other group members. Again, little interaction among the group members occurs.

However, the therapist deliberately can withdraw from the discussion and assume the role of coach rather than teacher–therapist. The group members are left to process an exercise or attempt to apply the ABC model to a focal client's problem. As long as the group does well and remains on target, the therapist does not intervene. When the group wanders or proposes practical solutions without attempting to work with the individual's belief system, the therapist can redirect their efforts. Simple comments such as "I wonder who can guess what John's beliefs are that lead to his anger?" can redirect the discussion.

The therapist also is active in seeing that one or two people do not dominate the discussion or that no one becomes disruptive. Since there is no assumption in RET that anyone "has" to talk or has a "right" to be heard, the therapist can manage the group discussion diplomatically and head it into productive areas.

Group members may socialize with each other outside the therapy sessions (and frequently do), but the therapist does not. The therapist's relationship is professional not social. The therapist may see individuals from the group for private sessions. Clients who require hospitalization for psychosis or suicide attempts are referred to a suitable facility, and their re-entry to the group is assessed upon their release. Occasionally, clients may be referred for medication, and this practice could be a condition for remaining in the group, depending on the attitude of the specific RET therapist.

APPLICATION

Group Selection and Composition

There are no special rules regarding group selection. Some practical guidelines are to exclude persons who are likely to be disruptive because of active psychosis or compulsive talking and to include members of both sexes, because many problems of interpersonal anxiety involve relations with the opposite sex. These guidelines might be disregarded if the person diagnosed psychotic were only occasionally disruptive or if therapy were combined with consciousness raising, for example, in a men's or women's sexuality group.

It is probably unwise to have all depressed persons in the same group, although a group having the same phobia (e.g., flying) might work well as a time-limited, topic-limited therapy group.

Group Setting

There are no special space requirements. A circular seating arrangement facilitates interactive communications. Sufficient space for role playing and psychodrama experiences also is desirable, and the space should be private enough to preserve confidentiality.

Group Size

No special rules apply. If there are fewer than 6 group members, discussions may lag. If there are more than about 12, it is difficult to include everyone.

For the teaching of RET principles and illustrating their application to selected problems, the group size could amount to several hundred. Ellis frequently demonstrates the use of rational principles in daily life to groups of 100 or more, although these demonstrations are not thought to be group therapy. Similarly, the public education workshops held at the Institute for Rational Living in New York City, Los Angeles, and elsewhere may be attended by scores of people. These workshops lie somewhere between therapy and education and focus on specific topics, for example, overcoming creative blocks and designing future life goals and plans.

Therapy Frequency, Length, Duration

Most RET groups meet weekly. They may be open ended with changes in membership or time limited. For time-limited workshops, about six to eight weeks seems typical. The length of session varies from an hour and a half to three hours. An exception is an RET group marathon, which might range from 10 to 14 hours or longer. There are no prescriptive guidelines for frequency, length, or duration.

Media Usage

There are no restrictions or requirements for media in RET groups. Videotape equipment might be used for giving feedback to participants about their mannerisms and style of presentation, but this probably is rarely done. Chalkboards and flip charts also could be used, but are not required. "Props," for example, foam bats, might be used. Ellis has conducted group therapy for years without any media aids, although he uses printed homework forms that clients may fill out. Some RET therapists (e.g., Maultsby, 1975) makes more extensive use of written forms.

Leader Qualifications

A leader should be professionally qualified to practice counseling and/or psychotherapy in his or her state and be competent in conducting rational–emotive psychotherapy. Although many professionals may meet these requirements and competently perform RET, certain ones are recognized by the International Training Standards and Review Committee in RET as associate fellows and fellows. They have demonstrated their abilities and are recognized as qualified in the practice of rational-emotive methods.

Ethics

Practitioners of RET are bound by the ethical code of their respective professional groups. The majority of recognized rational-emotive therapists are psychologists bound by the ethical code of the American Psychological Association. Violations of ethical standards also may be referred to the International Training Standards and Review Committee for action if the professional is certified to practice rational-emotive methods.

RESEARCH

There have been many research studies published that deal with RET and other cognitive-learning approaches to psychotherapy. These studies either focus on the cognitive hypothesis as a factor in psychological disturbance (Ellis, 1979), or therapeutic outcome studies (DiGiuseppe, Miller, & Trexler, 1979). Very few studies have investigated group therapy *per se.*

In general, the studies cited in these summaries lend support to the role of cognition in emotional–behavioral processes. The analog studies support RET treatment claims about the efficacy of its interventions. The problem with both these research summaries is that very few studies investigate pure or classical RET.

The studies that Ellis (1979) cites in support of his theoretical claims come from a wide variety of sources. Relatively few of them test hypotheses specifically derived from RET theory. It seems safe to conclude from the volume of studies cited by Ellis that cognitions play an important role in human behavior and experience; that neurotic behavior is correlated with unrealistic ideas and illogical thinking; and that mood is affected by cognitive processes. However, the fundamental hypothesis of RET—that irrational beliefs lead to self-defeating emotions and that rational beliefs do not—has not been adequately investigated.

The outcome studies of RET suffer from the same deficiency: few of them have studied pure or classical RET as an independent variable. DiGuiseppe *et al.* (1979) review about 50 studies, noting their limitations. Some used no behavioral outcome measures, obtaining data only on changes in irrational beliefs as measured by a paper-and-pencil test, a practice Wessler (1976) warned against. Some study the outcome of educational efforts, not psychotherapy or counseling. Others were studies that report outcomes of cognate approaches, not pure RET. Comprehensive RET is the kind actually practiced, and it overlaps significantly with the approaches of Meichenbaum (1974), Beck (1976), and others. Although some of the outcome research is impressive (especially Rush, Beck, Kovacs, & Hollon, 1977), the therapy is not exclusive RET in nature. The few RET studies support its effectiveness with such specific problems as public-speaking anxiety and test-taking anxiety.

One difficulty in conducting research on RET, whether group or individual, is that RET is not a single technique in the sense that, for example, desensitization is. RET is a theory of disturbance that emphasizes the roles of maladaptive perceptions, misconceptions, and evaluations. RET is a growing collection of tactics for helping people change their maladaptive cognitions; some tactics are very direct, some indirect. What makes research difficult is that a skilled RET therapist may use several cognitive, behavioral, and affective-expressive tactics within a few minutes while working with a client (Wessler & Ellis, 1980). If the direct disputing of irrational beliefs seems to get nowhere, the therapist quickly can switch to imagery or role reversal, or analogies, or even parables and poetry. It is very difficult to duplicate this therapeutic flexibility under controlled conditions.

If one accepts RET as an attitudinal theory of neurotic disturbance, then a different research question emerges: namely, can attitudes be influenced in dyads and larger groups? The answer is yes, and it is supported by several decades of research in attitude change and persuasion. RET employs these tactics to bring about evaluative and other cognitive changes (Wessler & Wessler, 1980).

STRENGTHS AND LIMITATIONS

RET takes the individual and his or her problems as its focus. It can be used for specific problems, for example, a phobia, and thus functions very much like behavior therapy. Or, it can take personality exploration and self-awareness as its goal, as do traditional psychotherapy, non-directive counseling, and other self-awareness approaches. As a system of therapy, RET easily incorporates specific techniques developed in other systems into its tactics of therapeutic dissuasion. Versatility and applicability to a wide range of neurotic problems of living are among RET's outstanding strengths.

RET is most easily used with clients who recognize their own responsibility in creating their difficulties or who readily come to accept this fact. RET makes no claim that the person was a victim of his or her parents, society, or past passive conditionings. Clients who wish to become undisturbed, rather than discovering on whom to place blame for disturbance, benefit most quickly.

RET works well with clients of at least average intelligence, but can be used with other people in a more or less rote fashion (which is probably how they learned their philosophy of living initially). Clients who are rigidly religious often resist the humanistic ethical message central to RET, but one need not give up all religion to do RET or to benefit from it. Almost all religions offer a rational version that de-emphasizes or eliminates the absolutistic thinking found in its very conversative or orthodox counterparts.

RET is no cure-all. It does not cure psychosis or psychopathy. It will not stop crime, delinquency, or social problems. Since RET depends on the cooperation of the client, it will not help the uncooperative. Therapists may try to encourage cooperation by many means, including their personal charisma, but not everyone is willing to cooperate.

Group RET has additional limits. The very disturbed client may be better helped in individual sessions. A client whose activities require weekly or more frequent monitoring would benefit more from individual sessions than from group.

On the other hand, for certain clients, particularly shy ones, group treatment is better than individual treatment. For many clients, the advantages of group therapy far outweigh the disadvantages. Most clients' problems involve other people, and therefore the group is an ideal setting in which to work on their problems. True, there is the disadvantage that there will be lesser amounts of attention from the therapist, but the advantages of group therapy are many:

1. They are cost efficient; the therapist can see several clients at one time and teach rational principles to many people at one time.
2. Members of the group can learn that they are not unique in having a problem or in having specific kinds of problems.
3. The group can provide a forum for preventative psychotherapy since members can hear others discussing problems that they may not have faced or may not be currently facing in their lives.
4. Group members can learn to help each other. It is a well established educational principle that one of the best ways to learn a skill is to try to teach it to someone else. Clients learn rational thinking while trying to teach it to others in a group setting.
5. Some experiences, activities, and exercises can be done only in groups. The group also provides forum for practicing shame-attacking or risk-taking exercises.
6. Some group exercises may be advantageous in bringing out specific emotions that then can be dealt with *in vivo* in the group setting.
7. Certain problems are more effectively dealt with in a group, for example, interpersonal or social-skills deficits. The client can practice new social behaviors and ways of relating to people.
8. A group setting allows clients to receive a great deal of feedback about their behavior, which may be more persuasive in motivating them to change than that of a single therapist in an individual situation.
9. When therapeutic efforts are focused on practical solutions to life problems, the presence of many heads in a room may result in more suggestions than an individual therapist could muster.
10. The group members can provide a source of peer pressure that may be more effective in promoting compliance with homework assignments than that of the individual therapist.

Finally, the group can provide a phasing out experience for clients who have been in individual therapy. Such clients may have discovered their irrational ideas and how to dispute them but require additional practice to complete the process.

REFERENCES

Beck, A. T. *Cognitive therapy and the emotional disorders.* New York: International Universities Press, 1976.

DiGiuseppe, R., Miller, N. J., & Trexler, L. D. A review of rational–emotive psychology outcome studies. In A. Ellis & J. M. Whiteley (Eds.), *Theoretical and empirical foundations of rational–emotive therapy.* Monterey, Calif.: Brooks/Cole, 1979.

Ellis, A. *Reason and emotion in psychotherapy.* New York: Lyle Stuart, 1962.

Ellis, A. *Growth through reason.* Palo Alto: Science and Behavior Books, 1971.

Ellis, A. The biological basis of irrational thinking. *Journal of Individual Psychology,* 1976, *32,* 145–168.

Ellis, A. The basic clinical theory of rational–emotive therapy. In A. Ellis & R. Grieger (Eds.), *Handbook of rational emotive therapy.* New York: Springer, 1977.

Ellis, A. Rational–emotive therapy: Research data that support the clinical and personality hypotheses of RET and other modes of cognitive–behavior therapy. In A. Ellis & J. M. Whiteley (Eds.) *Theoretical and empirical foundations of rational–emotive therapy.* Monterey, Calif.: Brooks/Cole, 1979.

Festinger, L. *A theory of cognitive dissonance.* Evanston, Ill.: Row, Peterson, 1957.

Frank, J. D. *Psychotherapy and the human predicament.* New York: Schocken, 1978.

Maultsby, M. C., Jr. *Help yourself to happiness,* New York: Institute for Rational Living, 1975.

McGuire, W. M. The nature of attitudes and attitude change. In G. L. Lindzey & E. Aronson (Eds.), *The handbook of social psychology* (Vol. 2). Reading, Mass.: Addison-Wesley, 1969.

Meichenbaum, D. H. *Cognitive–behavior modification.* Morristown: N.J.: General Learning Press, 1974.

Nardi, T. J. The use of psychodrama in RET. *Rational Living,* 1979, *14* (1), 35–38.

Rush, A., Beck, A. T., Kovacs, M., & Hollon, S. Comparative efficacy of cognitive therapy and pharmacotherapy in the treatment of depressed outpatients. *Cognitive Therapy and Research,* 1977, *1,* 1–8.

Walen, S., DiGiuseppe, R., & Wessler, R. L. *A practitioner's guide to rational–emotive therapy.* New York: Oxford University Press, 1980.

Wessler, R. L. On measuring rationality. *Rational Living,* 1976, *11* (1), 25.

Wessler, R. L., & Ellis, A. Supervision in rational-emotive therapy. In A. K. Hess (Ed.), *Psychotherapy supervision.* New York: Wiley-Interscience, 1980.

Wessler, R. A., & Wessler, R. L. *The principles and practice of rational-emotive therapy.* San Francisco: Jossey-Bass, 1980.

Zimbardo, P., & Ebbesen, E.G. *Influencing attitudes and changing behavior.* Reading, Mass.: Addison-Wesley, 1969.

ADDITIONAL READING

Arnold, M. B. *Emotion and personality: Psychological aspects.* New York: Columbia University Press, 1960.

Berkowitz, L. *Roots of aggression.* New York: Atherton, 1969.

Davison, G., & Neale, J. *Abnormal psychology: A cognitive experimental approach.* New York: Wiley, 1974.

Ellis, A. *Humanistic psychotherapy: The rational–emotive approach.* New York: Julian, 1973.

Ellis, A. The basic clinical theory of rational–emotive therapy. In A. Ellis & R. Grieger (Eds.), *Handbook of rational emotive therapy.* New York: Springer, 1977.

Ellis, A. Discomfort anxiety: A new cognitive behavioral construct. *Rational Living*, 1979, 14 (2), 1–7.

Ellis, A., & Geiger, R. *Handbook of rational–emotive therapy.* New York: Springer, 1977.

Ellis, A., & Harper, R. A. *A new guide to rational living.* Englewood Cliffs, N.J.: Prentice-Hall, 1975.

Hauck, P. A. *Overcoming depression.* Philadelphia: Westminster, 1973.

Hauck, P. A. *Overcoming frustration and anger.* Philadelphia: Westminster, 1974.

Hauck, P. A. *Overcoming worry and fear.* Philadelphia: Westminster, 1975.

Horney, K. *The neurotic personality for our time.* New York: Norton, 1939.

Izard, C. E. *Human emotions.* New York, Plenum, 1977.

Karlins, M., & Abelson, N. I. *Persuasion* (2nd ed.) New York: Springer, 1970.

Katz, D., & Kahn, R. L. *Social psychology of organizations* (2nd ed.). New York: Wiley, 1978.

Knaus, W. J. *Rational emotive education.* New York: Institute for Rational Living, 1974.

Knaus, W. J. *Do it now: How to stop procrastinating.* Englewood Cliffs, N.J.: Prentice-Hall, 1979.

Lazarus, A. *Multimodal behavior therapy.* New York: Springer, 1976.

Lazarus, A. *In the mind's eye.* New York: Rawson Associates, 1977.

Lazarus, R. S. *Psychological stress and the coping process.* New York: McGraw Hill, 1966.

Mahoney, M. J. Reflections on the cognitive–learning trend in psychotherapy. *American Psychologist*, January 1977, 32, 5–13.

Mahoney, M. J. A critical analysis of rational–emotive therapy and therapy. In A. Ellis & J. M. Whiteley (Eds.), *Theoretical and empirical foundations of rational-emotive therapy.* Monterey, Calif.: Brooks/Cole, 1979.

Moore, R. The E-priming of Albert Ellis. In J. Wolfe & E. Brand (Eds.), *Twenty years of rational–emotive therapy.* New York: Institute for Rational Living, 1975.

Raimy, V. *Misunderstandings of the self.* San Francisco: Jossey-Bass, 1975.

Rimm, D. C., & Masters, J. C. *Behavior therapy: Techniques and empirical findings.* New York: Academic, 1974.

Schachter, S., & Singer, J. E. Cognitive, social and physiological determinants of emotional states. *Psychological Review*, 1962, 9, 379–399.

Watzlawick, P. *The language of change: Elements of therapeutic communication.* New York: Basic, 1978.

Self-Control Group Therapy of Depression

MICHAEL W. O'HARA AND LYNN P. REHM

The purpose of this chapter is to describe in some detail a self-control therapy program for depression. To this end we will provide the rationale and context for the development of the treatment program. Second, we will discuss briefly the model of depression on which the treatment program is based. Third, will be a description of subject/client characteristics. Fourth, the nature of the research support for the effectiveness of this program will be indicated. Finally, we will describe on a session-by-session basis the elements of the treatment program.

The self-control therapy program has evolved over the past seven years in the context of five therapy outcome studies as well as trials in various community mental health centers. The original therapy package was developed by Fuchs and Rehm (1977) in an effort to determine the efficacy of a treatment based on Rehm's (1977) self-control model of depression.

SELF-CONTROL MODEL AND ITS IMPLICATIONS IN THE THERAPY OF DEPRESSION

The self-control model of depression (Rehm, 1977) derived from a more general model of self-regulation proposed by Kanfer (1970, 1971; Kanfer & Karoly, 1972). The model describes the cognitive-behavioral

MICHAEL W. O'HARA • Department of Psychology, University of Iowa, Iowa City, Iowa 52242. LYNN P. REHM • Department of Psychology, University of Houston, Houston, Texas 77004. Preparation of this chapter was supported in part by NIMH grant 2R01 MH27822 to Lynn P. Rehm.

processes that maintain certain behaviors that lack environmental support. Thus, adaptive self-control functioning may explain behavioral persistence despite environmental consequences that seem to mitigate against it (e.g., dieting, quitting smoking, writing a book). The model posits three interconnected processes (self-monitoring, self-evaluation, and self-reinforcement) operating in a closed loop feedback system.

Self-monitoring refers to the observation of one's own behavior and its situational antecedents and consequences. Self-evaluation involves a comparison between an estimate of one's performance derived from self-monitoring and an internal criterion. Rehm (1977) has elaborated Kanfer and Karoly's model by considering the importance of causal attribution in the self-evaluation phase. Positive and negative self-evaluations are mediated by the extent to which an individual attributes causality for important outcomes to him or herself as opposed to external factors over which he has little control. Self-reinforcement generally refers to the self-application of overt or covert rewards and punishments contingent upon positive or negative self-evaluations.

Rehm suggested that dysfunctions at any of these stages may be implicated in the development of depression. Specifically, he identified six self-control dysfunctions: (1) excessive monitoring of negative events; (2) attention to immediate versus delayed consequences of behavior; (3) setting stringent standards in self-evaluation; (4) inaccurate attributions of causality; (5) insufficient self-reward; and (6) excessive self-punishment. Rehm (1981) has reviewed evidence that supports the role of the various self-control dysfunctions in the etiology of depression as well as the links between self-control dysfunctions and depressive symptomatology.

Characteristics of depressed subjects who have benefited from self-control therapy as well as documentation of the program's effectiveness have been presented elsewhere (Fuchs & Rehm, 1977; Rehm, Fuchs, Roth, Kornblith, & Romano, 1979; Rehm, Kornblith, O'Hara, Lamparski, Romano, & Volkin, 1981); however, we will summarize them very briefly here. Subjects have been women ranging in age from late teens to mid-fifties. They have been predominantly Caucasian and middle class; nevertheless, there has been considerable variability along the lines of social class and race. Education level has varied from ninth grade to the Ph.D. level with a median and mode around 12 to 13 years. About 60 to 70% of the subjects were married.

Subjects met stringent depression criteria in order to be admitted into the therapy groups. Criteria have varied but in early studies subjects were required to have had MMPI-depression scale scores of at least 70. In later studies a Beck Depression Inventory score (Beck, Ward,

Mendelson, Mock, & Erbaugh, 1961) of at least 20 was required. Subjects in later studies also were required to meet Research Diagnostic Criteria (Spitzer, Endicott, & Robins, 1978) for Major Affective Disorder. Though subjects were solicited volunteers from the community, they were equivalent in most respects to a moderately to severely depressed outpatient population.

Five outcome studies have documented the effectiveness of the program provided in between 6 and 12 sessions. A variety of control groups have been employed including no treatment, nondirective group therapy, active instigational group therapy, and assertiveness training. A one year follow-up of subjects from two early studies (Romano & Rehm, 1979) indicated a persistence of treatment effects.

APPLICATION OF SELF-CONTROL THERAPY

Self-control treatment programs have ranged in length from 6 to 12 sessions; all have followed the same basic sequence both within and across sessions. Across sessions our strategy has been to focus on self-monitoring, self-evaluation, and self-reinforcement in a sequential fashion. The assumption is that each may be conceptualized as a therapy module and that self-evaluation builds on self-monitoring, and that self-reinforcement builds on self-evaluation. The number of sessions alloted for each component may vary both as a function of the needs of the clients and the exigencies of clinical practice.

Therapy sessions generally last between an hour and one half and two hours. The beginning of each is devoted to two activities. Clients fill out either a Depression Adjective Check List (Lubin, 1967), or the Beck Depression Inventory and perhaps the Self-Control Questionnaire (Rehm, et al., 1981). These periodic assessments of mood and self-control attitudes provide feedback on the progress of each client in therapy.

Following completion of self-report instruments, the therapist reviews with the group homework assigned the previous week. This period of homework review fulfills several purposes. First, program compliance readily may be assessed. Our basic assumption has always been that compliance with therapeutic homework assignments is crucial to the success of the group program. Group members typically have a variety of experiences with their homework so that we encourage members whose homework experience was positive to share their successful strategies with other group members. Members model appropriate self-control behaviors for each other as well as providing support to each other for making efforts at cognitive and behavioral change.

Our experience has been that the power of group therapy is most evident during the review stage. Up to a third of the entire session may be devoted to this process. A depressed client often does not believe he or she can meet the goals the therapist has set for him or her. The group allows the individual to interact with others who are similar in terms of how they feel. As group members see each other making changes, their own sense of hopelessness usually diminishes enough so that they try out new ways of thinking and new behaviors. Despite the relatively brief duration of these groups, a surprising degree of cohesion develops as these women work together to overcome their depression.

Following homework review, new material is presented to the group members didactically. The group switches to a psychoeducational mode at this point. In each session the therapist will discuss an aspect of depression from a self-control perspective. Each of the six self-control dysfunctions are described over the course of the group program. The therapist discusses how a particular dysfunction is causally related to depression and what can be done to rectify the dysfunction. At this stage it is important for the therapist to present the self-control rationale in a convincing fashion since each group member is likely to have his or her own understanding of the causes of his or her depression. Sometimes it is necessary to request that clients suspend belief and, in the nature of an experiment, act as if our analysis of their depression is congruent with their own. Again, group members, who have found that changing their self-control strategies has an impact on their mood, also will be helpful in influencing the belief system of doubting clients.

The group discusses the session's material both during and after the therapist's presentation. The therapist especially encourages members to provide examples from their own daily life as to how a particular self-control dysfunction impacts on their thinking and behavior.

In order to illustrate and concretize the session rationale an in-group exercise is completed. For example, during the week between the first and second session group members are requested to monitor their daily mood, positive self-statements, and activities. The exercise for the second session is for clients to graph their daily mood ratings and daily frequency of positive self-statements plus positive activities. What clients often observe doing this exercise is that the graphs are parallel, indicating that their mood is related to the frequency of their positive self-statements and activities.

The in-group exercises serve to clarify the didactic presentation as well as to make the material more personally relevant. Group members usually complete the exercises alone or with the help of the therapist. Time is alloted in group to discuss any new learning resulting from the exercises as well as any new confusion. The exercises also serve as a preparation for the homework assignment that follows directly from them.

The homework assignment is one of the most important elements of the therapy group. Based on the material presented and the exercise, homework is prescribed, the purpose of which is to encourage group members to put into practice self-control concepts to which they have been exposed in group. In the early stages of the group a therapist will contact each group member by phone to assess compliance with homework instructions as well as to clear up any confusion from the previous group. Given the relatively brief duration of the therapy program, prompt assessment of client problems with homework is essential.

SELF-CONTROL THERAPY MANUAL

We will present the 10-session version of the self-control program which includes three sessions each devoted to self-monitoring and self-evaluation and two sessions each of self-reinforcement and program review. The program will be described session by session following the structure outlined above. Sections that are in quotes and are attributed to the therapist are paraphrases only of material that is presented in session. Dialogue that is presented is for illustration of points only.

Session 1: Self-Monitoring

The self-monitoring module is the base on which the rest of the program is built. At the beginning of the session, the therapist presents a general overview of the 10-session program. The presentation of the program rationale might be presented in the following way.

THERAPIST: The therapy program in which you are going to participate probably will differ from any previous experience that you have had with group therapy. We will take a directive problem-solving approach to help you deal with your depression. The program in many ways will be course-like and we will be providing instruction, doing in-group exercises, and homework to help you develop new cognitive and behavioral strategies for overcoming depression. Over the next 10 weeks, we will be working with one central idea and that is that mood is related to your cognitions and your activities. You can control your mood and depression by changing your cognitions as well as your activities. We will help you to develop effective cognitive strategies as a way of increasing both positive cognitions and activities. You also will learn new goal-setting strategies as well as ways of motivating yourself toward those goals.

Rationale. Three points form the basis of the first-session rationale: (1) Mood is related to cognitions and activities. (2) Depressed persons selectively attend to unpleasant events in their lives. (3) Learning to pay more attention to pleasant events and increasing positive self-statements and activities will help in overcoming depression. The first two points are the principles around which the session revolves and the third point describes what the clients do with the information. In every session we elaborate points with examples and further explanation until we believe that each client appreciates the significance of the point.

In developing the rationale that mood is related to cognitions and activities we provide examples of their relationship.

THERAPIST: Both what we think about and what we do influence our mood. Many of you have had the experience of feeling sad after thinking about a personal failure or a family problem; or other times, for example, you may have chastised yourself for some real or imagined failing such as being five pounds overweight. The influence of thoughts on mood works the other way as well. Thinking of a past success or pleasant experience often has the effect of enhancing mood.

What we do also influences mood. For example, I'm sure you have all had days when you started out feeling depressed, but several good things occurred that left you in a good mood. You may have talked to a friend, had a pleasant interaction with one of your children, or a gratifying experience at work. The reverse may happen as well; for example, an argument with a friend can quickly ruin a positive mood state. In order to overcome depression it is important to recognize the relationship between what you think and do and your mood.

We attach a great deal of importance to the therapist presenting the rationale convincingly. Clients come to therapy with a variety of notions regarding their depression and we try to present our rationale so that they will understand their depression in a way congruent with the program. Removing the mystery of mood change also may be of value for many clients. We provide "good reasons" for why they may be depressed and offer strategies for change.

The second point of the rationale, "mood is also influenced by what we attend to," is one of the crucial anchors of the program. Changes in self-monitoring patterns often precede positive changes in mood. We attempt to modify the way in which clients self-monitor their own positive and negative cognitions and events on a daily basis.

THERAPIST: I also want to stress that depressed persons often pay attention only to the negative events in their life, ignoring positive ones. Imagine two persons, both of whom experienced an equal mix of positive and negative events. If one of the persons focused mainly on positive events and the other primarily on negative events, we would have little doubt as to which person would feel more depressed. Many depressed persons find it difficult to identify any positive experiences in their life.

The therapist encourages discussion of the first two points of rationale and prompts for examples from group members.

THERAPIST: Mrs. B., I noticed you seemed a little sad when I talked about attending to negative events. Would you share your thoughts with the rest of the group?

MRS. B.: My life seems to be full of bad things. I have problems with my husband and kids and even my own parents don't leave me alone. All I think about and everything I do is unpleasant.

THERAPIST: From what you have said, you seem to believe that the difficulties that you experience are causing you to feel down. Take a minute and think of a pleasant interaction with a friend that occurred in the past month. How did you feel?

MRS. B.: I can think of one and I felt good. I wasn't thinking of all my troubles. I seemed to forget them.

One of the goals during group discussion is for clients to reframe their current problems. The therapist would point out to Mrs. B. that she does have positive experiences and that they do affect her mood. Pointing out to clients how the way they think and behave is related to depression prepares them to accept our prescriptions for change.

The third point of rationale suggests the first stage in our strategy for overcoming depression.

THERAPIST: Learning to pay more attention to positive events and increasing cognitions and activities that bring up mood level will be our goal. By learning that your mood is affected by what you do and how and what you think rather than by uncontrollable forces, you will gain a sense of control over your mood.

The initial interviews and first-session introductions provide information for the therapist regarding what problems brought each client into therapy. The therapist, whenever possible, reframes each client's presenting complaints into our cognitive–behavioral framework and encourages the group members to do the same for each other.

Homework Assignment. In an earlier section we discussed the importance of the homework assignment. The therapist stresses that homework assignments are given at the end of each session and that they are crucial to the success of this type of therapy.

THERAPIST: Your first assignment will be to start paying particular attention to positive self-statements and activities. We want you also to observe how your mood varies with the types and numbers of positive self-statements and activities that you experience each day. You will have a chance to learn which cognitions and behaviors are most important for you in determining your mood.

Take a look at the log sheets and lists of examples of positive self-statements and activities. The following principles should be employed in doing your self-monitoring: (1) Keep the self-monitoring logs with you throughout the day, and record as often as possible. Make sure that you have recorded all your positive self-statements and activities in your log by the end of each day. (2) Record in a few words the actual self-statement or activity. Emphasis should be on trivial as well as large ones. (3) The lists should serve as a guide for types of self-statements and activities you otherwise may have missed. Review your list every now and then as a reminder. (4) At the end of each day record your day's mood. Although it may not seem so, everyone's mood varies from day to day and even from hour to hour. Try to rate your mood on a scale from 0 to 10. Zero stands for the worst mood you have ever experienced for a day and 10 stands for the happiest mood you have ever experienced for a day. Use any and all points in between and remember to record even small changes from one day to the next. (5) Use a separate log for each day; more than one if you need. (6) Bring your logs to each session! The rest of the program will build on this information.

We usually will ask group members to take a few minutes to recall both *trivial* and important positive self-statements and activities from the day. We emphasize paying attention to trivial activities and self-statements (i.e., small, often-overlooked) so that the group members do not wait around for a major positive event or an important positive self-statement to occur in order to log something positive. When the therapist is confident that all group members understand the logging procedure, he or she will let them know that they will be contacted by phone during the week to check on their homework assignments and to see if they are having any problems with them.

In the first session, time allocation is as follows for the 90-minute group: (1) introductions by group members and therapist—30 minutes; (2) program overview—5 minutes; (3) session rationale—35 minutes; and (4) homework assignment—20 minutes. Clinicians sometimes question how necessary it is to stick to these time guidelines. The guidelines

TABLE 1
Positive Self-Statements and Activities List

Self-statements
  1. I like people.
  2. I really feel great.
  3. People like me.
  4. I've got more good things in life than the average person.
  5. I deserve credit for trying hard.
  6. That was a nice thing for me to do.
  7. I'm a good person.
  8. I have good self-control.
  9. I am considerate of others.
 10. Someday I'll look back on these days and smile.
 11. My health is pretty good.
 12. I am an open and sensitive person.
 13. My experiences have prepared me well for the future.
 14. I have worked long enough—now is time for fun.
 15. Even though things are bad right now, they are bound to get better.

Activities
 16. Planning something that you will enjoy
 17. Going out for entertainment
 18. Attending a social gathering
 19. Playing a sport or game
 20. Entertaining yourself at home (e.g., reading, listening to music, watching TV)
 21. Doing something just for yourself (e.g., buying something, cooking something, dressing comfortably)
 22. Persisting at a difficult task
 23. Doing a job well
 24. Cooperating with someone else on a common task
 25. Doing something special for someone else, generosity, going out of your way
 26. Seeking out people (e.g., calling, stopping by, making a date or appointment, going to a meeting)
 27. Initiating conversation (e.g., store, party, class)
 28. Playing with children or animals
 29. Complimenting or praising someone
 30. Showing physical affection or love

are somewhat arbitrary; nevertheless, they reflect our estimation of the amount of time needed adequately to cover material and allow for group discussion. Coverage of the entire first session material in the initial meeting allows group members to start homework right away. Later sessions may themselves be expanded as much as the clinician desires and homework simply may be repeated. We might note at this point that we have no data suggesting additional therapeutic value for groups, on the average, as number of sessions increase from 7 to 12.

Day: _____   Date: _____

	Positive self-statement or activity	Positive self-statement or activity list number	
1.			
2.			
3.			
4.			
5.			
6.			
7.			
8.			
9.			
10.			
11.			
12.			
13.			
14.			
15.			
16.			
17.			
18.			
19.			
20.			

Day's mood rating: 0   1   2   3   4   5   6   7   8   9   10
               unhappiest   happiest
               ever   ever

FIGURE 1. Self-monitoring log.

Session 2: Mood and Events

The relationship between mood and self-statements and activities is further developed in the second session. Clients have spent a week monitoring positive self-statements and activities as well as rating their mood on a daily basis. Sessions 2 through 10 begin with a review of the previous week's homework as well as the rationale from the previous session.

Homework Review. The therapist begins the session by reiterating that mood is improved by increasing one's attention to positive self-statements and activities and increasing them. Group members are encouraged to bring up any problems that they may have had in completing the self-monitoring assignment. Each subject is asked to report on any positive experiences she may have had in doing the self-monitoring. The therapist interprets any positive experiences in light of the program rationale. For example,

THERAPIST: Mrs. B., would you share with the group some of your experiences in doing the self-monitoring homework?

MRS. B.: I found it difficult to focus on the positive things I said to myself. Thinking about how unhappy I have been was much easier. It seemed that I have very few of the positive self-statements but more positive activities than I expected.

THERAPIST: I suspect that many of the other group members had a similar experience. One of my efforts in the group will be to help you pay more attention to the positive activities in your daily life and increase the frequency of the positive things that you say to yourself.

During the review phase the therapist asks each person to read examples from his or her list of positive self-statements and activities. If a group member presents very few examples, the therapist will prompt him or her to think of other kinds of positive self-statements or activities, perhaps smaller or more trivial ones, that the person may have forgotten to write down or dismissed as unimportant. The therapist encourages group members to focus on the positive in their lives and this orientation continues throughout the course of the group.

Mood and Behavior Exercise. The mood and behavior exercise is designed to demonstrate, in a graphic form, the relationship between the number and types of daily behavior (activities and self-statements) and mood. It also provides several alternatives for understanding the relationship between mood and behavior.

THERAPIST: Now that we have a week's worth of information on your behavior and your mood level, let's see if we can establish, in a more obvious form, how the two are related.

The purpose of this exercise is to look closely at the relationship between behavior and mood. The assumption is that mood is influenced by behavior level generally or by specific types of self-statements and activity.

1. *Mood and behavior graph:* Using your self-monitoring logs for the last week, graph the number of positive self-statements and activities for each day using the scale at the right. Now graph your week's mood using the scale at the left. Are the lines roughly parallel? Do the peaks and valleys correspond?

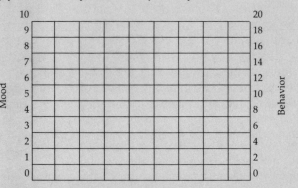

2. Pick out the 2 or 3 days on which your mood was the highest. Figure out the average number of positive behaviors for those days. Next, do the same for the 2 or 3 days on which your mood was the lowest. Is the average number of positive self-statements and activities higher on the better mood days?

3. Look at your self-monitoring logs for the 2 or 3 days on which your mood was the highest. What particular behavior happened on those days? Compare these logs to the logs for your 2 or 3 worst mood days. What happened on the high mood days that did not happen on the low mood days?

4. Can you see a connection between your self-statements and activities and your mood? People usually find a connection between mood and either general behavior level or some specific type of behavior. One week's records may not show this relationship clearly but the program is based on the idea that mood can be changed by changing self-statements and activities.

5. Repeat this exercise on next week's records.

FIGURE 2. Mood and behavior exercise.

Did most of you find that your mood level mirrored what you were doing? Remember that there will not be a perfect one– to–one correspondence between mood and the number of self-statements or activities since you may on some days have a few very enjoyable events, and on others have many events that are only moderately pleasurable. I want to emphasize that in the long run the relationships between your self-statements and activities and how you feel is quite clear. Your mood can be changed by paying more attention to the positive and increasing the number of your positive activities.

Isolating Mood-Related Self-Statements and Activities. The mood and behavior exercise served to underscore the general relationships between mood and behavior. The group members are asked to identify specific self-statements or activities that have the greatest impact on mood.

THERAPIST: Now that you see that your mood and behavior are related, let's try to isolate the behaviors that have the greatest effect on your mood. Take a few minutes right now to go back over the log sheets for the past week. Look at those days when your mood was the best. Are there particular self-statements or activities that stand out as responsible for better mood on those days? Are there particular classes of behavior that are checked off more often on those days? Do you have some idea already as to which self-statements or activities do most for your mood?

Which of those positive behaviors that were infrequent do you feel would make you feel good but right now occur at a very low frequency or not at all?

Group members are taught to become aware of effective self-statements or activities that help to bring their mood up. The therapist encourages discussion among the clients as they explore which behaviors help them to feel better.

Homework Assignment. Group members continue monitoring positive self-statements and activities as well as mood. The therapist asks that they pay particular attention to those behaviors that seem most influential in changing mood.

Session 3: Immediate versus Delayed Consequences

This session wraps up the self-monitoring module. The rationale for the session is that depressed persons often focus on the immediate "negative" consequences of an activity rather than delayed "positive" ones. Immediate consequences are often "effortful behaviors" (e.g., getting dressed and made up) and delayed consequences are often pleasant experiences (e.g., being at a party with friends). Again, keeping with the theme of the program the therapist attempts to instigate a change in attentional set from the negative (difficult arduous task) to the positive (pleasant delayed consequence).

Homework Review. Group members have continued to monitor their positive self-statements and activities and have graphed them as well in the same manner as in the previous session.

THERAPIST: A number of you found that your mood and behaviors seem to parallel each other quite closely. Others have found a definite relationship although not quite as strong. What you need to remember from this exercise is that you have a clear demonstration that your moods are not mysterious or uncontrollable. In fact, what you are doing and what you are saying to yourself have great influence on how you feel. The rest of the therapy sessions will build on this initial principle.

Group members are encouraged to discuss problems with their monitoring during the past week. The therapist will prompt members to describe any changes that they noticed in their mood due to the monitoring especially of the targeted positive self-statements and activities. Again, the therapist tries to help each group member identify classes of self-statements and activities that are especially related to positive mood.

Rationale. The therapist stresses that depressed persons tend to focus on negative rather than positive events in their lives and that their self-statements usually have a negative cast. The negative focus is often a distorted and unrealistic assessment of what is going on. Group members are told that over the next several weeks they will learn new ways to perceive events accurately and realistically and that this process will have the effect of lessening their depression. The explicit rationale for the current session is then developed and later extended in the session exercise.

THERAPIST: Events often are defined as positive or negative in terms of their consequences. For example, painting the house is negative because it is exhausting and unpleasant. Eating an ice cream cone is negative because of self-statements about gaining weight. Finishing a job is positive because it is over and you can relax for a while. These consequences or self-statements about them often make an event pleasant or unpleasant. Virtually all activities or events have many consequences: some are negative and some are positive, some are immediate and some are delayed. People who tend to be depressed focus on the negative consequences and miss positive consequences, especially if they are delayed.

Immediate versus Delayed Effects Exercise. Group members are taken through the example on the exercise worksheet. They discuss with the therapist and among themselves the issues raised in the exercise. Emphasis is given to the identification of delayed positive consequences of effortful behavior.

1. Choose four different activities that you recorded during the past week on your Self-Monitoring Logs. Write them in on the spaces at left on the worksheet.

2. For each activity fill in the effects in the four spaces to the right. Effects can be payoffs or consequences of an activity, that is, the reason you do it, the meaning it has for you. Effects can be either positive or negative. Most activity has both positive and negative effects (rewards and punishments, benefits and costs). Effects can also be immediate or delayed. Most activity has an effect at the moment but also may have a long-range cost or benefit. See the examples below.

3. Examples:

    Activity—

		Immediate	Delayed
(A) *Ate an ice cream cone*	Positive	Good taste nice break rested	Get more done if take breaks
	Negative	Expense	Gain weight

(B) *Called friend to come over for coffee*	Positive	enjoy talk	Better friendship
	Negative	Nervous about call	Less work done

4. Which were easier to think of? Immediate or long-term effects? Positive or negative effects? Which are you more likely to be aware of at the time you are doing something? Did you think of effects that had not occurred to you before? Are there instances where you might do things differently if you concentrate more on the delayed than on the immediate effects or vice versa?

5. During the coming week, use the extra column on your self-monitoring log to fill in a positive delayed effect of at least one positive activity per day.

FIGURE 3. Immediate versus delayed effects exercise.

(continued)

Worksheet

Activity		Effects	
		Immediate	Delayed
1. _____ _____ _____ _____	Positive		
	Negative		
2. _____ _____ _____	Positive		
	Negative		
3. _____ _____ _____ _____	Positive		
	Negative		
4. _____ _____ _____ _____	Positive		
	Negative		
5. _____ _____ _____ _____	Positive		
	Negative		

FIGURE 3. *Continued*

Homework Assignment. Group members continue to monitor positive self-statements and activities. In addition, they are requested to identify a delayed positive consequence of at least one positive activity each day and log it in the extra column of their self-monitoring log.

Session 4: Attribution of Causality

In this session the program changes its focus somewhat. The group begins to address problems that depressed persons have in self-evaluation. The attributional styles of depressed and nondepressed persons are described and a strategy to counteract group members' tendency toward dysfunctional attributions is elaborated.

Homework Review. The previous week's homework is reviewed and problems with it are discussed. If group members have had a difficult time identifying delayed positive consequences of daily activities, the group is invited to collaborate to assist every participant in completing her assignment.

Rationale. Dysfunctions in attributional style serve to maintain dysphoric mood for the depressed person. Self-statements about the causes of positive and negative experiences are the direct target of intervention. The therapist explains that the group will explore together examples of how their attributions about causes of success and failure influence their mood.

THERAPIST: People who are depressed tend to distort the nature of events and make them negative by the way in which they attribute the causes of events. Here are some examples:

1. After a minor quarrel with a friend, a woman feels depressed because "I'm always making people mad at me."
2. A woman's work is praised by her boss and she says, "He's just trying to make me feel better after the criticism he gave me the other day."
3. A friend in a hurry rushes by without stopping to say hello. The depressed self-statement is "She doesn't like me any more."
4. A woman who has just gone back to school gets an *A* on her first exam. She says, "The exam was just easy. I'll never do well on a hard one."

In each of the examples the woman involved made an attribution that made positive outcomes negative and negative ones worse.

The therapist goes on to explain the way in which depressed persons make attributions about the causes of success and failure (positive and negative events). Depressed persons view their successes as due to external, unstable, and specific causes.

THERAPIST: External causes are ones such as someone else or luck (for example, "Oh, I was just lucky"). An unstable attribution means that you believe that the cause may not be present in the future ("Just because I did well this time doesn't mean I'll do well next time"). A specific attribution for success refers to your belief that the cause of the success was unrelated to anything else going on in your life ("Doing well on this doesn't mean I'll do well on that"). As children we are taught to make these external, specific, unstable attributions about success. It is the "modest" thing to say, whether or not it is true.

Nondepressed attributions about successes are usually (1) internal, (2) general, and (3) stable. For example, 'I did a good job, didn't I?' 'I can do a lot of things well when I try' and 'I'm confident in my ability to do this.' These are all 'immodest' self-statements, but when true, they contribute to a sense of control over your life, to positive self-esteem, and lessen depression. What I am talking about is not bragging. It is important for you to recognize your skills, abilities, effort, and accomplishments. The majority of the successes you experience are things that you plan and work for and you deserve credit.

Self-Statements About Success Exercise. The purpose of the exercise is to help group members take credit for successes. The therapist should actively assist group members in assigning percentages to the three dimensions of causality and developing positive self-statements.

Self-Statements About Failure Rationale and Exercise. Depressed persons also show a pattern of self-statements characterized by internal, general, and stable attributions for failure.

THERAPIST: Statements like "It was my fault" or "I let him down" are typical internal statements about failure. People who are depressed tend to accept guilt and responsibility for negative events. "I can't win whatever I do" or "I can't do anything right" reflect general attributions about failure. People who are depressed also tend to overgeneralize about negative events. Statements such as "I'll never get this right" or "This *always* happens to me!" are reflections of another depressive tendency, to see negative events as constant and inevitable.

The therapist emphasizes that these types of attributions regarding failure are learned at an early age and often prevent individuals from attempting change. They are told that if a problem is due to a general and stable aspect of themselves, there is nothing they can do about it. If the cause is external, specific, or unstable, there is more likelihood that they can do something. Group members complete the remainder of the attribution exercise for negative events.

Homework Assignment. Group members continue to monitor positive self-statements and activities. In addition, members are asked to log

The purpose of the exercise is to help you make *realistic* self-statements about your successes and failures.

1. List two positive events that may have occurred for you in the past week. They need not be major events; many trivial occurrences can be considered successes.

   Event A: _____
   Event B: _____

2. Now rate each event as to whether its causes were (1) internal or external, (2) general or specific, and (3) stable or unstable. If you were completely responsible, you would rate 100%. If you shared some responsibility with other factors, you might rate near 50%. And if you were not at all responsible, you would rate 0%.

   Rate the degree to which the cause of the event was general or specific. If it was caused by something that determines many things that happen to you, rate the event 100% general. If it was something that only influences some things, use a figure around 50%. If it was an unusual, specific cause, rate at or near 0%.

   Rate the degree to which the event was caused by something that is stable or unstable. Rate it stable if the cause was something that will be constant or persistent and affect other things in the future. Rate it around 50% if it may or may not operate in the future. Rate it 0% if it was a unique cause unlikely to occur again.

   Event A: _____% internal   _____% general   _____% stable
   Event B: _____% internal   _____% general   _____% stable

3. Now write a positive self-statement about each event that reflects its cause or causes. These statements should be positive *and* true, that is, realistic and accurate. Note that most statements fit under more than one (usually all three) dimension of attribution, for example, "I was lucky" is external, specific, unstable.

   Event A: _____
   Event B: _____

4. Now list two unpleasant or negative events that may have occurred over the past week.

   Event A: _____
   Event B: _____

5. In the same way as for your positive events rate the degree to which the events were internal, general, and stable.

   Event A: _____% internal   _____% general   _____% stable
   Event B: _____% internal   _____% general   _____% stable

6. Now write a positive self-statement about each event that accurately reflects its cause or causes. The events that you list will probably be attributable to others or to chance. Those unpleasant events that are attributable to you may reveal targets for change, an issue that we will address next week.

   Event A: _____
   Event B: _____

FIGURE 4. Attribution of responsibility exercise.

at least one positive self-statement about one success (positive event) and one failure (negative event) each day.

Session 5: Goal Setting

Two sessions devoted to goal setting conclude the self-evaluation module. The program aims to remedy two common dysfunctions of the depressed group member with the goal-setting intervention: the stringent standards of performance that they set, and their difficulty in mobilizing personal resources to accomplish important goals.

Homework Review. The important concepts from the session on attribution are reviewed and difficulties with the homework are discussed. Group members often resist taking responsibility for success and the therapist will explore with them their various reactions to the homework. Group members who experienced positive outcomes with the homework serve as useful models for those who had problems with the assignment.

Rationale.

THERAPIST: People who are depressed tend to set unrealistically stringent goals or standards for themselves. Depressed persons are often perfectionistic and they set goals that are distant, abstract, overly general, and unobtainable. Partial accomplishment of goals is not fulfilling and the result for the person is a constant sense of failure. For example, a woman might feel depressed if she were unable to complete all the work her boss had given her that day even if it were an unreasonable amount. Our effort will be to help you to set goals that are realistic.

Four criteria for realistic goal setting are discussed with the group members. A general strategy for the selection of goals within the immediate therapy context is to select a class of activities related to good mood that may be occurring infrequently. A minor goal may be selected first with more important serious goals being selected later. Goals should be: (a) positive, increasing something in frequency or duration, not decreasing or getting rid of something; (b) attainable, a goal should be within group member's realistic possibilities, that is, something he or she actually could expect to occur; (c) in the individual's control, that is, something that is within the span of a group member's abilities and efforts. It should not be something that depends on the whim of others.

Goals should be broken down into subgoals meeting the same criteria as for goals with one addition. Subgoals should be operational. The

Goal: Broad or long range:

   "I want to increase _____

   _____

   _____

Subgoals:

   1. _____
   2. _____
   3. _____
   4. _____
   5. _____
   others_____

Assignment:

   1. Establish goals and subgoals. The general idea is to break down the overall goal into small, individual steps. To begin with, you may have to generate a whole list of possible steps and then select out of this list the best and most orderly steps. Subgoals should be defined such that they are (A) positive, (B) attainable, (C) in your control, and (D) operational.

   2. Revise or make up additional worksheets for the above or different targets (2 at most for now).

   3. Continue monitoring as in previous weeks *all* positive activities.

   4. If an activity falls within your goal category, make a check mark in the extra column of your self-monitoring log.

   5. Try to increase goal-related activities.

FIGURE 5. Self-evaluation worksheet.

subgoal should be defined in terms that identify specifically what behavior is to be performed in a way that would allow anyone to recognize when it has been met. This will mean that criteria for successful completion are built in. Examples of goals that meet the above criteria are discussed by the therapist.

Goal-Setting Exercise. The self-evaluation worksheet is completed by group members as they develop their own goals and subgoals. The therapist and the rest of the group provide feedback to each group member regarding his or her goals so that the goals of all group members meet the criteria that they had discussed.

Homework Assignment. The homework is to revise or make up additional goals meeting the criteria of being (a) positive, (b) attainable, (c) in your control, and (d) for subgoals, operational. Self-monitoring also continues with special reference to subgoal behavior.

Session 6: Goal Setting Continued

The rationale and strategy of effective goal setting are thoroughly reviewed in this session. Goals and subgoals that group members have developed are reviewed with the entire group.

Homework Review. Group members are asked individually to discuss their progress toward their goals and subgoals. They are encouraged to give feedback and support to each other, especially regarding work on subgoals. The therapist also reviews material from the previous week. Three points are emphasized: (1) depressed persons set criteria for goal accomplishment that are too stringent (i.e., too high or too broad); (2) they do not give themselves enough time to accomplish a goal; or (3) they do not recognize when they have made progress toward a goal.

Rationale and Exercise. Typically, group members have difficulty in two areas in attempting to do the goal-setting homework. First, they often select goals that are too problematic or large (e.g., finishing college or saving my marriage). The second problem that often develops is a subgoal that is too ambitious (e.g., contact 20 businesses a day where the goal is to get a job). In the first case the group member is encouraged to start with a smaller goal that is more likely to be attainable in the short run or to scale the goal down somewhat. In the second case, the member is encouraged to break down complex, difficult, or important subgoal activities into smaller steps. Ocassionally, an insufficient number of subgoals are developed so that they do not readily lead to the achievement of the overall goal. In this case, group members develop further subgoals.

Homework Assignment. Group members continue to monitor positive self-statements and activities with special reference to goal-related behaviors.

Session 7: Overt Self-Reinforcement

Up to this point in the program group members have learned to monitor positive activities and self-statements, to make accurate attributions for success and failure, and to develop realistic goals and subgoals. The self-reinforcement module is concerned with the maintenance of difficult or arduous behaviors through the contingent application of overt and covert self-rewards.

Homework Review. The therapist reviews with each of the group members their progress on goals that they have set. In addition, subgoals are further broken down if need be to make them more manageable.

Rationale. Group members are told that up to this point we have focused on paying attention to and increasing positive self-statements and activities. Mood responds positively to increases in these activities. The therapist also discusses another class of events that is important in overcoming depression.

THERAPIST: There is another class of events that also has a powerful effect on mood, that is, engaging in activities that, though not pleasurable in and of themselves, are either necessary or very desirable to accomplish. These are the kinds of tasks that give you a sense of accomplishment or relief to finish. They may be anything from household chores to school term papers to writing letters. They are often tasks that hang over you and that you think of frequently with guilt or anxiety or some other negative statement to yourself about your inability to get them done. These tasks, if swiftly finished, could lead to a significantly improved mood level, since you could then see tangible evidence of progress in problem areas. The focus of our next section will be to help you to accomplish some of these difficult but important tasks as well as subgoals that are difficult for you.

At this point the therapist explains some basic concepts about how behavior is controlled by rewards and punishers. The point is made that reward comes only after a desired behavior has occurred. People can control their own behavior by giving themselves rewards and punishers. These rewards may be overt (providing a tangible reward such as a new dress) or covert (verbalizing to themselves a positive statement such as "Boy, I really did a nice job"). Self-punishment is accomplished in much the same way, although it is probably more often a self-statement (e.g., "That was pretty dumb" or "I was a real idiot to have failed at that task").

THERAPIST: People who are depressed tend to punish themselves too much and reward themselves too little. They tend to be down on themselves and consistently seem to punish their behavior. They will downgrade their own accomplishments (for example, the woman who says "This old thing?" or the woman who does not reward herself for having done well in a course at school but instead becomes angry with herself for not having done better on the final exam). These same people find it difficult to reward themselves or to feel that they are deserving of any kind of positive activity or event in their life. The result is that they are not motivated to be more active in pursuing their goals. The depressed woman is more likely to focus on what has not been accomplished than on what has been done. This notion relates back to what we have been stressing all along regarding self-monitoring. If you are continually monitoring your failures and other shortcomings, it is not surprising that you frequently would get down on yourself in the form of self-punishment. Of course, the more often you punish yourself the less likely it is that you will do the things that are necessary to help you feel less depressed. Under these circumstances it is easy to allow yourself to engage in only the most basic and necessary activities. Often these activities are accomplished only with great difficulty or in some cases, not at all. In the absence of rewards for difficult tasks, there is little motivation to continue to do them.

Reward-Menu Exercise. Group members develop for themselves a reward menu from which they will select rewards for increasing goal-related behavior. On the reward menu group members should list as many potential rewards as possible. The rewards should be (a) truly enjoyable, (b) varying in magnitude from large to small, and (c) capable of free administration. Activities as well as things can be rewards and the self-monitoring logs may provide examples of both. The principle to be used is that easy activities can be used to reward hard positive activities.

THERAPIST: The idea of the "reward menu" is that each time you accomplish one of your difficult subgoal activities, you should reward your progress toward your goal with something from the "reward menu." You want to *motivate* yourself to work on the difficult subgoals with the added incentive of the reward. It may sound unnecessary or "improper" to do something nice for yourself, but at the moment we are interested in producing change, that is, a shift in your usual habitual pattern of behavior, and reward is one way to facilitate change.

Homework Assignment. Group members continue to monitor positive self-statements and activities. In addition, each time a difficult subgoal activity is accomplished, they reward it with a positive activity from their reward menu. They are instructed to match the size of the reward to the difficulty of the task that is accomplished.

Session 8: Covert Self-Reinforcement

The previous session focused on the application of overt reinforcers to reward difficult behaviors. It often is impractical or inappropriate to reinforce goal-directed behavior with concrete reinforcers. The use of covert reinforcers (positive self-statements) is developed in this session as a portable alternative.

Homework Review. The therapist reviews with each group member his or her efforts to increase goal-related activities and the use of contingent reward menus. Group members read examples of the subgoals accomplished and the items they chose from their reward menus. If any group member reports difficulty with the assignment, the therapist, with input from the rest of the group, will troubleshoot.

Rationale. A review of the rationale from the previous session will serve to prepare group members for the concept that changing their self-statements may have a positive impact on their mood.

THERAPIST: This week I want to talk about rewarding and punishing self-statements. Last week we talked about object or activity self-reward. This week we will concentrate on verbal self-reward. People can and most often do reward themselves with a positive thoughts or self-statements. Such self-statements focus your attention on accomplishments, strengthen that behavior, and serve as the basis for positive self-evaluation and self-esteem.

In order to overcome long-held biases most group members will have against self-praise, the therapist will develop the following rationale.

THERAPIST: Self-reward *is not* bragging or excessive pride. Bragging is trying to elicit compliments (rewards) from others by publicizing your accomplishments. Excessive pride is unrealistically overestimating your achievements and ignoring your limitations. Self-reward is a realistic recognition of your skills and efforts. It is the basis for self-esteem and it makes you partly independent of the evaluations of others. It is always nice to be recognized or complimented by others but it is essential to self-esteem to be able to recognize and evaluate your own behavior.

Covert Self-Reward Exercise. Group members develop at least five statements that are positive and true about themselves, that is, five positive characteristics. For example, I am good at . . . being a mother, my job, cooking, or solving problems. Or I am . . . friendly, sincere, hardworking, or loyal. Again, prompting and exploration with each member may be necessary to aid group members in developing at least five positive self-statements.

Homework Assignment. In addition to self-monitoring, group members are asked to include on their daily log at least two self-statements that are self-rewards that contingently follow a subgoal that is successful and/or difficult. They also are encouraged to add to their log any additional positive characteristics during the week.

Sessions 9 and 10: Review and Consolidation

New material has been presented practically every week and the last two sessions afford an opportunity for group members to consolidate their new learning. The therapist may find it useful to review with the group its progress toward the goals that the members set for themselves.

It is important to emphasize that the group has learned skills that may continue to be applied after the termination of therapy. Group members may want to share with each other some of their strategies for maintaining their gains from therapy. The therapist also may ask questions such as, "What areas may prove troublesome in maintaining freedom from depression?" It is important to emphasize that the increase in their self-control skills is the key to prevention of future episodes of depression or ameliorating those episodes before they become so serious as to require professional help again.

CASE EXAMPLE

The following case example illustrates the treatment course of one client who is typical of those we have treated.

> Mary S. was a 47-year-old mother of two children and was moderately depressed (BDI = 28). One of her children was married and had moved away; the other was a high school senior still living at home. Mary had been a housewife most of the past 25 years, occasionally working part time as well as frequently doing volunteer work in the community.
> When Mrs. S. was asked what she believed accounted for her current depression, she said that she and her husband had not been getting along for the last couple of years and that she was feeling useless and bored. Mrs. S. never had been in therapy before, though her private physician had frequently prescribed Valium for her anxiety and depression.
> During the first session Mrs. S. was surprised to find other women who were experiencing similar problems. The group also evidenced support and understanding of her difficulties. The therapist called her in the middle of the week to troubleshoot any problems and she reported that she had logged only a few positive self-statements and activities. She was reminded to log all positive self-statements and activities, particularly trivial ones, and at the thera-

pist's prompting she was able to recall several that she had not logged.

In the second group she complained that even though logging positive self-statements and activities did have some positive impact on her mood, she could not see how that would help her with her "real problems" of being bored and feeling useless and with her difficulties with her husband. However, she was able to see on the Mood and Behavior exercise that there were parallels and that she could identify both self-statements and activities that were especially related to positive mood.

Throughout the next several sessions the therapist continued to prompt her to log the trivial self-statements and activities as well as the more important ones. She had difficulty accepting the attribution rationale, particularly taking credit (internal attribution) for positive outcomes in her life. At this point she was still moderately depressed (BDI = 25) and continued to need extra encouragement from the other group members and the therapist.

During the goal-setting sessions, she learned to set realistic goals for herself, particularly in the area of improving her relationship with her husband and finding a part-time job. Earlier in the group she complained that her relationship with her husband had deteriorated and that there was nothing she could do about it. Her subgoals were to arrange for them to engage in pleasurable activities together and to increase the number of questions she asked him about his work activities. Within a couple of weeks she reported that her husband was much more responsive toward her and she took credit for the change. By this time, her mood also was improving.

By the last three sessions, she felt committed to change and used both material rewards and positive self-statements to reinforce her job-finding efforts. By the end of the group her depression had abated (BDI = 6) and she expressed satisfaction and surprise that she could make such a difference in her own life.

REFERENCES

Beck, A. T., Ward, C. H., Mendelson, M., Mock, J., & Erbaugh, J. An inventory for measuring depression. *Archives of General Psychiatry*, 1961, *4*, 561–571.

Fuchs, C. Z., & Rehm, L. P. A self-control behavior therapy program for depression. *Journal of Consulting and Clinical Psychology*, 1977, *45*, 206–215.

Kanfer, F. H. Self-regulation: Research issues and speculations. In C. Neuringer & J. L. Michael (Eds.), *Behavior modification in clinical psychology*. New York: Appleton-Century-Crofts, 1970.

Kanfer, F. H. The maintenance of behavior by self-generated stimuli and reinforcement. In

A. Jacobs & L. B. Sachs (Eds.), *The psychology of private events: Perspectives on covert response systems*. New York: Academic, 1971.

Kanfer, F. H., & Karoly, P. Self-control: A behavioristic excursion into the lion's den. *Behavior Therapy*, 1972, *3*, 398–416.

Lubin, B. *Manual for the depression adjective check lists*. San Diego: Educational and Industrial Testing Service, 1967.

Rehm, L. P. A self-control model of depression. *Behavior Therapy*, 1977, *8*, 787–804.

Rehm, L. P. A self-control therapy program for the treatment of depression. In J. F. Clarkin & H. Glazer (Eds.), *Depression: Behavioral and directive treatment strategies*. New York: Garland, 1981.

Rehm, L. P., Fuchs, C. Z., Roth, D., Kornblith, S. J., & Romano, J. M. A comparison of self-control and assertion skills treatments for depression. *Behavior Therapy*, 1979, *10*, 429–442.

Rehm, L. P., Kornblith, S. J., O'Hara, M. W., Lamparski, D. M., Romano, J. M., & Volkin, J. An evaluation of the major elements in a self-control therapy program for depression. *Behavior Modification*, 1981, *5*, 459–489.

Romano, J. M., & Rehm, L. P. Self-control treatment of depression: One year follow-up. In A. T. Beck (Chairperson), *Factors affecting the outcome and maintenances of cognitive therapy*. Symposium at the meeting of the Eastern Psychological Association, Philadelphia, April 18–21, 1979.

Spitzer, R. L., Endicott, J., & Robins, E. Research diagnostic criteria: Rationale and reliability. *Archives of General Psychiatry*, 1978, *36*, 773–782.

5

Cognitive Therapy in the Family System

RICHARD C. BEDROSIAN

COGNITIVE THERAPY IN THE FAMILY SYSTEM

Cognitive therapists generally treat patients in individual or group sessions, but rarely work with marital or family units. An underlying premise of individual therapy is that the problem resides within the psyche of the particular patient and that recovery can occur to the extent that his or her cognitive distortions change in the course of treatment. For many patients, the premise is at least partially valid in that they experience symptom relief as a result of individual sessions with a therapist. In other cases, however, the cognitive therapist will find it necessary to modify both cognitions *and* relationships by including other family members in the treatment process (Bedrosian, 1981).

The Relationship between Individual Symptoms and Family Interaction Patterns

The most radical family systems position views all or most manifestations of individual psychopathology as reflective of dysfunctional family interaction patterns. At best, the research literature offers minimal support for such a viewpoint (Jacob, 1975). A more conservative position, which acknowledges the process of reciprocal influence between the individual patient and significant others in the environment, is detailed in the following propositions.

RICHARD C. BEDROSIAN • Massachusetts Center for Cognitive Therapy, Westborough, Massachusetts 01581.

Proposition 1: Family systems can reorganize quickly in response to individual psychopathology.

Imagine how the day-to-day management of your household would change if your spouse became severely depressed or agoraphobic for even a month of two. You would begin to assume many of your spouse's chores and responsibilities. As time progressed, the role of your spouse in major household decisions would tend to diminish. The added burdens would create stress for you, but you also would become accustomed to running the family in your own way. Eventually you would face the difficult choice of curtailing your social life and any other activities you enjoyed outside the home or risk isolating your spouse further. As you withdrew from your network of friends and extrafamilial interests, you would struggle with feelings of resentment toward your spouse.

The preceding actually represents a benign version of the family situations that emerge in clinical practice. Loved ones repeatedly demonstrate a willingness to accommodate to the most troublesome, incapacitating individual symptoms. Consequently, what may begin as an individual problem ends up as a way of life for an entire family. The more chronic the symptom, the greater the disruption in the household.

Proposition 2: Good intentions notwithstanding, the family organization that accompanies individual psychopathology may not support improved adjustment on the part of the identified patient.

Family members often unwittingly help to maintain passivity and avoidance behavior. The mother of a depressed, highly anxious young man would serve her son meals in his room, where he sat watching television all day, despite the fact that the rest of the family ate together in the dining room. If his friends called or came to the house, she obeyed his request to tell them he was out. Rather than encourage her son to use the self-control techniques his therapist had suggested to him, the mother would dispense narcotics to him from her own supply of medication whenever he found it difficult to cope with his anxiety.

Proposition 3: Ongoing family interactions can exacerbate symptoms and trigger or intensify maladaptive cognitions.

Examples in which family conflicts aggravate individual symptoms are numerous in clinical practice. Some depressed patients, for instance, are prone to blame themselves for *any* problems in the family that may occur. On the other hand, interacting with depressed individuals can exert a noxious influence on others, as research has indicated (Coyne, 1976).

The manner in which interpersonal processes influence belief systems has been (and probably will continue to be) a source of controversy among social psychologists. Nonetheless, we can assume that an individual will retain a profound sense of hopelessness or a decidedly negative self-image if these attitudes constantly are being reinforced either implicitly or explicitly by family members.

On the other hand, a process that resembles "psychological reactance" (Brehm, 1966), seems to occur in the families of some clinic patients. Brehm postulates that when an individual is faced with elimination or threatened elimination of behaviors he or she originally felt free to perform, a motivational state, labeled psychological reactance, is aroused. The theory predicts that when an individual feels free to reject or adopt any of a number of attitudinal positions, pressure to adopt or reject any one position threatens that freedom, thereby arousing reactance and leading to efforts to restore the freedom by resisting persuasion or adopting a position at variance with the one recommended (Hass & Linder, 1972).

As observed among clinic families, psychological reactance occurs when the identified patient clings all the more tenaciously to a dysfunctional belief system in response to persuasion or pressure from family members. A woman viewed isolated incidents as proof that she was performing poorly at her job and ruminated constantly about being fired. The hours she spent at home discussing her job worries put a severe strain on her marital relationship. Her husband would attempt to talk her out of her beliefs in a pedantic, condescending manner. When he became exasperated with his wife, he would simply attack her ideas as "stupid." The more her husband attacked her, the more the woman defended her beliefs, as well as her right to hold them. At one point she protested, "What do you know about my job? You're on easy street where you work!" It was necessary to modify the interactional pattern that produced the husband's aversive comments and the wife's righteous indignation, before the therapist could focus on the anxiety over work.

Proposition 4: Improvement on the part of the identified patient can produce an increase in stress for other family members.

Imagine again that you have reorganized your household in response to your spouse's emotional problems. As your partner recovers from his or her difficulties, the two of you will find it necessary to renegotiate the distribution of power and responsibility in the household. Suddenly you find that you cannot make major decisions unilaterally without antagonizing your spouse. Temporarily at least, even the most routine family matters may require debate and discussion.

At times, treatment can lead to greater assertiveness on the part of the identified patient, as well as other forms of behavior that can be troublesome for family members. In order to preserve his health, a middle-aged cardiac patient began to curtail his business activities, since he recognized that his attitudes toward work had contributed to his heart problems. He allowed himself more leisure time and planned several lengthy vacations with his family. As he spent more time at home with his wife and his adolescent daughters, tensions rose sharply in the household. Accustomed to occupying a position of leadership in the business world, the man behaved in a bossy, intrusive manner at home, which rapidly alienated the rest of the family.

Proposition 5: Individuals in family systems often behave on the basis of assumptions about one another that may have little or no basis in reality.

Married couples and other individuals who are in close contact engage frequently in "mind reading," in that they anticipate one another's tastes, attitudes, and moods in advance, *without ever validating their hypotheses.* When "mind reading" is accurate, it tends to save time and effort for the members of a family system. Unfortunately, when an individual becomes depressed or anxious, cognitive distortions tend to interfere with his or her ability to make inferences about the motives or reactions of others, particularly in the absence of direct feedback. Spouses who experience marital distress are likely to do a poor job of communicating on an explicit level, so they fall back too often on dysfunctional assumptions in order to make predictions about their partner's internal states.

A woman in her twenties who experienced symptoms of depression and anxiety, complained about daily phone calls and visits from her aged father-in-law. The man behaved in a rude, critical fashion during his visits and often impeded her work in the home. Since she had assumed that her husband knew and approved of the visits, she felt powerless to alter the situation. During subsequent marital sessions, she overcame her reluctance to raise the matter with her husband. She found that he was unaware of the frequency and noxiousness of his father's visits, and that he was supportive of her efforts to set greater limits on the man's behavior.

GUIDELINES FOR ESTABLISHING CONTACT WITH SIGNIFICANT OTHERS

1. The therapist should interview the spouse or other relevant family members as early as possible in the course of treatment. Early contact

with significant others provides the therapist with a broader data base. The identified patient's account of the family situation, which may be the product of his or her cognitive distortions, can mislead the therapist, particularly in the absence of information from other observers. Even when they do not participate in subsequent treatment, family members can use the interview to become acquainted with therapy and the therapist. If they meet the therapist early on, significant others are more likely to cooperate if he or she requests their presence during a later stage in treatment.

2. As Haley (1976) recommends, early contacts with family members should concentrate on the presenting problems of the identified patient. In the early interviews, the therapist avoids tinkering with the marriage or other relationships in the family unless he or she has made an explicit contract to do so with the parties involved. The initial family interview can be aimed at assessing the impact of the presenting problem upon the relevant family members, their reactions to the patient's difficulties, and any solutions that they attempted to implement. The therapist should avoid implying in any way that the family is to blame for the patient's complaints.

3. Whenever possible, the therapist should speak *directly* to the relevant family member(s) about attending a session. Delegating such a task to the identified patient, which is generally the path of least resistance for the therapist, can yield confusing results. If the family member comes in for an interview, the therapist does not know what stimulated the appearance unless he or she actually made the request. Perhaps the identified patient has said, "My therapist wants to meet the person who's driving me crazy," or "The doctor thinks you're sicker than I am, so he wants to talk to you." If the family member fails to come in, the therapist also will not know why. Some patients will speak to their families about entering treatment in an unassertive or otherwise inappropriate manner; others simply will fail to raise the issue at all, only to tell the therapist that the family members are unwilling or unable to participate. Clinical experience indicates that the majority of family members will respond favorably to the therapist's request for their involvement in the treatment.

MODIFYING INTERACTION PATTERNS THAT AGGRAVATE COGNITIVE DISTORTIONS

An unemployed college graduate in his early twenties sought treatment for severe bouts of depression and anxiety. He complained of a wide range of symptoms, including low self-esteem, social isolation, and impotence. Through the standard cognitive therapy techniques, he was able to curb his anxiety attacks and improve his morale. As his depression began to lift he established a sexual relationship with a woman 20 years his senior, much to the dismay of his parents. The woman's behavior tended to support the parents' objections. She repeatedly manipulated the young man by capriciously terminating the relationship, only to resume it again at a moment's notice. His moods alternated between elation and despair, depending upon the status of the relationship. The patient realized that it would be better for him in the long run to sever the relationship, but held a number of dysfunctional beliefs, such as "No other woman would want me" and "I hunger for love," which prevented him from taking decisive action.

The young man lived with his parents, who supported him financially and paid for his treatment. His relationship with the older woman became the object of constant family conflict. Although their arguments were quite sound, the more his parents attacked the relationship, the more the son would defend his right to maintain it. He began reaching out spontaneously to other women, but retreated quickly when his parents began pressuring him to date others. Rather than pursue his evident interest in other women, he responded to the pressure from his parents by reaffirming the dysfunctional belief, "There's only one woman I can ever love." As the parents stepped up their efforts to influence their son, they broadened their criticisms to include attacks on his worth as a person. In addition to intensifying his depressogenic cognitions, the family quarrels distracted the young man from his own concerns about the relationship and diverted him from other important issues in his life, such as job hunting.

After the parents had threatened to stop paying for treatment unless the relationship ended, the therapist invited both the father and son in for a session. In a private meeting with the father, the therapist asked the man to describe the worst that could happen to his son if the relationship were to continue. Would he have children with her? No. Marry her? No. According to the father, his worst fear was that his son could lose valuable time by remaining in the relationship. The man recognized that neither he nor his wife were able to influence their son at all on the issue. In fact, the father admitted that by pressuring his son he actually made it more difficult for the young man to evaluate the relationship on its own merits. Moreover, he expressed the belief that given time, the son inevitably would break off the relationship. The father agreed that by attempting to coerce the son, the parents actually were causing him to lose time, which was just what they had feared to begin with.

The therapist met with the father and son together, and asked them to avoid any further discussion of the relationship. He suggested that the young man try to discuss only vocational issues with his father, who was highly qualified to serve as a resource on the subject. The pair talked about job hunting during the remainder of the session, while the therapist helped to divert them away from any further comments about their disagreements. A similar meeting with the father and son occurred a week later. Once again, the therapist encouraged the two of them to focus on employment issues and intervened when the conversation drifted back to the son's social life.

Since the family was able to avoid serious conflict over the son's relationship, friction in the household began to subside. The parents then were able to support their son in his attempts to resolve other significant problems in his life. After considerable internal debate and a few false starts, the young man subsequently broke off the relationship of his own accord and began to date other women again.

TESTING AND MODIFYING ASSUMPTIONS ABOUT RELATIONSHIPS

In individual treatment, the cognitive therapist often encourages the patient to test actively the validity of his or her assumptions concerning significant others. When a particular relationship seems to be a focal point for the patient's distress, the process of "reality testing" can be accelerated if the therapist includes the relevant individual(s) in the session.

As discussed earlier, all of us conduct our social relationships on the basis of innumerable inferences and assumptions that have varying levels of accuracy. Clinical experience indicates that three types of cognitions about relationships may require therapeutic attention:

1. *Inferences about the Internal States of Others.* Inferences of this sort can focus on emotions ("I know you're angry because you're biting your nails"), motivation ("You came home late because you knew my mother was here"), attributional processes ("You'll think I'm to blame if we don't enjoy our vacation"), and so on. To make matters even more complicated, partners in intimate relationships often attempt to *infer one another's inferences,* for example, "You think that I think you're stupid, but it's not true." Individuals can become highly abstract and convoluted in their assumptions about one another's internal processes, as illustrated by Laing (1961) and by Ralph Cramden of "The Honeymooners" ("You know that I know that you know that I know what's going on").

It would appear to be a simple matter for a person to test out his or her assumptions about the inner experiences of a significant other. In fact, the process can be quite involved, particularly if the relevant individuals are unwilling or unable to self-disclose. Moreover, some persons can maintain considerable leverage in a relationship simply by creating a state of ambiguity regarding their feelings toward their spouses.

2. *Expectations of the Other.* We all possess a multitude of implicit and explicit expectations regarding our partners in intimate relationships. The content of such expectations can be highly idiosyncratic. Some examples include: "I thought that when you changed jobs you'd be spending more time at home" or "I want you to stay away from me when I'm tired" or "I want you to accept my family as they are;" and so on. As Lederer and Jackson (1968) point out, every intimate relationship involves the establishment of a *quid pro quo,* which means, literally, something for something. Unfortunately, when partners interact with one another on the basis of *implicit* expectations or "unspoken convenants" (Sager, 1978) the potential for dissatisfaction increases. Some spouses often assume that their partners *know* what their unstated expectations are. When an unspoken demand goes unfulfilled, the spouse may react as if his or her partner had refused to comply with a direct, unambiguous request. For example, after working late, a psychologist missed his commuter train. When he called his wife to inform her of the delay in his return from work, he made it a point to mention that after a long day at the office, he would now have to wait an hour until the next train arrived. In the past, a similar line of conversation generally led to his wife "spontaneously" offering to drive him home, but on this occasion she merely offered her condolences and hung up. While waiting in the train station, the psychologist began to ruminate about how nonsupportive, noncaring, and nongiving his wife was, and thereby managed to arrive home in a surly, belligerent state. Only after a period of bickering did he recognize the connection between his present emotional state and his clumsy attempt to provoke his wife's sympathy earlier. A major goal in cognitive therapy with couples or families is to encourage the participants to make all their demands and expectations of one another as *explicit* and *concrete* as possible. The therapist adopts the stance that only through making direct requests of one another can individuals learn (1) if their demands are realistic or appropriate and (2) if the significant other(s) will comply. Note that in the example in the preceding paragraph the psychologist made his request in an indirect manner which precluded the possibility of feedback.

3. *Rules about Relationships.* In addition to rather specific expectations, individuals also hold generalized assumptions about the nature of

their relationships with other family members. Such assumptions, like other dysfunctional cognitions, can lead to inappropriate emotional reactions and a lack of behavioral flexibility. For example, the individual who believes that people in love automatically should sense one another's needs will find it difficult to communicate his or her demands directly to loved ones. Some relationship rules reflect all-or-nothing thinking, for example, "If you love someone, you never get angry with him" or "A wife always stands by her husband, whether he's right or wrong." Relationship rules that reflect the individual's familial or subcultural background, particularly those concerning the nature of male and female roles, may be at variance with the current social context of the family. As with other dysfunctlonal cognitions, the therapist strives to make the individual's rules about relationship explicit, so that he or she can examine their validity and/or utility.

The following case example illustrates how conjoint family or marital sessions can be used to correct cognitive distortions and faulty relationship patterns. A depressed business executive sought individual treatment for chornic symptoms of anxiety and depression that originated primarily in the work setting. At first, the therapist worked with him individually in order to modify the man's perfectionism and self-denigration. As the work situation began to improve, the patient reiterated the concerns about his marriage that the therapist had deferred earlier in treatment. Characteristically, he blamed himself fully for the difficulties that he perceived in the marital relationship. On the other hand, he portrayed his wife as blameless, devoted to him, and perfectly content with their life together.

If the therapist had continued to see the patient individually, he eventually might have accepted the man's account of the domestic situation at face value and gone on to help the executive weigh the advantages and disadvantages of a trial separation. Instead the therapist called the wife and arranged a meeting with the couple. During the first conjoint session, the wife seemed glib, sarcastic, and hardly contented with the marriage. While meeting alone with the therapist, she said of her husband at one point, "I've been protecting him all his life."

The therapist's first task was to redefine the marital dissatisfaction of the husband as a *relationship problem* rather than an individual problem. To accomplish such a goal, the therapist had to help the executive stop attributing the marital problems solely to himself. The therapist encouraged the wife to explain to her husband *exactly* how she felt about the marriage in a way that reflected the intensity of her own dissatisfaction and disappointment. Gradually the husband began to view the marital difficulties as a *shared* problem.

The therapist observed that although each spouse indicated dissatisfaction with the marriage, neither partner made many direct requests for behavioral changes from the other. Neither partner seemed to lack assertiveness in other social or work relationships. In the marriage, however, both spouses maintained a detached, unassertive position. Consequently, the therapist began to explore the spouse's dysfunctional cognitions, using their requests and demands as the starting point. He found that each partner held a number of beliefs that prevented direct communication in the relationship.

The husband believed that his wife should be more "exciting and spontaneous," that she somehow should be able to satisfy all his needs instinctively, without any prompting on his part. Gradually, he realized that his expectation for "spontaneous" behavior from his wife was both unrealistic and unproductive. In fact, both partners cited instances in which he had failed to respond to spur-of-the-moment suggestions (e.g., "Let's go out dancing tonight") from his wife. Another dysfunctional assumption that surfaced repeatedly on the husband's part was the idea that if his wife complied with one of his requests he would be obligated to her thereafter. Thus, if his wife responded to a desire on his part for sexual relations, he would think, "She really doesn't want to do this for me and she'll think I owe her." Nonetheless, his wife seemed quite candid in her feedback whenever she found his requests unacceptable.

Dysfunctional cognitions also interfered with the wife's ability to ask her husband for what she wanted. Because her husband had suffered depressive symptoms, she believed that he might experience additional psychological problems if she pushed him to satisfy her needs. If she expressed her wishes, by attempting to initiate sex for example, the wife would distort the meaning of any negative response from her husband. If her husband turned down her request for lovemaking she would think, "He probably doesn't want me anymore" or "Now it's up to *him* to make the first move, because I won't ask him for *anything* now." The wife selectively attended to instances of coldness or rejection on the part of her spouse, while overlooking situations in which he had been warm and attentive to her needs.

Session after session, the therapist pursued the same strategy with the couple. He would urge one of the spouses to make explicit, concrete requests of the other. The requests had to involve *observable behaviors*, rather than attitudes. Thus, "I want you to come to realtor's on Sunday" was acceptable; "I want you to show an interest in house hunting" was not. Once they began making appropriate requests, the spouses then were able to test out their dysfunctional assumptions about the relationship and one another. The husband quickly realized that his demands for "spontaneous" behavior from his wife created a situation in which compliance was impossible. As therapy continued, he grew less distrustful of his wife's reactions to him. He found that she truly enjoyed doing things *simply to please him*. The wife, on the other hand, discovered that her husband could tolerate a good deal more pressure from her than she had anticipated. Indeed, by behaving more assertively, she actually began to provide her husband with the sense of spontaneity and excitement that he had wanted. With practice, she began to resist her tendency to overreact when he refused her requests. With the therapist's help, the couple communicated more effectively and directly on a number of issues, such as sexual relations, childrearing, and social interactions, which they had avoided due to prior disagreements.

COPING WITH STRESSES INDUCED BY POSITIVE TREATMENT EFFECTS

It is desirable to prepare family members for new stresses that may arise as a result of symptom reduction in the identified patient. Such stresses may necessitate a shift in the focus of therapy from individual to relationship issues. In forewarning the family, the therapist can explain that the new tensions within the household are not catastrophic, and can be alleviated in the course of treatment.

A married woman in her late twenties experienced a rapid onset of severe agoraphobic symptoms as she recovered from a long-standing depression. It is noteworthy that her agoraphobia began just after she and her husband made their annual move to the resort town where he ran a seasonal business. While the husband worked extremely long hours in the business, the wife experienced boredom and social isolation. Nonetheless, the husband was very helpful and considerate to his wife during her most symptomatic period, when she was unable to drive or enter public places alone.

The therapist believed that the patient's problems were closely related to unarticulated grievances within the marital relationship. Both spouses denied the presence of any marital difficulties, but the therapist warned them that conflicts at home *might* occur once the wife no longer occupied such a helpless position.

Through a combination of group and individual cognitive therapy, the woman learned to control her anxiety symptoms. As she improved, conflicts did in fact emerge in the marriage. The major issues were the husband's summer business, which the patient felt constrained their life-style unnecessarily, and his parents, whom the patient perceived as intrusive and domineering. It was clear that the spouses held widely divergent attitudes about male–female relationships, stemming in part from the differences in their backgrounds.

Once her symptoms diminished, the woman was urged to be more assertive in her marriage. She began to acknowledge, grudgingly at first, the effects of her marriage upon her symptoms. As his wife began to demand equal time for her needs, the husband became more irritable and withdrawn, uncharacteristically so for him. Through the use of conjoint sessions, however, the couple achieved a more equitable balance of power and rewards in their relationship.

CONCLUSION

The present chapter explored the interface between cognitive therapy and family therapy. The author's experiences to date indicate that the two approaches blend readily with one another. The territory of "cognitive family therapy" remains largely uncharted, so that innumerable adventures and mysteries await future explorers there.

REFERENCES

Bedrosian, R. C. Ecological factors in cognitive therapy: The use of significant others. In G. Emery, S. Hollon, & R. Bedrosian (Eds.), *New directions in cognitive therapy*. New York: Guilford, 1981.

Brehm, J. W. *A theory of psychological reactance*. New York: Academic, 1966.

Coyne, J. C. Toward an interactional description of depression. *Archives of General Psychiatry*, 1976, *39*, 29–40.

Haley, J. *Problem solving therapy*. San Francisco: Jossey-Bass, 1976.

Hass, R. G., & Linder, D. E. Counterarguement availability and the effects of message structure on persuasion, *Journal of Personality and Social Psychology*, 1972, *23*, 219–233.

Jacob, T. Family interaction in disturbed and normal families: A methodological and substantive review. *Psychological Bulletin*, 1975, *82*, 33–65.

Laing, R. D. *Self and others*. London: Tavistock, 1961.

Lederer, W. J., & Jackson, D. D. *Mirages of marriage*. New York: Norton, 1968.

Sager, C. J. *Marriage contracts and couple therapy*. New York: Brunner/Mazel, 1978.

6

Cognitive Therapy with Couples

NORMAN EPSTEIN

(handwritten annotations) (Internal and External Stimuli) ↑ PERCEPTION (+ interpretation) ↓ Emotional Responses / Behavioral Responses

Although behavior therapists who treat distressed marriages traditionally have acknowledged that spouses' cognitive appraisals of each other's behavior play a role in relationship dysfunction, interventions focusing on cognitive components of relationship problems clearly have played a secondary or even a minor role in formal behavioral approaches. However, due to the influence of a general growth of interest in cognitive variables in behavioral models and to the recognition that spouses' negative beliefs and attitudes easily can undermine even the best conceived behavior-change programs (Jacobson & Margolin, 1979), significant attention now is being paid to the development of assessment and treatment procedures for cognitive factors. In the general cognitive model, an individual's emotional and behavioral responses to a stimulus (internal or external) are mediated by his or her perception and interpretation of the stimulus rather than elicited directly by objective characteristics of the stimulus (Beck, 1976; Meichenbaum, 1977). In an interpersonal system such as a marriage, the members of the relationship continuously provide stimuli for each other and actively construe the behaviors they exchange. Because marital satisfaction is a *subjective* state that is related to proportions of idiosyncratically defined pleasing and displeasing behaviors exchanged by spouses (Jacobson & Margolin,

This chapter is from "Cognitive Therapy with Couples" by Norman Epstein, *The American Journal of Family Therapy*, 1982, *10*, 5–16. Copyright 1982 by Brunner/Mazel, Inc. Reprinted by permission.

NORMAN EPSTEIN • Center for Cognitive Therapy, 133 South 36th Street, University of Pennsylvania, Philadelphia, Pennsylvania 19104.

1979; Weiss, 1978), understanding and changing a distressed relationship necessitates attention to cognitive events in the marriage.

This chapter examines three major approaches to cognitive therapy for marital problems: modification of unrealistic expectations of relationships, correction of faulty attributions in marital interaction, and use of self-instructional procedures to decrease destructive interaction. Means for integrating cognitive and behavioral approaches to marital therapy are described, and the extent to which cognitive approaches are consistent with a systems view of marriage and marital therapy is discussed.

APPROACHES TO COGNITIVE THERAPY WITH COUPLES

The three forms of cognitive therapy described below traditionally have been used to treat the problematic behavioral (e.g., impulsivity) and emotional (e.g., depression) responses of individuals. However, these cognitive approaches offer means of intervening in a dysfunctional marital system where spouses' subjective distress and their exchanges of negative behaviors are linked. In the discussion that follows, ways in which cognitive interventions can be used both to alter subjective distress and to control expression of destructive behaviors in dyads will be stressed.

Modifying Unrealistic Expectations

The expectations that each member of a couple brings to the marriage regarding the nature of an intimate relationship and the roles of its members are important foci of cognitive interventions with distressed couples (Jacobson & Margolin, 1979; O'Leary & Turkewitz, 1978). The impetus for treatment of unrealistic or exaggerated expectations has been Ellis's view (Ellis & Harper, 1975) that disturbed marriages result when one or both spouses hold irrational beliefs (e.g., other's approval is necessary; one *must* get one's way).[1] Ellis suggests that these unrealistic, demanding expectations inevitably produce disappointment and frustration, with associated negative emotions such as anger, and counterproductive behaviors such as nagging. His rational-emotive therapy (RET) is intended to challenge the validity of these irrational beliefs

[1]In the present chapter, the practice in the literature of using the terms *irrational belief* and *unrealistic expectation* interchangeably to describe extreme or distorted standards that a person applies to self, partner, or relationship will be followed.

directly. Distressed spouses are taught that particular expectations produce disturbed emotions and behavior, and they are coached in substituting more realistic thinking about themselves and their partners. For example, it is stressed that blaming one's partner for his or her mistakes only elicits counterproductive defensiveness, that it is human to make mistakes, and that the important point is learning from one's mistakes.

Ellis's approach to marital dysfunction tends not to be an interactive systems view but an extension of his model of individual psychopathology. However, it is likely that spouses reared in the same society will share and reinforce each other's unrealistic expectations. Conjoint treatment can be quite useful for identifying and challenging mutually held dysfunctional expectations. Second, partners may have complementary irrational beliefs, as when one spouse believes he or she must get his or her way and the other believes that he or she must perform perfectly. Such a couple may enact a destructive spiral in which the former nags and the latter defends or withdraws in frustration. Also, it is important to assess whether one spouse may in fact elicit and reinforce the other's expectations (e.g., excessive need for approval) when this leads to compliance with the former's wishes.

Ellis assumes that 10 core irrational beliefs mediate people's dysfunctional responses to their environments (Ellis, 1962). Although measures of these beliefs have been found to correlate with indices of psychopathology such as depression (LaPointe & Crandell, 1980; Nelson, 1977), restricting one's assessment and treatment to that set of cognitions may result in overlooking other unrealistic expectations that play important roles in marital dysfunction. Epstein and Eidelson (1981) found that self-report scales designed specifically to measure unrealistic expectations about relationships were better predictors of clinical couples' levels of marital distress, desire to maintain rather than terminate the relationship, preference for marital versus individually-oriented treatment, and self-perceived chance for improvement of the marital problem than were scales from Jones's (1968) measure of Ellis's irrational beliefs about self. Consequently, cognitive assessment in marital therapy is likely to be more comprehensive if it includes such expectations about relationships (e.g., disagreement between partners is destructive to the relationship, partners should be able to sense each other's needs and moods as if they could reach each other's mind, and partners are not capable of changing). Other relevant expectations regarding relationships involve qualities of romantic love, marital roles, and the amount and quality of time partners will spend together (Jacobson & Margolin, 1979; Stuart, 1980).

Stuart (1980) notes that an individual's negative (or positive) expectations easily can become self-fulfilling prophecies, as these expectations guide actions toward the partner and elicit the anticipated responses from him or her. Although negative self-fulfilling prophecies make the couple's world more predictable, they are likely to exacerbate marital conflict and dissatisfaction. Unrealistically positive expectations also are likely to generate distress when the realities of married life fail to meet one or both partners' standards.

Sager's (1976) concept of "marriage contracts" is consistent with a cognitive view of marital conflict. According to Sager, each partner brings to the relationship a set of expectations, both conscious and beyond awareness, regarding the benefits he or she will give and receive. These expectations, whether realistic or unrealistic, often are unspoken, but when the realities of the couple's interactions do not meet such implicit expectations spouses respond (e.g., with disappointment, anger, attack) as if an explicit agreement had been violated. Sager's therapeutic interventions are intended to make the spouses aware of their individual expectations or "contracts" and how these mesh or conflict with the partner's contract and with their actual marital interactions. Foci for change may include individual expectations (e.g., a spouse's assumption that he or she must receive unqualified acceptance from the partner might be challenged and modified) or the couple's pattern of interaction (e.g., an overly critical spouse may be coached in expressing criticism in a constructive manner that is palatable to a sensitive partner).

A comprehensive assessment of expectations relevant to marital dysfunction should include commonly held irrational beliefs such as those postulated by Ellis (1962), common unrealistic expectations about relationships (Epstein & Eidelson, 1981; Jacobson & Margolin, 1979), and expectations that are more idiosyncratic to the members of a particular couple. Beck's idiographic approach to assessing dysfunctional cognitions (Beck, 1976; Beck, Rush, Shaw, & Emery, 1979) consists of systematic inquiry in clinical interviews, combined with clients' record keeping regarding their cognitions (thoughts and visual images), emotions, and behaviors in particular situations. Assessment is designed to identify specific cognitive distortions of events (*automatic thoughts*) and basic underlying assumptions. Applying this approach to marital interaction, a therapist may, for example, note a husband's negative mood in response to his wife's criticism and may draw out the husband's distorted appraisal that his wife thinks he is an inadequate husband. Identification of similar instances in which the husband interprets his wife's disagreement or criticism as total rejection may lead the therapist and husband to explore expectations underlying these negative interpretations, such as, "In order to be a successful, adequate husband, I must satisfy my wife in every way." Accurate assessment of underlying expectations requires that the interviewer use questions carefully in order to go beyond superficial descriptions of thoughts and thereby obtain samples of the central meanings that events have for the individual (Beck *et al.*, 1979).

Modification of unrealistic expectations involves systematic reality testing and examination of how spouses' beliefs inevitably produce disappointment or restrict their ability to solve problems. On the one hand, a therapist can suggest directly to a spouse that a particular expectation is extreme and contributes to marital distress. Bibliotherapy can be used as an adjunct to therapist interventions; for example, couples who have sexual dysfunctions and hold unrealistic expectations regarding sexual performance may be instructed to read literature espousing more realistic views of sex, such as the volumes by Barbach (1976); McCarthy, Ryan, and Johnson (1975); and Zilbergeld (1978). Such material can be assigned as homework and discussed during marital therapy sessions. Clients may be more highly motivated to challenge their own beliefs if the therapist guides them in exploring how these cognitions exacerbate frustration and conflict in their marriage.

Systematic and repeated reality testing often is necessary to modify firmly established cognitions that may have served as self-fulfilling prophecies in the past. Beck *et al.* (1979) note that the effectiveness of directly telling a client that his or her expectations are invalid may be limited because an individual's cognitions may lack external validity but may be internally valid (consistent with his or her other cognitions and experiences). Therefore, a direct verbal attack on the person's way of organizing reality may elicit confusion and anxiety. Confusion and defensiveness can be minimized by interventions in which the couple learns through here-and-now experiences the degree to which their expectations are accurate.

Beck *et al.* (1979) note that reality testing is not intended to produce unrealistically optimistic expectations on the part of clients but to test the validity of negative or extreme expectations. Therapists and clients collaborate in examining specific evidence that is consistent or inconsistent with each cognition associated with a presenting problem. The therapist can ask a series of questions that guide the client in testing expectations against logic and his or her life experiences. Eliciting facts that clients may have overlooked or discounted in jumping to conclusions may facilitate a reassessment of such dysfunctional cognitions. Although the task of modifying unrealistic expectations may be difficult when they are shared by two spouses, the potential for uncovering evidence contradictory to the beliefs can be greater when the therapist can use both spouses as sources of data.

A major approach for challenging unrealistic expectations is reality testing by means of behavioral experiments in which spouses are guided in creating *new* data bearing on the validity of their negative cognitions (Beck *et al.*, 1979; Stuart, 1980). Stuart stresses that changes in micro-behaviors, high-frequency events in a couple's daily interaction pattern, contribute significantly to changes in the spouses' perceptions of each other's level of interest and acceptance. By focusing the couple's attention on positive behavior exchanges and by translating global complaints into specific behavioral goals, the therapist works to instill a belief that change is possible and to counteract negative expectations about the relationship (Jacobson & Margolin, 1979; Stuart, 1980). Similarly, spouses can be coached in experimenting with alternative ways of interacting in order to determine the differential consequences. For example, spouses who expect that open disagreement will damage their marriage can be trained in communication skills (e.g., Guerney, 1977) that facilitate expressiveness without negative consequences. The degree to which the effects of open communication disconfirm spouses' negative expectations can be monitored during therapy sessions and at home. Beck *et al.* (1979) note that in order to subject a belief to experimental test, it must be translated into operational terms; for example, the expectation that "My husband wants to dominate me and will fight my attempts to assert myself" could be operationalized as "My husband will yell at me and refuse to negotiate if I tell him I want to take turns drawing up the monthly family budget." The client's task is to carry out the prescribed behavior and keep a detailed record of the behavioral, cognitive, and emotional consequences. An advantage of constructing such behavioral experiments during conjoint marital therapy sessions is that the other spouse is at least indirectly challenged to behave in a manner that will disconfirm the partner's negative expectation.

Another method for increasing flexibility in a couple's expectations regarding relationships is the modeling of alternative relationship patterns by a co-therapist pair. Although co-therapy is expensive and may require that the therapists invest considerable effort in the development of their own working relationship (Luthman & Kirschenbaum, 1974), interaction patterns modeled by co-therapists can facilitate couples' experimentation with alternative behaviors and expectations regarding marriage (Epstein, Jayne-Lazarus, & DeGiovanni, 1979; Epstein & Jayne, 1981).

It should be noted that some of the above interventions focus directly on cognitive content (identifying distortions and errors in thinking) and other procedures use behavioral experiences to shift problematic expectations. The common goal of the predominantly cognitive and the behaviorally-oriented interventions is reality testing of faulty cognitions.

Therapists also need to identify when negative expectations are reality-based; for example, when a spouse expects the partner to reject his or her attempts at assertiveness and in fact the partner reacts quite negatively. In such situations, procedures to modify the quality of the individual's assertive behavior, the partner's interpretations of that behavior, and the partner's social skills (e.g., for negotiating) would be appropriate.

In addition to specifying and modifying spouses' unrealistic expectations regarding themselves and their relationship, it is important for the course of therapy to consider potentially problematic expectations regarding the process of therapy itself. Jacobson and Margolin (1979) stress that behavior change programs are unlikely to be successful unless members of a couple expect to work collaboratively toward *mutual* change, with a minimum of blaming. In order to instill such a collaborative set during the initial stage of therapy, Jacobson and Margolin increase the couple's attention to relationship strengths, facilitate some positive interaction between partners in the first session (e.g., by asking them to recount how they met and what attracted them to each other), express optimism about the outcome of therapy, and emphasize how the partners can elicit more positive behaviors from each other by behaving positively themselves. When spouses expect that feelings must change before behaviors can be changed, this assumption is challenged as well, and they are encouraged to enact behavior changes that can elicit more positive feelings.

Doherty (1981) presents a cognitive model in which spouses' expectations of efficacy or mastery in solving their problems are a function of their attributions regarding the causes and characteristics of the problems. For example, the expectation that a problem behavior can be changed is likely to be stronger when the behavior is seen as voluntary rather than involuntary and transitory rather than stable. The next section of this paper discusses dimensions with which couples attribute meaning to their behaviors and describes approaches to modifying dysfunctional attributions.

Correcting Faulty Attributions

Distressed spouses not only tend to exchange high rates of negative behaviors but also are prone to making negative attributions about each other's behavior. These attributions often are generalized to the extent that the individual applies a narrow range of primarily negative dimensions in evaluating the partner (Beck, 1980) and tends to notice or "track" the partner's negative behaviors while failing to notice positive behaviors (Jacobson & Margolin, 1979). Another common cognitive process that can interfere with a behavior change program occurs when a spouse notices a desired change on the part of the partner yet discounts its value, concluding that the partner's underlying personality or intent has not changed. Behavior changes that are attributed to coercion or impression management (e.g., "He's doing more chores around the house because he's afraid I'll leave him if he doesn't") are less likely to be received as positives, and Jacobson and Margolin (1979) suggest that such negative attributions even can be fostered by contingency contracting procedures in behavioral marital therapy. Gelles and Straus (1979) note that, at the extreme, attributions of malevolent intent can contribute to violence among family members. Consequently, correction of spouses' faulty attributions and perceptions of each other is an important step in establishing and maintaining a mutually satisfying relationship.

The attributions that couples make regarding the source(s) of their problems are likely to influence their optimism and motivation for therapy. For example, attributing responsibility for the problem to one's partner, particularly when the attribution involves negative intent, is likely to elicit destructive blaming (Doherty, 1981). When problems are attributed to stable or global (trait) characteristics of the partner, the individual's confidence that the problem can be resolved will be lower and his or her negative response to the partner may be generalized to various aspects of the relationship. An example of the latter phenomenon is when a husband interprets his wife's getting a job as reflecting a general lack of respect for his ality as a provider (and therefore his masculinity) and then becomes quite jealous whenever she talks to another man. Attributing the responsibility for marital dysfunction primarily to oneself can be problematic as well. On the positive side, the tendency to blame the partner should be lower. Similarly, the estimate of potential for solving the problem should be higher when one's own problematic behaviors are perceived as voluntary (Doherty, 1981). However, attributions to global or stable characteristics of the self are likely to lead the individual to perceive generalized problems (e.g., "I am not only impotent sexually, but probably cannot please my wife in any aspect of our relationship") for which there is limited hope of improvement.

Hurvitz (1970) systematically challenges attributions that involve "terminal hypotheses," explanations suggesting no avenues for change. By asking a series of "Why?" questions, Hurvitz stresses to a couple how their terminal hypotheses (e.g., "He inherited a bad temper") are inconsistent with their participation in change-oriented therapy and challenges them to generate "instrumental hypotheses" that imply potential for problem solving (e.g., "We seem to snap at each other when we have had little time for relaxation"). Rush, Shaw, and Khatami (1980) ask each member of a couple to keep a log of marital interactions associated with unpleasant emotional responses. They then elicit each member's assumptions and interpretations about each event during conjoint sessions and test these against the partner's cognitions. This reality testing of interpretations each spouse had feared to express can reduce negative views of self and other, anxiety about rejection, and hostility.

In order to reduce mutual blaming, Baucom (1981) explains to couples how marital problems can be attributed to internal factors (self) or to external factors (e.g., partner) and coaches them in assessing how their own cognitions and behaviors contribute to specific problems in their relationships. On the other hand, Beck *et al.* (1979) guide overly self-critical depressed individuals toward reattributing causes of problems to factors outside themselves. The techniques used include identifying and evaluating the validity of "facts" the person uses in assigning blame, demonstrating how the person applies harsher standards for his or her own behavior than for others' behavior, and challenging the belief in *total* responsibility for negative consequences. Baucom (1981) also works to counteract attributions made to global and stable factors by having couples analyze their marital problems in terms of specific and unstable determinants. The common goal in all of the above interventions is to shift and expand spouses' perspectives in interpreting the meanings and causes of their behavior.

Some misattributions in marital interaction can be due to systematic distortions in thinking such as those described by Beck (1976). Personalization, the tendency to overestimate the degree to which events are related to oneself, may lead an individual to assume indiscriminately that he or she has caused the partner's bad moods. Dysfunctional consequences of personalization include aversive self-derogation, defensiveness, and depression. The partner who receives such an egocentric response is likely to feel misunderstood and frustrated.

A second form of distorted thinking is polarized or dichotomous thinking, in which people attribute extreme characteristics to themselves and their partners. The individual whose perceptions are channeled by such absolutes (e.g., "He *never* pays any attention to me") may overlook gradations of behavior and have a low expectancy for change in the marriage. Partners who are accused of extreme behavior tend to respond in anger when they perceive that their "good efforts" have been overlooked. Other thinking distortions that can lead to inaccurate attributions regarding a partner's behavior include selective abstraction (focusing on a detail out of context), arbitrary inference (jumping to a conclusion in the absence of evidence or in the face of contradictory evidence), and unjustified overgeneralization from a single incident. Beck (1976) suggests that when people apply these absolute, broad, personalized cognitive "rules" in interpreting, evaluating, and attempting to influence their own behavior and that of others, the consequences are disturbed emotions and behaviors. The therapeutic task is a collaboration between therapist and clients in identifying problematic thinking distortions and substituting more realistic, adaptive rules. The therapist works to instill the idea that thoughts are hypotheses rather than facts, helps the client(s) identify attitudes and assumptions that seem to elicit negative emotions and behaviors, and coaches clients in challenging distorted cognitions through logic and *in vivo* reality testing. As suggested earlier in the present paper, the monitoring of spouses' cognitions during marital interactions in conjoint therapy sessions offers repeated opportunities for identifying and modifying problematic distortions.

A common cognitive restructuring procedure used with couples (Jacobson & Margolin, 1979; Stuart, 1980) involves relabeling (or finding a new attribution for) behaviors that spouses find distressing. For example, Jacobson and Margolin describe how a wife misattributed her husband's lack of expessiveness to a lack of trust or love, when in fact it was due to a deficit in expressive skills. In such a case, relabeling itself may reduce the couple's distress by identifying a more benign explanation for a distressing behavior. However, it also is important to address the wife's desire for verbalizations of love by means of appropriate interventions such as communication training. The process of relabeling begins with identification of the intent attributed to the partner. It is particularly useful to elicit descriptions of the negative attributions made about specific instances of the partner's behavior during conjoint therapy sessions. The partner can then provide feedback regarding his or her own intentions, feelings, and goals associated with the behavior (Rush, Shaw, & Khatami, 1980). Of course, the attributions the partner makes about his or her own behavior themselves may involve problematic distortions that must be addressed (e.g., trait attributions that imply inability to change). Nevertheless, at times it may be less important to determine which attribution is more accurate than to instill the attitude that attributions are subjective and susceptible to error. Couples can be coached in the use of communication skills (e.g., Gottman, Notarius, Gonso, & Markman, 1976; Guerney, 1977) designed to increase each spouse's understanding of the other's perspective and thereby decrease misinterpretation.

Stuart (1980) suggests that it can be beneficial for therapists to distort attributions for spouses' behaviors in a positive direction, in the interest of eliciting positive emotions and interactions. It seems that this approach should be applied quite judiciously, because it could backfire by leading a spouse to perceive the therapist as allying with a negative partner or by leading one or both spouses to question the therapist's observational ability.

The goal of decreasing aversive interaction and increasing positive interaction in behavioral marital therapy is likely to be facilitated significantly by the assessment and modification of attributions that contribute to the perception of behaviors as negative or unchangeable. Such an approach involves teaching couples that marital satisfaction is a subjective state influenced by idiosyncratic interpretations of day-to-day interactions. Attributional change can be both a prerequisite for and a consequence of positive behavior change.

Teaching Self-Instructional Procedures

Interactions of highly distressed couples commonly are marked by emotional outbursts and escalating exchanges of aversive behavior. Although such behavior may be determined in part by distorted expectations and attributions that elicit negative emotions such as anger and anxiety, the particular impulsive form of the behavioral response is itself problematic in that it impedes the reflective processes needed to test faulty cognitions. Impulsive interaction between emotionally aroused spouses also interferes with systematic problem-solving skills that could reduce distressing conflict. Behavioral marital therapy procedures such as communication training, problem-solving training, and contingency contracting, which are intended to decrease exchanges of aversive behaviors, can be difficult to implement unless spouses are able to direct and control their responses to each other. A communication training program such as Guerney's (1977) Relationship Enhancement helps slow impulsiveness by imposing strict interaction rules, but success with such an intervention presumes a certain level of self-control under stressful conditions; that is, the mere presence of the partner can elicit strong, task-interfering emotional and behavioral responses in highly distressed couples (Epstein & Williams, 1981).

In marital treatment, conjoint sessions provide opportunities to assess cognitive excesses and deficits. However, in cases where a spouse's self-regulatory ability is so impeded that he or she continually disrupts conjoint sessions, individual self-instructional training may be a necessary prerequisite.

Meichenbaum (1976, 1977) describes procedures for assessment and training of self-instructional skills for use in inhibiting impulsive responses, focusing attention on task-relevant cues, attending to task goals, coping with frustration and failure, and controlling specific verbal and nonverbal behaviors needed to accomplish the task. Couples who respond impulsively toward each other can be taught how their unregulated behavior interferes with fulfillment of their needs in the relationship, trained to recognize cues of impulsive or otherwise unconstructive behavior early, and coached in the development of positive cognitive and behavioral coping responses. Each spouse has the task of noticing cues on his or her own part (e.g., anger, anxiety, confusion, rapid speech, interrupting the partner, and thoughts about winning an argument) and cues exhibited by the partner (Epstein & Williams 1981). The therapist initially can provide the couple with feedback regarding such cues, and videotape replay of sessions can be used to "relive" situations that elicited maladaptive cognitions, emotions, and behaviors. Spouses then are instructed to use the identified cues as discriminative stimuli for positive self-instruction, which can include statements describing the steps involved in a task and how to accomplish them. For example, self-instruction during a communication training task might include (1) identification of impulsive responses (e.g., "I am interrupting my partner") and task-interfering cognitions (e.g., "I am thinking about how my partner's ideas are incorrect"), and (2) self-instruction for effective completion of the task (e.g., "Stay calm. Listen carefully to my partner and try to understand how she views things. Do not respond with my ideas until I have communicated understanding of my partner's views to her"). Interventions by the therapist include specific instructions for generating positive self-statements, modeling of overt self-instruction, and coaching of clients' own rehearsals. There should be a progression from overt to covert self-instruction, and couples are more likely to develop proficiency with these skills if they have opportunities to practice them while discussing relatively benign topics before progressing to emotion-laden relationship topics.

Stress inoculation training, which teaches clients to cope with stressors by means of self-instruction, imagery, and behavioral skills (Meichenbaum, 1977), can be used to reduce spouses' maladaptive responses to stressful marital conflict and its concomitant negative emotions such as anger and anxiety. Meichenbaum (1977) describes a three-phase model of stress inoculation in which clients are educated in a conceptual framework regarding stress responses, rehearse a variety of cognitive and behavioral coping techniques, and then apply the skills with real stressors. The training and rehearsal phase includes coping techniques for four stages: preparing for a stressor, confronting and handling it, coping in the event of being overwhelmed by the stressor, and reinforcing oneself for successful coping. Behavioral coping techniques include planning an "escape route" (e.g., going out for a walk) and use of physical relaxation. Cognitive coping involves monitoring one's negative self-statements (e.g., "I'll lose control") and using their occurrence as cues for emitting positive, coping self-statements (e.g., "Just relax and take one step at a time").

Stress inoculation training can be applied with distressed couples for whom interaction has come to elicit anxiety sufficient to impede communication and problem-solving. Novaco's (1975) use of stress inoculation for controlling anger arousal also can be valuable in reducing spouses' destructive ways of responding to marital conflict. Clients are taught relaxation skills to reduce arousal and cognitive skills for coping with provocations. They are taught to identify anger-eliciting self-statements (e.g., intolerance for the partner's mistakes, perceived threats to self-worth) and to substitute constructive self-statements.

Assessment of the need for stress inoculation training to reduce problematic anxiety and anger in marital conflict is best accomplished in a conjoint session, where the therapist can observe how debilitated each spouse is when interacting with the other. In fact, the couple's own negative experiences during the interaction can be used to support the rationale for the training. The initial rehearsal of self-instructional skills is best done individually rather than with *in vivo* marital interaction, and some spouses with severe anxiety or anger responses may need individual therapy before they can work collaboratively with their partners. However, with many couples even the initial rehearsal of skills can be conducted with both partners present but working individually with the therapist rather than interacting. Advantages of this format are that spouses learn coping skills both by rehearsing and by observing their partners rehearsing, and they increase their understanding of each other's cognitions and emotional reactions. Individual skills then can be monitored and practiced in actual marital interaction, with the therapist instructing, providing feedback, modeling, and coaching the couple as needed.

Cognitive Interventions, Behavioral Interventions and Systems Theory

Cognitive and behavioral approaches to therapy traditionally have been designed to modify the dysfunctional thoughts and skills of individuals through processes of relearning. Although cognitive and behavioral interventions with *individuals* may not seem consistent with goals of marital therapists who are guided by concepts of systems theory, a cognitive-behavioral model of marital *interaction* has some important areas of overlap with a systems orientation.

The cognitive interventions described in this paper are intended to modify distortions, deficits, and excesses characteristic of the individual spouse, but it is assumed that these dysfunctional cognitions continually influence and are influenced by interdependent sequences of behaviors between spouses. Each partner's emotional and behavioral responses to the other are mediated by his or her cognitive appraisal of the partner's behavior. In terms of marital conflict, negative behaviors elicit negative cognitions, and vice versa. The argument that behavioral change will produce attitudinal change (Stuart, 1980) is limited with highly distressed couples whose expectations and attributions are very negative.

Reduction of behaviors identified by spouses as distressing may not produce greater marital satisfaction if negative cognitions have not been changed (e.g., "He helps more around the house now, but he still doesn't *want* to help"). Cognitive interventions such as relabeling of behaviors for which there are negative attributions may be necessary before spouses will be motivated to change their behavior (Jacobson & Margolin, 1979). Similarly, negative cognitions are unlikely to change if they are supported by the "evidence" of continued negative behavior. Change in the marital system depends on changes in sequences of cognitions and behaviors occurring between spouses.

Feldman (1976) describes how cognitions and behaviors interact in a marital system, such that complementary cognitive schemata (e.g., attitudes and expectations about oneself and relationships) are elicited in the two spouses in the course of their behavioral interplay. Each behavior on the part of one spouse simultaneously is a response to the partner's behavior and the person's own cognitive schemata, a stimulus for the partner's subsequent behavior and schemata, and a reinforcer of the preceding couple interaction. Feldman identifies a circular pattern in couples involving a depressed member, such that the nondepressed member's behavior (perhaps a critical remark) elicits self-depreciation and dysphoria in the depressed partner, which then elicits overprotective cognitions and behavior on the part of the nondepressed member. However, the depressed partner finds the oversolicitousness not only reinforcing, but also frustrating to his or her own desire for competence. Any consequent withdrawal or hostility expressed by the depressed partner then elicits cognitions of self-depreciation in the nondepressed partner, who is likely to engage in depression-inducing behavior and thereby begin the cycle once again. Spouses can initiate the repetitive *[handwritten annotations at top: "Non-depressed Spouse's behavior (Critical comment)" / "Depressed withdrawal Non-depressed: overprotectiveness" / "Depressed spouse: Self-depreciation & dysphoria"]*

pattern at any behavioral or cognitive point in the sequence, and treatment should take into account each step in the sequence: the non-depressed spouse's cognitions (threats to the self-image of rescuer) and behaviors (criticism, oversolicitousness), and the depressed spouse's cognitions (self-depreciation) and behaviors (self-criticism, withdrawal). The determinants of any one component of the cycle are understood by examining the total interactive system.

Dryden (1981) suggests that cognitive, behavioral, and systems orientations to the treatment of couples' problems can be integrated by challenging spouses' faulty inferences and beliefs regarding their relationship, teaching them social skills to reduce negative interactions, and modifying the responses of each partner that may reinforce undesirable behavior on the other's part. Stuart (1980) describes a sequential model of cognitive and behavioral interventions, in which cognitive changes are induced in order to facilitate new behaviors, behavior changes are initiated to produce new (more positive) subjective experiences, and cognitions likely to encourage repetition of new desired behaviors (e.g., recognition of a partner's positive response; attribution of positive intent) are developed.

Thus, the marital therapist must be skilled in modifying both internal cognitions and overt interactions between spouses. The cognitive approaches presented in this chapter can be combined with behavioral marital therapy procedures such as communication training and problem-solving training in order to produce positive cognitive and behavioral changes in distressed couples. For example, relabeling negative attributions can decrease hostility and facilitate empathic communication, and development of clear communication can provide evidence to contradict negative expectations about one's relationship. Similarly, self-instructional training can facilitate behavioral problem-solving skills by focusing performance and decreasing task-interfering thoughts and emotions, and cooperative efforts in problem solving can build positive expectations and attributions regarding one's partner. The therapist's task is to implement mutually enhancing changes in spouses' cognitions and behaviors.

By integrating cognitive and behavioral interventions in a conjoint setting, the martial therapist has the advantage of a multidimensional approach to complex marital interactions. Although the cognitive approaches described in this chapter represent extensions of established cognitive therapies for individuals, their application with couples has been derived in clinical practice and has yet to be tested empirically. Consequently, they should be applied with caution until their efficacy has been investigated in treatment outcome studies. In order to do justice to the complexity of intervening in a marital system involving inter-dependent behaviors and cognitive structures, such studies should not fail to include multidimensional assessment and examination of sequences of cognitive and behavioral responses in the dyad.

REFERENCES

Barbach, L. G. *For yourself: The fulfillment of female sexuality.* New York: Anchor, 1976.

Baucom, D. H. *Cognitive behavioral strategies in the treatment of marital discord.* Paper presented at the annual meeting of the Association for the Advancement of Behavior Therapy, Toronto, 1981.

Beck, A. T. *Cognitive therapy and the emotional disorders.* New York: International Universities Press, 1976.

Beck, A. T. *Cognitive aspects of marital interaction.* Paper presented at the annual meeting of the Association for the Advancement of Behavior Therapy, New York, November 1980.

Beck, A. T., Rush, A. J., Shaw, B. F., & Emery, G. *Cognitive therapy of depression.* New York: Guilford, 1979.

Doherty, W. J. Cognitive processes in intimate conflict: I. Extending attribution theory. *American Journal of Family Therapy,* 1981, *9*, 3–13.

Dryden, W. The relationships of depressed persons. In S. Duck & R. Gilmour (Eds.), *Personal relationships 3: Personal relationships in disorder.* New York: Academic, 1981.

Ellis, A. *Reason and emotion in psychotherapy.* New York: Lyle Stuart, 1962.

Ellis, A., & Harper, R. A. *A new guide to rational living.* Englewood Cliffs, N.J.: Prentice-Hall, 1975.

Epstein, N., & Eidelson, R. J. Unrealistic beliefs of clinical couples: Their relationship to expectations, goals, and satisfaction. *American Journal of Family Therapy,* 1981, *9*(4), 13–22.

Epstein, N., & Jayne, C. Perceptions of cotherapists as a function of therapist sex roles and observer sex roles. *Sex Roles,* 1981, *7*, 497–509.

Epstein, N., Jayne-Lazarus, C., & DeGiovanni, I. S. Cotherapists as models of relationships: Effects on the outcome of couples' therapy. *Journal of Marital and Family Therapy,* 1979, *5*, 53–60.

Epstein, N., & Williams, A. M. Behavioral approaches to the treatment of marital discord. In G. P. Sholevar (Ed.), *Handbook of marriage and marital therapy.* New York: Spectrum, 1981.

Feldman, L. B. Depression and marital interaction. *Family Process,* 1976, *15*, 389–395.

Gelles, R. J., & Straus, M. A. Determinants of violence in the family: Toward a theoretical integration. In W. R. Burr, R. Hill, F. I. Nye, & I. L. Reiss (Eds.), *Contemporary theories about the family* (Vol. 1). New York: Free Press, 1979.

Gottman, J., Notarius, C., Gonso, J., & Markman, H. *A couple's guide to communication.* Champaign, Ill.: Research Press, 1976.

Guerney, B. G., Jr. *Relationship enhancement.* San Francisco: Jossey-Bass, 1977.

Hurvitz, N. Interaction hypotheses in marriage counseling. *The Family Coordinator,* 1970, *19*, 64–75.

Jacobson, N. S., & Margolin, G. *Marital therapy: Strategies based on social learning and behavior exchange principles.* New York: Brunner/Mazel, 1979.

Jones, R. G. *A factored measure of Ellis' irrational belief system, with personality and maladjustment correlates.* Unpublished doctoral dissertation, Texas Technological College, 1968.

LaPointe, K. A., & Crandell, C. J. Relationship of irrational beliefs to self-reported depression. *Cognitive Therapy and Research*, 1980, *4*, 247–250.

Luthman, S. G., & Kirschenbaum, M. *The dynamic family.* Palo Alto, Calif.: Science and Behavior Books, 1974.

McCarthy, B. W., Ryan, M., & Johnson, F. A. *Sexual awareness: A practical approach.* San Francisco: Boyd & Fraser, 1975.

Meichenbaum, D. A cognitive-behavior modification approach to assessment. In M. Hersen & A. S. Bellack (Eds.), *Behavioral assessment: A practical handbook.* New York: Pergamon, 1976.

Meichenbaum, D. *Cognitive–behavior modification: An integrative approach.* New York: Plenum, 1977.

Nelson, R. E. Irrational beliefs in depression. *Journal of Consulting and Clinical Psychology*, 1977, *45*, 1190–1191.

Novaco, R. *Anger control: The development and evaluation of an experimental treatment.* Lexington, Mass.: Heath, 1975.

O'Leary, K. D., & Turkewitz, H. Marital therapy from a behavioral perspective. In T. J. Paolino & B. S. McCrady (Eds.), *Marriage and marital therapy: Psychoanalytic, behavioral, and systems theory perspectives.* New York: Brunner/Mazel, 1978.

Rush, A. J., Shaw, B., & Khatami, M. Cognitive therapy of depression: Utilizing the couples system. *Cognitive Therapy and Research*, 1980, *4*, 103–113.

Sager, C. J. *Marriage contracts and couple therapy: Hidden forces in intimate relationships.* New York: Brunner/Mazel, 1976.

Stuart, R. B. *Helping couples change: A social learning approach to marital therapy.* New York: Guilford, 1980.

Weiss, R. L. The conceptualization of marriage from a behavioral perspective. In T. J. Paolino & B. S. McCrady (Eds.), *Marriage and marital therapy: Psychoanalytic, behavioral, and systems theory perspectives.* New York: Brunner/Mazel, 1978.

Zilbergeld, B. *Male sexuality.* Boston: Little, Brown, 1978.

Cognitive-Behavioral Strategies to Induce and Enhance a Collaborative Set in Distressed Couples

Janis Lieff Abrahms

This chapter illustrates the complexity of interpersonal conflict. Relationship dissatisfaction often is a product of both intrapersonal and interpersonal deficiencies. Both cognitive and behavioral interventions, therefore, may be uniquely suited to increase partners' subjective valuation of their relationship.

When both spouses first are treated in individual therapy, they are encouraged to focus on themselves, to examine thoughtfully the futility of their present attitudes and behaviors, and to make appropriate changes vis-à-vis their marital partner. Subsequent conjoint sessions may be indicated, as will be discussed later. Cognitive and behavioral interventions intermesh to produce a cogent, comprehensive treatment package.

Whether to treat individuals separately or together as a couple, and to focus on idiosyncratic and dysfunctional needs and expectations versus interpersonal behavioral deficits and excesses, involves decisions that are highly intricate, delicate, and controversial. The ideas presented admittedly are speculative, based on the author's clinical experience with distressed couples.

Janis Lieff Abrahms • Department of Psychology, Yale University, New Haven, Connecticut 06520.

Collaborative Set

The term *collaborative set* recently was defined by Jacobson and Margolin (1979) according to a social learning and behavior exchange model: "Both spouses must conduct themselves as if they viewed their relationship difficulties as a common problem which can be solved only if they work together" (p. 108). The *Random House Dictionary* (1966) employs the interpersonal connotation of the word *collaborate* with this definition: "to work together . . . to co-operate with the enemy" (p. 289).

In the cognitive-behavioral (CB) treatment of couples, the individual is assisted in realizing the full complex of factors which contribute to marital disease, along with the degree to which ones' own maladaptive cognitions constitute "the enemy." Such cognitions consist mainly of dysfunctional expectations, attributions, and ideas regarding oneself, one's partner, and one's relationship. Collaboration in this context is viewed as an individual's conscious decision, responsibility, and effort, a demonstrated willingness to work for the good of the relationship regardless of one's spouse's alleged feelings or reciprocated actions.

Building a Collaborative Set through Individual Cognitive Restructuring

Problem solving and communication training are virtually impossible to accomplish if a couple is unwilling to collaborate. According to Jacobson and Margolin (1979), "faulty attributions [e.g., "my spouse is the enemy"] often need to be corrected before spouses will enthusiastically engage in a collaborative effort to modify undesirable relationship behavior" (p. 142). Couples often enter therapy viciously blaming each other for the problems in the marriage and stubbornly waiting for their partner to initiate positive change.

Maladaptive, interpersonal attitudes must be sensitively exposed immediately. Behavior therapists who begin sessions by having couples trade off "low cost" behaviors may not be cognizant of the fact that any positive behavior change for some spouses is simply too risky and unpleasant. Too many cognitive obstacles may exist for marital partners to be willing to experiment with behavior change—particularly in front of each other. Therefore, if the therapist tries to induce an experimental attitude by encouraging the couple to *act* more constructively toward one another, his or her effectiveness may be deflated or sabotaged unnecessarily and unfortunately.

Individual versus conjoint sessions may provide a more conducive, therapeutic environment for each spouse to focus on himself or herself (Abrahms, 1982) and to consider with less distraction the basic thrust of the cognitive model: one's individual responsibility in creating dissatisfaction by adhering to dysfunctional relationship expectations and ideas. Premature conjoint sessions may create a no-win trap: either the partners reject the therapy and continue to blame each other for their misery (a self-defeating point of view which originally may have brought the couple into therapy), or they must admit their culpability to their spouse.

Particularly in the early stage of treatment, CB therapy may be more efficacious if persons are seen individually rather than as couples. As spouses identify and challenge their flawed cognitions, they might loosen their ingrained, bitter, pessimistic postures and allow themselves to establish a motivational commitment to the marriage and therapy. Many people need time to review the advantages and disadvantages of blaming their partner for their unhappiness, harboring grudges, and refusing to initiate positive action. Couples often are mentally unable and unwilling to engage in an experimental "as if" attitude, acting "as if" the marriage were viable and "as if" they felt loving. It is the therapist's task to break through this resistance by restructuring the couple's defeatist attitude. Moreover, the therapist should make every attempt to structure successful marital interactions, minimizing aversive contacts between spouses.

For some couples, individual treatment sessions might be superfluous; for others, however, the establishment of a constructive attitude might facilitate achievement of the primary, preliminary therapeutic goals of CB marital therapy: to focus on oneself, to build positive expectations regarding the viability of the marriage, and to build credibility in the therapist's competency and usefulness of the therapy.

COGNITIVE CHANGE POTENTIATING BEHAVIOR CHANGE

Proponents of behavior exchange principles (e.g., Stuart, 1980) posit repeatedly that the best way to change Partner B's behavior is to change Partner A's behavior. Retreating one step, cognitive-behaviorists (e.g., Epstein, 1982) assert that the most effective way to change Partner A's behavior is first to change Partner A's cognitions. That is, instead of trying to modify the undesirable behavior of Partner B, an alternative solution is to increase Partner A's tolerance of his or her spouse's undesirable behavior—particularly since people frequently do not change long-standing, well rehearsed habits easily or consistently just because other people find them annoying. Once Partner A realistically assesses the proportions, meaning, and underlying intent of Partner B's behavior, the objectionability and importance of the behavior in question may become dramatically reduced.

For instance, if a husband believes, "If my wife doesn't listen to me the way I would like her to, she doesn't care about me," one approach would be to change the wife's listening abilities. A cognitive strategy, however, would be to modify the husband's perceived need for complete, undivided attention by helping him to identify the inaccurate meaning he imposes onto his wife's episodic inattentiveness.

The following example illustrates how cognitive restructuring techniques facilitate behavioral solutions. Sam continually dropped wet towels on the bathroom floor, although he was personally well groomed and kept other household areas quite neat. Every morning, when his wife Sara entered the bathroom, she became infuriated because she thought, "What does he think I am? The maid? I work hard, too. He treats me shabbily. He doesn't give a damn about me." She mistakenly interpreted his careless habit as a deliberate insult by assuming: "If I ask my husband to do something important for me, he should listen. If he doesn't listen and change his behavior, it's because he chooses to disregard me. Thus, he must not respect me or value the marriage."

By directly checking the validity of these thoughts with Sam or by exploring alternative explanations for his behavior in her own mind, the upset spouse would discover the true reason for her husband's actions. In the early morning, he was usually preoccupied. Her mindreading, therefore, had been off base.

Sara also erroneously assumed that (1) people have free will, and (2) people change easily and quickly. She consistently upset herself if her husband deviated from his promises. To challenge her silent assumptions, the therapist instructed her to change instantly and permanently several of her more entrenched habits: binge eating, smoking, nail biting, nagging, and thinking negative thoughts about her neighbors. A week later, when she was asked about the ease and degree of compliance in changing these habits, she confronted the unrealistic nature of her excessive demands.

Once her husband's habit seemed less abusive, her anger diminished. She then could entertain the following constructive behavioral options: (1) She could continue to ask her husband to pick up the towels but not expect him to remember. (2) She could post notes with the hope that he would read and follow them but, again, not expect him to remember. (3) She could let him remind himself and try not to upset herself when he forgot. (4) She could positively reinforce him if he did remember, in an attempt to increase the probability that he might remember in the future.

Here the sequential use of cognitive followed by behavioral methods illuminated and sustained each strategy's beneficial effects. As spouses take more responsibility for their own negative feelings, they achieve better control over their emotions, increase their capabilities to act more positively toward their partner, and potentially increase the probability of eliciting more positive reactions from their partner.

Three detailed examples are presented below to demonstrate the usefulness of (1) individual cognitive restructuring to develop a collaborative set prior to conjoint therapy and (2) integrating cognitive and behavioral interventions to facilitate positive change within couples. The first example, a clear case failure, describes a couple that was insufficiently induced to accept their individual contribution to their marital dissatisfaction. When brought together, they became embroiled in accusatory, deprecating, interpersonal attacks that ultimately aborted the therapy sessions. The second example represents a more successful intertwining of individual self-examination and behavioral exchange. Finally, a third example illustrates how dysfunctional relationship expectations depress a relationship's perceived viability.

Case 1. Failure to Induce Adequately a Collaborative Set

John and Nancy Smith, a couple in their mid-forties, entered therapy complaining that their marriage was deficient across all areas of functioning: sexual, affectionate, communicative, and recreational. What existed between them was a sizzling rage, triggered by a traumatic incident that had occurred three years earlier while consulting a psychiatrist about their son Joel's delinquent behavior. In front of their son, Nancy had attacked John verbally for destroying Joel's self-concept, controlling her life, and deserving the family's hatred.

John apparently did not attempt to dispute her accusations. Feeling ashamed and ruthlessly abused, he silently castigated his wife for creating an irreparable schism between them and between him and his children. Since that incident, the couple continued to move apart, leading parallel lives and making contact only through fighting.

Two years elapsed, during which time the couple's two daughters demonstrated significant improvement in individual CB therapy. At a family session on behalf of the children, the parents expressed interest in couples therapy. They seemed somewhat motivated to repair their relationship, yet skeptical that anything or anyone could reverse its erosive decay.

The Interfering Effect of Underlying Cognitions on a Behavioral Experiment

At the first session, a gestalt of the couple's relationship evolved that included both strengths and deficiencies during various stages of the marriage. The therapist explained behavior exchange and cognitive principles and attempted to generate a present-oriented, experimental, nonevaluative attitude on the part of the couple. The Smiths identified concrete and positive areas of change and agreed as a first homework assignment to exchange relatively low-cost behaviors. Each spouse agreed to take responsibility for his or her own behavior assignment, making such change noncontingent on the other's behavior. This clause was intended to cut through the typical "you, first" attitudinal impediment. Specifically, John agreed to discard his cigarette at the half-way mark. Nancy agreed to invite a mutually chosen neighborhood couple to a movie the following weekend. Thus the exchange entailed improvement in John's personal grooming habits and in Nancy's involvement in their leisure time activities. Both partners expressed credibility in the feasibility and significance of the experiment.

The therapist further explained that any outcome would yield valuable information that would be used in the next session. This statement was made to encourage the return of both partners, regardless of their cognitive and emotional reactions to the results of the experiment. Implicitly, the experiment was designed to inject fresh blood into the relationship and/or to assess the couple's ability to collaborate.

When the couple returned the following week, Nancy had not completed her homework assignment. She said she felt manipulated by the experiment and did not want to collaborate for John's sake. It is interesting that the first experiment highlighted what was later found to be a series of core obstructionist assumptions. Both partners had acted according to their underlying beliefs. John believed that only he was genuinely interested in improving the marriage. All failure thereby was attributed to Nancy. It might be hypothesized that to substantiate this self-righteous attitude, he was obliged to complete the homework. John conveniently used the failure of the first experiment to confirm his prevailing belief.

Nancy believed that to collaborate meant to give up control, and to give up control was a sign of weakness. The therapist unwittingly had designed an exercise that presented her with an unbeatable formula: either she cooperated and experienced a self-devaluation, or she rejected the task and was blamed by her spouse for ruining their relationship. Although the therapist tried to elicit potential obstacles at the time of assignment, the wife had not objected. She may not have been aware of her silent assumptions or of their potency in affecting her behavior. It is also possible that she passively agreed to cooperate in order to avoid momentarily her husband's anticipated wrath.

Purpose of Individual Sessions

The therapist decided to see the couple individually for a number of reasons: (1) The couple had adopted a fixed, blaming framework that undermined each partner's ability and willingness to consider independently the impact of his or her own attitude and behavior. Pressing self-scrutiny in the presence of the other partner seemed to exacerbate their competitive, combative stance. Each continually shifted the focus of responsibility back onto the other person. (2) Given the couple's reluctance to continue therapy and their pessimism regarding the viability of the relationship, further perceived failure might have precipitated their dropping out of therapy permaturely.

Individual cognitive strategies were presented with the following basic treatment rationale: "Beliefs often paralyze actions. Therefore, it is important to identify and correct these ideas before partners can work effectively together."

Both spouses agreed to come in for individual sessions to deal with their cognitive blocks and resultant resentment prior to learning communication and problem-solving skills. At this point, Nancy seemed more eager to begin than John. He blatantly admitted that his only reason for being in therapy was to engage Nancy in therapy. He insisted that for the marriage to survive, she would have to apologize for her unfair and unpardonable actions in the psychiatrist's office. Nancy would barely speak to John, never mind apologize.

To perk John's interest in therapy, the therapist suggested that if Nancy realized his interest in improving the marriage, she might be more willing to meet his request. John agreed to attend eight individual sessions, after which he insisted on another conjoint meeting to evaluate changes in his wife. John wholeheartedly believed he needed Nancy to vindicate him of his guilt and repair his damaged self-image.

Cognitive-Behavioral Interventions

In order to objectify their hostility and blame, the spouses were taught to record automatic thoughts and eventually to identify silent assumptions using the Dysfunctional Thought Form (Beck, Rush, Shaw, & Emery, 1979). This exercise quickly illustrated that at moments of intense rage, both partners framed the other as uncaring and condemnable. For example, when John refused to lend his car to one of the children, Nancy thought, "He's unwilling to inconvenience himself for his family. He's selfish." The couple learned to identify such cognitive errors as mislabeling and selective negative focusing which discolored their perceptions of each other.

To revise more accurately their perspective of each other, they were asked to record instances of how their spouse demonstrated caring and interest in his or her *own* way. This clause prevented disqualifications or the ignoring of behaviors that challenged the "uncaring" hypothesis. Nancy listed such items as "asking me about my day at work, taking the kids to school when they missed their bus, and sharing his view of the daily news." John listed, among other items: "buying me my favorite kind of bagel for Sunday morning breakfast, laundering my clothes, and asking me about my work day." Thus both were able to see how each had viewed the other as 100% self-centered. They had exaggerated the frequency with which their spouse demonstrated unacceptable behavior and their sense of deprivation. It is interesting to note that whereas the focus of this exercise was clearly behavioral, its impact was cognitive in that an unsavory relationship was injected with positive highlights. The couple was forced to reconcile the incongruity between a list of their partner's pleasing behaviors and their own global dissatisfaction with that partner.

To prepare for the rapidly approaching conjoint session, Nancy worked on reattributing her children's problems to a number of factors besides John's mismanagement of his anger. She identified advantages and disadvantages of adhering to her prevailing belief: "Joel's emotional and social problems today are John's fault." The advantages were that (1) she would not have to relinquish her resentment for John, (2) she could use John as a scapegoat and blame him for Joel's shortcomings, (3) she could blame John for Joel's future mishaps, (4) she did not have to recognize her complicity in Joel's development, (5) by expressing dissatisfaction with John, she created a view of herself as the more benevolent, rational, well adjusted parent, and (6) she did not have to take responsibility for improving the marriage. The disadvantages were: (1) by feeling resentful toward John, she guaranteed no improvement in her relationship and discouraged herself from initiating better interactions, (2) she preserved a negatively biased view of the marriage, (3) she wasted time ruminating over rancorous thoughts, (4) she experienced a high level of dissatisfaction which eroded the quality of her everyday life, and (5) the marital situation was aversive to the children and provided poor role models for them.

This self-help exercise motivated Nancy to consider the ill effects that her past beliefs were having on her present marriage and moved her to desire actual readjustments in her attitude and behavior toward John. First, she concluded that the disadvantages of subscribing to the above dysfunctional belief outweighed the advantages by 80%. She then was asked to present evidence that disconfirmed the "John is solely to blame" assumption. She realized that (1) Joel had acted in difficult, disruptive, and aggressive ways since birth, (2) John had been provoked by Joel's stubborn defiance into overreacting in inflammatory ways, (3) this reaction was not based on his disregard for Joel, but rather John's inability to discipline with more adaptive tactics at the moment, and (4) although John had communication problems with his family, he showed them love in other ways.

Since her original blaming perspective was neither helpful nor totally valid, she rewrote it as follows:

> John's communication problems may have contributed to Joel's emotional and social problems, but John tries to be a loving and patient father. Joel, certainly as an adult, has a responsibility to change his own destructive attitudes and behaviors rather than to blame his father for his current situation. John did the best he could given an imperfect child, father, and relationship. I can try to take the initiative to improve the marriage, even if John's relationship with Joel does not improve.

Another major obstacle to be hurdled involved the pejorative meaning Nancy ascribed to making decisions jointly. Nancy firmly believed that to ask John for his opinion would be a sign of personal weakness, as if her independent judgment were defective. The couple's communication pattern could not be positively altered until she convinced herself that it was not helpful to achieve power by excluding John.

Nancy considered the advantages and disadvantages of ostracizing her husband from the rest of the family. She was unsure of what might occur if she did include him since it had been some time since she had acted collectively. Nancy was certain, however, that by systematically excluding him, she had to deal with his angry recriminations and brooding withdrawal.

She also realized that she had created a self-fulfilling prophecy. She withheld information and made unilateral decisions. John interpreted these actions as meaning, "My ideas are unimportant to my wife." He then withdrew and showed less interest in the family. Finally, she denounced him for having so few constructive familial interactions. In diagraming this pattern, she concluded that she did not have to be magnanimous, but merely self-interested to act more positively toward John. John also was shown how this negative reinforcing cycle yielded results that were dichtomously opposed to his wishes.

The therapist further diluted her "cooperation–weakness" formula by asking the following questions:

THERAPIST: If a person subscribes to a belief that is frequently self-defeating, is it a sign of strength to continue to subscribe to it?

PATIENT: Of course not. It's not very heroic to maintain crummy habits.

THERAPIST: If a person is willing to experiment empirically with a belief and to develop a more beneficial belief, even if it takes a great deal of effort, might she be viewed as acting from a mature and healthy vantage versus a position of weakness?

PATIENT: I see what you're getting at, but it's hard to accept.

These logical challenges helped Nancy to adopt gradually a more experimental attitude regarding her interactions with her husband. Knowing that John felt excluded from and victimized by the family, she decided to allow him to participate in decision-making and pleasure oriented activities. For instance, she once left a friendly note, informing him of the whereabouts of the family and of subsequent dinner plans. John decided to join the family at the specified site and reacted with conspicuous appreciation. Nancy realized how her dysfunctional beliefs had polarized John from the family, a reaction that ran counter to her desire for him to become more vitally involved. Moreover, his positive reaction reinforced Nancy's sense of positive control. She thus discovered that by making her husband feel important (according to his criteria), she gained control in that she positively influenced their marital experiences.

John's individual therapy progressed along similar lines. The Dysfunctional Thought Form underscored his basic maladaptive marital views: "I get nothing from the marriage. Nancy doesn't give a damn about me. She blames me for everything bad in the marriage. I refuse to change until she proves her love to me." Obscuring a more rational perspective was his tendency to use selective negative focus and overgeneralization. These cognitive errors were identified and corrected, as discussed earlier.

The greatest obstacle to John's progress was his defensive and accusatory posture. He adamantly believed that because he had been genuinely wronged, Nancy would have to make the relationship "right" for him. Typically, he acted in a sullen or vindictive manner while feeling quite sanctimonious. He believed that by threatening divorce and by viciously upbraiding his spouse for her apparent disinterest in him and blaming stance toward him, he could "punish her into line."

During the brief period for which the patient contracted, the therapist endeavored to examine and to weaken John's unwavoring philosophy. He listed the advantages and disadvantages of believing: "Nancy must show significant change before I agree to change. And, not only must she go first, but go first while I continue to punish her." One obvious disadvantage was that an entire generation could pass while he waited for her to initiate positive action. At that moment (although apparently not integrated over time), he agreed that he had been winning a Pyrrhic victory—in typecasting himself as the "hurt and abused victim," he had created both justification *and* misery.

By the end of the eighth session, both partners realized to some extent how corrosive and self-perpetuating their interactional patterns had become. Nancy had begun to modify her irrational views that (1) John was totally responsible for the family's problems, and that (2) collaboration on her part meant she personally was incapable of independent action. John had begun to perceive the value of controlling his rage attacks and of initiating positive changes noncontingent on Nancy's behavior. It was intended that these individual CB therapy sessions would provide a motivational and educational backdrop for future constructive interactions.

Purpose of Conjoint Session

A conjoint session was planned, as originally promised, so that Nancy could soften the effect of her previous accusations and John could show appreciation for Nancy's efforts to include him in important family matters. It was hoped that once this barrier had been successfully crossed, John could learn to handle criticisms more effectively, and Nancy could learn to handle John's angry outbursts more effectively. Furthermore, each partner could continue to take low-cost steps to enhance his or her value to one another while eventually acquiring more adaptive problem-solving and communication skills.

Admittedly, the therapist believed the timing of the conjoint session to be premature. Yet, because there was some evidence that the couple understood and embraced the major points made in their individual sessions, the therapist scheduled a highly structured couples session with a predetermined, mutually acceptable agenda.

Paradigmatic of cognitive-behavioral therapy, the conjoint session afforded an opportunity for the couple to gain a realistic perspective of each other, their marriage, and its potential. They could (1) expose and check out misassumptions, (2) revise faulty accusations, (3) recognize positive interactions and rebalance a selectively negative bias, and (4) reattribute a spouse's undesirable behavior to more emotionally defused and accurate explanations. For example, Nancy excluded John, not because she viewed him as unimportant, but because of the distorted meaning she attached to such cooperation. John fought, not because he despised Nancy, but because he was deficient in handling various frustrations and felt unloved. He also expected his verbal attacks to force her to abide with his demands. (5) Moreover, the spouses could correct their tendency to mislabel by learning to express their annoyance with the person's behavior rather than with the person himself or herself. (6) They also could recognize how their "should" statements reflected arbitrary, interpersonal expectations that fueled their anger when their spouse did not live up to them.

Results of the Conjoint Session

Unfortunately, what ensued in the conjoint session was a repeat performance of the same habitual attack–counterattack–withdraw cycle that marked the couple's previous interactional pattern. The couple had begun fighting the night before the session about matters to be discussed in it. Nancy told John that she recently had spoken to their son, suggesting that he leave the home (allegedly for the good of everyone involved). John became infuriated at the idea that she would take such significant action without first consulting him. This event triggered his insufficiently weakened belief that to be excluded was an unpardonable rejection, that the marriage was worthless if his wife did not confide in him on all major issues, and that she must not trust or respect his judgment.

It is unclear whether Nancy acted with intentional malice. She later admitted that she had planned to discuss this matter with John first, but had spontaneously spilled her negative feelings to her son in a moment of confrontation. Nonetheless, John's explosive reaction was perceived by Nancy as punishment for sharing information with him. John refused to participate further and the session was terminated. Both felt exceedingly discouraged and misunderstood.

Although the therapist convinced the couple to return for a follow-up session to illustrate the controlling effect their dysfunctional interpretations had on their emotions and behaviors, neither would agree to further sessions. Both blamed the other for the failure of the relationship and rejected any notion of using the backfired session as an *in vivo*, exemplary learning experience.

What exactly transpired between this couple is highly complex and speculative. Apparently, they had not sufficiently reconstructed their blaming philosophies nor acquired adequate interpersonal, coping skills to handle each other's destructive provocations.

Appropriateness of a Conjoint Session

The advantage of presenting this particular case, which embraces failure unabashedly, is that it abounds with opportunities for rich hypothetical debate. It is posited that, given the anger-inducing ideas of the husband, the antagonistic stance of the wife, and the couple's pervasive resistance to taking personal responsibility for their marital dissatisfaction or constructive experimentation, conjoint therapy had a high probability of failing. It seems possible, however, given the minor advances accomplished individually, that additional individual sessions could have reaped more productive benefits.

Individual therapy affords an opportunity analogous to a parallel or good faith contract (Weiss, Birchler, & Vincent, 1974), whereas conjoint therapy is encumbered with many of the disadvantages of a quid pro quo agreement (Lederer & Jackson, 1968). That is, in the former, a person's individual decision to change his or her behavior is independent rather than functionally related to the spouse's actions, thereby obscuring competitive comparisons of effort between partners. The Smiths' hypervigilance of each other's behavior, rather than their own, may have weakened their ability to tolerate regressions in their spouse.

Summary

The pivotal variables contributing to the failure of this couple's therapy were not investigated systematically. It seems reasonable, however, to identify the following components: (1) The couple's dysfunctional beliefs were deeply ingrained. (2) Some of the maladaptive beliefs created an aversion to collaborating. (3) The couple had a history of negative experiences that fortified their pessimism. (4) At least one member was significantly depressed with a high tendency to personalize negative interactions and to connect his or her happiness and self-esteem with how significant others perceived and treated him or her. (5) There had not been enough time for the couple to learn and to rehearse interpersonal, coping strategies to immunize them against their partner's verbal attacks. Finally, (6) it is possible that the therapist's own dysfunctional thoughts about her inability to help this couple in the agreed upon time framework and to integrate cognitive and behavioral strategies effectively interfered with her functioning and conveyed a defeatist outlook to the couple.

CASE 2: SUCCESSFUL INDUCTION AND ENHANCEMENT
OF A COLLABORATIVE SET

The next example illustrates a more successful induction and enhancement of a collaborative set in a distressed couple. First, the wife was treated individually to develop a constructive motivational set and attitude. Such preparatory inductions helped maximize the positive effect of subsequent conjoint sessions and increased the couple's expectation that they could effectively resolve their problems.

> Jean Saunders was referred by her family internist due to an anxious and depressed reaction to fertility problems. For two years she and her husband, Mark, had tried unsuccessfully to conceive. Innumerable tests showed no biological obstacle to conception.
>
> Upon intake, Jean's ideas about her infertility were extreme and depressogenic. She firmly believed that "it would be tragic if I couldn't have children. It's all I ever wanted. I couldn't give Mark what he wants." Jean not only felt disappointed; she felt decimated.
>
> When asked to recount her husband's viewpoint, she quickly discounted Mark's rational argument. Mark had told her that although he very much wanted to have a baby, he most highly valued his relationship with Jean. He was most concerned about the aversive effect the infertility problems had had on her health and on the marriage. Mark seemed to feel optimistic about alternative channels of obtaining a child (e.g., adoption), and allegedly believed that they could be happy regardless of whether they ultimately became parents. Jean disqualified these remarks by presuming that Mark was unable to express his "real" feelings. She also interpreted his healthy attitude as artificial hope and happiness designed to relieve pressure imposed on Jean to reproduce.
>
> With further questioning, it became apparent that Jean vehemently resented Mark. She felt deprived, hostile, and victimized because of her infertility problem. She viewed her situation as horrible and unfair and Mark as inattentive to and unsupportive of her needs.
>
> Several problems revolved around their sexual activity. Their obstetrician had advised them to have intercourse only on particular days and during specific moments. By strictly adhering to these orders, the couple sacrificed much of the spontaneity and enjoyability

of their previous sexual encounters. Jean became angry when Mark seemed tired or unexcited about having sex. She thought, "He's not interested in having a baby. If he loved me and wanted to have a baby, he would show more enthusiasm. He doesn't appreciate how difficult this situation is for me." On the other hand, when Mark was enthusiastic and romantically inclined, she again felt angry: "He expects me to enjoy this mechanistic act? He doesn't appreciate how difficult this situation is for me!"

Dealing with Competitive Feelings Aroused when Individual Sessions Are Recommended for Only One Spouse

The therapist decided to work with Jean on an individual basis to undercut her resentment toward her husband and to introduce her to the basic cognitive model of introspection and constructive thought criticism. But first, it was necessary to elicit and to deal with her competitive feelings about receiving such treatment. Jean verbalized apprehension and anger over the meaning she imputed to exclusive individual sessions—that she, rather than Mark or the infertility problem itself, was to blame for their anxiety and deterioration of the marriage.

The therapist asked her to define the difference between blame and responsibility. Jean stated that blame would probably lead to derogatory feelings about herself, whereas responsibility, a nonprejorative term, allowed for greater personal influence in a constructive manner. The "blame" ascription had blocked her capacity for self-examination.

Since the couple could not afford separate, individual sessions and since Jean was showing more obvious signs of distress, it seemed logical to offer her relief first. It was pointed out that she was "making a contest" between herself and Mark rather than questioning what she could do for herself that would be in her own best interest. To dilute further the apparent one-sidedness of the treatment program, the therapist added that in Mark's therapy he also would be held responsible for his portion of the experienced distress. At this point Jean seemed eagerly motivated to begin individual sessions, although various degrees of competitiveness had to be monitored continually throughout treatment.

Individual Sessions

As an initial intervention, Jean explored how her ideas and behaviors thwarted rather than advanced her goals. For example, the therapist challenged her assumption that "if Mark loved me, he'd always want to follow the doctor's orders." Playing the role of Mark, Jean was asked to "comprehend with accuracy" or to empathize (Burns, 1980) with Mark's perspective.

THERAPIST: I understand that there are times when you don't feel like having sex.
JEAN (as Mark): Sometimes I get fed up with our problems.
THERAPIST: Is that because you don't care about Jean?
JEAN: That's ridiculous. I love Jean, but this has been an ordeal for both of us. I sometimes feel pressured to perform.
THERAPIST: Is your lack of enthusiasm indicative of your disinterest in having children?
JEAN: That's also ridiculous. Besides, much of the time, I'm the enthusiastic one.
THERAPIST: Do you think you alone have experienced unpleasantness regarding the infertility problem?
JEAN: No. Actually, Jean is the one who has to monitor her temperature and take multiple tests.
THERAPIST: It sounds like you do have some appreciation for what both of you have gone through.
JEAN: I really think I do.

This empathy technique exemplifies how one spouse's maladaptive attributions can be refuted unilaterally and expeditiously. Jean composed the following statement upon seeing Mark more clearly in relation to herself: "Sometimes Mark doesn't feel like having sex because he's human. Like me, he has varying states of arousal. Neither he nor I is always capable of being responsive in a flash. Even if he is unenthusiastic about having sex at times, I know he loves me, and I know he very much wants to have a child." She gradually became more accepting of her own and her spouse's limitations and worked on accurately construing their disappointing sexual interactions.

Nonetheless, Jean recurrently felt infuriated when Mark fell short of her expectations. On one occasion, she chose to spend the day watching him run a marathon. She then expected him to join her for dinner that evening. Instead, he went to a pub with several friends and returned home two hours late. Jean was livid because this event had underlying, anger-inducing significance: "I overextend myself for him. He should reciprocate. If he doesn't, he stinks and so does the marriage."

The therapist pursued the logic of this argument: "In what percentage of marriages in the United States do the spouses do for each other exactly equally?" Jean laughed and answered, "Five percent." "And is it reasonable and fair to evaluate your marriage only on those occasions when Mark does not act as you had hoped?" "No," she replied, "I could expect to be disappointed quite often with that point of view." The therapist helped Jean to see that reciprocity is an ideal that can be approximated only through mutual trust, by making one's spouse feel important and by being a valuable companion and friend. Again, coercive and punitive recriminations obstructed rather than enhanced her spouse's desire to reciprocate.

Jean saw no advantages to insisting that reciprocity be instantaneous and perfectly balanced. She could not possibly meet his expectations nor would she want to, she would repeatedly feel let down, and possibly, she could make the marriage so unrewarding that he would abandon her.

Seriously considering the undesirable consequences of her assaultive communications, Jean returned the following week with a revised perspective:

> It's unreasonable for Mark to always provide for me the way I'd like him to. What stinks, then, is not Mark, me, or the marriage, but my unrealistic expectation that he must do for me exactly as I think he should. He is a free and autonomous person. If I only love him when he obeys my rules, my love is shallow. I can work on overcoming my deeply entrenched "should" statements and on allowing Mark to love me *his* way (at least, some of the time). Moreover, I have difficulty accepting the fact that it may be desirable to act selfishly some of the time. I both resent and admire him for thinking of himself. I sometimes wish I could do the same for myself.

Jean confronted her apparent "love addiction" (Ellis & Harper, 1975). She had an overriding and excessive need to be shown how important she was to Mark and how loved she was by him. Otherwise, she felt misunderstood, unappreciated, and inferior. She admitted that she often felt jealous of Mark's relationship with his mother and hurt when friends excluded her. By monitoring her automatic thoughts, she proved to herself that she often invoked the issue of love indiscriminately.

Three major interventions were used to break through her preemptory belief that she needed Mark to love her more or better. First, the therapist inquired, "How many times would Mark have to tell you forcefully and convincingly that he utterly despised you before you believed him?" Jean answered, "Not more than once." The therapist persisted, "And how many times does he have to tell you he loves you before you believe him?" Jean understood that as long as she needed constant reassurance, she would never feel confident about her relationship.

To explore her silent assumptions, the therapist then asked, "If

Mark, in fact, did not love you as much as you would like, why would this be upsetting to you?" Jean realized that she attached her capacity for pleasure to his demonstrations of love. Using the Pleasure Predicting Form (Beck et al., 1979), she soon produced evidence that refuted this mistaken belief.

Next, the therapist used a particular example to demonstrate how Jean mindread Mark's intentions, inferring lack of love from his behavior. Jean reported feeling jealous and resentful of Mark's mother because she assumed Mark loved his mother more than he loved her (90% believed). She then explored other, equally plausible, less personally hurtful explanations as to why he sometimes inconvenienced himself for his mother (against Jean's wishes): (1) He felt obligated to his mother (90%); (2) he believed Jean would be more forgiving than his mother (80%); (3) he wanted to act as he did because it seemed convenient or reasonable to him (90%); or, more generally, (4) Mark could not resist his mother's demands (100%). Her belief in the initial hypothesis immediately dropped to 5%. She realized that because she had a bottomless, self-destructive need for love, she tended to yoke Mark's regard for his mother to his disregard for her. When future incidents occurred, she tried to employ corrective thinking measures by reminding herself of his assertiveness deficiency with his mother, his right to act in ways that were discordant with her wishes, and her tendency to question his love inappropriately.

Conjoint Sessions

Restructuring the Couple's "Happiness Equals Parenthood" Formula

By the first conjoint session, Mark had read enough cognitive-behavioral literature to grasp its basic tenets. He empathically reiterated his adaptive view of their infertility problem, stating that they both had been gravely upset and terribly inconvenienced by sexual pressures. But he challenged Jean's idea that he would consider her a bad wife if she did not provide him with a child. In a poignant and loving tone of voice, he reconfirmed an invaluable point that, perhaps, no therapist could deliver so convincingly: "I'd like to regain our happiness, Jean. We've got a strong marriage. I married you for you, not for what you might give me at some future date."

In an attempt to free Mark from his rational role and to ally the spouses with each other, the therapist encouraged Mark to express any doubts or disturbances that sometimes crossed his mind. Both partners admitted that they occasionally still believed that they could not be "truly" happy without a baby. A variety of techniques were used to expose logical inconsistencies between the ostensible validity of this idea and the reality of their experiences.

Over the next four weeks, the couple sensitized themselves to enjoyment by recording events that they experienced at a 60% or higher level of pleasure. They were instructed to monitor closely their positive moods and to transcribe at least three pleasurable experiences a day that were *unrelated to parenting* and that represented a broad sampling of times when they were alone, with their spouse, or with other people. The couple received a copy of the Pleasant Events Schedule (Lewinsohn, Munoz, Youngren, & Zeiss, 1978) to augment their awareness of everyday pleasures that inadvertently might be discounted or overlooked.

Each spouse then shared with his or her partner the most pleasurable moments of the week. Jean noted such items as "going to bed early" (100%), "feeling competent at school" (90%), and "having dinner with Mark" (90%). Mark's responses included "taking a walk with Jean" (90%), "running" (90%), and "visiting friends" (90%). Here, couples therapy proved particularly valuable because both spouses were reminded of highly enjoyable events that the other had forgotten.

The therapist elicited the internal dialogue that accompanied several of the pleasurable events. The couple's positive mood was captured in thoughts that were completely unrelated to having a child (e.g., while jogging: "My body is working well today. The air smells great."). When asked to reconcile the results of the experiment with their initial idea, the couple drew the following reformulations: "Mark and I experience high levels of pleasure that are unrelated to having a baby."

Jean seemed perplexed and resistant. Believing the above restatement only 70%, she disqualified its validity by retorting, "We can be somewhat happy—I can't disregard the results of the experiment—but I don't experience real 'highs.'" Jean, an elementary school teacher, then was asked, "If you were grading an exam and divided final scores into high, medium, and low categories, what would constitute a 'high' range of scores on a scale of 0–100?" Jean replied, "85–100%." "And looking at your pleasure sheet," the therapist pursued, "have you had any experiences that fall into that category?" Jean realized how she had disqualified the positive evidence that rendered her predominant view inaccurate. The therapist had Jean read about disqualification errors to strengthen further her comprehension of corrective thinking.

Due to the nature of her prevailing belief, Jean predictably admitted that even in the face of concrete evidence that clearly did not confirm her existing belief, "I don't buy it emotionally." The therapist then explained emotional reasoning, or drawing conclusions based on the way one feels. In effect, Jean was thinking, "I feel doubtful about the legitimacy of the restructured statement; therefore, it must be wrong."

Jean still believed that the key to her misery was her childless state. The therapist zeroed in on how that destructive *belief* created her distress, rather than the condition itself. An analogous situation was presented to help Jean restore her objectivity.

> A woman once believed that she could not be happy as long as she was unmarried. Using the Pleasure Predicting Form, she tested out this hypothesis by going to a movie alone. She had expected a ten percent pleasure level and had recorded an actual ten percent pleasure level. She, therefore, thought she had proven her point. In the next therapy session, the therapist asked her to describe the movie. While doing so, the woman became quite animated and amused. The therapist again inquired about her low enjoyment level. In a moment of reevaluation, the woman admitted, "Actually, I loved the movie itself" (90% believed), "but as I was leaving the theater, I realized that I was the only person there who was alone. I thought I must be unattractive, inferior, and generally undesirable. My mood plummetted."

The therapist then asked Jean what made the woman miserable. She responded, "Being alone!" Once again, Jean selectively comprehended this event in a manner consistent with her own self-defeating, information-processing schema. The therapist persisted with another story.

> Another woman went to the theater alone. She also found the movie highly enjoyable. But as she was leaving, she thought, "I really respect myself for seeking pleasures alone. I feel I have a lot of courage. It's refreshing and freeing to know I don't need other people to make me happy."

Eventually, Jean realized that it was the idiosyncratic meaning that she ascribed to being alone or to having a child that dealt the devastating blow to an undesirable situation.

Next, the therapist helped the couple understand how negative beliefs perpetuate themselves by creating a self-fulfilling prophecy. Jean had menstruated on New Year's Eve, an event that precipitated a severe mood drop in both partners. She had wanted to avoid that evening's party but managed to go. From the pleasure sheets, the therapist discovered that she had had a wonderful time.

Figure 1 shows how avoidance of potentially gratifying situations could buttress a faulty belief system. The therapist asked Jean why it would have been contraindicated for her to have gone to bed. Jean discerned that she probably would have felt worse and that she might have reinforced her basic premise that she was miserable because she could not have a child. Jean then was asked to write rational disputa-

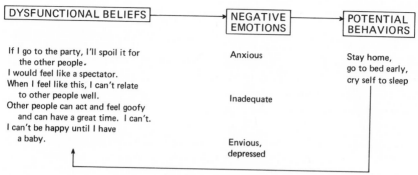

FIGURE 1. Dysfunctional belief cycle.

tions based on the reality of her experience that evening. She stated unequivocally, "People enjoyed my company. (One person asked me to stay past 2 A.M.) I related well to people. A couple of times I felt and acted goofy. The party was really fun." The credibility of Jean's dysphoric beliefs were shaken, again.

Another angle to the crux of the problem underlying Jean's resistance to change fortuitously was exposed when she began to have negative feelings toward her husband in the therapy session. She questioned how Mark could have wept bitterly when she had menstruated on New Year's Eve, yet believed he could be happy without a child. To Jean, giving up the misery was equated with giving up the desire to have a child. In essence, she was not free to enjoy her life without attaching a negative valence to that attitude.

The therapist inquired, "Do you see any errors in your belief, 'If I have fun today, I am no longer interested in having a child'?" Irrationally, Jean reasoned that if Mark could be happy without a child, then only several equally upsetting explanations existed for his behavior on New Year's: (1) Mark had been lying about how much he wanted to have a baby; (2) his display of unhappiness was ingenuine, a provision of false sympathy, or (3) he only wanted a baby to appease her. Jean simply could not fathom how Mark could have despaired over not having a child, yet see their present lives as satisfying.

Jean separated her beliefs into two analyzable statements. (1) "Mark is genuinely sad that we can't have a baby this month." (2) "If we don't conceive this month, Mark is committed to making his experiences highly gratifying." Jean agreed that these two ideas could coexist. One could be quite saddened about not procreating *and* know that one's life was rich in delightful moments. Jean also understood that people upset themselves to different degrees, not because of how absolutely important a particular issue is to them, but how important they make that issue relative to other areas of their life. Jean concluded, "I can see that it might be possible to give up the distress without giving up the desire to have a child." Ellis and Harper (1975) assert this point when they suggest giving up the desperate, neurotic component of an idea while retaining one's desire to attain a particular goal. The therapist corroborated that committing oneself to a vitally absorbing and enjoyable existence was exquisitely compatible with wanting to have a child. Both were life affirming.

Furthermore, Jean explored the advantages and disadvantages of believing, "I must be miserable as long as I'm childless." She realized that the advantages were few and antigrowth in nature. She could continue to blame her misery on her situation and not have to rethink her maladaptive ideas. The disadvantages were more weighty including burdening her prospective child with her happiness, thereby creating excessive power for and pressure on that child, and contaminating her present life. Given the uselessness and invalidity of her belief, Jean began to appreciate her marriage with new awareness.

Balancing the "Good" and "Bad" Partner

Competitive feelings, again, were being stirred up in Jean. She had stated earlier that she resented viewing the infertility problem as mainly her problem. And much of the discussion had thus far centered on Jean's inability to dispel her obsessive focus. To defuse potential polarization between the marital partners, a rationale was offered to help the couple accept the differential between their capacities to digest the newly presented "happiness in spite of parenthood" formula. First, the therapist elicited their ideas about Jean's "resistance." Jean said she might be too stupid to change, and Mark said she might not want to change. The therapist then presented a more reassuring, less pathological explanation: "It is the nature of a prevailing belief to seem eminently real and to pop reflexively into one's head regardless of one's motivation to change." Pointing to the green carpet in the conference room, the therapist observed,

> All your life you've [Jean] thought that this carpet is red. Now I'm telling you that it might help you to see it as green. This mix-up is confusing you. Don't expect yourself to accept this new hypothesis so easily. People don't change so instantaneously. I understand completely that what I am telling you today

is difficult to digest. But I also believe that you owe it to yourself to consider it.

To reduce further the couple's negative judgments regarding Jean's rejection of the corrective model, the therapist pointed to Jean's past experiences over which she had no control. The primary focus of her upbringing had been her family, whereas Mark's parents had suffered serious disappointment in their children (Mark's brothers). This information was used to clarify how she might have learned to magnify the importance of having children through repeated parental messages. Mark, fortunately, reinforced this point by facetiously adding, "Although I am the exception, of course, my parents never made me believe that children were the lifeline of their relationship."

These interventions helped create a therapeutic climate of acceptance in which each individual was granted the freedom to experience and to express his or her negativity. To push too hard or too soon for change would have forced Jean into a cognitively repugnant position. She either might have viewed herself with reproach or rejected the therapy, therapist, and her spouse for not being sensitive to her experience.

Dealing with the Couple's Sexual Problems

Cognitive-behavioral interventions were aimed at mitigating the couple's sexual frustration caused by a rigidly prescribed medical regimen. The Saunders also held several ideas about their sexual activity that significantly deflated its enjoyability while engendering pervasive feelings of inadequacy.

The couple was asked to record their dysfunctional thoughts during their next sexual encounter. Both believed that they always should have high levels of pleasure. They should never feel pressured or annoyed, but rather romantic and highly aroused. When questioned about the usefulness and validity of these "should" statements, it became evident that their underlying belief was somewhat superstitious: If the baby were conceived under less than optimal conditions, they would have an irreversibly negative feeling toward the child. The Saunders recalled friends who never forgot the unpleasantness of the evening during which successful fertilization took place. That experience, however, in no way lessened their love for their baby.

The therapist bolstered this point by asking, "In a child's lifetime, what percentage of pleasure is derived from the moment of conception versus the growth and development of the child?" The couple laughed and answered, "You're right. It's minor." They had magnified the importance of that moment and inadvertently imposed unrealistic pressure on themselves.

The couple also revised their "should" statements to reflect ideal circumstances "that can only be approximated." For instance, Jean said, "Instead of expecting that you should always be interested in sex at the prescribed time, it would be helpful if we both tried to be more accommodating to each other's moods." Mark saw that it was impossible to feel highly aroused at all times, especially with sex programmed according to day rather than physiological response.

As revealed earlier, both partners had equated their interest in making a child with their interest in having a child. Thus a spouse's reluctance to have intercourse was interpreted as disinterest in parenting. The couple worked together to compose a realistic attitude (which they reported as 95% believable) that disconnected their level of sexual arousal at any given moment from their long-standing desire to have a child.

Mark also had exaggerated the meaning of Jean's having an orgasm. The therapist asked him, "Why should Jean have an orgasm? What does it mean to you about you and about her if she does not?" Mark's performance anxiety was rooted in his assumptions that (1) he was inadequate as a lover and husband if Jean did not have an orgasm and (2) Jean could not enjoy herself without an orgasm. The personalization error in the first conclusion was challenged by having the couple generate alternative reasons for Jean's inorgasmic state—reasons that had nothing to do with Mark. In this exercise, Jean was extremely helpful in explaining what thoughts sometimes interfered with her arousability (e.g., "Here we go again. It's useless.") Jean also convinced Mark that pleasure was not all-or-nothing and that orgasm was not the sole route to relatively high levels of sexual pleasure. Thus by checking out his mistaken premises, Mark gained a more realistic and salutary perspective. He seemed to accept fully her refutations and reported great relief in their future, coital interactions.

"Antithwarting" interventions (Burns, 1980) also were employed. That is, instead of becoming angry, defensive, or sullen about their partner's sexual response, the couple learned to communicate more adaptively, affectionately, and empathically. Through role playing, they learned to accept each other's limitations and mutual frustrations rather than to impose further obstacles by trying to make the other feel guilty or inadequate.

By sharing each other's automatic thoughts, the Saunders realized that they both felt pressured and inconvenienced. Jean often thought, "I know this is important, but I don't want to have sex now. He acts as if we should be having a romantic time." Mark often thought, "This is such a pain in the ass. I hope she doesn't get too upset. Come on, Jean. Have an orgasm. It's important." The couple became partners rather than adversaries when they saw the problem through their spouse's eyes.

Following these cognitive changes, a behavior exchange program was implemented. The therapist asked each partner to write down three activities that he or she would like his or her spouse to do *more of*, being positive and specific (Stuart, 1980). After some negotiating, the couple traded behaviors, agreeing to try to act as the other wished. The main purpose was to increase their sexual satisfaction. For instance, Jean agreed to act "as if" she felt romantic, ignoring her "true" feelings. Mark agreed to approach Jean in a variety of locations around the house rather than just in the bedroom. One week later, the couple reported that their lovemaking had become exceedingly satisfying, even while adhering to the doctor's temperature-controlled recommendations. By the end of the week when the novelty had worn off, they still managed to humor each other and not to magnify the "intolerability" of the situation.

Summary

The combination of cognitive and behavioral techniques, unfolded with proper timing in individual and conjoint sessions, thus helped to rectify the childless couple's dysfunctional expectations about their ability to be happy individually and jointly, as well as to have satisfying sexual interactions. It is posited that the couple's adoption of a more positive, team-like attitude was crucial in facilitating their willingness to engage in subsequent, constructive behavioral experiments—experiments that served to expand their actual capacity for happiness.

IDENTIFYING AND RESTRUCTURING MALADAPTIVE FORMULAS REGARDING RELATIONSHIPS

By restructuring faulty relationship expectations or "should" statements, an individual may experience relief without needing to modify his or her spouse's undesirable behavior.

Examples of dysfunctional relationship formulas include: "Once the romance is gone, the relationship is worthless." "If my spouse is less motivated than I am in therapy, we have no chance of improving." "I'll be put in a demeaning position if I initiate positive action first." And, "If my spouse cared about me, X." This last idea could be completed with any number of unwarranted conclusions. Several deleterious relationship expectations will be discussed below.

One patient was irritated that her husband was not more affectionate. In actuality, she exaggerated how little she got out of the relationship and often discounted those times when her husband did act lovingly. Her anger sprang from several preemptive assumptions (Johnson, 1977): "My ideas about how you should act are right. You have free will. You should be able and willing to change your behavior to meet my expectations."

These assumptions obviously are presumptuous because there is no written, universal rule as to the degree of affection that one *should* show. Moreover, given different upbringings, the marital partners experienced the display of public affection differently. The wife relished it; the husband was embarrassed by it. One placed a positive, the other a negative value on the behavior. The husband's behaviors and emotional reactions were dictated by his value judgments and conditioned responses. He could not easily and quickly modify his behavior and, in fact, was not highly motivated to do so, even though he loved his wife. What is considered excessive or deficient about a behavior thus frequently is arbitrary and subjective. Through examination and correction of the couple's biased expectations, a more positive view of the marriage was developed independent of changes made in the partners' affectionate initiations.

Case 3: The Controlling Effect of a
Maladaptive Relationship Formula

The following case study exemplifies how a maladaptive formula critically instigated interpersonal conflict. Peter and Lois Reed entered therapy because after 16 years of marriage, the husband "no longer loved his wife." They were both greatly disturbed by this belief, partly because they were not sure whether to continue living together or to begin divorce proceedings. They had two children whom they both loved and did not want to disrupt unnecessarily. They also seemed interested in making the marriage work, if possible. The husband had sought medical advice, hoping for a physical explanation to account for his waning romantic feeling for his wife. Medical tests proved negative. He then thought he might be depressed and sought psychological counseling.

Thereapeutic interventions zeroed in on the couple's deleterious cognitions and behaviors. The therapist asked Peter to define the meaning of *love*. He replied vaguely, "A romantic, tingling, swept up feeling; security; clear assurance that this is the person with whom you want to spend the rest of your life; an overwhelming desire to be with someone."

To uncover underlying silent assumptions, the therapist then asked, "What does it mean to you about yourself, your wife, and your relationship in general that you no longer love your wife according to your definition?" Peter answered, "Because I no longer love my wife, but can't offer any valid reasons why, (A) something must be wrong with me; (B) Lois can't be happy in the marriage; and (C) the marriage is irremediable."

Lois made similar assumptions. She equated a genuine expression of love with a lifetime guarantee of a viable relationship. Emotional reasoning insidiously affected her perceptions: "If I don't feel loved (and I can't feel loved if Peter doesn't tell me he loves me), the marriage is rotten, my husband is rotten, and I've failed."

Lois also operated under the misassumption that her husband's insecurity created her insecurity. She was shown that it was, in fact, her own questioning about her lovability and capacity for experiencing pleasure without Peter's professed love that created her insecurity. Lois was trained to use a wrist clicker to catch her dysfunctional thoughts. She readily noticed the connection between her insecure ideas and her mood drops. Her husband's behavior merely contributed to but did not determine her affective response.

Spurred by their exacting relationship expectations, the couple interacted in severely punitive ways. Peter stopped making love to Lois because he believed his sexual advances would be misinterpreted as an admission of love. Reasoning that such action might confuse Lois and create false hope, he made a "humanitarian" decision to remain withdrawn until he was certain of his commitment. Lois, feeling apprehensive and threatened, exhorted him to make love to her to prove his heterosexuality. On a practical level, their actions further alienated each other.

Individual Sessions

Several individual sessions were spent discussing the couple's crippling ideas. Lois explored her fear of being divorced, contemplating how she could manage if this undesirable event became a reality. She earnestly believed: "If Peter leaves me, I wouldn't be able to cope. It would be evidence that I was defective. I would be devastated." But by reviewing her capabilities objectively, she realized that independent of Peter, she had made most of the major decisions regarding the children, had successfully run the household, and had functioned admirably in part-time jobs that supplemented her income. She gradually felt more confident of her ability to survive and less desperately in need of Peter's love.

In learning to reattribute more accurately Peter's loss of faith in the relationship, Lois realized that it was their definition of *love* and its alleged importance, not her inherent desirability as a wife, that had precipitated much of their uneasiness. Consequently, she became more tolerant of his uncertainty, less hateful of him, and less self-flagellating. She began to function more joyfully, continuing to hope that Peter would choose to remain in the marriage.

In Peter's individual sessions, he began to defuse his distress by first realizing that he had acceptable options. In order to assess realistically his interest in preserving the marriage, he had to feel free to terminate it without loathing himself. He confronted his double standard, that is, a nonjudgmental attitude toward divorced friends, yet condemnation of himself. He also realized that his children might fare better with divorced parents than with ones who resentfully protected the marriage for the children's sake. Paradoxically, by dissolving all coercion to commit himself to the marriage, he reduced his resistance and increased his desire to improve his marital situation.

Conjoint Sessions

Peter had remained withdrawn because he believed "it was better for Lois," and "to act romantically, I must feel romantic." He began to treat these beliefs as testable hypotheses, agreeing to initiate lovemaking again on a regular basis (which was operationalized in greater detail). Lois understood the nature of the experiment and agreed not to perceive his overtures as a guarantee of security, but as an attempt to develop the strengths of the relationship. She also agreed not to evoke the question of love for two months, after which time the effects of the therapy would be reviewed.

The therapist delved further into the couple's assumptions about love. "Why must you 'love' or 'be loved' to be gratified in the marriage?" "What percentage of couples in the United States today do you think experience gratification to the extent that you expect to?" The therapist asked Peter, "How much have you loved Lois in the last two weeks?" Peter replied, "50 to 70%." The therapist continued, "And how much have you liked Lois?" "75 to 100%," Peter answered. The therapist then inquired, "And how much would you have to like Lois in order to sustain comfortably the marriage?" This rational dialogue helped the couple to operationalize the viability of their relationship according to observable and testable indicators, for example, pleasure derived from mutually enjoyable activities and the willingness and ability to problem-solve satisfactorily. By focusing on specific, positive, behavior changes and concrete strengths of the marriage, the Reeds disengaged from vacuous debates about the relationship's worth.

Pleasure predicting was implemented by scheduling specific, potentially enjoyable, joint activities. The Reeds rated as highly pleasurable such events as going to a restaurant, taking the kids to the beach, watching a movie, doing yard work, and furniture shopping. They also independently rated their level of gratification in the marriage on a weekly basis. These levels consistently exceeded the 75% mark and chipped away at Peter's doubt.

The couple conducted a comparative study, asking two very close, seemingly happily married friends to rate their approximate range of marital gratification over each of the past five years. Their scores varied widely. The couple observed that they simplistically had viewed love and happiness as full or empty when, in fact, even in the best of marriages, there are bound to be arid spells.

Thus Peter and Lois identified and challenged the cognitive base that had eroded their trust in one another and produced noxious marital interactions while experimenting with more constructive behaviors. They concluded that things were not as bad as they had first thought, that they had proven their capacity to enjoy each other, and that the value of the relationship could not be subsumed under one nebulous, omnipresent sensation called *love*. The Reeds successfully terminated therapy following several communication skill training sessions.

Summary

This case presentation illustrates the sapping effect that faulty relationship expectations can have on a couple's adaptive functioning. Effective challenge of these cognitions again seemed to foster positive attitudinal changes that potentiated new, constructive actions.

Conclusion

Which, when, and with whom specific treatment strategies should be employed are questions that need to be investigated as an interpersonal model of cognitive-behavioral therapy is developed. Several issues will have to be addressed: (1) When are individual versus conjoint sessions most efficacious? (2) What is the unique value of cognitive strategies (designed to identify and challenge the belief system of partners) versus behavior exchange strategies (which focus more concretely on the modification and exchange of behaviors)? (3) How should cognitive and behavioral interventions be sequenced relative to each other to maximize their effects? (4) To what extent do cognitive and behavioral strategies facilitate the induction and enhancement of a collaborative set within partners? (5) In what way are the following factors relevant (a) the intransigency of each partner's maladaptive beliefs, (b) the pervasiveness of each partner's distress at the time of therapy, and (c) the premorbid constitution of each marital partner and the marriage itself ?

Whereas Jacobson and Margolin (1979) acknowledge that "behavior therapists might at times find a cognitive emphasis advantageous" (p. 149), the specifics remain undelineated. Future research may demonstrate empirically that the potency and scope of behavior therapy techniques are incrementally enhanced when key, underlying cognitions are explicitly treated. Effective cognitive revision seems to potentiate a collaborative set and new, constructive actions (Stuart, 1980). But a certified intermarriage of reconstructed attitudes and behaviors has yet to be arranged in any systematic fashion.

References

Abrahms, J. L. *Inducing a collaborative set in distressed couples: Nonspecific therapist–patient issues in cognitive therapy.* Paper presented at the annual meeting of the Association for the Advancement of Behavior Therapy, Los Angeles, November 1982.
Beck, A. T. *Cognitive aspects of marital interactions.* Paper presented at the annual meeting of the Association for the Advancement of Behavior Therapy, New York, November 1980.
Beck, A. T., Rush, A. J., Shaw, B. F., & Emery, G. *Cognitive therapy of depression.* New York: Guilford, 1979.
Burns, D. D. *Feeling good: The new mood therapy.* New York: Morrow, 1980.
Ellis, A., & Harper, R. *A new guide to rational living.* North Hollywood, Calif.: Wilshire, 1975.
Epstein, N. Cognitive therapy with couples. *American Journal of Family Therapy,* 1982, 10 (1), 5–16.
Jacobson, N. S., & Margolin, G. *Marital therapy: Strategies based on social learning and behavior exchange principles.* New York: Brunner/Mazel, 1979.
Johnson, S. M. *First person singular: Living the good life alone.* New York: Lippincott, 1977.
Lederer, W. J., & Jackson, D. D. *Mirages of marriage.* New York: Norton, 1968.
Lewinsohn, P. M., Munoz, R. G., Youngren, M. A., & Zeiss, A. M. *Control your depression.* Englewood Cliffs, N.J.: Prentice-Hall, 1978.

Stein, J. (Ed.). *The random house dictionary of the english language*. New York: Random House, 1966.

Stuart, R. B. *Helping couples change: A social learning approach to marital therapy*. New York: Guilford, 1980.

Weiss, R. L., Birchler, G. R., & Vincent, J. P. Contractual models for negotiation training in marital dyads. *Journal of Marriage and the Family*, 1974, 36, 321–331.

8

Cognitive Therapy in Groups with Alcoholics

Meyer D. Glantz and William McCourt

Alcoholics are a notoriously difficult population to treat. Typically, they seek treatment after interpersonal support systems, and economic and employment functioning have been severely disrupted or destroyed, and are, at best, poor candidates for psychotherapy. Their passive dependent personality characteristics and their abstraction-impaired cognitive functioning make them less amenable to most traditional therapeutic interventions. Relapses often involve extended periods of use of an addictive substance that removes the patient from even the possibility of therapeutic contacts; furthermore, relapses often result in the additional deterioration of the drinkers' circumstances and the destruction of resources necessary for the control of the drinking. Alcohol provides an immediate gratification and the ingestion of even a small amount of alcohol disrupts or inhibits exactly those cognitive functions that are necessary to exercise the self-control necessary to prevent further drinking and eventual inebriation. In addition, alcohol distorts the inebriate's self-perception and diminishes or even obliterates his or her memory of the period of drunkenness. Further, the use of alcohol is generally socially acceptable and it is a visible often encouraged behavior in many social settings. Despite these discouraging factors, however, a cognitively oriented intervention designed specifically for alcoholics can be successful. Important to this approach is some understanding of the personality and cognitive characteristics of alcoholics.

Meyer D. Glantz • National Institute on Drug Abuse, Division of Clinical Research, 5600 Fishers Lane, Rockville, Maryland 20857. William McCourt • Southwood Hospital, Norfolk, Massachusetts 02056. The development and practice of the therapy described here was done at the Center for Problem Drinking, Veterans Administration Outpatient Clinic, Boston, Massachusetts and was supported by the V. A. Medical Research Service.

PERSONALITY CHARACTERISTICS

Although there is a consensus that there is not a single or unique "alcoholic personality," and no single specific personality characteristic has been observed universally in alcoholics (Tarter, 1975b; Stein, Rozynko, & Puch, 1971) there are a number of traits that many alcohologists have come to associate with alcoholism. Based on his extensive review of the research literature, Cox (1979) concluded that the most salient characteristics of alcoholics are their passivity and their dependency. Catanzaro (1967) described 13 frequently observed and commonly attributed characteristics: low frustration capacity, grandiosity, anxiety, guilt, perfectionism, emotional immaturity, difficulties with authority, sex role confusion, poor anger modulation, excessive dependency, low self-esteem, feelings of isolation, and compulsiveness.

Although there is contradictory evidence regarding whether alcoholics have a generally good or poor opinion of themselves (Neuringer & Clopton, 1976), they usually are assumed to have a low self-concept. Berg (1971) found that alcoholics had a lower self-concept than normals and that, after drinking, the alcoholics' self-concept improved while the normals' self-concept worsened. Vannicelli (1972) found that alcoholics know less about their drunk selves than about their sober selves. Alcoholics demonstrate a greater than normal discrepancy between their perceptions of themselves and their ideal selves (Berg, 1971). They typically report themselves to be depressed (Gibson & Becker, 1973) and anxious (Smith & Layden, 1972) and they generally have been found to demonstrate an external locus of control (Rohsenow & O'Leary, 1978). McClelland and his associates (1972) report that alcoholics score at high levels on the n-power motivation scale and at low levels on the Activity Inhibition measure. Lisansky (1967), drawing on Halper's (1946) work, suggests that "alcoholism prone persons have not developed the usual neurotic mechanisms of defense against threat, at least not to an extent which makes such mechanisms effective" (p. 7).

COGNITIVE CHARACTERISTICS

In terms of cognitive functioning, a few factors commonly are agreed on. Alcoholics do not appear to exhibit intellectual decrement as measured by standard tests of intelligence; they frequently have been tested as functioning within the average to superior range on such tests as the WAIS and Wechsler-Bellevue scales (see reviews by Kleinknecht & Goldstein, 1972; Tarter, 1976, 1975a). There is a fair amount of evidence of deficit on some measures of abstracting ability and the ability to process environmental input requiring conceptualization, integration, and transformation of disparate elements in the perceptual field (Tarter, 1975a, 1976) and alcoholics fairly consistently have scored as highly field dependent on a number of field orientation measures (Goldstein, 1976; Tarter, 1976).

In a study investigating male alcoholics' conceptualizations of situations, Glantz and Burr (1981) found that when construing events that cannot be classified easily and clearly, alcoholics, as compared to normals, are more likely to continue to attempt to categorize these events in terms of the qualities that they typically employ even if they are inappropriate, rather than develop new more appropriate categories. In addition, they demonstrated a lesser tendency to discriminate between a range of events and the attribution of any given quality was more likely to be followed automatically by the attribution of other particular qualities even in the presence of neutral or contradictory evidence. Although the normals most commonly categorized situations in terms of affiliative qualities, the alcoholics most commonly categorized them in terms of positive or negative emotions and they seemed to have available fewer evaluative categorizations that are necessary to indicate the desirability of actions, events, and changes.

A Cognitive Model of Alcoholism

We view alcohol abuse as both a problem and a solution to a problem. It is obvious that alcohol abuse leads to problems, but it is less frequently recognized that alcohol abuse is in itself an attempt at problem-solving. These problems may be emotional (e.g., anger, helplessness), social (e.g., unemployment and poverty), or interpersonal (interpersonal conflict or isolation). Alcohol may serve as a problem-solving or coping mechanism in a number of ways. Although alcohol is pharmacologically a central nervous system depressant, its effect depends on a number of factors including dosage, expectation, circumstances of use, and physical state. It may reduce anxiety or other strong emotional states; disinhibit internal restrictions on behaviors; blur perception of one's self, of others, or of situations; stimulate fantasies; cause unconsciousness; and facilitate the forgetting of or distortion or memory of past events. It might be used as an excuse for failure or for other unacceptable behaviors, as a means of escaping situations or responsibilities, or as a facilitator of or a substitute for some aspect of normal functioning. We hypothesize that the alcoholic always has been a poor problem solver, (see, for example, the study by McCord & McCord 1960, 1962; McCord, 1972) due to his or her maladaptive thought processes. Failing to cope by using other problem-solving approaches, he or she turns more and more to the use of alcohol to solve problems. As alcohol is increasingly used as a problem-solving technique, the abuser becomes an increasingly ineffective problem solver. Faced with problems that cannot be affected, the only option left to the abuser is to affect him or herself, that is, his or her experience of the problem, through the use of alcohol. It is fairly easy to see how this problem-solving approach would lead to recurrent themes of helplessness, low self-esteem, guilt, and many of the other personality characteristics that have been associated with alcoholics. It has been our observation that the clients' problems are often rooted in their conceptualizations, that there are certain conceptualization patterns that are particularly common among the clients, that these thinking patterns are "maladaptive" or "unrealistic," and that a corrective change in these maladaptive thinking patterns might well lead to at least a partial resolution of the clients' problems.

It is important to consider the characteristics of the particular patient population that is to be treated. Almost all of the research cited above was conducted with male patients and the applicability of the findings to female alcoholics is as yet uncertain (Gomberg, 1976). Our model of alcoholism and its treatment is based on our clinical experiences with patients at the Boston VA Center for Problem Drinking. The maladaptive thinking patterns of the patients may be described in terms of the basic processes that underlie their conceptualization and the content themes that typically characterize their conceptualizations. Some of these themes may become highly prominent in the thinking and consequent behavior of the alcoholic and may be considered to be personality characteristics.

Beck (1972) has proposed a model of depression in which he emphasizes the role of thinking in this disorder. He has described errors in the process of thinking that are typical of depressed patients, for example, drawing conclusions in the absence of or contrary to the available evidence. He described how these processes can lead to a depressive thought content, for example, "John didn't call me tonight, he doesn't love me anymore." We feel Beck's model is relevant to the thinking of the alcoholic even though alcoholics are a far more heterogeneous population than depressives and their thought disorders are more difficult to specify. However, there are some characteristic thought processes and contents that seem to occur frequently among our patients.

The maladaptive thought processes that we have observed generally seem to involve a failure to utilize the typical parameters, range, content, number of, and relationship between categories or attribution classes.

We have observed in alcoholic patients the maladaptive processes that Beck (1972, 1976) has described for depressives. These would include drawing arbitrary inferences, making dichotomous (black–white) evaluations, and making gross overgeneralizations. We also have observed a number of other maladaptive processes. Our patients frequently exhibit thinking that is either global, abstract, and undifferentiated *or* thinking that is highly narrow, concretized, and specific. Often, patients' evaluations are emotionally dominated. Patients frequently are unable to identify and differentiate affects or the origin or object of the affect (e.g., "I don't know why, but I'm angry all the time at nothing in particular"). Evaluations often are based on a single criterion, standard or dimension, or the criteria and categories used in evaluations are not sufficiently discriminated from each other and/or are applied incorrectly (e.g., sobriety may be seen as the measure of entitlement). The alcoholics' beliefs and assumptions are often not tested or readily subject to disconfirmation by contradictory evidence and at least some of their attributions are likely to be unrealistic. Many patients fail to see interrelationships between factors in a situation and patients often demonstrate an arbitrary and narrow focus of attention on a single aspect of a situation or person. Partly in consequence of this, patients often are unable to generate or consider alternatives or to change their perspective or point of view. Of course, this is not an exhaustive list of maladaptive processes and we do not mean to imply that these processes are confined to or definitive of alcoholics. Also, no one patient exhibits all of these processes but, rather, they consistently appear to utilize a limited number.

The above processes lead to a number of frequently occurring maladaptive themes, or thought contents, in alcoholic patient populations. There is not, however, an invariant one-to-one relationship between each process and each theme; any process may lead to any one or more of the themes and conversely, any theme may be determined by any one or more of the processes.

We have observed a number of maladaptive theme contents. Some of our patients believe that they are totally powerless and/or victimized. Many of our patients have either very low *or* (less commonly) very high self-images, and many either overaccept *or* underaccept responsibility for either good *or* bad outcomes. Patients' evaluations and anticipations frequently are pervasively negative. Some patients have an overly high or overly low feeling of entitlement. Most of our patients believe that alcohol is the only alternative to bad feelings and problems. This list also is not meant to be an exhaustive one, nor are these content themes confined to or definitive of alcoholics. Again, no one patient exhibits all of these themes but each seems to consistently demonstrate a limited number.

Table 1 describes the more common maladaptive content themes that we have observed, the behaviors that are often associated with them, examples of self-statements that would characterize them, and an example of a way in which alcohol use might serve as a means of coping with the consequences of the maladaptive conceptualization.

We have taken one commonly occurring theme or thought content in the life of the individual alcoholic and have analyzed it to illustrate our hypothesized model of maladaptive thought processes and contents. The patient had been abstinent for six months and suddenly began to drink. He stated, "I don't know what happened. I just found myself in a bar and before I knew it, I had three drinks and ended up on a drunk." The patient's memory and understanding of this event is as if he was a passive participant in a series of accidental events.

We hypothesize that the following processes underlie the patient's thinking: The patient experiences a negative feeling such as anxiety or anger which he wishes to relieve by getting drunk. The desire to get drunk arouses guilt and must be denied. The patient compromises his desire to get drunk with its attendant guilt by selectively focusing his attention on the thought "I'll just have one drink." This selective focusing enables him to begin drinking and at the same time to deny the wish to get drunk. "Just one drink" is an allowable indulgence, even for an alcoholic. Failing to see the relationship between each individual drink and the inevitable drunkenness, the first drink is experienced as "just one drink" and not as the first on the road to intoxication. The second drink is experienced as "just one more," as are the third, the fourth, and all the drinks up to the point that the patient has ingested sufficient alcohol to remove all prohibitions and concerns about drinking. The selective focusing on the idea of having "only one drink" allows the drinker to dissociate his intent, actions, and responsibility from the outcome and this allows the drinker to experience and remember events in ways that minimize his active conscious participation and responsibility.

This model of alcoholism implies that the most effective therapy modality for alcoholics would be a cognitively-oriented therapy. This approach presumes that therapeutic interventions must be directed at the patient's thinking processes as well as the symptom-related behaviors and characteristics and that therapeutic change must be supported by the development of effective coping skills.

Alcoholics Anonymous has long recognized the important role of thought processes in alcoholism. "Stinking Thinking" is the catch-all phrase applied to the various thoughts and conceptualizations alcoholics have that reinforce and justify their drinking. AA members constantly advise their fellow members to pay close attention to the way they think and alert their members to thought patterns that often lead to drinking. For example, a member is warned against the consequences of indulging in thoughts of victimization and self-pity by the slogan "Poor me, poor me, pour me a drink." Another example is the way in which AA changes the overwhelming thought of "a life of sobriety" to the more manageable thought of being sober "one day at a time."

Sanchez-Craig (1975, 1980) has reported the use of a cognitively-oriented therapy with alcoholics. In her articles, she describes a treatment strategy that involves: (1) the *identification* and analysis of drinking episodes, (2) *exposure* to the drinking stimulus situation in imagination and desensitization of unpleasant aspects, (3) *generation* of alternative thoughts and coping strategies, particularly self-statements, and (4) *cognitive rehearsal* of new coping responses. Sanchez-Craig also describes several case studies of individuals with whom this approach has succeeded.

Marlatt (1976, 1978, 1979) has developed a cognitive-behavioral model of alcoholism, craving for alcohol, and relapse. Questioning the tension-reduction hypothesis as an explanation of alcohol's reinforcing properties, he hypothesizes that alcohol reinforces by increasing perceptions of personal control and efficacy. Marlatt recommends an intervention strategy for use with alcoholics that combines D'Zurilla and Goldfried's (1971) training in problem-solving skills with the encouragement of alternative positive activities such as meditation and physical exercise and an inoculation-type approach to relapse prevention. Marlatt reports that preliminary experience indicates that this skills training approach has "utility" as one component of a multimodal behavioral approach to relapse in problem drinking (Chaney, O'Leary, & Marlatt, 1978).

The success that Beck, Meichenbaum, and others have had in using cognitively-oriented therapies with various patient populations, the compatibility of the proposed model of alcoholism with the modality, and the favorable experience that Glantz had in using cognitively oriented techniques with a group of alcoholics encouraged the development of a cognitively-oriented therapy program at the Boston Veterans Administration Center for Problem Drinking. The program was designed for small groups of alcoholic patients. Although group therapy with alcoholics can be difficult even for experienced therapists (e.g., Yalom, 1974), we felt that the cognitive therapy techniques could compensate for the disadvantages of a group method with alcoholics and could benefit from the possibility of the interactions of the patients. The

TABLE 1

Common Maladaptive Conceptualization Themes of Alcoholics

Theme	Behavioral characteristics	Example of automatic thought	Example of coping function of alcohol use
High self-image	Conceit, feeling of superiority, rejection and conflict with others	I'm better than they are. I don't have any problems. This job is beneath me.	1) Combat feelings of inferiority 2) Reduce anger when not treated as superior
Low self-image	Depression, self-denigration	I'm no good. I'm worthless.	1) Tranquilize or deaden feelings 2) Distort self-image 3) Create fantasy of a better self
High power/control	Unwarranted optimism and meglomania, attempt impossible	I can do anything. It's not impossible for me.	1) Create fantasy and feeling of power 2) Tranquilize when fail
Low power/control	Feeling helpless and hopeless, no attempts, no alternatives, depression and anxiety	I can't do anything. There is nothing I can do.	1) Create fantasy and feeling of power 2) Tranquilize or deaden feelings 3) Provide means to control others 4) Relieve inhibitions to act
Under acceptance of responsibility for bad outcome	Denial of responsibility, seeing self as innocent/helpless victim, blame and resent others	It wasn't my fault. They were responsible. I couldn't help it. He gets me so mad I had to drink.	1) Provide excuse—"Did cause drunk" 2) Tranquilize or deaden feelings
Overacceptance of re-	Accept all blame	It's all my fault.	1) Tranquilize or deaden feelings

Category	Description	Cognitions	Functions
...sponsibility for bad outcome		I'm to blame. I ruined everything.	2) Distort perceptions of self or situation 3) Disinhibit expression of anger and resentment
Under acceptance of responsibility for good outcome	Denigration of own achievements, not reward self	It was luck. It's not much. I didn't really do it. I don't deserve it. That's too good for me.	1) Tranquilize or deaden feelings 2) Create fantasy of success 3) Disinhibit expression of pride
Low entitlement	No self reward or acceptance of good things, self denigration and depression	I don't deserve better.	1) Tranquilize or deaden feelings 2) Distort perception of situation or self 3) Permit self-reward
High entitlement	Expectation of too much for little effort, resentment of others, angry and demanding attitude	I deserve better. I should have gotten that. They owe it to me.	1) Create fantasy of distorted situation 2) Tranquilize or deaden feelings
Overly negative evaluations/anticipations	Unwarranted pessimism, highly critical, not enjoy available positive things, not try new things, insufficient effort, quit easily	Nothing is any good. It won't work no matter what I do. Things will never be better.	1) Tranquilize or deaden feelings 2) Distort perceptions of self or situation
Overly positive evaluations/anticipations	Unwarranted optimism, not recognize or anticipate problems, poor judgments, set self up for failure	I don't need to worry. This will set me up for life. Those problems will work out.	1) Tranquilize when disappointed 2) Create fantasy of success 3) Distort perceptions of self or situations
Alcohol is the *only* solution	Inability to confront and cope with problems and/or negative and strong feelings (e.g., anger, anxiety, depression, loneliness)	It's the only way to handle it. What else can I do? It's so bad I must drink.	1) Tranquilize or deaden feelings 2) Disinhibit expression of emotions 3) Provide means of seeking help

therapy protocol to be described was developed and used over a three-year period at the clinic.

COGNITIVE THERAPY FOR ALCOHOLICS

The stated goals of the group are to demonstrate the importance that thought processes play in the lives and behavior of the members, to demonstrate that these thought processes are subject to change, and to demonstrate further that this change is within the patient's control. The group attempts to identify problem areas of conceptualizations and to work out alternative and more constructive patterns that will lead to more desirable feelings and behaviors. Although the topics of the group discussions and exercises always focus on content (theme) oriented goals, the therapists use these activities as an opportunity to attempt to modify the patients' underlying maladaptive processes.

In addition, the therapists help the patients to develop alternative and more successful coping and self-regulatory skills and encourage the patients to substitute more adaptive behaviors for those that support maladaptive conceptualizations and symptom patterns. Although the therapy is specifically intended for alcoholics, its focus is on maladaptive conceptualizations and behaviors, only some of which are related to alcohol use. The use of alcohol by the group members is discussed in the same way as their other maladaptive behaviors and unsuccessful coping techniques. It is expected that few, if any, of the patients will be able to develop a controlled pattern of social drinking; this is particularly true for patients who have not established social support systems and stable living situations and developed alternate coping techniques. For this reason, complete abstinence from alcohol use is encouraged.

The general principles on which therapy is based and many of the techniques that are used are drawn from established cognitive therapy procedures. We have relied particularly on the general strategies and techniques developed by Beck (1976, 1979) and Meichenbaum (1975, 1977; Meichenbaum & Turk, 1976) and the skills training procedures developed by D'Zurilla and Goldfried (1971) and Novaco (1977). We encourage psychotherapists who wish to employ the therapy protocol for alcoholics to familiarize themselves with these works.

The therapy also relies on the development of a facilitative group process of open interaction among the group members. This requires skill and experience on the part of the therapists and it is recommended that the protocol be used by therapists who have had at least some experience with group intervention approaches.

Although the use of a group format usually implies that the patients share the same fundamental problem and can, therefore, all be treated with basically the same intervention, we have found that it is necessary to develop an individual treatment plan for each patient. Although the same intervention strategy is applied to each case, specific goals and intervention attempts are worked out for each patient based on his particular maladaptive coping mechanisms; his temperament, beliefs, and social and intellectual abilities; his social and economic situation; and the nature and history of his drinking behavior. Although patients are screened only to exclude those demonstrating evidence of gross organic brain dysfunction or evidence of being inappropriate for referral to a therapy group, they are given an extensive series of tests for diagnostic and planning purposes. Each patient is asked to complete a Beck Depression Inventory, a Spielberger Trait Anxiety Inventory, a California Psychological Inventory, a detailed problem drinking history report, a measure of assertiveness, and a Situations Rep Test (Glantz, 1980, 1982), which provides information about the organization and content of the subject's conceptualizations. As part of the therapy activities, the patients also describe their beliefs about themselves, make a short presentation introducing themselves to the group, fill out a Goal Attainment Scale which describes the current status of four important areas of their lives and the goals they would like to reach in each, and give information about themselves through the normal activities of the group meetings. The information from these assessments is organized into a diagnostic picture and the problems and strengths of the patients and therapeutic goals and potential interventions are determined. This planning is then coordinated with the therapy protocol and the therapists attempt to accomplish the scheduled tasks for each therapy session, while at the same time taking advantage of presented opportunities to advance the therapeutic plans developed for the individual patients. This requires extensive preparation on the part of the therapists and frequently is more time consuming than the group meetings themselves.

An example of an intervention that was planned for a particular patient is presented below. It was determined in advance that this particular patient typically took responsibility for negative outcomes for which he was not responsible. The most salient of his maladaptive thought processes was his tendency toward overgeneralization. A general strategy was selected and when the patient related to the group a relevant incident, the therapists used the opportunity to implement the strategy.

The patient was a 42-year-old white man, a high school graduate who had been drinking heavily for 20 years. He was separated from his wife, whom he visited once a week. When she saw him she frequently became upset and angrily accused him of ruining her life and not supporting her financially, and thereby making her miserable. The patient responded with intense feelings of guilt and responsibility, usually followed by his getting drunk. In discussion, he said, "I've ruined her life. I'm a bum because I don't give her money. I make her feel bad."

The patient's evaluation of the situation, totally dominated by his feelings of guilt, focused solely on himself. Furthermore, he took his wife's accusation as a statement of fact rather than opinion. In other words, the patient accepted too much responsibility for his wife's distress. His feelings of guilt were exacerbated by an extremely critical self-evaluation.

An attempt was made to show the patient that each person is responsible for his own moods and feelings. The patient was asked whether he was or ever had been responsible for his wife's good moods. He answered "no." He was then asked how he could be responsible for the bad but not the good moods. He said he did not know. When he was asked who was responsible for his moods, he replied that he was. A group member asked, "If you're responsible for your moods, how come she's not responsible for hers?" He answered, "I guess she is." He then volunteered that even when he was making a lot of money, his wife made the same accusations. He said that he supposed she was an angry and depressed person before she met him. When asked whether there was anything he could do to make her happy, he said, "No, I guess only she can do that."[1] The patient subsequently reported that he no longer reacted to his wife with guilt.

Group Treatment

As conducted at the VA, the groups consisted of 8 to 10 patients and were led by two therapists. As both of the therapists in the program were males, a female therapist at the clinic occasionally was asked to assist in role-playing exercises. Patients attending the outpatient clinic were offered the opportunity to participate in a cognitive-behavior therapy group as part of their regular treatment program. Each group met twice weekly for 10 weeks. Each meeting, which was videotaped, lasted for 1½ hours. Most of the patients were white, unmarried, unemployed

[1]This case study is reprinted by permission from *Journal of Studies on Alcohol* (1980, Vol. 41, pp. 338–346.). Copyright Journal of Studies on Alcohol, New Brunswick, New Jersey.

men between the ages of 40 and 50. All were veterans. Most had experienced the breakup of their marriage and family, and most had had multiple arrests, blackouts, seizures, and hospitalizations for the treatment of alcoholism. The typical patient lived alone and was supported by some form of public assistance, had a history of alcohol misuse spanning 10 to 20 years, and had problems similar to, but more serious than, the "heavy intake" and "binge drinking" problem drinkers described by Cahalan and Room (1974).

Although only some patients maintain sobriety throughout the course of the 20 group meetings, a rule is established that any patient who comes to a meeting in an intoxicated state will not be permitted to attend that meeting. An agreement is made with the patients that they will attend all 20 meetings. If a patient misses three meetings or more, he is able to continue as a group member only if the other members are willing to allow him to continue.

COGNITIVE THERAPY PROTOCOL

Following is the therapy protocol that describes the session-by-session treatment plan for the typical course of therapy.

Sessions 1 and 2

Goals 1. To have patients complete several exercises that will be used in future groups and also will aid in the evaluation of the effectiveness of the group

2. To introduce the patients to the group and to establish certain expectations and conventions for the group

Each patient completes two exercises. The first is the Goal Attainment Scale (GAS), for which each patient, with the help of a therapist, defines his current status, his 5 week, 10 week, and 3 to 6 month goals in four areas of his life: (1) residence, (2) leisure activities, (3) employment–education–skills, (4) social-interpersonal-affiliative relationships and activities. All of the goals must be stated in specific concrete behavioral terms. Our patients have great difficulty with this task; they have a tendency to define goals in a general, amorphous fashion with little thought of how the goals might be achieved. Goals often are far beyond the patient's ability. Nevertheless this exercise is useful in teaching patients to think in a concrete, goal-directed, and realistic fashion about their lives.

The second exercise is the self-presentation. During the first session each patient is asked to prepare to give a three-minute talk about himself. During the second meeting, the patients go one at a time to another room where there are three staff members. They deliver their self-presentation to the "audience" and it is recorded on videotape. This produces an objective sample of the way in which the patient presents himself to others. Many of our patients are publicly self-denegrating and many are unaware of the manner in which they present themselves in social situations.

After the completion of the exercises the patients and therapists introduce themselves and the patients are each asked to answer three questions: (1) When were you most happy? (2) When were you most sad? (3) How do you feel about the future? This allows the patients to find out a little about each other and feel more comfortable with each other and develops the expectation that the group members will share personal and usually private information. During these sessions, the patients also are told a little bit about the orientation and objectives of the group and a little about the two exercises and they are given an opportunity to discuss them.

In all of the sessions the group process is developed and used to facilitate the tasks and goals. This helps to develop objective observation skills, interpersonal interactions, a less egocentric focus, a feeling of sharing and of having common experiences, a feeling of caring for others and an opportunity to first comprehend an idea in relation to another and then to see how that idea might apply to oneself. Patients are encouraged to participate very actively in discussions focused on other patients in the group and to help each other to identify, understand, and correct maladaptive thoughts and behaviors.

The assignment for the second session is to complete the Speilberger State Anxiety Scale and the Beck Depression Inventory.

Sessions 3 and 4

Goals 1. To teach patients the underlying philosophy of cognitive therapy
2. To demonstrate to patients that their concept of themselves is not necessarily shared by the world at large, that is, there are different ways of viewing oneself
3. To demonstrate that one's conception of oneself is only an opinion and not a fact; to contradict the common conception, "It's not that I think I'm a bum; it's that I am a bum"
4. To demonstrate the notion of "reality testing"

To achieve the first goal, the therapists role play a vignette. One therapist plays the role of the other therapist's employer; he role plays calling his secretary and asking her to send in the employee. The purpose is to tell the employee that he has received a raise. The employer instructs the secretary not to tell the employee about the raise as he wants to surprise him. The employee comes into the employer's office in a hostile and belligerent way and continues to be so for the remainder of the vignette. Clients are asked to describe what they have seen. They usually respond with the feelings that they have observed and then with the behavior. The patients are usually unable to think of a reason for the employee's hostility. Only with direction from the therapists are they able to consider what possible thoughts that participant had before entering the office. In simple schema, plausible thoughts, feelings, and behavior of the employee in the vignette are written out on the blackboard. It is stressed repeatedly that it was the thoughts and expectations that determined the feelings and behavior of the employee. It is further pointed out that many other thoughts and expectations were available to the employee and that had he chosen them, his feelings and behavior would have been different. Lastly, it is explained that one of the major foci for each individual member of the group will be "how he thinks, how he can think differently, and the benefits of thinking differently." The group is told that they will accomplish this through the use of homework assignments and through experiences in the group. It is important to note that a lot of time is spent in differentiating between thoughts and feelings. Many patients seem to be unaware of their thinking processes, and some patients seem to have difficulty understanding what "thoughts" are. A definition that we have found helpful for patients is that "thoughts" are self-talk or that which you say to yourself, about yourself, or about some other subject; the self-talk sometimes may be in the form of images instead of words.

To accomplish the second goal, group members view their videotaped self-presentation and each is asked to comment about it. Following their comments, they elicit opinions about the self-presentation from other group members. Frequently, the group's opinions are at odds with the presenter's view of the presentation and of himself.

The discussion also is directed toward the third goal of showing that one's self-image is only an opinion and focuses on the validity of other people's view versus one's own. This is a fundamentally important issue with people whose concept of themselves is either above or below that which seems realistic. A common example is the patient with poor self-esteem who is convinced his own estimation of himself is the only true one. Exposure to alternate points of view tends to make him doubt the absolute conviction.

To accomplish the fourth goal, the notion of reality testing is discussed and the exercises of checking one's opinions with the videotape recording and with other group members are used as examples. During all sessions, patients often are asked to compare an opinion with a tape or the group's opinion.

The assignment given at Session 4 is for each patient to write the five most important beliefs he has about himself.

Sessions 5 and 6

Goals 1. To explore each patient's basic beliefs about himself, to show how they agree or disagree with other people's beliefs about him
2. To explore the relationship between the patient's basic beliefs about himself and other aspects of his life
3. To demonstrate to patients how readily apparent their own beliefs about themselves are and the effects this would have on their relationship with others
4. To demonstrate and discuss responsibility avoiding
5. To explain the general model that thoughts determine feelings that together determine behavior and to explain the rationale and the potential benefits of cognitive restructuring

The first three goals are the object of an exercise using the "five most important beliefs about myself" assignment. A patient is selected and the other group members attempt to guess what the patient listed as his beliefs about himself. Then, the group describes their own opinions about the patient. Although the group members usually have not had much contact with each other before the group was formed, they usually have opinions about each other and are able to make a guess about each others self image. Each patient's own list of beliefs is read and in a discussion, guided by the therapists, the group compares the three lists, and explores the patient's self-image, its similarity to the group opinion, the accuracy of the group's "guess" of the patient's self-image (usually very high), and the implications of each to the patient's life. This is done with each patient in turn.

There is usually at least one patient who has not done the assignment. The patient almost invariably presents an excuse that avoids responsibility for the assignment (e.g., "There was no time to do it"). The excuse is discussed and provides an opportunity to demonstrate the difference between responsibility avoiding and responsibility accepting for any action or inaction.

The therapists make a brief presentation of the model that thoughts determine feelings which together determine behavior and a number of examples are given which pertain to the group members. Following this, the therapists discuss the potential benefits of controlling and determining one's feelings and behaviors and explain how this is possible by controlling one's thoughts.

Two cognitively oriented self-help guides, the Ellis and Harper book (1975) and the Beck and Greenberg article (1974) are made available to those who are interested and a "monitoring" assignment is given. The patients are asked to describe in writing for the seventh session two strong feelings they have had, the thoughts that preceded the feelings, and the behavior that followed.

Sessions 7 and 8

Goals 1. To review the patients' progress in reaching the goals they selected in the Goal Attainment Scale, to discuss the relationship of different thinking patterns to the accomplishing of goals, and to identify specific conceptualization problems that the patients have in relation to their goals
    2. To help patients to understand and accept the Thought→ Feeling→ Behavior model
    3. To help patients to become aware of their own Thought→ Feeling→ Behavior patterns, to identify and help them to become aware of irrational or maladaptive thoughts, and to demonstrate the relationship of these to their feelings and behaviors
    4. To develop further the distinction of facts from opinions and of maladaptive or irrational thoughts from adaptive or rational thoughts and to demonstrate the consequences of each
    5. To help patients to develop a continuous awareness (or monitoring) of their thoughts

Patients are given a copy of their Goal Attainment Scale and are asked to report on the progress they have made. They discuss the difficulties they are having in reaching their goals and the discussion focuses on these difficulties in terms of the cognitive model of feelings and behavior.

The patients' monitoring homework assignments then are analyzed. This is accomplished by writing the patient's assignment on a blackboard and having the group discuss it. The therapists conduct the discussion in which emphasis is placed on the organic connection between thoughts and feelings and the behaviors that follow. The focus of attention is turned to the thoughts themselves. These are discussed in terms of their internal logic, their hidden assumptions, their relationship to reality, their adaptiveness or maladaptiveness to the patient's life, alternative thoughts the patient might have, and the potential benefits of these alternative thoughts. Approximately one-third of the time the thoughts are ones that lead to a feeling of wanting to drink. During the sessions, the therapists often apply the above analysis to the feelings that arise during the group meetings. If a patient displays any noticeable emotion, he immediately is asked to share with the group the thoughts that preceded this emotion. Imaginal role playing often is used to explore Thought→ Feeling→ Behavior (TFB) patterns and role playing and reenacting by the patients are also used.

The monitoring assignment is given for the ninth session.

In order to help the therapists and the patients learn more about the conceptualizations of the group members, the patients are asked to meet individually with one of the therapists and to take a modified version of the Kelly Rep Test (Kelly, 1955). The modification is called the Situations Rep Test (Glantz, 1982) and focuses on thoughts about interpersonal and noninterpersonal experiences and situations. The results are discussed with the patient.

Sessions 9–12
Goals 1. To continue the analysis of thoughts, feelings, and behaviors
     2. To develop the idea of alternative thoughts with the goal of determining one's own feelings and behaviors
     3. To instill in the patients the habit of utilizing alternative modes of thinking as a countermeasure to negative thoughts and feelings and to learn to do so using negative thoughts or feelings as a cue to begin the process of using alternative self-statements

Monitoring assignments and in-group experiences are analyzed by the group using the TFB model. As the patients develop an understanding of the model and its application, they are encouraged to explore the idea of determining and controlling their feelings and behavior. The group discusses the feelings and behaviors that would result from various modes of thinking and considers the benefits of the more "adaptive" thoughts and the possibility of substituting the more adaptive thoughts for the maladaptive ones. This leads to the idea of using adaptive thoughts, in the form of self-statements, as a countermeasure to the maladaptive thoughts and their feelings and behavior. As the patients accept these ideas and become aware of their own maladaptive thoughts, they are encouraged to practice and develop the habits of utilizing the more adaptive modes of thinking.

Attention is devoted to the utilization of the onset of negative feelings or behavior or maladaptive thoughts as cues to the individual to begin the alternative and more adaptive thoughts in the form of self-statements. Once a patient has had the experience of an alternative and more adaptive thought leading to a more positive feeling and/or behavior, then he usually has passed a critical point and will adopt and benefit from the therapy and its philosophy relatively easily. For this reason, patients are often encouraged to "try an experiment" in which they attempt to think about something "differently" or at least try to behave as if they had a different conceptualization of a person or a situation.

In order to concretize comments about the patients' thoughts and self-image, the therapists and the group often rate them on a 1 to 10 scale, indicating a range between high and low self-image, extreme optimism and extreme pessimism, overacceptance of responsibility and underacceptance, maladaptive and adaptive thinking, and so forth. This rating technique also is used to concretize the difference between an individual's opinion and the groups opinion and to concretize change and progress.

A monitoring assignment is given for the eleventh session.

Sessions 13 and 14

Goals 1. To review the patients' progress in reaching the goals they selected in the Goal Attainment Scale, to discuss the relationship of different thinking patterns to the accomplishment of goals, to identify specific conceptualization problems that the patients have in relation to their goals, and to develop alternate and more adaptive thought patterns that will facilitate selecting and reaching a desirable and realistic goal

2. To demonstrate how physical-somatic factors relate to conceptualizations and to demonstrate some techniques for controlling some somatic responses

3. To demonstrate a model for understanding and controlling impulsive and explosive behaviors such as angry rages

The patients' Goal Attainments Scales are discussed as before. A strong emphasis is placed on thought patterns and alternate conceptualizations and their relation to selecting and reaching goals.

In a discussion format, the therapists demonstrate how internal behaviors or physical reactions also fit into the TFB model. It is explained that thoughts determine these behaviors and, as is often the case with TFB patterns, there is a feedback effect. Once the behaviors are initiated, awareness of and thoughts about the behaviors reinforce and amplify the original thoughts, which lead to a greater reaction and so on.

Alcoholics almost seem "to think with their bodies" in that they are especially sensitive to somatic feedback and frequently follow this cyclical pattern. Many alcoholics report having a feeling of overwhelming anxiety and physical tension or deep depression and physical lassitude.

The TFB model is used to explain these experiences and emphasis is placed on the idea that these feelings are produced by and are controllable by thoughts. The idea of a feedback system is explained and a version of Schacter and Singer's (1962) model of affective reaction is presented. As the therapists and group members explore particular patients' TFB patterns, the therapists demonstrate specific behavioral techniques to help combat the habituated response patterns. Tense patients are encouraged to take a few deep breaths or use muscle relaxation techniques that are taught in training classes at the clinic. Inactive patients are encouraged to become physically active.

A number of our patients report that they are subject to impulsive and explosive behaviors such as angry, often violent, rages. These behaviors also are discussed with the above ideas and an approach in controlling impulsive behaviors is taught. Novaco (1977) has developed Meichenbaum's stress inoculation procedure (1975) for use in anger control and the therapists teach a version of this procedure. The approach involves three basic phases. The first is a cognitive preparation stage that essentially is the application of the above cognitive model to the experience of anger. The second phase involves skills acquisition and rehearsal which includes the learning of alternative conceptualizations and self-statements, the development of a task orientation or problem-solving approach to anger situations, and the utilization of the above somatic techniques. The third phase involves application practice.

The assignments for the fifteenth session are practicing and applying the tension, lassitude and anger control techniques and identifying two important problems to work on.

Session 15–18
Goals 1. To teach patients problem-solving skills and strategies, to demonstrate the relationships between thoughts and feelings, and problems and problem solving, and to help the patient to work out particular problems

Most of our patients do not really know how to go about solving real world problems in a rational organized way. They typically act in an ineffective, impulsive manner and feel that their problems are insoluble. Building on the model of TFB, a modified version of D'Zurilla and Goldfried's (1971) problem-solving strategy is taught. Patients are presented with the idea that there are five basic steps that they should take when solving a problem:

1. *a)* Determine that there is a problem and that it is a problem that you want to solve.
    b) Define the problem in specific, concrete, operational terms.

2. *a)* Determine the possible goals or resolutions.
   b) Evaluate each and select one.
3. *a)* Determine the possible paths to the goal or resolution.
   b) Evaluate each and select one (or more).
4. *a)* Take the first step on the path to the goal or resolution.
   b) Continue to work toward goal or resolution.
5. As you are working toward the goal or resolution, check to make sure that the path you are on is leading to the goal or resolution.

During these sessions each patient presents at least one important problem and, with the help of the therapists and the other group members, works toward solving it using D'Zurilla and Goldfried's strategy. This is an extremely difficult exercise for the patients and requires a great deal of help from the therapists and often involves consideration of TFB patterns. The most difficult step for the patients seems to be the definition of the problem in specific concrete, operational, objective terms. They typically think of problems in global amorphous ways that have no implied resolutions or courses of action and, in fact, often imply irresolvability (e.g., "I want things to be the way they were 20 years ago"). Not infrequently a problem is identified and thought of by the patient in terms of a vague wish-fulfilling fantasy (e.g., "I want to meet the woman of my dreams"), a poorly articulated conflict (e.g., "Why can't I work like everyone else"), or one problem that serves as an expression of a number of poorly thought out interrelated problems, (e.g., "I haven't been able to finish building a chair for my girlfriend," which encompassed problems related to the patient's relationship to his girlfriend's family and his lack of an apartment of his own which stemmed from his lack of a job). By working on specific problems, patients learn the problem-solving strategy. The patients' Goal Attainment Scales also are utilized in these problem-solving exercises.

Assignments are given during these sessions that involve having the patients work on a step of the problem solving.

Sessions 19 and 20
Goals 1. To review and integrate the material and the exercises of the group, to answer any questions or discuss any issues that the patients might have, and to help patients to plan to continue the tasks and ideas they began in the group
2. To have the patients complete (for a second time) the assessment exercises for a pre–post comparison

After the patients have completed the exercises, they discuss what they have learned from the group, issues that they are concerned about, and their plans for the future.

Discussion

The goal of the cognitive therapy groups is the teaching of generalized coping and reconceptualizing skills that go beyond the specific content of the problems that are dealt with in the group. It is for this reason that maladaptive thought processes are such an important target of the therapy. If these are ameliorated, then not only may the concomitant maladaptive themes be remedied, but the patient is more likely to develop an enduring generalized adaptive conceptualizing system that will enable him to avoid the development of other maladaptive themes and enable him to cope successfully with both his current environment and new situations. An important goal of the therapy is to teach the patient the philosophy of the cognitive approach to behavior and the means by which he can identify and change maladaptive thoughts so that he can, in effect, become his own therapist and continue the beneficial changes on his own after the termination of the group.

Although the topics of the group discussions and exercises are often oriented around affects and behaviors, the ultimate target of the therapy and the modality through which it operates are cognitive in nature. Although the therapy involves some behavioral skills training, for the most part it is assumed that the patients have, at least to some degree, the necessary adaptive practical and interpersonal skills and it is further assumed that the problem is to help them to identify and use those skills when appropriate. This approach usually means that the patient is helped to learn to substitute one behavior for another rather than encouraged simply to stop a particular behavior, such as drinking. For a number of patients, however, we have found that instruction in relaxation training and assertiveness training can provide an important supplement to the patients' repertoire of adaptive alternative behaviors and, perhaps more importantly, increases their confidence in their ability to initiate an alternative adaptive response.

Initially, we anticipated that the patients who would benefit most from the cognitive therapy group would be those who were verbal, reflective, intelligent, educated, and have a belief in the potency of thought. Our expectations have not been verified. Although the therapy did not work equally well with all patients, we are unable at this time to preselect those patients who will benefit most. We are, however, able to describe some of the characteristics of the responsive patients that are observable during the therapy. The patients who appeared to benefit from the cognitive therapy seemed to have three characteristics in common: (1) They were motivated toward change. (2) They accepted the cognitive-behavior philosophy and its implications. (3) They had some experience in which they benefited from a reconceptualization and the application of the cognitive techniques. As much as possible, each patient should be an active collaborator in the attempt to bring about therapeutic change rather than a passive recipient of a treatment.

Although some patients readily accepted the cognitive–behavior philosophy, others resisted it. Despite repeated efforts to make the philosophy concrete, it remains too abstract and esoteric for some patients. Other patients resist because accepting the model would mean accepting responsibility for their thoughts, feelings, actions, and problems. Some patient's feelings are so dominantly pervasive and overwhelming that they believe that their thoughts have little if any impact and that the therapy was, therefore, useless to them.

We believe that patients learn best through a process of doing and experiencing. Although the didactic presentation of concepts and discussion obviously is necessary, ideas must be assimilated both experientially and behaviorally. For many of our patients, talk alone appears to have minimal impact. Therefore, it is essential that discussion be supplemented by *in vivo* experiences, role playing, homework assignments, reality testing and behavior change "experiments" and the development of self and other monitoring skills. We would agree with Beck (1976), Meichenbaum (1977), and others who have advocated the use of a multimodal therapy strategy. We have found the 20-session group cognitive therapy to be a potent intervention strategy. For most patients, however, it is necessary for them to participate in some form of treatment after the 10-week course of therapy.

For most of our patients, the severity of their psychopathology, the magnitude of the disruption and/or impoverishment of their social networks and interpersonal relationships, the deterioration of their employment and financial situations, and the relative inaccessibility of social support, and tangible resources combine to make positive change and recovery a long and difficult process. Although the cognitive therapy can ameliorate much of their psychopathology and can increase their coping skills, it cannot bring about direct remediation of those other problematic factors. Therefore, we recommend that after the cognitive therapy groups, patients continue in some form of counseling support (such as Alcoholics Anonymous) or individual cognitive therapy. Our patients typically are referred for individual therapy which is sometimes supplemented by attendance at AA meetings or other support or therapy groups at the clinic. While we believe that the cognitive therapy approach, using a structured format and a relatively small predetermined number of therapy sessions, is very effective, we have been considering expanding the protocol to 25 or 30 sessions or creating a follow-up or maintenance group to provide additional therapeutic support. Also, while the protocol is fairly structured, we do not believe that the cognitive therapy can be an invariant procedure that is the same for all patients. We try to be flexible and to create an individual therapy plan for each patient and to adapt the therapy plan for each new group to the particular members of the group. We are considering ways to increase the flexibility and the responsivity of the protocol. Despite our desire to improve the cognitive therapy protocol we have had considerable success with this program of therapy and feel that it can be used successfully by others.

REFERENCES

Beck, A. *Depression: Clinical, experimental, and theoretical aspects.* Philadelphia: University of Pennsylvania Press, 1972.

Beck, A. *Cognitive therapy and the emotional disorders.* New York: International Universities Press, 1976.

Beck, A., & Greenberg, R. *Coping with depression.* New York: Institute for Rational Living, 1974.

Beck, A., Rush, A., Shaw, B., & Emery, G. *Cognitive therapy of depression.* New York: Guilford, 1979.

Berg, N. Effects of alcohol intoxication on self concepts. *Quarterly Journal of Studies on Alcohol,* 1971, *32,* 442–453,

Cahalan, D., & Room, R. *Problem drinking among American men.* New Brunswick, N.J.: Rutgers Center of Alcohol Studies, 1974.

Catanzaro, R. Psychiatric aspects of alcoholism. In D. Pittman (Ed.), *Alcoholism.* New York: Harper & Row, 1967.

Chaney, E. F., O'Leary, M. R., & Marlatt, G. A. Skill training with alcoholics. *Journal of Consulting and Clinical Psychology,* 1978, *46,* 1092–1104.

Cox, W. The alcoholic personality: A review of the evidence. In B. Maher (Ed.), *Progress in experimental personality research* (Vol. 9). New York: Academic, 1979.

D'Zurilla, T., & Goldfried, M., Problem solving and behavior modification. *Journal of Abnormal Psychology,* 1971, *78,* 107–126.

Ellis, A., & Harper, R. *A new guide to rational living.* North Hollywood, Calif.: Wilshire, 1975.

Gibson, S., & Becker, J. Alcoholism and depression: The factor structure of alcoholics' responses to depression inventories. *Quarterly Journal of Studies on Alcohol,* 1973, *34,* 400–408.

Glantz, M. Developments in the elicitation and analysis of constructs. Paper presented at the American Psychological Association Meeting, Montreal, September 1980.

Glantz, M. *Diagnosis and assessment for cognitive behavior therapies: A Rep Test approach.* Paper presented at the Eastern Psychological Association Meeting, Baltimore, April 1982.

Glantz, M., & Burr, W. *A comparative study of neurotics', alcoholics', and normals', conceptualizations of situations.* Paper presented at the Fourth International Congress on Personal Construct Psychology, St. Catharines, Ontario, August 1981.

Goldstein, G. Perceptual and cognitive deficit in alcoholics. In G. Goldstein & C. Neu-ringer (Eds.), *Empirical studies of alcoholism*. Cambridge, Mass.: Ballinger, 1976.

Gomberg, E. The female alcoholic. In R. Tarter & A. Sugerman (Eds.), *Alcoholism: Inter-disciplinary approaches to an enduring problem*. Reading, Mass.: Addison-Wesley, 1976.

Halpern, F. Studies of compulsive drinkers: Psychological test results. *Quarterly Journal of Studies on Alcohol*, 1946, *6*, 468–479.

Kelly, G. *The psychology of personal constructs* (Vols. 1 and 2). New York: Norton, 1955.

Kleinknecht, R., & Goldstein, S. Neuropsychological deficits associated with alcoholism: A review and discussion. *Quarterly Journal of Studies on Alcohol*, 1972, *33*, 999–1019.

Lisansky, E. Clinical research in alcoholism and the use of psychological tests. A reevalua-tion. In R. Fox (Ed.), *Alcoholism: Behavioral, research, and therapeutic approaches*. New York: Springer, 1967.

Marlatt, G. A. Alcohol, stress, and cognitive control. In I. G. Sarason & C. D. Speilberger (Eds.), *Stress and anxiety* (Vol. 3). New York: Wiley, 1976.

Marlatt, G. A. Craving for alcohol, loss of control, & relapse: A cognitive–behavioral analysis. In P. E. Nathan, G. A. Marlatt, & T. Løberg (Eds.), *Alcoholism: New directions in behavioral research and treatment*. New York: Plenum, 1978.

Marlatt, G. A. Alcohol use & problem drinking: A cognitive–behavioral analysis. In P. C. Kendall & S. P. Hollon (Eds.), *Cognitive–behavioral interventions: Theory, research and procedures*. New York: Academic, 1979.

McClelland, D., Davis, W., Kalin, R., & Wanner, E. *The drinking man: Alcohol and human motivation*. New York: Free Press, 1972.

McCord, J. Etiological factors in alcoholism: Family and personal characteristics. *Quarterly Journal of Studies on Alcohol*, 1972, *33*, 1020–1027.

McCord, W., & McCord, J. *Origins of alcoholism*. Stanford: Stanford University Press, 1960.

McCord, W., & McCord, J. A longitudinal study of the personality of alcoholics. In D. Pittmann & C. Snyder (Eds.), *Society, culture and drinking patterns*. New York: Wiley, 1962.

Meichenbaum, D. A self-instructional approach to stress management: A proposal for stress inoculation training. In C. Spielberger & I. Sarason (Eds.), *Stress and anxiety* (Vol. 2). New York: Wiley, 1975.

Meichenbaum, D. *Cognitive-behavior modification*. New York: Plenum, 1977.

Meichenbaum, D., & Turk, D. The cognitive–behavioral management of anxiety, anger, and pain. In P. Davidson (Ed.), *The behavioral management of anxiety, depression and pain*. New York: Brunner/Mazel, 1976.

Neuringer, C., & Clopton, R. The use of psychological tests for the study of the identifica-tion, prediction and treatment of alcoholism. In G. Goldstein & C. Neuringer (Eds.), *Empirical studies of alcoholism*. Cambridge, Mass.: Ballinger, 1976.

Novaco, R. Stress inoculation: A cognitive therapy for anger and its application to a case of depression. *Journal of Consulting and Clinical Psychology*, 1977, *45*, 600–608.

Rohsenow, D., & O'Leary, M. Locus of control research on alcoholic populations: A review. I. Development, scales, and treatment. *The International Journal of the Addic-tions*, 1978, *13*, 55–78.

Sanchez-Craig, M., A self-control strategy for drinking tendencies. *Ontario Psychologist*, 1975, *7*, 25–29.

Sanchez-Craig, M. Random assignment to abstinence or controlled drinking in a cognitive-behavioral program: Short term effects on drinking behavior. *Addictive Behaviors*, 1980, *5*, 35–39.

Schacter, S., & Singer, J. Cognitive, social and physiological determinants of emotional states. *Psychological Review*, 1962, *69*, 379–399.

Smith, J. W., & Layden, T. A. Changes in psychological performance and blood chemistry in alcoholics during and after hospital treatment. *Quarterly Journal of Studies on Alcohol,* 1972, *33,* 379–394.

Stein, K., Rozynko, V., & Pugh, L. The heterogeneity of personality among alcoholics. *British Journal of Social and Clinical Psychology,* 1971, *10.* 253–259.

Tarter, R. Psychological deficit in chronic alcoholics: A review. *International Journal of the Addictions,* 1975a, *10,* 327–368.

Tarter, R. Personality characteristics of male alcoholics. *Psychological Reports,* 1975b, *37,* 91–96.

Tarter, R. Neuropsychological investigations of alcoholism. In G. Goldstein & C. Neuringer (Eds.), *Empirical studies of alcoholism.* Cambridge, Mass.: Ballinger, 1976.

Vannicelli, M. Mood and self-perception of alcoholics when sober and intoxicated: I. Mood Change, II. Accuracy of self-prediction. *Quarterly Journal of Studies on Alcoholism,* 1972, *33,* 341–357.

Yalom, I. Group therapy and alcoholism. *Annals of the New York Academy of Sciences,* 1974, *233,* 85–103.

9

Cognitive Therapy with the
Young Adult Chronic Patient

Vincent B. Greenwood

Recently, there has been an effort to extend the application of cognitive therapy to different patient populations (Emery, Hollon, & Bedrosian, 1981). In that spirit, I should like to share my experiences and observations in applying group cognitive therapy to a very difficult patient population, the young adult chronic patient. To my knowledge, this is the first attempt to apply cognitive group therapy to this patient population.

PATIENT POPULATION

Since the advent of deinstitutionalization, a difficult patient group has emerged, known as the young adult chronic or "revolving door" patient. These are patients—mostly in their 20s and 30s—with serious psychiatric disabilities. They are the first generation of mental patients forced to cope with the stresses and demands of community living (Pepper, Kirshner, & Ryglewicz, 1981). They do not cope well, and consequently become perpetual or recurrent clients of mental health systems, social service agencies, and—frequently—the legal-penal system. They pose treatment and service delivery system dilemmas that are significantly different from those posed by earlier generations of the severely mentally disabled.

The great majority of these patients carry an Axis I diagnosis of schizophrenia. In addition, many display severe borderline pathology.

Vincent B. Greenwood • Center for Cognitive-Behavioral Therapy, 5225 Connecticut Avenue, N.W., Washington, D.C. 20015

Although their symptom pictures vary greatly, there is considerable similarity in their functional characteristics. All these patients display severe difficulties in social functioning. They have few social or vocational skills and no natural support systems. Thus, what is an everyday problem in living for us becomes a crisis for them. When under such stress, they show serious disorders in reality testing, affect modulation, and impulse control, exhibiting both aggressive and self-destructive behavior (Schwartz & Goldfinger, 1981).

Perhaps the most problematic characteristic of these patients is their lack of involvement in treatment. They do not define themselves as mental patients. They typically are brought to the hospital against their will and often feel victimized by the mental health system. Their hospitalizations are often stormy and they end up rejecting treatment—vehemently or passively. The burden, consequently, rests with the mental health system to design treatments that will be responsive to this new class of psychiatric "untouchables."

In attempting to tailor cognitive therapy to this patient group, I have observed different stages over the course of psychotherapy. (I am defining *stage* as a set of therapist operations designed to effect reliable changes in the patient.) Detailing treatment in stages seems particularly useful with this patient population who are notorious for their lack of involvement with and adherence to psychotherapeutic approaches.

Anthony, a leader in the development and evaluation of rehabilitation treatment packages for the severely psychiatrically disabled, has recently (Anthony, 1980) proposed an innovative outcome evaluation model that incorporates specific stages of involvement and understanding. In this model, it is crucial that evaluators assess the extent to which patients become involved with and understand treatment before attempting to evaluate outcome. Likewise, clinicians working with this patient group need to address specifically these issues of involvement and understanding. It would be unfortunate to reject a particular treatment modality merely because the patient has not been sufficiently "exposed" to the essential ingredients of the treatment. It would be equally unfortunate if practitioners did not make modifications in a particular treatment approach in order to ensure that patients are exposed to the more potent aspects of the treatment.

Thus, the straightforward application of cognitive therapy, as, for example, outlined in the *Cognitive Therapy of Depression* (Beck, Rush, Shaw, & Emery, 1979) rests on a number of assumptions that are invalid with the young chronic patient. Engaging the patient in a collaborative analysis and treatment of his or her problematic behavior and cognitive distortions rests on the following premises:

1. The patient is motivated to seek treatment.
2. The patient acknowledges he or she has a psychological problem (i.e., patient has a minimal degree of insight).
3. The patient has the belief that it is acceptable to self-disclose.
4. The patient is capable of attending to and understanding the treatment that is being offered.
5. The patient is capable of acquiring some of the fundamental skills that are the focus of cognitive therapy (e.g., introspection, disputational skills, an empirical problem-solving style), (Beck *et al.*, 1979).

The above-noted qualities typically are present at the outset of treatment with those suffering affective or anxiety-based disorders. With psychotic patients, they are not present. Consequently, the cognitive therapist who is unwilling to actively seek appropriate modifications will be frustrated in his or her attempts to administer the armamentarium of behavioral and cognitive change strategies.

STAGES OF TREATMENT

Three stages of group cognitive therapy with the young chronic patient have been abstracted. The first stage has an explicit agenda of securing the patient's involvement in treatment. The second stage tries to facilitate the patient's understanding of the cognitive therapy treatment process—what Beck *et al.* (1979) and others have termed the "socialization" stage. The third stage involves the application of specific cognitive and behavioral change strategies with the primary goal of helping patients change their maladaptive perceptions and ideas.

These stages, as just described, are generic stages, which probably would be utilized in the treatment of almost any clinical disorder. When compared with the course of therapy for neurotic disorders, however, significant differences arise with regard to the timing, effort, and techniques involved in consummating each stage.

THERAPY GUIDELINES

The major guideline for therapists in conducting this kind of group is to develop a sophisticated appreciation of the cognitive viewpoint (Beck, 1976) so that group phenomena and change strategies can be conceptualized in cognitive terms. It would be useful at this point to reiterate and highlight the distinctions made by Glass and Arnkoff (1981) and others between therapy process and therapy procedure. Therapy process refers to the model of change that underlies a course of therapy, while therapy procedures refer to specific techniques used to bring about change. The cognitive therapist will find this distinction particularly useful with this patient group. Given the "multimodal" nature of pathology in these patients, it is important for the therapist to delineate an internally consistent view of the therapy process. This will allow the therapist to experiment with a wide range of techniques in an orderly and coherent fashion. Perhaps more so than with other disorders, therapists must "think cognitive" and yet operate in a multimodal fashion in order to exploit opportunities for constructive change.

Another guideline in the group treatment of these patients is the desirability of multiple therapists. There are a number of reasons for this recommendation. The psychological make-up of these patients is best apprehended by both a group-process and a problem-oriented focus. Patients become more keenly aware of their distorted perceptions and unrealistic premises when they arise in the group process. When such distortions are triggered, a vigorous, directive, and often didactic approach is required to help patients disengage from, and then critically evaluate, their cognitive distortions. The use of co-therapists provides a division of therapeutic attention and labor that helps ensure that distortions are first attended to, and then challenged. In addition, given the attentional difficulties and volatile interpersonal styles of many of these patients, management of the group (e.g., gate-keeping functions, limit-setting, etc.) could overwhelm a single therapist. Finally, some of the most useful techniques, such as modeling and role playing, require the presence of at least two therapists.

The outline of treatment strategies for the cognitive group therapy of psychotics are elaborated to include: (A) the goal of the stage, (B) the guiding principles or basic schemata in the therapist's mind that guide his or her behavior, (C) process criteria—specifically, the cognitive change or shift desired in patients—that enable the therapist to judge when the stage is completed, and (D) specific techniques found useful.

The group itself consisted of 8 patients recruited from a ward for young adult chronic patients at a large public psychiatric hospital. Two therapists conducted the group. With a maximum of 8 patients at any one time, the group met once weekly for 10 months. Turnover in the group was minimal with a total of 12 patients involved during the life of the group. The therapists were supervised on a weekly basis by the director of training at the Center for Cognitive Therapy in Philadelphia.

Stage I: Involvement

The first stage of therapy aims to secure the patient's involvement in treatment. In order to underline the need for this state, I would like to portray the quality of the resistance that these patients revealed when anticipating involvement in group treatment. Comments from the first few sessions reveal concerns more intense and of a different degree than the usual neurotic fears regarding involvement in groups.

- "When I talk, I feel obsolete."
- "I can't sit in the same group with these people, since they are sinful."
- "If I reveal my problems, others will catch them."

Almost all patients indicated that they would suffer serious harm, or inflict serious harm, by becoming involved in group treatment. Such concerns include but go beyond the approval and performance anxiety preoccupations of neurotics. Concerns over fusion, disintegration of one's identity, persecution, and loss of control were aroused by the invitation to group treatment.

Given the intensity and interpersonal nature of these anxieties, the guiding principle at the outset of treatment was to create a trusting emotional climate in the group by achieving strong patient–therapist rapport. While acknowledging that the establishment of a warm and genuine patient–therapist relationship is a time-tested treatment principle applicable to almost all disorders, it is particularly salient for this patient group.

Initially, the group itself must acquire motivating properties for the patient. These patients, unlike neurotics, do not identify problems in their social lives that they feel motivated to solve. Both the primitive nature of their prominent defense mechanisms and the apathy and despair that dominate the conscious life of these patients emphasize the need to make the group experience itself gratifying. These patients seem unable to perceive a better way to live their lives. Until such hope is instilled, the group needs to be a haven of interpersonal nourishment.

Although I agree with Ellis (1959) that the realization of a warm and genuine patient–therapist relationship characterized by unconditional positive regard is not a necessary condition in working effectively with neurotics, it appears to be a necessary, although by no means sufficient, condition for change with this severely disabled group. When patients link their heightened involvement in the therapy process with their liking for the therapist, it is fair to assume that the realization of the core facilitative interpersonal conditions can ameliorate significantly the often noted motivational and attentional problems of these patients.

The cognitive shift desired in patients during this stage would be from rejection to acceptance, from "I can't tolerate this group . . . it is irrelevant . . . I don't need it" to "This is a relatively safe place where I can get help for some of my problems."

To establish rapport and secure the patient's involvement in treatment, the therapist needs to seek behaviors consonant with the core facilitative conditions of respect, genuineness, and empathy as originally highlighted by Rogers (1957). These strategies are advocated after having observed that they lead to change in the patient's cognitions of involvement in treatment and not because they represent necessary and sufficient conditions of change.

The following are some of the guidelines and specific therapist behaviors found particularly beneficial with psychotic patients.

Two guidelines are advocated in the expression of empathy at the beginning of treatment: (1) err on the side of ensuring that the patient feels understood, rather than articulating beliefs or implicit attitudes that are out of his awareness; and (2) when the therapist's comments "go beyond" what the patient is immediately expressing and experiencing, they always should be in the service of reducing, rather than increasing, the patient's anxiety.

I have found therapist self-disclosure to be a potent intervention in cutting through patient denial. Particularly when therapists reveal they have problems similar to patients' (e.g., communicating with others, feeling put down, loneliness), a very open discussion of these issues often ensues. After such a discussion it is much easier to illuminate the cognitions that contributed to the denial (e.g., "If I admit my difficulties, people will think I'm homosexual").

Therapist self-disclosure in the initial stage of treatment should convey the cognitive view, provide structure, and invite—rather than demand—participation. An illustration:

> When I'm in groups, I often get scared. I worry that I will appear foolish. If I tell people some of the things I am thinking, they may not like or respect me. I'd like to know if others have this fear also. But first, let me say I try to fight off this fear by reminding myself people are usually more understanding and sympathetic. Also, when I force myself to speak up, I often find others have similar problems and can be quite helpful to me.

Communicating understanding and tolerance for the patient's self-defeating behavior also seems to be essential for future collaboration. An immediate or zealous focus on change automatically can elicit severe resistance to, if not actual flight from, the group.

Other interviewing guidelines that would be suggested at the beginning of treatment include reinforcing reality testing; supporting ambiguous defenses of the patient; keeping comments brief and directive (avoid open-ended interpretations); and accentuating friendly nonverbal behavior, such as shaking hands.

Because psychotic patients often can bring such intense resistance to therapy, it is somewhat surprising that such patients exhibit a good deal of cognitive and behavioral change regarding their involvement in group treatment after a relatively brief period of time. After eight sessions attendance was stable. As for the patient's involvement in treatment, the following comments provide anecdotal evidence of a cognitive shift.

- "People in here don't look so mean anymore."
- "This group is like a family."
- "I wish we could meet more often."
- "You can really talk about anything in here."

What counts for such dramatic behavior change? The following quote by Beels (1980), a leading spokesman in the treatment of this patient group, captures the poignant experience of such patients at the outset of treatment and provides some understanding as to why patients can change their group behavior significantly in a brief period of time.

> In the psychotic state, and to some degree after it has subsided, a person's experience of initiative, distance and exchange has changed. Schizophrenics often feel great anxiety at the simplest initiatives. Their difficulty in carrying out greetings and negotiations with strangers is famous and the reason why evidences of thought disorder are especially present in the psychiatric interview. There is difficulty over control with social distance. Feelings of pursuit and rejection may overwhelm the patient in situations where for most of us there is merely the problem of encouraging someone or putting someone off. What is manners for us, is for him an operatic nightmare. (p. 10)

Once psychotic patients perceive the therapist as someone they can rely on to respond sensitively to and guide their awkward and anxiety-laden attempts to communicate with others, they seem willing to risk much greater involvement in the therapy process.

Stage II: Understanding

The next objective is to facilitate the patient's understanding of the cognitive therapy process and to create a working alliance focused on how problems can be solved. Again, it would be unwarranted to assume that these patients possess insight into the cognitive therapy process. Doses of time and creativity are required to impart this understanding.

Recently (Gardner, 1980; Heitler, 1976; Lorion, 1974), there has been empirical support for the unfortunate clinical observation that low-income, poor prognosis patients tend to have very little idea what psychotherapy is, how it can help them, and how they can involve themselves in the therapy process. The skills required to become meaningfully engaged in the therapy process very often are lacking. In Stage I, it was not that patients did not possess the skills to become involved in group treatment, rather that they had "negative" cognitions regarding such involvement. In this next stage, it is not that patients had negative cognitions about the therapy process, rather that they had very few cognitions at all.

In the second stage of treatment, the therapist must become much more directive and didactic. However, as he or she is trying to bring to life the cognitive viewpoint—specifically, that people create their own feelings and determine their own behavior by the way they think and perceive—he or she quickly collides with one of the cardinal features of this patient group; namely, their ingrained projective defenses. At this stage, patients acknowledge that they have serious problems in living and suffer from some searing emotional states. The cause of their suffering, however, does not reside in their maladaptive thinking but somewhere "out there," in the real or imagined environment. The notion that people can control their own destiny is a radical notion for neurotics and normals. For psychotics, it is revolutionary.

The guiding principles in the therapy during Stage II are, first, to convey the central role of thinking on the person's affect and behavior; and, second, to encourage self-attributions of internal causation. In each session, after important interchanges or role-playing exercises, care would be taken to highlight the cognitive underpinnings (e.g., "If you think _____, then you'll feel/behave _____. Whereas, if you think _____, then you'll feel/behave _____"). The cognitive shift desired in patients during this stage is from mystification (e.g., "I don't understand what therapy is") and helplessness (e.g. "He, she, it or they are causing my suffering") to understanding and control (e.g., "I can reduce my suffering and achieve my goals by changing the way I think about and interpret life experiences").

Before listing some of the specific techniques we found to be most useful in the socialization process, I would like to abstract a broad strategic principle that applies throughout the course of treatment, but which is particularly noteworthy in this stage: *Employ techniques that take into account the attentional difficulties of these patients.* Of the broad range of cognitive deficits in this patient group, the most problematic is their inability to attend, and to filter out irrelevant stimuli in their environment. It is therefore important to use strategies that capture the patient's attention and involve him or her actively. This is particularly true in the group situation where it is difficult to monitor and solicit constantly each patient's attention throughout the session.

To convey the cognitive view, one of the most helpful techniques was modeling. One teaching technique was for the therapists to plan "skits" to demonstrate the essential role of cognitions in determining one's reactions to an event. We would, for example, act out the same scene—waiting for a friend who was late—a number of times, modeling self-talk indicative of anger, self-disparagement, or indifference. After the skit, we would highlight the cognitive viewpoint by comparing various concrete reactions.

The ABC model (Ellis, 1962), because of its simplicity, proved to be an effective vehicle to teach the cognitive view. One strategy that mobilized group members' attention would involve the therapist clearly labeling the A (activating event) and C (emotional consequence) components of an emotional episode, and then asking all group members to figure out possible self-statements (B) that would have led to the emotional consequence (C).

An important objective during this stage of treatment was to help patients disengage from the self-defeating automatic perceptions and reactions that occurred in the group. Therapists would offer a model on how to disengage by constantly "collecting data" regarding how patients were reacting to one another and to the therapists and by probing for the implicit assumptions that are fueling such reactions (e.g., "Mary, you look crushed when I cut you off. What are you thinking and feeling right now?").

"Checking it out" soon became part of the group culture as indicated in the following comments by patients:

- "I'd like to know when others are reading my mind."
- "Why are people always looking at me in here?"
- "You must think I'm a sissy now that you know I was molested as a child."

After approximately 12 sessions, a majority of patients in the group were demonstrating a rudimentary understanding of the cognitive model by initiating attempts to analyze problems in terms of self-statements. I also was heartened by reports from other staff members that this behavior was generalizing beyond the cognitive therapy group.

Stage III: Cognitive Restructuring

It was at this point that I believed it was time to introduce cognitive and behavior change strategies—specifically designed to alter the maladaptive thinking of group members—with some confidence that such strategies would not be met with confusion or resistance.

The cognitive shift desired in patients during this stage is difficult to capsulize or parsimoniously summarize as I have tried to do in Stages I and II. The range of information processing distortions and of dysfunctional underlying assumptions is much greater than in other disorders. I will, however, list some of the most common information processing distortions that occurred in the group with examples of some of the basic assumptions or core beliefs that accompanied these distortions.

1. *Selective Abstraction and Arbitrary Inference.* These distortions usually occur simultaneously and refer to the process whereby the patient first focuses on a particular detail in the environment and then draws a conclusion that is unwarranted if he or she were to consider other relevant data. In depression, this type of dysfunctional thinking usually takes the form of a disparaging personalization. In the group there was a more ominous theme. Patients were vigilantly scanning the environment for "clues" to support hypotheses concerning danger and threat. A major primary assumption that fuels this style of thinking is that everything has meaning; or, specifically, that people constantly are sending messages of hatred to me.

2. *Dichotomous, That Is, All-or-None Thinking.* This refers to the tendency to think in absolute terms. This characteristic, which many contemporary theorists label "splitting," is a thinking pattern that is well ingrained with this group. It is seen vividly when patients describe themselves or significant others in their life. They frequently describe themselves and others as all good and powerful, or as all evil and utterly ineffectual. Some of the primary assumptions that underlie this thinking pattern include: If part of me is bad, all of me is bad; and, If you do not love me, you hate me.

3. *Magnification, That Is, Catastrophizing.* This refers to the tendencies to exaggerate or overestimate the meaning of a particular event, or its future negative consequences. This cognitive predisposition represents one of the most devastating components of schizophrenic illness. This pattern frequently is elicited when such patients make tentative steps to face themselves and their limitations more realistically, or when they begin to take some initiative in overcoming their withdrawal tendencies. Such steps take on what appears to be a life and death struggle. The predominant underlying assumption accompanying the cata-

strophizing response is: Psychological and behavioral risk taking results in annihilation.

4. *Faulty Attribution.* This is the process whereby the patient severely underestimates or overestimates the extent to which he can control his or her behavior, the behavior of others, and events in the world. The basic assumptions here seem to be: I have no control over my thoughts, feelings, or behavior. Voices, demons, and so forth have control. If I wish something, it will happen.

Because the pathology in the new chronic patient is so severe and in some respects intractable, it is essential for the cognitive therapist to develop a realistic framework to gauge change. It quickly was discovered that certain constraints and qualifications had to be added to those cognitive change principles proven effective with other patient groups. These qualifications can be translated into the following strategic principle: *The focus of cognitive restructuring strategies should not be on the central characteristics of the patient's thought disorder.*

This principle dictates trying to avoid interactions that require the patient to overcome some of the cardinal features of his or her disability. Thus, strategies that are contingent upon the patient's ability to introspect, to make subtle semantic distinctions, to employ an empirical problem-solving style, to generate and sustain a continuous cognitive horizon of alternative hypotheses, or to dispassionately challenge delusional thinking are unlikely to succeed. It is unclear at the present time whether such deficits are absolutely refractory to change or whether they might be ameliorated in a later stage of treatment. It is evident that socialization to the cognitive therapy model itself is not sufficient to produce change in these areas.

One implication of this viewpoint is to focus on the patient's distortion of events and interactions rather than upon his underlying beliefs and premises. Given the very real impoverished existence of most of these patients, the more "elegant" cognitive therapy goal of getting the patient to challenge irrational premises regarding personal worth or achievement is unrealistic. Distinctions between "awful" as opposed to "quite frustrating" circumstances have little meaning for this group. What does appear to have a great deal of meaning is to demonstrate that, although mired in a truly sorry state of affairs, they do distort events in a way that reinforces their avoidance tendencies and sense of worthlessness.

Once patients in the group reduced their reliance on the defenses of denial and projection, they revealed that they rather consistently overreacted to interpersonal stimuli in a negative fashion. Things really are not as miserable or threatening as they construe them. Thus, a good deal of time is spent helping patients discriminate between what Walen, DiGiuseppe, and Wessler (1980) have termed "confirmable" reality and "perceived" (i.e., distorted) reality. The following examples illustrate this point.

KATHY: When you said patients on the ward bothered you, I guess you meant me.
ROBERT: No, not you Kathy, I was talking about . . .
KATHY: That's a relief.
THERAPIST: Kathy, I notice when someone mentions something negative, you often assume you're to blame.

CHARLES: I stopped the conversation because I knew Deloris was bored with me and didn't want to talk.
THERAPIST: Is that true?
DELORIS: Not really. I was preoccupied with something else . . . I sort of wish we had talked longer.
THERAPIST: Charles, when a conversation doesn't go well you assume it's because there's something wrong with you and you end it.

The above examples reflect how these patients have deep-rooted premises that greatly contribute to their avoidance of others. The desired outcome of such interventions is slowing down the patient's automatic responses to interpersonal stimuli and introducing into their consciousness alternative, more realistic ways of interpreting events.

Another effective intervention during this stage was stress innoculation training (Meichenbaum, 1977), using modeling and role playing as a teaching medium. First, therapists would articulate some of the distortions and irrational assumptions triggered when faced with a stressful encounter (e.g., approaching someone to initiate a conversation). Therapists would then model coping self-statements before, during, and after the encounter. Patients were then asked to role play the same social situations using the coping self-statements.

The strategic principle applies to delusional thinking. Our attempts to encourage patients to re-evaluate aspects of their delusional system typically result in increased guardedness. Jacobs (1980) recently has introduced the distinction between thinking and knowing. Thinking is characterized as an endless dialogue we constantly carry on with ourselves in solitude. Thinking is governed by reason. Knowing, on the other hand, is more of an awareness of truths, such as knowing one is a man or woman. Jacobs contends that knowing cannot be directly altered by thinking or metathinking (i.e., thinking about thinking). It is likewise our clinical experience that delusional thinking, particularly grandiose delusions of the self, are never fully surrendered. The patient's delusional interpretations of self and others often recede when the patient is functioning well. However, they typically re-emerge when the patient is under stress.

The implication of this view for the cognitive therapist is that waging a frontal cognitive assault on what appears to be a chronic—if fluctuating—intrinsic impairment is unlikely to succeed. When delusional material is presented attempts are made to translate it into consensually validated interpersonal or intrapersonal concerns (e.g., "Sam, it seems like you can't accept yourself as someone who gets angry." rather than "Sam, what evidence do you have that a demon is possessing you?").

CONCLUSION

A stage theory of group cognitive therapy with the young adult chronic patient has been presented. I am very encouraged regarding the potential of group cognitive therapy with this patient group. With it, cognitive therapy appears to possess a number of advantages over traditional psychotherapy.

1. Because cognitive therapy emanates from a clearcut theory of human functioning and behavior change, and offers specific strategies for change, a greater isomorphism between psychotherapy process and procedure is achieved. Conceptualizing severe psychopathology in cognitive terms—specifically, detailing information processing distortions and concomitant underlying assumptions—allows for a more precise and operational definition of such pathology. This results in enhanced clarity and concreteness in the actual practice· of cognitive therapy, which are essential dimensions in the treatment of this patient group. Payoffs include not only more vivid learning experiences in therapy, but also laying the groundwork for the application of skills learned in therapy without the guidance of therapist.

2. Cognitive therapy has the technical advantage of flexibility as well as precision. Given the extreme variability of the symptom picture, and cognitive and behavioral deficits of the young chronic patient, it is noteworthy that cognitive therapy passes the test of utility in that it can be applied by people in the field working with this patient population. It thus avoids the pitfalls of methodologically sound, but to date clinically irrelevant, discrete social skills approaches (Wallace, Nelson, & Liberman, 1979) and the documented (Mosher & Keith, 1980) inadequacy of traditional therapy approaches.

3. The structure of cognitive therapy—specifically, the emphasis on collaboration and on the powerful role of cognitions in influencing be-

havior—is an antidote to two of the most problematic features of this patient group: their lack of self-reliance and their tendency to disown and project responsibility for their behavior. Cognitive therapy stands in stark contrast to analytic and object–relations approaches which, because of their conceptual ambiguity and emphasis on transference, appear to exacerbate these tendencies. Unlike these approaches, the cognitive view does not hold that ingrained ways of thinking and perceiving will whither away as the vicissitudes of the patient–therapist relationship are worked out. Rather, an active and directive approach that provides repeated learning experiences to supplant distorted thinking and perceiving—the hallmark of cognitive therapy—is deemed necessary to produce change in this patient group.

It also is hypothesized that group treatment holds unique advantages for this patient group.

4. Some of the basic dysfunctional assumptions of this patient group are so powerful that it may not be possible to dispute them without the immediate raw data provided by the group interaction as disconfirming evidence. Psychotic patients are not aware of believing they are fused, persecuted, and so forth. Rather, they experience these states directly and acutely with others. It is necessary to create some uncertainty in the experiencing of these feelings and perceptions before illuminating the dysfunctional underlying assumptions.

5. There is mounting evidence (e.g., Brown, Birley, & Wing, 1972; Leff, Hirsh, & Gaind, 1973) that the most potent triggers to psychotic behavior are interpersonal. It is possible that the most effective learning, and best opportunities to modify perceptions and maladaptive assumptions, can take place in the emotionally charged atmosphere built into the group treatment format. Learning experiences can be linked to one of the most crippling handicaps of this patient group; namely, their difficulty in forming interpersonal relationships.

SUMMARY

The purpose of this chapter was to report on the application of a group cognitive therapy approach with the young adult chronic patient. Given the (impoverished) state of the psychotherapy art with this patient group, the intention was to experiment with a range of cognitive therapy strategies and then observe the results. In that spirit, this chapter focused on modifications in the cognitive therapy approach found useful with this patient group. Observations were presented in the context of a stage theory that emphasized the need to secure the patient's involvement with, and socialization to, the treatment process. It is our hope that the speculative clinical observations presented will motivate others to attempt more rigorous study of the application of cognitive therapy to this difficult patient group.

Acknowledgments

The author is grateful to Arthur Freeman, director of training at the Center for Cognitive Therapy in Philadelphia, for his support and helpful discussion of some of the issues raised in this manuscript.

References

Anthony, W. A. *A client outcome planning model for assessing psychiatric rehabilitation interventions.* Working paper for NIMH-sponsored conference on Outcome Research with the Severely Mentally Disabled, Portsmouth, N.H., 1980.

Beck, A. T. *Cognitive therapy and the emotional disorders.* New York: International Universities Press, 1976.

Beck, A. T., Rush, A. J., Shaw, B. F., & Emery, G. *Cognitive therapy of depression: A treatment manual.* New York: Guilford, 1979.

Beels, C. *The measurement of social support in schizophrenia.* Unpublished manuscript, Columbia University, 1980.

Brown, G., Birley, J. L., & Wing, J. K. Influence of family life on the course of schizophrenia. *British Journal of Psychiatry,* 1972, *121,* 241–258.

Ellis, A. Requisite conditions for basic personality change. *Journal of Consulting Psychology,* 1959, *23,* 538–540.

Ellis, A. *Reason and emotion in psychotherapy.* New York: Lyle Stuart, 1962.

Emery, G., Hollon, S. D., & Bedrosian, R. D. *New directions in cognitive therapy—A casebook,* New York: Guilford, 1981.

Gardner, L. H. Racial, ethnic and social class considerations in psychotherapy supervision. In A. K. Hess (Ed.), *Psychotherapy supervision: Theory, research and practice.* New York: Wiley, 1980.

Glass, C. R. & Arnkoff, D. B. Thinking it through: Selected issues in cognitive assessment and therapy. In P. C. Kendall (Ed.), *Advances in cognitive–behavioral research and therapy* (Vol. 1). New York: Academic, 1981.

Heitler, J. B. Preparatory techniques in initiating expressive psychotherapy with lower-class, unsophisticated patients. *Psychological Bulletin, 1976, 83,* 339–352.

Jacobs, L. I. A cognitive approach to persistent delusions. *American Journal of Psychotherapy,* 1980, *4,* 556–563.

Leff, J. P., Hirsh, S. R., & Gaind. Life events and maintenance therapy in schizophrenic relapse. *British Journal of Psychiatry,* 1973, *123,* 659–660.

Lorion, R. P. Patients and therapist variables in the treatment of low-income patients. *Psychological Bulletin, 1974, 81,* 334–354.

Meichenbaum, D. *Cognitive-behavior modification: An integrative approach.* New York: Plenum, 1977.

Mosher, L. R., & Keith, S. J. Psychosocial treatment: Individual, group, family and community support approaches. *Schizophrenia Bulletin,* 1980, *6,* 10–43.

Pepper, B., Kirshner, M. C., & Ryglewicz, H. The young adult chronic patient: Overview of a population. *Hospital and Community Psychiatry*, 1981, *32*, 463–469.

Rogers, C. R. The necessary and sufficient conditions of therapeutic personality change. *Journal of Consulting Psychology*, 1957, *21*, 459–461.

Schwartz, S. R., & Goldfinger, S. M. The new chronic patient: Clinical characteristics of an emerging subgroup. *Hospital and Community Psychiatry*, 1981, *32*, 470–474.

Walen, S. R., DiGiuseppe, R., & Wessler, R. L. *A practitioner's guide to rational–emotive therapy*. New York: Oxford University Press, 1980.

Wallace, C. J., Nelson, C. J., & Liberman, R. P. A review and critique of social skills training with schizophrenic patients. *Schizophrenia Bulletin*, 1979, *5*, 88–121.

10

Cognitive-Behavioral Treatment of Agoraphobia in Groups

Susan Jasin

Introduction

Although agoraphobia has often been viewed as a learned disorder, no author to date has emphasized the cognitive components nor suggested treatment that is both behavioral and cognitive.

Behavioral explanations of agoraphobia have been offered by a number of leading theorists (Lazarus, 1966; Wolpe, 1970). Undoubtedly the most adequate learning formulation was developed by Goldstein and Chambless (1978). Their landmark article "Reanalysis of Agoraphobia" describes the core learned feature of agoraphobia as "fear of fear" and suggests three other defining features: (1) onset during interpersonal conflict; (2) low self sufficiency and assertiveness; and (3) hysterical response style. Their explanation is most adequate from a behavioral perspective and can be enhanced by greater attention to cognitive factors.

Goldstein and Chambless (1978) contend that agoraphobics experience initial anxiety attacks in the context of interpersonal conflict, rather than from clear-cut conditioning events like an auto accident or entrapment in an elevator.[1] This conflict model suggests that clients' am-

---

[1]Pseudoagoraphobics present much like agoraphobics in that they avoid a number of public places and/or are reluctant to venture far away from a safe person or zone. The reasons for their restriction, however, do not involve fear of fear and may be related to one of the following: (1) Traumatic experiences like rape that can create conditional and generalized anxiety about travel beyond a safe zone; (2) social phobia with anxiety about social consequences like criticism or scrutiny; (3) severe depression; (4) paranoia; (5) borderline personality disorder.

Susan Jasin • California School of Professional Psychology, 3974 Sorrento Valley Boulevard, San Diego, California 92121.

bivalence about experiencing grief, addressing marital dissatisfaction, resolving developmentally inappropriate dependence, or expressing anger generates physical sensations like heart palpitations, dizziness, shortness of breath, tingling in limbs, nausea, and the like. Because agoraphobics hold what Goldstein (Goldstein & Chambless, 1978) calls a "hysterical response style" they fail to connect these physical anxiety sensations to their environmental ancedents and worry instead that symptoms will lead to some catastrophic consequence like heart attack, passing out, or insanity. This fear of bodily sensations or fear of fear is negatively reinforced each time an agoraphobic either avoids or flees from a situation while experiencing an attack. In addition this fear quickly generalizes, promoting progressively greater and greater travel restrictions. Free-floating anxiety ensues as agoraphobics develop conditioned anxiety to their own body sensations and anticipate the possibility of additional attack. Furthermore, Goldstein and Chambless (1978) have documented that lack of adequate assertive skills, a behavioral deficit, that correlates with agoraphobia and is a significant descriptive factor. The implication is that people who are unassertive and lack self-management skills are more likely to have difficulty resolving conflicts and will be more anxious.[2] Thus the Goldstein and Chambless model refers to the major learning theory components of agoraphobia but does not emphasize cognitive deficits and distortions. The Goldstein and Chambless explanation rests heavily on the occurence of anxiety attacks, negative reinforcement of avoidance and generalization of effect.

However, observation indicates that something beyond anxiety attacks must lead to agoraphobia. Many people who have anxiety attacks and the opportunity to develop fear of fear do not become agoraphobic. In order to fully understand the disorder, it would be helpful to know what makes agoraphobics different from normals. This author believes that the functional difference lies in agoraphobics rather unique cognitive deficits and distortions. Goldstein and Chambless (1978) allude to this, in part, when they mention "hysterical response style." *Hysterical*

---

[2]A smaller but still important group have been called simple agoraphobics since interpersonal conflict, low self-sufficiency, lack of assertiveness, and a hysterical response style are not part of their makeup and/or are not involved in the development of their symptoms. The simple agoraphobic's early attacks were biochemically induced as a function of anesthesia, hypoglycemia, street drugs, or post-operative reactions to medication. They experience fear of fear and need to be flooded, but exploration of dynamics and modification of characteristic coping patterns is unnecessary. For these clients, travel group alone will be sufficient. However, the vast majority of agoraphobics need to challenge their dysfunctional thinking, improve the ability to label and express feelings, and learn to deal more effectively with life conflicts and stresses. The purpose of the psychotherapy group is to learn those skills.

response style, the cognitive precursor to fear of fear, has been defined as failure to connect anxiety to its true antecedents or misapprehending the true antecedents of one's anxiety. Validating hysterical response style has presented an interesting measurement problem. Using the Minnesota Multiphasic Personality Inventory (MMPI), Jasin (1981) found elevations (group mean above 70) on the Hysteria scale for agoraphobic males and females but since this trait has multiple descriptors it is not clear that the elevations obtained truly reflect the intended cognitive response. Clinical observations in hundreds of agoraphobics, however, bear out the existence of a gap or error in the agoraphobic perceptual system.

Nonagoraphobic clients usually respond to attacks by thinking "What's going on to produce these symptoms?" That is, what are the antecedents to distress. When antecedent conditions are identified, problem solving ensues and conflicts are resolved, anger is expressed, and so on. In contrast, agoraphobics having both poor insight, low assertiveness and weak problem solving skills, and are obsessive about the consequences of their discomfort. Since agoraphobics generally have few appropriate responses they can make, it is not surprising that they respond in a self-defeating way. Perhaps as much by default as anything else they distort the meaning of their distress and fallaciously conclude that some dire consequence is encroaching. Clinical interviews reveal that those who are obsessive about heart attack often have a relative or friend who has suffered from the condition. Ruminating about insanity has frequently been preceded by a model who has been hospitalized for an emotional disorder or a breakdown. Taken together the agoraphobics' perceptual deficits about antecedents and cognitive distortions about consequences distinguish them from others who have anxiety attacks. These cognitive factors seem critical to the development of the disorder (see Figure 1).

Considering the interplay of cognitive, behavioral, and environmental factors discussed, a multifaceted treatment approach is recommended. In order to attain lasting improvement, treatment must attend to both the symptoms (anxiety attacks and avoidance) and the underlying causes of agoraphobia including content issues (grief, marital dynamics, etc.) as well as intrapersonal issues like low assertiveness, problem solving, and misperceptions. The two-stage treatment program developed at Temple Medical School attends to these factors and has been shown to be a highly preferred and desirable model. This chapter excludes reference to the content issues mentioned earlier and focuses on the development of a group model for the treatment of the symptoms of agoraphobia and intrapersonal processes as they have been previously defined.

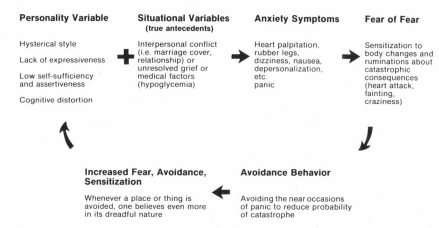

FIGURE 1. Agoraphobic cycle.

Many authors have espoused the psychological advantages of group treatment. Yalom (1975) has listed 10 curative factors offered by group psychotherapy. Of particular interest to agoraphobics are *universality* and *cohesiveness*. Almost by definition agoraphobia insures emotional and social isolation and depression. Phobic anxiety and travel restrictions often prevent what seems to be the simpler kinds of duties— grocery shopping, PTA meetings, making deposits at the bank, and so on. As a result, agoraphobics often feel incompetent and worthless. Lack of sympathy from friends and relatives, who cannot possibly understand or make sense of the agoraphobics difficulties reinforces further the agoraphobics' isolation and self-downing cognitions. In addition, agoraphobics are often connected only by their auditory umbilical cord to neighbors and acquaintances and the telephone is no substitute for physical contact and human warmth. Moving from this isolation into a group of fellow sufferers and therapists who are understanding and accepting can be a joyous experience. Another advantage to group treatment is simply financial. From a practical standpoint, a group format can be offered more inexpensively hour per hour than individual treatment. Hopefully, this savings allows more clients to be treated and facilitates both stages of a multifaceted treatment (referred to earlier).

TRAVEL GROUP: RATIONALE, METHODOLOGY AND PURPOSE

In the beginning stages of treatment each client is assigned to a travel group. This group is basically an *in vivo* flooding group. It is important to pause and reflect upon the choice of *in vivo* flooding over *in vitro* flooding or desensitization. Several considerations may be reviewed in order to understand this decision. Although desensitization has been used for years in the treatment of agoraphobia (Wolpe, 1970), it has been remarkably ineffective for several reasons. First, the hierarchy of phobic stimuli used in the procedure has been composed of places where the client is likely to be anxious. According to the previous analysis, the primary phobic cues are interoceptive. Agoraphobics are most afraid, not of planes and lines, but the internal sensations of anxiety that occur in such places and are imagined to lead to catastrophic consequences. If desensitization were used, the appropriate hierarchy would be made up of physiological sensations and imagined catastrophic consequences not of freeways, department stores, auditoriums and so forth. A second consideration is that even if the hierarchy were based on an adequate behavioral analysis, agoraphobics are not easily trained to relax. Because of their cognitive distortions most are so concerned about losing control that relaxation (either deep muscle or chemically-induced) becomes aversive rather than comfortable and is blocked at its earliest stages. Third, the method of desensitization (approach the phobic situation bit by bit and back off and relax whenever discomfort arises) reinforces the misbelief that unpleasant physiological sensations are bad or dangerous and should be avoided. Quite to the contrary, clients would benefit from learning that anxiety is an important and helpful signal (feedback from the body) that something is distressing and in need of attention. Densensitization is incompatible with that very important message and is therefore contraindicative. Flooding, on the other hand, can be directed at fear of fear (rather than the bogus hierarchy of places) and shows excellent and predictably rapid results. In addition, recent literature helps substantiate the notion that interventions directed at the phobia as it exists in its natural context, that is "contextual therapy," are superior in speed and generalizability to imaginal procedures (Rachman, 1978). In light of these considerations *in vivo* over imaginal procedures and flooding over desensitization has been selected.

Flooding calls for prolonged exposure to moderate or intense anxiety-provoking stimuli. To accomplish this result, travel group clients visit sites that allow them to experience internal sensations producing moderate to intense anxiety. Clients remain in these places and focus on the phobic stimuli that lie within them until habituation occurs. When this procedure is repeated over and over, agoraphobics learn that anxiety does not drive them out of control and their inaccurate cognitions change. They realize that at worst they will feel uncomfortable. When these corrected perceptions are obtained, fear of fear diminishes, conditioned anxiety to places diminishes, sensitization levels go down, and frequency of panic attacks drop. It is at this point that the therapist may best begin a new series of interventions aimed at identifying and dealing with the true antecedents or underlying causes of anxiety. This constitutes the second level of treatment. In sum, providing re-educative experience promotes more reality-based cognitions and diminishes anxiety and avoidance. These cognitive and behavioral changes peel away the outer layers of the agoraphobic onion and allow access to the underlying causes.

The Travel Group

The size of the travel group may vary, but a range of 3 to 7 persons with one leader and one or more helpers has consistently proven to be quiet manageable and cost effective. Given the nature of the procedures and resultant distress experienced by the client, it is advisable to have a ratio of no more than 3 clients to 1 therapist or helper.

Groups may be homogeneous or heterogeneous; however, it may be most effective to cluster clients who share similar educational and socioeconomic backgrounds rather than those who are at a similar stage of recovery. "Seeding" the group with more advanced clients provides beginners in treatment a coping model as well as a source of inspiration.

The helpers provided are trained members of the staff and may be either psychological or psychiatric interns or former agoraphobics who have completed treatment. Helpers without either of these two backgrounds often are not well received, as clients perceive them as not understanding. Perhaps because they have "been there" former clients, who have been trained adequately, seem to be the most trusted and most engaging therapeutic assistants. The preparation they are given consits of: (1) their own experience and recovery; (2) a thorough technical orientation to the two levels of the program; (3) a series of helper workshops where the helpers role play the therapist; and (4) several months of apprenticeship with experienced leaders in a number of different groups. In this apprenticeship period, the helpers practice coaching clients in the use of coping strategies and gather on-the-spot feedback and supervision from the group leader. Although it is tempting to assign paraprofessionals or newly recovered clients directly to the role of helper, this procedure can and often does lead to bewilderment, distress and, at best, retarded progress for the client.

Frequency and Duration of Groups

Several options exist for scheduling travel groups. Massed practice alone (e.g., a two-week intensive program) produces rapid, visible progress that may both generalize poorly to the clients' home setting and lack durability over time. Spaced practice alone (e.g. weekly sessions) generally yields less dramatic improvement and less motivation for continuation. In its favor, spaced practice produces more durable change and generalizability of results when the time between sessions is used to complete travel homework assignments. A combination of massed and spaced sessions may be the best format. A two-week daily program followed up by weekly meetings allows the client "to get off to a flying start" by seeing immediate and dramatic improvements and also promoting permanent change by incorporating coping strategies and exposure methods into the client's daily routine.

In addition to the spacing of sessions, decisions must be made as to the length of each session. Following the guidelines for flooding, a group meeting must be long enough to provide a minimum of 1½ hours of exposure to the phobic stimuli so that habituation can occur (Levis, 1980). Since the structure of the group (see "Structure and Format" section) includes homework review as well as post-exposure processing, a minimum of three hours is recommended. Shorter groups are markedly less effective and longer groups show increased habituation that seems to reach the point of diminishing returns after six hours.

Structure and Format

Prior to the first group meeting, it is desirable, though not necessary, for the client to meet individually once or twice with her[3] primary therapist. During that time the therapist can begin to establish rapport and build trust while getting a full account of the client's symptoms and fears. Initially, the use of the Severity of Agoraphobic Scale can provide a measure of agoraphobic avoidance (Chambless, Caputo, & Jasin, 1982). Once a description of the presenting complaint has been obtained, short and long-term goals may be set and the initial *in vivo* training can begin. (It is also worth noting that the Severity of Agoraphobic Scale can be used post-treatment in order to verify results.)

After this pretraining and during the first group meeting, an hour is spent on introductions. Each client tells her story—how the symptoms began and developed, and what her limitations and fears are at the present. In the second hour, the primary therapist gives a non-technical explanation of the development and maintenance of agoraphobia. Since most clients and their families view agoraphobic behavior as sick, weak,

---

[3]Feminine pronouns are used when referring to the agoraphobic client (1) for simplicity; and (2) at present approximately 80% of agoraphobic clients reporting for treatment are female. As sex-role persecutions relax more male agoraphobics will probably report for treatment.

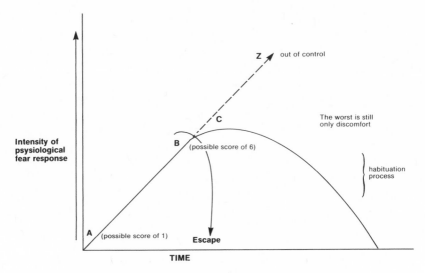

FIGURE 2. Panic/anxiety attacks: habituation versus escape.

or at best stupid, it is important to correct these inaccurate perceptions immediately. Such judgmental explanations of agoraphobia only reduce further the self-esteem, perceived self-efficacy, and motivation of the already depressed and fearful agoraphobic. In place of a pathology model, a behavioral anlaysis is given. Emphasis is placed upon the accidental nature of the cognitive and behavioral learnings that have led the client to her present set of maladaptive thoughts and habits. Reference is made to cognitive and behavioral deficits as predisposing factors, classical conditioning of anxiety to neutral places, adventitious reinforcement of avoidance behavior and so on. These explanations lack the judgmental quality of the pathology model and help the client to begin to gather some vestige of self-esteem. In addition, a cognitive-behavioral orientation allows the client to modify her thoughts about treatment—to see it as straightforward retraining rather than the mysterious task of "sanitizing one's psyche."

After the first wave of questions have been answered, the leader introduces the rationale and the design of the flooding model as well as the need for cognitive coping strategies to promote habituation. Figure 2 depicting panic–anxiety attacks may be helpful in explaining the importance of habituation versus escape. An explanation such as the following may be given to the group concerning Figure 2.

> At Point A, you begin to experience the first signs of mounting anxiety, perhaps tingling in the arms and legs, and nausea. As time passes, the level

of distress increases and at Point B you feel heart palpitations, dizziness, sweating, shaking, and "jelly legs." Uncomfortable and frightened, you think about how your sensations will continue to worsen until you go completely out of control. You worry that your distress will escalate and you picture yourself losing control, having a heart attack, or passing out. As a result of this catastrophic thinking and imagery, you terminate the upward spiral of anxiety, at first by distraction and finally by escape. Your flight is negatively reinforced because it stops your discomfort. You learn to escape and eventually avoid simply because it feels better than suffering discomfort, terror, and the chance to go crazy, faint, or die. At the same time you learn to be anxious and run more and more frequently. You also learn to fear the place where you have had the attack. This place becomes frightening because of its association with past attacks and just being there in the future will be enough to bring on another one. What you need to learn instead is that your attacks can go to a peak of panic and great discomfort (see Point C) *but no further*. Unless you persist in picturing yourself dying or going out of control, once your anxiety reaches its peak your body's natural adaptation will take over and you will begin to feel better. As time passes you will adapt more and more and feel progressively less anxious and more comfortable. After some time the attack will end all by itself. I know you don't believe me. That's okay. I'm not asking you to. You need to know, not because I have told you, but from experience, that the *worst is still only discomfort*. The only way to know and trust the safety of adaptation is to block avoidance and escape and to experience a full panic attack again and again until you can believe for yourself that you won't go crazy.

This rationale for flooding is made available to the client in the first group meeting, as well as on subsequent occasions.

In the second group meeting, the client is acquainted with a coping technique that will help her manage anxiety both during flooding sessions and on her own. This method if called *focusing* and it is explained, role played, and practiced in a short *in vivo* exposure module. Although only one of several strategies, focusing, like other strategies, keeps the agoraphobic exposed to the fearful internal sensations so that over time, fear of fear dissipates. Although simple in essence, many clients new to treatment are so afraid of their symptoms that they cannot identify or describe them. Many others are so fearful that they cannot bear to experience their symptoms for more than a few seconds before some form of distraction like talking, singing, smoking, or ruminating takes over. The first coping technique is simple to "be inside your body" for as long as you can stand it while focusing on all unpleasant sensations, describing them verbally to the coach.

The therapist may first model focusing, then ask the client to reenact a typical attack. The therapist or coach sets the stage (department store, checkout line, etc.) than asks the client to begin describing out loud the body sensations that would be likely to occur. As the role play begins, she is asked to "go through her body" reporting all current symptoms. She is first asked to focus on how her head feels. Does she have blurred vision, headache or pressure, dizziness, depersonalization, dry mouth, a lump in the throat, or some other form of discomfort? Reports such as, "I feel like I'm going to choke" or "I know that I am going to pass out" are future-oriented and catastrophic. When such a remark is made, the client is asked, "How does it feel right now? Please describe the lump in your throat. What are the exact dimensions? Describe the dizziness. Does your head feel like it's spinning or floating?" Next she is asked to move her attention down her body, reporting anything out of the ordinary such as chest pressure, heaviness, hollowness, palpitations, tachycardia, knotted or fluttery stomach, nausea, blood racing or curdling. Again, futuristic catastrophic statements like "What if I suffocate?" or "What if I have a stroke?" must be modified immediately by asking "Please, what are you feeling right now." A client who is allowed to continue catastrophizing will have a virtually impossible time habituating. Catastrophizing feeds anxiety—not just for agoraphobics—but for all of us. A later section reports other more confrontive strategies for anxiety reduction. In the beginning of treatment, however, simply focusing on immediate body sensations will begin to decondition the agoraphobic's fear of fear.

After the client role plays "going through her body," she is asked to pick only one symptom, the most frightening, and stay focused on it, describing it aloud if necessary, until her fear of it or the sensation itself subsides. Optimally, she stays focused on the experience until it is no longer frightening and then continues to focus until the experience goes beyond extinction to boredom. Often as one's body sensation diminishes another will peak, causing the agoraphobic renewed distress. Again, she is asked to simply stay with it. Although distractions and obsessions will automatically recur, the skilled coach repeatedly refocuses the client on current sensations. This method not only hastens habituation and extinction of fear of fear, but also gives the client a task or strategy to combat helplessness. It provides a semblance of control much like pointing in the direction that the traffic is moving while at the same time commanding "Go that way!"

In order to offset the discomfort of focusing, a self-support method called *grounding* is also taught. This Gestalt technique involves attending to non-phobic immediate stimuli, both outside and inside the client's body, especially those that promote the feeling of stability and connectedness. For example, the agoraphobic can begin by describing her exact location. "Right now I am halfway up the bridge on Route 42 headed toward Center City. I see the car lights coming toward me. I am aware of the Schlitz sign to my right and the field to my left. The sky is clear and there are stars overhead. The traffic is light and mostly in the opposite direction." Next the client describes and feels the supports within and against her body. "I feel my buttocks and back pressing against the car seat. The seat feels solid and a little lumpy and I also feel my hands wrapped around the steering wheel. It is cool and has ridges. I am aware of my own backbone as well and that it is supporting my trunk. It feels solid even though I am trembling." Grounding alternates with focusing so that in this example the client will again describe internal phobic stimuli saying "I am aware of the shaking in my arms and legs, my heart is racing. I can feel sweat under my arms and on my palms. My legs are weak and rubbery." These two descriptions lock the client into the present, insure contact with the true phobic stimuli (internal sensations), and provide appropriate counter-conditioning agents. Though simple, grounding and focusing are incredibly effective.

After several role plays, a short trip outside the group room is made to do some real focusing and grounding. Guided individually by therapists or helpers, each agoraphobic practices focusing in a minimally threatening situation, perhaps walking a block from the building, climbing the stairs, or taking short elevator trips, and grounding to the supports in that environment. At this time, as always, success is defined as having symptoms and practicing effective coping. Clients are told that once they master these techniques they will be able to travel freely, though not necessarily comfortably. They also know that ultimately the elimination of their excessive symptomology can be accomplished only when the underlying reasons for their anxiety have been identified and eliminated.

Once focusing and grounding have been mastered and in the succeeding sessions, clients learn important cognitive strategies to diminish catastrophizing and further reduce anxiety. Among these are *echoing* or repeating a catastrophic self-statement. Catastrophic thinking includes statements such as "What if *this* time I really flip out?" "What if I pass out and no one cares for me?" "What if my heart can't take the strain and I have a heart attack?" Several steps are used to attack this kind of maladaptive thinking. First, the client is encouraged to pay attention to her futuristic, horrific thoughts and their subsequent effects. To facilitate the process, the agoraphobic may be asked to think out loud, having her coach identify the maladaptive self-sentences. Then she may be asked to repeat each one five times, noting how her anxiety level varies as a result. It soon becomes clear that this thinking is hurtful because it intensifies her anxiety, gets her out of the "here and now," slows habituation, and thrusts her into future traumas she cannot possibly deal with in the present. Since each of us can only deal with what is presently happening, catastrophizing makes an agoraphobic virtually powerless and defenseless. It is suggested that if an individual can deal with what is here now and now and now and now, the future will be handled.

After recognizing that catastrophizing is a foundation for increased anxiety and ultimate failure, the client tries out active ways to challenge it. They include first of all questioning the data and rational self-dialogue (Beck, 1979). Examples of this include:

> I know it feels like I can't get enough air, but I'm really just hyperventilating.

> Although it feels like I am going crazy I have felt this way before and I have not been locked up yet.

> I know it feels like I am going to have a heart attack, but the doctor says my heart is fine and that I am in no danger when I get palpitations.

A second cognitive technique is verbal or visual thought stopping—interrupting catastrophisizing by thinking the word "stop", then snapping a rubber band around the wrist to eliminate destructive self-talk. Other clients visually empty their head of thoughts by putting them in a "mental garbage can". Third, the self instructional procedures suggested by Meichenbaum can be adapted (Meichenbaum, 1977). Clients are encouraged to develop and test coping statements that are self-instructional in nature. Figure 3 portrays a list developed by one such client.[4] It is important to insure that clients do not use these cognitive strategies as avoidance but rather interpose them with focusing on their internal phobia stimuli. Last of all *paradoxical intention* is an advanced cognitive strategy that may be taught after four or more flooding sessions to those who are particularly courageous and/or have a good sense of humor. Specifically, the client is asked to make the most frightening symptom worse, not by catastrophizing, but by focusing on it and talking to it. "OK heart, let's go, beat faster! Come on pop out of my chest, faster, faster! I dare you. Let's go over the top. Give me your worst! Come on, pass out! Let's go. Get dizzier. Head be a balloon. Float to the ceiling." The impact of this cognitive strategy is enormous as it displaces the catastrophizing with a kind of bravado that is not only functional but also amusing—and who can forget what an effective counter conditioning agent humor is! After a full description of these procedures is made and questions have been answered, clients rehearse by working in dyads, each playing the role of both client and coach. Therapists circu-

---

[4]A special thanks to Carmen G. for allowing publication of her personal list.

Stay with the feeling—don't fight it.
The worst that could happen is discomfort.
I've lived through this before and I'll make it this time.
It only *feels* threatening.
It *will* pass.
The best thing that can happen is when it's over I won't be as afraid of it next time!
I only *feel* out of control:
    Than a positive—I'm driving OK. I'm walking OK
By letting go I am in control.
I may feel out of control, but I'm in control.
The way to get out of this is to go thru it.
I am not going to die.
I have done this before and I'm going to do it again and nothing bad will happen.
The worst thing that can happen is I'll panic (and that hasn't hurt me yet).
The best thing that can happen is that I'll be one step closer to recovery.
I *will* make it home. I've always made it home.
I can do this and I will do this because I want to do this.
If I have to feel high symptoms to get better, I will.
Feeling the symptoms is good—it means I am working toward recovery.
I'll never get better if I keep running from the symptoms.
I am getting better.
I am a brave, hard working person and I'm proud of me.

FIGURE 3. Cognitive coping strategies designed by agoraphobics.

late among the dyads giving feedback and reinforcement and standing in as coach or client whenever necessary.

In the second half of the practice session, the group once again visits minimally distressing locations and practices using coping strategies *in vivo*. Upon the return to the therapy room, each client has an opportunity to "process" what has happened—to review her experience while traveling. This processing module is exceptionally important as it allows clients to clarify what worked for them and what did not. In the midst of a panic attack it is difficult, if not impossible, to get a sense of what is going on. Processing afterward affords the opportunity to step back and sort out what has gone on and also reinforces the pattern of planned strategies for dealing with panic rather than blind flight. Recall as well, that the definition for success has changed from comfort and skillful avoidance to coping effectively with symptoms. This too, is a cognitive shift of prime importance as it activates avoiders, turning them into seekers.

The last work in the group meeting involves each client, with the help of the leader, planning homework to consolidate gains. Homework may consist of repeating the same travel task without the support of a therapist. Another support person may be used or the client may make an attempt to go it alone. Generally it is important not to ask too much since a victorious client in a group often cowers at the thought of doing exactly the same task without "an expert" along or in the vicinity. The laws of shaping are followed—little steps and big rewards. Overlearning or extinction beyond zero is another useful guide. The client may be asked to practice going to shopping malls until she is bored before she shifts to another, more difficult task. Always program for success. Figure 4 is a sample homework sheet that encourages agoraphobics to develop a written plan of action, self-generated feedback, and a permanent record of improvement.

Later meetings follow a different schedule agenda. The first forty-five minutes is spent going over homework assignments to further shape risk-taking, practice, and the effective use of coping strategies. Group- as well as self-reinforcement is taught. The topics of secondary gain, self-esteem and independence are developed. Figure 5 provides a data keeping sheet on which clients may record anxiety episodes and their antecedents. These sheets allow the client to begin developing "insight" into the onset of their discomfort. They are either discussed in the travel group or taken with the client into individual or group psychotherapy. The second 1½ hours of the session are devoted to exposure. Subgroups may be formed so that each client can work on becoming accustomed to a variety of places while reducing her sensitivity and fear of internal sensations.

Included in group activities are trips to shopping locales, bridges, elevators, theatres, open spaces and so on—doing almost anything that the client is agoraphobically afraid to do. For advanced groups, long train or car trips, even airplane flights, as well as the ultimate agoraphobic experience, an amusement park, may be included.

Following travel, the group reconvenes so that members can "process" their experience, laugh, congratulate each other, draw support when they need it, and finally plan their upcoming homework. Over

	Task 1	Task 2	Task 3	Task 4	Task 5
DATE _____ **NAME** _____					
Goal					
Mode of transport					
Time of day/night					
Companion (s)					
Medication: before, during task					
Distance from home or other challenge involved					
Emotional/physical reactions					
Rewards and satisfactions experienced					
Additional comments					
Discomfort score (0–5) at end of task					

Figure 4. Homework sheet.

Time and date	Symptoms (physical and mental)	Duration in minutes	Highest SUDS	Setting or circumstances	Possible antecedents

FIGURE 5. Client record of panic attacks.

time, the therapist's role is reduced as clients need less and less coaching and take the initiative in planning group activities. As this happens, the client surely experiences herself as more effective and competent, as well as less phobic. At the end of each 5 or 10 week block of groups, each client's stated goals are evaluated. New goals are set when old ones are attained. In order to prompt group leader attention to a number of preferred interventions, a Travel Group Leader Checklist has been improvised and is included in Figure 6.

Of special note is that skillfully coached flooding may provoke important visual, verbal, and kinesthetic recollections. These memories may relate to relevant historical or current dynamics. Often at the very peak of intense feelings, one may ask the client "In what other situations do you recall having felt like this?" An immediate response might be "The night my father died" or "When I am with my husband I feel just this way—trapped." Another intervention is to ask the client to experience what emotion she feels "beneath" the fear. Often the therapist can readily see that intense anger, grief, or loneliness are operating. These strong affective states terrify most agoraphobics by nature of their sheer intensity. A fairly significant portion of agoraphobics, perhaps 20–30%, have unresolved grief as the true antecedent to their distress. Perhaps another 20–30% are angry and confused about their relationships and their resultant ambivalence precipitates distress that they do not connect to an interpersonal cause. These kinds of data are certainly grist for the therapeutic mill and should be recapitulated in the psychotherapy sessions.

Psychotherapy Group

Prior to treatment, most agoraphobics believe that their symptoms come from "out of the blue" and probably reflect some underlying weakness or craziness. In the psychotherapy group, this belief is supplanted by the more accurate notion that excessive anxiety symptoms[5] often mask other deeper and more frightening emotions. The group

[5]The adjective "excessive" is used to imply that some anxiety symptoms are normal and adaptive. They are signals from our bodies that we are experiencing distress and should take a look at the factors that cause it. Hence, anxiety in small doses is an important cue to scan the environment (inside and outside) to look for an adaptive change or instrumental response. Unfortunately, most agoraphobics envision cure as life without anxiety of symptoms. Even some that are "cured" refuse to recognize the fact because they "still have symptoms." To correct this misconception, clarification of the utility of anxiety (in appropriate amounts) must be made repeatedly.

LEADERS' NAME _____   DATE _____

☐ Homework reports for each client and social reinforcement.

☐ Instruction on how to better cope with difficulties
encountered in the last week.

Note here questions you had trouble answering or
difficulties you had trouble resolving:

☐ Work on client self-reinforcement.

☐ Work on countering the client's tendency to minimize
accomplishment.

☐ Developing individual task(s) for travel segment.

☐ Coaching in the use of paradoxical intention.

☐ Repeated restatement of Rule 1: Don't turn back
when you are feeling panicky. Stop and use the
technique or just wait until you feel better—then
proceed or return home.

☐ Report on successes of the day.

☐ Development of next weeks homework.

FIGURE 6. Checklist and feedback sheet for travel group leaders.

exists so that clients experience contact and assimilation of interpersonal
issues rather than interruption and inhibition. The group begins with
exercises to increase sensory and affective awareness. Members are
guided through a process that begins with experiencing basic sensations
and emotions and ends ideally with expression and need satisfaction.

Then, just as in a travel group, clients learn to stay with their feelings rather than utilizing distraction and intellectualization to diffuse them. The dysfunctional belief that feelings are dangerous diminishes quickly with repetitive group training and group practice.

As the client's fear of anxiety is reduced she should begin to make connections between her discomfort, antecedent events and other kinds of affect. For between-session practice in making these connections, the record sheet depicted in Figure 5 is suggested. As this progresses expressiveness training can begin. The client is taught not only that her feelings are all right but that she has the basic human right to experience and express them. She is trained to use expressions that are clear, direct and appropriate with regard to the social context and the level of intimacy needed in the situation.

Coupled with assertiveness/expressiveness training, the therapist continues to work on changing the agoraphobics hysterical style. Methodologically, a therapist makes every attempt to work with the affect that arises in the session rather than talking about past feelings and problems. Although the exploration of past traumas and conflicts may be necessary, the emphasis is on coping with current feelings and difficulties even if they arise in historical context. Inevitably, this experiential modality produces better relearning than interventions made on an intellectual level.

Two of the more common feelins that arise in the psychotherapy group are anger and grief. Even though it may appear that unresolved grief could be handled in a group, individual flooding sessions are somewhat more effective as they provide massed extinction trials. This work should be scheduled in addition to or in place of group psychotherapy. On the other hand, anger is an affect that is more appropriate to psychotherapy groups. If anger is current, but primarily the result of past or cumulative turmoil, it can be productive to express anger in the session by reliving old scenes. A discussion of basic human rights may be helpful and guidelines for acting assertively rather than aggressively or passively can be provided. Role playing, expressiveness, and using feedback from the group and its leader further help the client to develop confidence and expertise in assertiveness (see Lange & Jakubowski, 1978). As Fodor (1974) suggests female agoraphobics are often traditionally feminine and rigidly sex typed. They often put others first and themselves last, as many women have been taught to do. Many of their emotional and physical needs remain unfulfilled as they passively wait for others to be as giving to them as they are to others. Resentment, depression, restricted activity, and interest, as well as low self-esteem, frequently follow. Improving one's ability to cope not only involves expressing feelings, but also doing things about those feelings and for oneself. This "enlightened self-interest" as Ellis (1962) calls it must be shaped carefully. It may begin with the simple task of taking one hour a week to do something for oneself.

Although the treatment just described is composed of two parts which naturally complement each other, it would be misleading to suggest that improvement is linear. An important and complicating factor is the role of the significant other and the effect of symptom reduction on the agoraphobic's family system. As the identified client becomes more mobile and expressive, the significant others in her life react with surprise, pleasure, and often a good deal of discomfort. Understanding of this diversity of reactions is easier if one thinks of the agoraphobic family as a system: Because of her "illness," others have learned to protect, accompany, support, and in many ways, accommodate the behavioral and emotional limitations and difficulties of the agoraphobic. At least one significant other has served as a "phobic companion," a personal representative of safety who travels with the client by promising to care for her if she should be overwhelmed by an attack. This role is time-consuming, inconvenient, and demands a great deal of patience and effort. In addition to his or her caretaking duties, the phobic companion generally has accepted the role of therapist. By the time the client has entered therapy, the phobic companion has tried a variety of common-sense treatment techniques such as reasoning, joking, and finally, pressuring the phobic to push through her fear. When these methods fail to work and the client seeks professional help, the phobic companion or "therapist" feels displaced and diminished. As the agoraphobic improves, the significant other experiences elation as well as confusing and contradictory feelings. Most experience some sense of failure for not having brought about a cure themselves. Often the companion is angry at the therapist or program for displacing him and fears that the agoraphobic's growing independence ultimately may lead to disruptive changes in their relationship and the family unit (e.g. fear of extramarital affairs, divorce, etc.). Sabotaging the therapist's effort is a common result of the significant other's mixed feelings.

CONCLUSION

As self-care and assertiveness skills develop and travel anxiety and panic attacks subside clients approach the seemingly unresolvable conflicts in their lives. Many join a couples group or enter individual therapy. Some eventually separate or divorce. Almost all can become more autonomous, fully functioning adults. As these personality changes take place, the client's mobility continues to improve quite spontaneously. It would seem that the client's ability to cope with life enhances her perceived self-competancy and self-esteem, and allows her to feel more in control, rather than fearful of going out of control. In addition, as her independence grows, so does her ability to separate from the program.

A number of recovered agoraphobics, perhaps as a function of their special sensitivity to separation, do not leave. They stay with the program to become office aides, helpers, travel group leaders, even psychologists. They seem eager to share with others what they have gained through therapy. They may form a fairly extensive volunteer staff that helps provide the kind of coverage necessary to make superior two-phase treatment of agoraphobic possible.

REFERENCES

Beck, A. T. *Cognitive therapy of depression.* New York: Guilford Press, 1979.
Chambless, D. L., & Goldstein, A. J. The treatment of agoraphobia. In A. Goldstein & E. Foa (Eds.) *Handbook of behavioral interventions.* New York: Wiley, 1980.
Chambless, D. L., Caputo, G. C., & Jasin, S. E. *The Severity of Agoraphobia Scale.* Manuscript submitted for publication, 1983. (Available from D. Chambless, Dept. of Psychology, American University, Washington, D.C. 20016.)
Ellis, A. *Reason and emotion in psychotherapy.* New York: Stuart, 1962.
Fodor, I. G. The phobic syndrome in women: Implications for treatment. In V. Franks & V. Burtle (Eds.), *Women in therapy.* New York: Bruner/Mazel, 1974.
Goldstein, A. J., & Chambless, D. L. A reanalysis of agoraphobia. *Behavior Therapy,* 1978, *9,* 47–59.
Jasin, S. E. *A comparison of agoraphobics, anxiety neurotics and depressive neurotics using the MMPI and Beck Depression Inventory.* Unpublished doctoral dissertation, Temple University, 1981.
Lange, A. J., & Jakubowski, P. *Responsible assertive behavior.* Champaign, Ill. : Research Press, 1976.
Lazarus, A. A. Broad-spectrum behavior therapy and the treatment of agoraphobia.*Behavior Research and Therapy,* 1966, *4,* 95–97.
Levis, D. J. Implementing the technique of implosive therapy. In A. Goldstein & E. Foa (Eds.), *Handbook of behavioral interventions.* New York: Wiley, 1980.
Meichenbaum, D. *Cognitive-behavior modification: An integrative approach.* New York: Plenum Press, 1977.
Rachman, S. J. *Fear and courage.* San Francisco: W. H. Freeman, 1978.
Wolpe, J. W. Unravelling the antecedents of an agoraphobic reaction:A transcript. *Behavior Research and Therapy,* 1970, *1,* 259–264.
Yalom, I.D. *The theory and practice of group psychotherapy.* New York: Basic Books, 1975.

11

Sexual Enhancement Groups for Women

SUSAN R. WALEN AND JANET L. WOLFE

Despite the so-called sexual revolution, large numbers of sexually confused and frustrated women still abound. Kinsey (Kinsey, Pomeroy, Martin, & Gebhard, 1953), Hunt (1974), and Hite (1976), arriving at strikingly similar figures, report that approximately 10% of American women never experience orgasm and that well over half of sexually active women do not regularly reach orgasm in their coital experiences. The woman who sought treatment often has gone to professionals who, following Freudian tradition, questioned her feminine identification or tried to help her transfer her erotic sensitivity from her sexual organ, the clitoris, to her vaginal canal—usually, in the process, exacerbating her problem.

Masters and Johnson's (1970) pioneering work in the development of behaviorally-oriented treatment (which viewed orgasmic dysfunction as due largely to faulty learning rather than as a sign of severe neurosis), was more on the mark but frequently required costly conjoint therapy and a cooperating partner, thus leaving a large percentage of women out in the cold. In the wake of an alleged sexual revolution—which has left many with the impression that everyone is having (or should be having) a sexual ball—the woman who does not see herself as fitting into the popular stereotype of the sexually emancipated woman often is left with increased feelings of despair. As one client put it: "I think I should be oozing and juicing all over the place, having multiple orgasms. I felt better a few years ago, when I thought I was supposed to be bored."

SUSAN R. WALEN • Department of Psychology, Towson State University, Towson, Maryland 21204. JANET L. WOLFE • Institute for Rational Living, 45 East 65th Street, New York, New York 10021.

Time-limited all-women's sexual enhancement groups and pre-orgasmic groups have provided a powerful demonstration of how effectively and efficiently sex therapy can be done when the appropriate learning conditions are provided. Barbach (1974) has reported the most extensive data on group treatment of preorgasmic women. Of 83 women treated, 91.6% learned to reach orgasm with masturbation, and a majority were able to generalize their sexual skills to partner situations without specific programming for such transfer. Heinrich (1976) reports that 100% of 15 women became orgasmic with masturbation within 10 sessions; at two-month follow-up, 13 of the women were orgasmic in partner sex, additionally reporting increased frequency and pleasure in sexual activity. Lieblum and Eisner-Hershfield (1977) found an increased frequency of masturbation and orgasmic response, increased comfort in discussing sex, in body exploration, and in the use of vibrators as a function of group treatment. Schneidman and McGuire (1976) reported that 70% of formerly nonorgasmic women under age 35 learned to reach orgasm with self or partner manual stimulation in a 10-week group. Although only 40% of the women over 35 accomplished this goal within the 10 weeks, 60% had done so by the 6-month follow-up. Research by Barbach (1974), Heinrich (1976), Kuriansky, Sharpe, and O'Connor (1976) has demonstrated that women who participate in preorgasmic groups feel far better about their bodies and feel they have better control over their lives after therapy. As Barbach (1980) indicates,

> though relatively few transfer their orgasmic ability to relationships before the end of the group, most do so within seven or eight months after the sessions have ended, without any further therapy. This result suggests that the women do more than solve a narrowly-focused problem; they learn concepts and tools for approaching a broad range of problems, and can utilize these techniques at a later date.

In addition to increased orgasmic responsiveness, other results that are consistently reported to occur as a function of group treatment are reduction of sexual anxiety, reduction of sexual inhibitions, enhanced body image, increased self-acceptance, increased confidence in the ability to feel pleasurable and sensual feelings, and increased desire for sex.

The effectiveness of *individual* and *conjoint* sex therapy for women with sexual dysfunctions has been well documented (Walen, Hauserman, & Lavin, 1977). Behavior therapists (Brady, 1966; Chapman, 1968; Lazarus, 1963; Madsen & Ullman, 1967; Wolpe, 1969) have reported 85% to 100% success in the individual treatment of female orgasmic dysfunctions. Individual therapy results from nonbehaviorally oriented therapists have been far less well documented. In a study of 61 partially or totally "frigid" women treated four times a week in psychoanalytically-oriented therapy for a minimum of two years, 25% of the cases were cured (O'Connor & Stern, 1972). In a sample that excluded women without partners and couples without serious marital or psychological difficulties, Masters and Johnson (1970), following a *conjoint* behavioral treatment model, found that 83.4% of a group of 193 anorgasmic women became orgasmic after two weeks of therapy. Although research directly comparing the efficacy of individual versus group treatment is not available, our clinical experience suggests that group treatment is to be preferred. In addition to being less costly than individual therapy, and not requiring a cooperating partner, the group format is more efficient, enhances motivation, and generally seems to provide a context most ideally suited to women's unlearning old maladaptive attitudes, feelings, and behaviors, and supplanting them with newer and more adaptive ones.

A major therapeutic element that has been identified in group therapy is the relief from self-blame and anxiety that comes from the discovery of the group members' shared suffering and the acceptance by others despite one's flaws (Yalom, 1970). All-women's groups seem to offer ingredients that help provide their members with an especially powerful corrective emotional experience and an especially facilitative learning environment. A major ingredient in this is the increased communicational freedom that the same-sexed group seems to provide. Meador, Solomon, and Bowen (1972) found that "women together talk differently from the way they do in the presence of men. The cultural conditioning which most women have assimilated rises to the fore if only one man is present" (p. 338).

An important influence in women's difficulties in sexual enjoyment has been their sex role scripting that has taught them to be passive, dependent, to value themselves and their bodies largely on the basis of their ability to lure and secure a male, and to rely on a male to come along and light their orgasmic fire. The all-women's sexuality group is seen as providing a place where a woman can come and, shutting out the psychosocial influences of her past, enter a supportive and protective place where she can discuss, learn, and practice an entirely different set of attitudes about herself and her sexuality. In the climate of warmth, support, playfulness, and caring that rapidly occurs in the women's group, a powerful and at times almost magical appearing development of abilities occurs. A woman can experience her own power as a person, develop a more positive relationship with herself and her body, and take responsibility for her orgasms.

Between sessions, when she is doing her masturbatory homework, the group member is comforted at the thought that there are at least six other women in her community who are also masturbating. Back in the group, she is provided with a set of reinforcement contingencies that are often the reverse of those in the "outside world." In contrast to the impatience or blame she may have gotten from her spouse or lover, she receives hugs and cheers from other group members for the first tingle in her vulva, or for her first stumbling attempts at asserting herself. A plain-looking unpartnered woman in her 50s—often not seen as a sexual person on the outside (by others and herself)—experiences herself for the first time as an envied sexpot and is complimented on her new "glow" when she reports to the group her sexual experimentation with water-massagers and new masturbation positions. Group members are reinforced and supported in a new belief system that is the basis of their sexual self-determination—that they have a right to get satisfaction for their own wants (sexual and nonsexual), rather than merely taking care of others, and that they are in charge of their lives and their sexuality. And finally, in a group whose members all have the same kinds of genitals and essentially the same long-time freeze on sexual discussion, they receive much-needed practice in sharing sexual feelings and communicating about sex that will become the bridge to their communicating these feelings to their partners with greater facility and comfort.

A Cognitive-Behavioral Group Model

A variety of styles of women's groups have been reported in the literature. Often, however, little detail about the structure or format of the groups is given, so that a therapist may not have very clear guidelines for conducting them. It is our purpose in this chapter to describe in some detail how we conduct our own women's groups and to outline procedures for dealing with typical kinds of problems. Since an important ingredient in the groups is dealing with problems in a flexible, individualized manner, it is recommended that the chapter be used not as a rigid blueprint for how one must run the group, but rather as a set of suggestions on procedures and issues emerging from the groups we have conducted. Although research has not yet been done dismantling the effective components of the treatment, it is our belief that our groups are most distinguishable from many of those run by other professionals because of their heavy focus not merely on behavior change or skill acquisition through the use of sex therapy techniques, but on teaching a more expanded set of skills for restructuring the attitudes and cognitions that are seen as underlying sexual dysfunctioning and attendant emotional distress. It is this teaching of a general disturbance–combatting cognitive self-help approach that accounts for what appears to be our unusually rapid elimination of the target problem (90 to 100% of the women in our groups orgasm in only six two-hour sessions) and for the heavy generalization to other areas of the women's lives (Wolfe, 1976).

The goals of the group encompass a broad range of cognitive and behavioral changes:

1. Becoming more comfortable talking about sexuality with others
2. Unveiling and debunking erroneous sexual myths and sex role programming that interfere with autonomy and self-determination in sexual and nonsexual areas
3. Increasing knowledge of anatomy and physiology of female sexuality
4. Learning more about and becoming more comfortable with one's own body via self-exploration and directed masturbation
5. Permission-giving to increase sexual pleasure and playfulness; information-giving to expand the sexual repertoire
6. Overcoming emotional blocks to sexual freedom (guilt, anxiety, self-downing, anger) by challenging dysfunctional cognitions
7. Improving ability to assert oneself and to communicate sexual preferences to one's partner
8. Developing plans for continuing sexual enhancement when the group concludes

GROUP COMPOSITION AND SELECTION

We generally have found the optimal group size to be between six and nine women. Although having two female co-therapists tends to facilitate the group (and especially the construction and troubleshooting of homework assignments), it is possible for one therapist who is highly experienced in sex therapy and in conducting groups to lead a sexuality group. Since the existence of a mastery model with perceived similarity to group members appears to be a powerful factor in the groups' success (Yalom, 1970), a female rather than a male therapist is seen as mandatory. The all-female membership also reinforces the important idea that women are the best authorities on their own sexuality.

Members in both the settings in which we operate (Walen in private practice and a university setting; Wolfe in an outpatient clinic) generally are self-referred or referred by colleagues. Although prescreening might appear to be an absolute requirement of such groups, the fact is that in several years of running the groups we have not encountered anyone

who was not able to participate in them. Those who have never participated in therapy groups, women who previously have had difficulties in
relating in mixed-gender groups, and even borderline clients have, in
the unusually supportive atmosphere of the theme-centered all-wom-
en's group, been able to open up fairly readily and to participate actively, abetted considerably by a "go around" format that allows each
woman to speak up at least two or three times during each session.

Although we run two kinds of groups, preorgasmic groups and
sexual enchancement groups, group composition is not rigidly restricted
to women with the same problem. Typically, there will be two or three
women in the preorgasmic group who define themselves as anorgasmic
either because they are having orgasms but not labeling them as such, or
are having orgasms in masturbation but not in intercourse. There also
will be two or three anorgasmic women in the sexual enhancement
groups. Not only have we not encountered any real difficulties in running mixed problem groups, but rather, we have experienced the mixing
as beneficial in that the members often derive encouragement from the
presence of coping models. Not uncommonly, for example, a preorgasmic group member will encourage another by saying, "I used to be
where you are, and now I can do it. Here's something that worked for
me that maybe you might want to try." The already orgasmic member in
a preorgasmic group also illustrates the important lesson that orgasmic
ability is not a panacea—that having the ability to reach orgasm is no
guarantee of a problem-free sex life.

Ages of the group members generally range from early 20s through
the 60s. Although it is not mandatory to have each age group represented, it is generally helpful, where possible, to have an approximate
matching in order to avoid a feeling of being "the odd woman." Thus,
having two women in the 50 to 70 age group, or two women with
orthodox religious backgrounds, can enhance feelings of belonging and
support and provide better opportunities for vicarious learning. Ultimately, however, the increasing awareness that there are more com-
monalities than differences among group members despite disparate
ages and backgrounds wins out over alienation. In our experience, having at least two of any age group or background comes about naturally,
without any need for deliberate matching or additional recruitment.

Portrait of a Typical Group

Looking at a woman in her 60s who has been married for 40 years,
another in her 30s who recently "came out" as a lesbian, another a

young woman who lives alone and has few friends, and a fourth a bubbly, active person with two lovers, one might at first wonder what they have in common and how they are going to identify with each other. Common elements quickly become apparent as they introduce themselves and discuss what they think they "should" be doing sexually. The following is a sample of the presenting problems taken from some of our most recent sexual enhancement groups:

- "I should be having orgasms during intercourse—my boyfriend says so. Otherwise, I'm denying him the pleasure of giving me an orgasm."
- "I'm not sure if I have orgasms. I've heard that if you don't know for sure, you haven't had one."
- "My husband's and my sex life has gotten dull and routine; I know I should be enjoying sex with him and giving more to him."
- "I should be able to have sex without fantasy . . . come faster . . . and have multiple orgasms."
- "I should be having vaginal orgasms."
- "I shouldn't take so long to come."
- "I should be able to express my needs—but I'm uncomfortable because I think it's unfeminine and I'm afraid because if I tell him now—after seven years of faking—he'll really be hurt."
- "I should want sex as much as my partner."
- "I only have orgasms with a vibrator, and think if I were really healthy, I wouldn't need it and could come in 'sex.'"
- "I almost never feel turned on. I could take sex or leave it."

Most readily apparent—even in the most highly educated members—is a great deal of sexual ignorance and inappropriate expectations. The group member has feelings of shame and disgust toward her genitals and basically dislikes her body. She is looking for the earth to move, for stars exploding, for "coming" during intercourse. She does not trust her own experience and does not think she is a "real" woman. She has labeled herself as frigid, as has (frequently) her doctor if she is not having orgasms in intercourse. She then thinks she is sick and incapable of a good sex-love relationship. As a result, she has become more uptight, finding it harder than ever to let go and thus anticipating sex with dread and experiencing arousal in terms of fright and cutting off. There is at least one sexual practice (fantacizing, extramarital sex, oral stimulation) that she has set up as the *sine qua non* of sexual health and for which she condemns herself—for doing it, for not doing it, or for both. Her facial expression changes from amused to moved to relieved as she listens to each woman in turn provide a description of a set of problems overlapping remarkably with hers. She expresses genuine surprise as she becomes aware that all of her well-put-together-looking, "normal"-appearing groupmates are not the perfect, emotionally integrated creatures she has imagined them to be in other settings—but in fact are very much like her. She thus experiences tremendous relief within the first hour of the group at discovering she is not the terrible and inadequate sexual "freak" she always had imagined herself to be. She has received and given to herself few positive messages about her sexuality and has had few good models. The group will need to provide her with correct information, to help her redefine her problems without the cognitive castigation she usually imposes on herself, and to help her replace her negative attitudes and feelings with more positive ones—all in a climate of support and permission giving.

TREATMENT FORMAT AND ROLE OF THE LEADER(S)

Both the sexual enhancement groups and preorgasmic groups are conducted on a time-limited, topic-centered basis. The range of time for such groups as revealed in literature reports is 6–12 weeks, with the group meeting one or two times each week for 1½ to 2 hours. Although our own groups are conducted for six weeks, meeting once a week for a two-hour session, we strongly recommend that therapists who are not highly experienced in working with groups and/or in the area of female sexuality schedule a longer (8 to 12 week) group. With increasing experience, the therapist can conduct the workshop more efficiently. We have found that with a 6-session format, the pressure of the limited time encourages clients to come to the point, be more quickly self-disclosing, and accomplish the work of therapy more efficiently and directly. The greater efficiency of therapy when clients know it is to be time-limited has been reported by Muench (1964) and Paul (1966). In our groups, the bibliotherapy and behavioral homework assignments, as well as encouragements to keep sharing histories and discoveries with other women friends outside the group, are seen as greatly helping to extend the amount of therapy time the group members are getting beyond the 12 hours spent in the group.

The initial sessions of the groups that we conduct are more highly structured than later sessions. In the first three meetings particularly, the therapists contribute the majority of the agenda items in order to (a) define each client's problems and socialize the client to the group and to the cognitive focus of therapy; (b) provide experiences that will encourage group members to evaluate specific attitudes; and (c) teach clients correct facts about sexuality. Throughout each session, however—more so from the third session on (after the didactic groundwork has been laid)—members are encouraged to present and work on their own individual sexual problems.

During the course of the group the therapists utilize a number of styles of presentation, including brief lectures, experiential exercises, group discussion, individual problem focus, handouts, audio visual aids, and assignment and review of homework. (Examples of these techniques will be described later.) Varying the format in this way maintains the interest of group members at a high level and thus maximizes learning and retention.

The role of the therapist is a difficult but challenging one, and it is preferable that she be highly skilled and flexible. It is up to her to create a climate of permission-giving, support, and encouragement while still confronting resistances. She will be giving permission to push on and try new things; or not to try so hard, to slow down and relax. She is to serve as a participant–model, yet keep the group moving efficiently and, maximizing opportunities for vicarious learning by picking up on group process issues, tying together themes and people with similar problems. She would do well to be highly skilled clinically in order to pick up underlying issues and work with such areas as depression, couples communication, and low self-esteem. To maximize her value as an educator, she needs to be highly informed about female sexuality, birth control, and other female sexual health issues.

One of the leader's first tasks is to state clearly the theme that will be reiterated again and again in the course of the group—sex is a *natural function* that has been inhibited in them by psychosocial blocks; their goal in the group will be to *work together* to help each other erase their old inaccurate information and destructive attitudes and feelings in order to reclaim and take control of their sexual identities and feelings. This is facilitated from the start by the leaders helping the group members to accurately label their problems. "Bad communication," for example, really may mean a bad marriage. Very commonly, the therapist needs to clarify and correct the woman's self-imposed diagnosis. Many women come to the group defining themselves as *frigid*, meaning suffering from primary anorgasmia. Typically, this label really means that the woman does not experience orgasm during intercourse, but in fact is orgasmic in other ways. Although some sex therapists would label this complaint as situational anorgasmia, it is seen more correctly as normal sexual functioning and clearly identified as such to the group·members, with the explanation that 70% of women do not regularly orgasm during intercourse (Hite, 1976). By this kind of reconceptualization, the leader is able to correct misinformation, help the woman set a more realistic goal, point out the role of "should-ing" and other cognitive components in producing some of her distress, and begin to challenge during the first session some of the traditional role scripting and cognitive self-castigation.

GENERAL THEMES

Before describing the session-by-session content of the groups, we will outline a number of general themes that recur across sessions in order to give the reader a sense of the flavor of the workshop.

Use of a Flooding Model. From the first moments of the first session, the therapists actively and directively move to encourage frank and open discussions of sexuality. Via modeling by the therapists, a flooding rather than a cautious desensitization model is used. The cognitive message transmitted by this model is that sex is neither taboo nor frightening and that the group members are not fragile infants who must approach a dangerous topic obliquely. Further desensitization is encouraged by having the women discuss a list of topics back and forth with at least one outside woman friend and by reading as much material on the sexuality reading list as they can.

Use of Informal and Lusty Language. An examination of the language of sexuality proves very revealing. In English, we have a relative paucity of terms for many aspects of sexual functioning. For example, there are no direct synonyms for *clitoris*, the female sex organ. This fact suggests the cultural devaluation of the woman's sexuality and may, in part, account for the difficulty many women experience in talking about sex. Similarly, the majority of colloquialisms used for *masturbation* are descriptive only of male masturbation (e.g., "beat the meat" or "pull the pud"). In addition, many of the terms for female masturbation seem to have been coined by men (e.g., "finger fuck") and are not accurate representations of how women masturbate.

An additional problem of our language of female sexuality is that terms are used loosely and with inaccurate referents. When asked for synonyms for the word *vagina*, for example, the words most frequently cited by students were "cunt" and "pussy" (Walen, 1978). Yet these words were meant to convey the entire genital area, not merely the vaginal canal. As Hite (1976) reports, even when women are describing an activity they have positive feelings about (e.g., cunnilingus), they tend to describe it in "spare, tight, unenthusiastic and secretive language." It is pointed out to group members that if a hallmark of good partner sex is good communication—the ability to express sexual preferences clearly, directly, and comfortably—then developing and practicing a new sexual vocabulary is very important. When people think about their own genitalia and the sex acts in which they engage, they do not think in technical or medical terminology. We believe strongly that therepists should be prepared to accept this fact and freely model such behavior. When therapists comfortably use the informal and lusty language of sex, they may illustrate meaningfully a different attitude toward sexuality—the playful, demystified attitude we wish to project. In addition, since many women have only passive sexual vocabularies, the therapists' modeling may help clients move these terms from passive to active vocabulary. The most common words to describe male and female genitalia are *cock* and *cunt*, and these are the words we use most frequently in the groups.

Focus on Sex-Role Socialization Messages. An important theme in our workshops is consciousness raising about the unequal position of women in our society. We stress that it is unlikely that women will obtain sexual equality if they are not working toward human equality. For example, many women grow up with the cultural notion that most of their worth as people depends on their "feminine allure." They are encouraged to use their sexuality indirectly to get what they want from men, but at the same time are not supposed to take an active role or to enjoy sex. Whenever it is relevant, we point out the importance of such socialization messages that is continuing to interfere with the women's sexual enjoyment and general self-actualization, and encourage group members (especially those with no previous exposure to feminist writings) to read some of the recommended "consciousness-raising" literature on the effects of traditional female sex-role socialization.

Focus on Changing Cognitions. Group members are consistently aided in identifying and challenging the dysfunctional thoughts that result in emotional turmoil and that block sexual functioning. They are helped to examine their perceptions and evaluations of their own sexual functioning, their partner's behavior, and environmental events. The cognitive focus is taught by mini-lectures on the techniques of cognitive and rational-emotive therapy, and its techniques are demonstrated on individual problems brought up by the group members. *A New Guide to Rational Living* (Ellis & Harper, 1975) is recommended to all group members for further elaboration of cognitive self-help procedures.

Focus on Changing Behavior. One way to feel better, to change attitudes, or to reinforce attitude change is to behave differently. This message is presented repeatedly at all sessions. Group members are encouraged to practice new behaviors and challenge themselves with new behavioral risks both within the group sessions (e.g., asking for clarification or help with a problem) and in homework assignments. These new behaviors may be sexual or nonsexual in nature.

Focus on Self-Acceptance. Whether or not group members want to change their attitudes or learn new skills, we believe that an important first step is *acceptance of the now.* By this term we mean acceptance of oneself, acceptance of one's partner, and acceptance of reality. Very commonly, group members may be blaming themselves heavily or blaming their partners for not doing what they want them to do. The resultant emotions, whether anger or depression, are incompatible with good sexual functioning. We therefore encourage the women to focus first on feeling better about the sex they are doing, rather than merely on doing better sex. Once this nondemanding philosophy is accepted, they can move forward far more efficiently.

Focus on Hedonism. Many of the cognitive and behavioral assignments used in the group are designed to inculcate and implement a generalized hedonic philosophy. Assignments are not merely sexual, therefore, but are broadly self-pleasuring, designed especially to reinforce the idea that "I have a right to have pleasure." Until a woman adopts this broader notion, she often will have difficulty allowing herself pleasure in sexuality.

The impact of sex-role socialization is seen clearly in this area, and is often particularly strong in women with strict religious upbringing or those who are deeply embedded in their roles as wives and mothers. Such women define their role as that of taking care of other people, and often have grossly neglected the habit of doing nice things for themselves. Assignments such as taking a leisurely bubble bath or buying flowers for oneself may serve to combat guilt or thoughts of "selfishness," and may encourage a more general acceptance of hedonic self-pleasuring.

Use of Humor. Humor is another way in which the hedonic philosophy is asserted. We attempt to keep a light, playful attitude, replete with puns and witticisms, whenever it seems appropriate. Humor is another way of teaching women that it is appropriate and healthy to have fun. Humor also is an important desensitizer. Not only is it all right to have fun, but to make fun of things. Obviously, the group members are never the butt of a joke, although their cognitive distortions may be. It is our experience that an efficient way to explode myths and attack taboos is to help clients realize the absurdity of some of these notions.

Focus on Women's Health Issues. Because of the large amount of ignorance regarding their bodies and what happens to them, time always is taken in the groups to inform women about such issues as the relative risks of the different birth control methods, how to detect some of the common "female problems" (such as vaginal infections), and proper ways to go about treating them. Frequently this involves some further demystification of the role of "doctors as sex experts" as the women become aware of the inadequate treatment almost all of them have received at one time or another, and learn new ways of dealing more assertively with physicians in the future so as to receive better care. *Our Bodies, Ourselves* (Boston Women's Health Collective, 1976) is highly recommended as a handbook for helping the women become more educated about and responsible for the healthy functioning of their bodies.

Leaders as Participants. The co-therapists in our groups function very much as participant models rather than as distant or aloof experts. As leaders, we are very self-disclosing about our own sexuality. In fact, on every exercise in which group members are asked to self-disclose intimately (e.g., sharing details of how we masturbate), the group leaders participate and demonstrate free disclosure and a coping (or successfully "coped") model. As Yalom (1970) points out, a therapist who is self-disclosing; who models open, direct, and uninhibited communication; and who has had similar problems, but overcome them, greatly increases the therapeutic power of the group.

Participants as Leaders. One of the most significant themes of the group is that other women are the best source of information about female sexuality—not male PhD's, doctors, or other "sex experts." An important cognitive message given to the group is that there is no "right way" to have sex, but that it is up to each woman to define her sexuality and sexual preferences for herself. Both within and outside the group, members are encouraged to find out how other women think and feel about sexuality and how they go about it. They learn to acquire the capacity to abstract personally relevant information and helpful hints even when the spotlight of attention is not directly focused on them. They give each other substantial support and permission to be sexual. They share with each other by providing in-group practice in taking risks, communicating feelings, and sharing their own specific sexual practices. This in-session sharing helps enormously in building better facility in talking to and dealing with their partners outside the group. *The Hite Report* (1976), which is a compilation of the questionnaire responses of over 3,000 women, is recommended reading because it serves to amplify the theme of women as experts. It provides new insights and techniques while increasing their awareness that they are not alone but part of an ever growing "army" of women struggling together for sexual self-determination.

SESSION-BY-SESSION FORMAT: A SAMPLE MODEL

The following format is used in both types of groups we conduct, the preorgasmic and the sexual enhancement groups. The main difference between the two types is that the amount of time spent on troubleshooting masturbatory practice sessions understandably is shortened in the enhancement groups, which generally have only two or three anorgasmic women (as opposed to the preorgasmic groups, in which they represent the majority); and the intensive individual problem solving tends to begin in the second or third session in the enhancement groups, with a correspondingly heavier focus on partner problems.

Session 1

Once the group is convened, the therapist opens the first meeting by congratulating the women for attending and challenging their first sexual stereotype—sex should be naturally perfect. We ask the members to give their first names, and set forth the group rule of absolute confidentiality, explaining its importance in allowing the women to be as free as possible to express themselves. Each participant then is asked to tell the group something about herself, incorporating the following information into her responses: What are you worried or concerned about sexually? Are you orgasmic? Are you currently in a relationship or not, and what are your feelings about this? How does your partner feel about your being here? Each woman typically speaks for 5 to 10 minutes. If the target questions are not answered or if the client digresses or speaks for a prolonged time, the therapists guide her back to task.

The next phase of the meeting is devoted to illustrating some of the detrimental sexual stereotypes that women encounter. An exercise that we find especially useful is to ask the women to call out words or phrases that come to mind for each of the following categories: (1) women who are sexually active; (2) women who prefer not to be sexually active; (3) men who are sexually active; (4) men who prefer not to be sexually active; and (5) women who are very self-determined about their sexuality. The responses are written in columns on a blackboard or tagboard, and the women are asked what trends they notice in the responses. What clearly emerges from this "nasty name" exercise is that men who are sexually active are prized (e.g., called *swingers* or *macho*), while women who are sexually active are condemned (e.g., referred to as *whores, promiscuous,* or *loose*). Women who are inactive are castigated (e.g., *dyke, frigid*), while men who are inactive are derogated by associating them with females (e.g., *momma's boy, fairy*). Finally, women who are self-determined are seen as pushy or aggressive and destructive of male sexual prowess (e.g., *ball buster* or *castrating woman*). This exercise—a powerful consciousness raiser (Kellogg, 1973)— is followed by a discussion of the lack of adequate models for healthy sexuality in women, including a review of some statistics on the sexual oppression of women. The goal in this section of the workshop is to provide women with valid understanding of their problems in dealing with their sexuality. The message is that *they* are not deficient, but have been raised in a culture where different standards exist for men and for women and where the missionary position in sex serves as a dramatic metaphor for women's position in this society; lying flat on her back, on the bottom, getting fucked (over). Some brief data citing on some of the facts of women's oppression is done, with active contributions from the group members, at least 50% of whom generally have been raped or sexually molested at some time, who have worked as hard and long as men but for less money (the median income of full-time working females is approximately $5,000 a year less than it is for males); who have been patronized and been told "not to bother your pretty little head" about financial and mechanical things. Slowly, the women come to see that although they certainly have collaborated in perpetuating their helplessness and dependency, the facts of reduced power and respect in a male-dominated society do not make things easier and that they will need to work long and hard at countering both internal and external forces in order to claim their fullness, strength, and autonomy.

During the second hour of the first session, basic education about the anatomy and physiology of sex is provided. Because there are so few adequate illustrations of female genitalia, we have had local artists prepare very large, softly colored drawings of female external genitals in which the clitoris and clitoral head and shaft are depicted clearly. During the anatomy lesson, the therapists continue to stress the role of the clitoris by referring to it as "the clitoris, *your sex organ.*" The message passed down in the culture and often reinforced by the male partner is that the vagina is "where it's at." In sex education classes, girls still for the most part are taught that they have two ovaries, a uterus, and a vagina. Group members frequently report that they never even masturbated or heard of the clitoris until they were in their 20s, 30s, or even 50s or 60s. (Boys generally are taught about their sex organs and about masturbation in sex education classes.) An image that many group members report as powerful and corrective is viewing intercourse as male masturbation (i.e., rubbing of his sex organ against the walls of her reproductive organ) thus making it a small wonder that the woman often finds this stimulation insufficient to induce orgasm. It is stressed again and again that orgasm is a learned response and that failure to experience it is not a sign of neurosis but of faulty or inadequate early learning, and that in a culture in which millions of men and women barely recognize women or their organs, it is no surprise that women have not learned how to reach orgasm. In the end, failure to achieve that shining, male-established goal of female orgasm in intercourse is, as Hite (1976) points out, not a deficiency but a normal response to insufficient stimulation.

We review the physiology of the sexual response cycle, drawing principally on the work of Masters and Johnson (1970) and Kaplan (1974). In this segment we particularly stress the fact that vaginal lubrication is a very early sign of sexual arousal and does not mean that the woman is near her orgasmic threshold. This bit of information may be corrective for her partner who, in many cases, tests her readiness for intercourse by inserting his finger into her vagina to see if it is wet. In this as in all phases of the group we avoid the use of technical language. Thus, rather than clinically describing the "formation of the orgasmic platform at the lower third of the vaginal entroitus," we simply describe the arousal and plateau stages in terms of "blood flowing to the cunt and swelling the tissues, much in the same way as blood flows to the man's cock and causes it to swell."

If time allows, we explore the group members' attitudes and feelings about their bodies, following the "go-around" format that allows all the women to talk at least two or three times, from the first session on. They may be asked to imagine themselves looking at themselves in the mirror nude, and to share with the group whether their feelings were positive or negative; to what extent their feelings about their bodies influence how they feel about themselves as a sexual person; and to what extent they feel they are valued (or devalued) by others for their bodies. They are encouraged to work on accepting themselves and on giving themselves the right to be sexual persons, whether or not they have perfect bodies. We conclude the first session by encouraging the women to "ask any dumb questions you've ever had about sex and were afraid to ask . . . you can even ask an intelligent question!" We are thereby accomplishing several tasks at once: (1) picking up on loose ends, (2) allowing the group members to take responsibility for their own sex education, and thus their own sexuality, (3) providing practice in verbally communicating about their sexual wants, and (4) reinforcing the message that it is all right to sound "dumb," to make mistakes, to show you are imperfect. At the end of the question-and-answer period, we hand out the first homework assignment (below).

HOMEWORK[1]

Session 1

1. *Exploring your attitudes and development as a sexual being*
   Sit down and discuss with a female friend the following experiences you had while growing up:

   (a) What were your parents' (or parent-substitutes') attitudes toward sex? Your mother's? Your father's? How were they communicated to you?

   (b) What was the attitude of your peers toward sex as you were growing up?

   (c) When and how did you learn about menstruation? What was the attitude of the person who told you? Were you frequently very uncomfortable—for example, have cramps? Did you ever feel embarrassed by an incident involving menstruation?

   (d) When and how did you learn about masturbation? What is the earliest self-pleasuring or masturbation experience you can remember?

   (e) When and how did you first learn what sex really was? Were you shocked?

   (f) What were the circumstances of your first real sexual experience and what was it like for you?

   (g) Did you ever have "crushes" on a girlfriend or any romantic/physical feelings for another girl or woman?

   (h) When did you first hear the name of your sex organ, the clitoris?

   (i) Do you remember any sexual traumas such as child–adult sexual contact, rape, or other frightenig sexual experiences?
   Spend 5 to 10 minutes with your friend on each question.

[1]Adapted from Lonnie G. Barbach's *For Yourself* (New York: Doubleday, 1975).

2. *Explore your genitals*

Get yourself relaxed and comfortable. Bathe or shower if you wish. Spend 20 minutes to half an hour, in a quiet room where you will not be disturbed, examining your genitals with a hand mirror. Get to know them. Identify all parts of them and touch each with your fingers, using the attached drawing as a guide. Notice the colors and textures. See if you can determine any differences in sensitivities between the different areas. Place your fingers inside your vagina to feel the pubococcygeal muscle and to see if some areas are more sensitive to touch than others. Separate the labia and look at all the details. Notice the three parts of the clitoris: the shaft (the tube-like structure just below the pubic hair—you can find it by rolling your fingers from side to side over it); the glans (the little pea-like structure); and the foreskin (the movable hood overhanging the glans). Try moving the hood of the clitoris back and forth over the glans. Repeat this exercise on subsequent days, until you feel comfortable.

3. *Exercise your pubococcygeal muscle (optional)*

This is the large muscle that surrounds the vaginal opening, and covers the whole pelvic floor. To locate it, urinate with your legs slightly apart; the muscle you squeeze to stop the flow is the pubococcygeal (or PC) muscle. Lie down and put your finger in the opening of your vagina and contract the PC muscle; feel the contraction around your fingers. Practice contracting this muscle at least three different times over the next week, spending about two to three minutes each time. Do each contraction to a count of approximately 6 seconds, until you have done it about 6 to 10 times. Flexing this muscle can be another way to help you tune into your genital sensations.

4. *Beginning masturbation*

Pick a time when you can relax, unwind, and be sure of not being interrupted. Lie comfortably on your bed, without clothes. Using a lubricant such as massage oil, baby oil, or your own natural saliva or vaginal juices, begin to explore your vaginal area, slowly and gently. Experiment with different types of strokes and pressures: light, feathery touches, harder rubbing, in-between strokes. Try massaging your clitoral area with your fingertips by making gentle, firm, circular motions. Find out what feels best for you: Direct stimulation of the glans? Massaging the areas directly surrounding the clitoris above, below, or to the sides? You may try massaging the clitoris between your forefinger and middle finger or massaging the whole area.

Feel what there is to feel. Don't hold back, don't measure your sensations. At first you may not feel very many sensations; but continue, and take notice of even slight feelings. Focus on what is *there,*

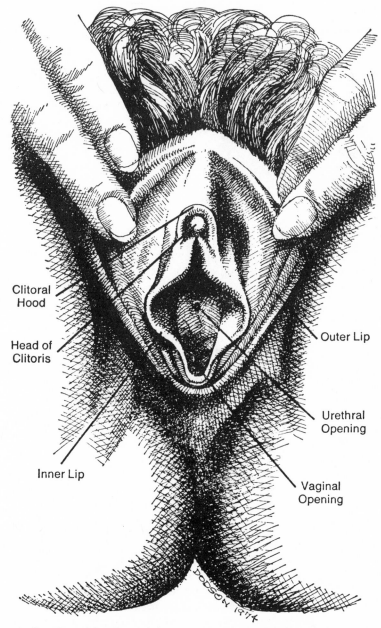

FIGURE 1. Drawing of female genital anatomy used as a handout in women's sexual enhancement groups. (From *For Yourself: The Fulfillment of Female Sexuality* by Lonnie Barbach. Copyright 1975 by Lonnie Garfield Barbach. Reprinted by permission of Doubleday & Company, Inc.)

not on what is not there. You are looking to get to know your body and how you feel and react, not for instant orgasm. Use mental aphrodisiacs if you wish: fantasize or read an erotic book or magazine. Repeat this exercise at least two or three times (for at least 15 minutes each time) over the next week. Move slowly; do not push yourself. There is no need to discover the whole range of feelings in one day or even one week. Little by little, you will learn to feel safe with your sensations and with your sexual responses. Do not shoot for orgasm. Slowly, quietly allow sexual tensions to build up, ebb, build up, ebb.

We begin the second session by asking the group members for their reactions to the first session. If they experienced any distress we help them to challenge their automatic thoughts. Typically, however, there is a warm expression of relief and encouragement that is strengthened as the group discusses the first meeting. We then review their homework assignments, thereby learning more about each participant and helping the women who had difficulty in doing the homework to identify their emotional blocks and other resistances and to develop specific plans for working against them. Not uncommonly, several members will plead that they were "too busy," their kids were underfoot, or they were "too tired" to do the exercises. Low frustration tolerance (avoiding the anxiety accompanying difficult and uncomfortable situations) and lack of belief in their right to take time and space for themselves are pinpointed by the leaders as being contributory to these resistances, and appropriate cognitive and behavioral homework assignments are suggested, along with practical advice (such as borrowing a friend's empty apartment).

The focus of Session 2 is on masturbation—learning to be one's own best sex partner—and on increasing comfort with their bodies. Group members are asked for their feelings about touching their bodies and about being their own sex partners. A great deal of the ensuing discussion entails cognitive challenges to feelings of guilt, anxiety, or revulsion. The claim made by members that sex is so much better with a partner than alone is met with the explanation that 95% of women who masturbate have orgasms most of the time—a far higher percentage than occurs in partner sex and thus a more reliable way to reach orgasm. Other advantages given are the freedom from being observed and its frequent attendant anxieties; the fact that one does not need to have an available partner to have sexual pleasure and that women tend to have difficulty in seeing themselves as having sexual feelings and desires other than those resulting from male initiation. Finally, it is explained that if one can learn comfortably and reliably to reach orgasm with oneself, one is likely to enjoy it all the more with a cooperating partner.

During the final segment of this session in the sexual enhancement groups, each woman describes in detail the various ways she masturbates. (In the preorgasmic groups, this discussion would normally not take place until session three, as group members tend to have had relatively little masturbatory practice, and thus might feel inadequate about their descriptions.) All members are encouraged to ask each other as many direct questions as they wish. For most women, this exercise may be the first time they ever have spoken to anyone about the subject of masturbation and is almost always the first time they have verbalized their masturbatory procedures. Our members often decide to give themselves the assignment of trying out someone else's method just for fun, thereby providing the originator with perhaps her first exhilarating experience in being a *teacher* in sexuality. This exercise allows us to identify any potentially troublesome styles of masturbation. For example, one woman had trained herself since early childhood to reach orgasm only while in a tightly curled position, one which clearly would make good partner sex quite difficult. Additionally, we can provide cognitive corrections about masturbation (e.g., "I'm probably the only person who masturbates—or doesn't masturbate" or "I'm doing it the wrong way"). Finally, we can help the group members to identify and correct their cognitive blocks to orgasm.

The women in the sexual enhancement and preorgasmic groups are asked to share with the group a description of "the sexiest experience you ever had with yourself." As in all such disclosure exercises, the leaders share one of their own experiences. The women then are asked "what prevents you from doing more of that for yourself?" Again, guilt reduction is the typical therapeutic focus. Since many of the women's sexiest experiences tend to be their more unusual ones (e.g., masturbating on a secluded beach or with a cucumber), the group members (talking for perhaps the first time about their "dark secrets") receive practice in seeing that the "freaky" things they have done sexually were in fact not so freaky or shameful after all. This tends to pave the way for increasing levels of self-disclosure. At the next session, for example, a woman may share the information that she is having her first affair and is almost sick with anxiety and guilt about it. The group members' reaction almost invariably is support and empathy and not the condemnation and rejection she had imagined would occur.

At the end of the session, the second homework assignment is given out (see below), and the women are encouraged to bring to the next session any sex "toys," sex books, magazines, or vibrators they may have.

Homework[2]

Session 2

Welcome to Masturbation Week!

Remember—it's important to make an agreement with yourself that if improving your sex life is important, you'll have to set aside enough time for you to work on it. A minimum of four separate 20-minute to 45-minute sessions this week is recommended.

Pick a time of day when you're relaxed, and feeling reasonably good about yourself. Find a place (your bed, in front of the fireplace, in the bathtub, wherever) that's quiet, comfortable, and where you won't be interrupted. (Turn off the phone!) Create a sensuous atmosphere; turn down the lights, turn on background music, if you wish. Feel free to do whatever may help you to get in a more sensuous mood and arouse your sexual fantasies. This may include looking at sexy pictures in a magazine, reading an erotic book, or thinking up sexy experiences or fantasies.

Remember some of the places that felt particularly good when you touched them last week. Remember, too, that masturbation is a natural body function, and is GOOD for you; give yourself permission, out loud, if you wish, to enjoy it.

Now, all you need is a little perseverence. You might not get excited for quite a while, or might not have any orgasm. These kinds of responses take practice. DON'T WORRY.

Using some oil (or secretions) for lubrication, find an enjoyable place to stroke. When you've found one, keep rubbing, alternating the pressure and the rate. Try stroking up and down; try stroking sideways, in circles, back and forth. Try rubbing as though you were massaging yourself to reach the parts below the skin. Don't worry if you temporarily lose the pleasurable feeling. If a place becomes tender, or numb, switch to a new place. Stop when you want, start when you want. Do what feels O.K. for you. Try whatever positions, movements, or stimulation you want (with pillow, objects, whatever). Use one hand or

---

[2]For additional reference material see Barbach (1975); Heimann, LoPiccolo, & LoPiccolo (1976); Dodson (1974); SAR Guide (1975).

both. Touch yourself elsewhere on your body—your breasts, inside of legs and arms, face—experiment. Find what feels good. Make as much or as little noise as you want. And try to remember that there is no "right" or "best" way to masturbate—there's *your* way. And finding your way takes trying out lots and lots of different things. YOU HAVE THE RIGHT TO PLEASURE . . . but even pleasure takes practice.

Why Masturbate?

Masturbation or self-stimulation for sexual pleasure is liberating for men and women. It's a most natural function—children do it—developing guilt mainly when others start telling them it's wrong. Looking at and touching your genitals helps you gain greater comfort and acceptance of your sexuality and your body. And it helps you become more attuned to what feels good and better able to enjoy your sexual responses—both with your most reliable sex partner (yourself!) and with others. It is the best way to learn about your own sexual responses so that you can communicate them more clearly and effectively to your partner.

Masturbation can, if you so choose, be your primary sexual outlet. It's a great way to relieve sexual and other tensions (and a good nightcap to help you sleep!) With a partner, it can take the pressure off your partner (and you) to perform. It is one of many ways to share sexual experiences and techniques and to develop greater sexual honesty with your partner. It can be a tremendous turn-on to see someone you care about give themselves pleasure. Finally, people who feel good about pleasuring themselves and who take responsibility for their sexual responses are less likely to have sexual problems.

Session 3

Goals in this session are to continue to troubleshoot the factors interfering with orgasmic response and body comfort and to help extend the members' awareness of new things they might try to expand their sexual repertoires. The session begins with the women sharing their sexual paraphernalia with each other and leaders encouraging swapping of books or magazines. The leaders also bring in a variety of vibrators for demonstration and discuss their various advantages and disadvantages. Those requesting it are given information on places where they may obtain such sex toys and materials. A dam seems to have broken during this "show and tell" section: many of the women previously had considered such devices but never had tried them, out of shame and anxiety. Again, the message is: "Sexual experimentation is healthy and natural.

I'm not a pervert or an inadequate person if I go into a department store to buy a vibrator." We continue with a review of the homework assignments and continue to stress the need for taking time for ourselves for our pleasure. We also initiate a discussion of sexual fantasies, stressing the positive value of fantasies, discriminating between fantasy and reality (e.g., one may enjoy a particular fantasy—such as having sex with the entire church choir—without having to worry about acting it out), and encouraging women to develop and expand their fantasy life. Books that women tend to find erotic, such as Friday's *My Secret Garden* (1975), are recommended.

The focus of the latter part of this session is on clarifying the role of cognitive therapy techniques in dispelling emotional blocks to sexuality. The theory of cognitive therapy is described, and by working with individual members of the group, the members learn directly and vicariously how to apply these methods to their problems of anger, anxiety, guilt, depression, and especially, low frustration tolerance. One way we have found particularly effective in helping group members identify their main dysfunctional cognitions is to give them a handout with Ellis's (1975) "Twelve Irrational Ideas that Cause Disturbance" in the left column and his corresponding rational countermessages in the right column. Each women is asked to identify to the group two of these self-messages she plans to work on over the next week (via overt and covert rehearsal) and is encouraged by the leaders to work on this new programming "every hour on the hour," if possible.

The session concludes with individualized assignments to the members involving self-nurturance and/or the taking of new behavioral risks. For example, one woman assigned herself the task of telling her partner that she wanted him to "go down on her." Another assigned herself the task of getting a lock put on the inside of her bedroom door and informing her children that she wanted them to knock if they wanted to enter. If there is time at the end of the group we may show parts of the series of films *Becoming Orgasmic* by LoPiccolo and Heiman (1976). This film series provides a useful coping model of a woman learning to be orgasmic and, in the later segments, communicating her new skills to her partner.

Session 4

We begin this session by asking for "reports from the field." By such an open-ended structure we allow more opportunity for group members to use this session to bring out their individual problems for therapeutic intervention. The majority of this session is spent in this individual focus.

The main agenda item we introduce in the latter part of the second hour is bridging the gap between what the women are learning about their own sexuality and their partner(s). We define assertive behavior and discuss the factors responsible for women's especially heavy problems in this area, focussing on sex-role socialization messages (e.g., "Be sweet," "Don't rock the boat," "Take care of others," "Don't express anger—it's unfeminine"). Part of taking charge of one's sexuality, it is pointed out, involves challenging the old notion that it is up to a man to satisfy a woman, that he will do so if he really loves her, without any coaching, and that if she lets him know what she wants, she will "hurt" him or be "castrating." Particular attention is paid to handling sexual initiations and refusals and asking your partner for what you want. Other areas raised by participants include dealing with a partner's resistance to doing the kind of stimulation she wants or to having a vibrator join them in bed; expressing negative feelings about her partner's behavior in nonsexual areas; asking for more snuggling and cuddling; and expressing positive feelings. A belief system that supports assertive behavior is developed by the group, typically including the following: (1) I am in control of the way I feel about my partner; (2) I am able to make appropriate choices about how I relate to my partner; (3) I am a strong and centered person, with the right to be treated with respect, to have my desires considered, and to have my time taken seriously. Role playing and feedback are used to help members get practice in communicating their thoughts and feelings in more appropriate ways, along with modeling by the therapist or other group members, where appropriate.

Homework assignments are, by this session, usually given by the women to themselves, with other group members supplementing them and the leader picking up any loose ends or making additional suggestions. This process underscores the group members' ability to create their own solutions and fades out some more of their reliance on the "authority figures." As an additional assignment, each member is asked to think about the following questions: What do you want done to you? What, if anything, do you want to do for your partner? Members are asked especially to think of things that they never have tried before and then to try at least one of them out during the week, thus incorporating risk taking and assertiveness assignments into one.

Session 5

This session basically is unstructured by the therapists, allowing the participants maximum opportunity to bring up their own agenda items.

Two topics generally emerge: dealing with (sex-interfering) anger at one's partner for inconsiderate sexual or nonsexual behavior, and handling difficulties in dealing with their partner's focus on goal-directed sex (orgasm) rather than on intimacy, kissing, cuddling, sensuous stroking, and the other activities they love. (Almost invariably, the group sighs in unison when asked to get in touch with their feelings about snuggling via an experiential exercise often introduced at this point.) Anger issues are dealt with by a mini-lecture on the cognitive bases of anger and by role playing and feedback. The problem of getting off a "fuck focus" is dealt with by introducing how to do mutual "information massages" and other sensate focus procedures. A handout with instructions for some of these is given out to group members with a caution not to go ahead with them if there is a significant relationship problem or a partner who flatly refuses to participate in nonorgasmic sex. In these situations, members are encouraged to go for couples counseling.

Another focus provided by the therapists during the second hour is preparation for the future, since the sixth session is usually scheduled after an interlude of three to six weeks. Each member is asked to respond to the following questions: How will you try to make sure that you don't backslide? What will you plan to do for yourself in the next month? What are your future goals for yourself? For your sexuality? Additional risk-taking exercises and other supplementary assignments also may be suggested by the other group members and the leaders. The follow-up meeting is then scheduled, and the women are asked if they wish to arrange to bring refreshments to it.

Session 6

The follow-up session usually is conducted in a very relaxed atmosphere, typically with wine and refreshments provided by the leaders and group members. The first agenda item is a review of each woman's progress, checking for backsliding, stability, or new progress. Not uncommonly, significant changes have occurred in the women's lives (e.g., loss of a partner, change of job, etc.), and the impact of these changes on sexuality is assessed. Often, therefore, the follow-up meeting revolves around general life-change stresses and developing coping strategies for handling them. In such cases, sex may be the frosting on the cake. If there are emotional problems relating to such issues as health, finances, or relationship crises, it generally is best to deal with these first.

Another common focus of the follow-up meeting is to provide what amounts to an advanced course in sexuality. Since the group's inception, many of the women will have taken new risks, tried new sexual experiences, and read a great deal on the topic of sexuality—all of which may open new areas for questions. We therefore ask group members at some point in the meeting to pick some item, hopefully one that always has been particularly difficult or embarrassing for them to discuss, and to throw it out to the other group members for their response. For example, in a recent follow-up group, questions such as the following were raised: "Do you swallow your partner's cum when you go down on him," "How do you protect yourself against VD if you know your lover is sleeping with other women?" and "Is anal sex bad for you?"

During this final meeting it is common for the members—by now closely involved in each others' lives—to express sadness that the group is ending. The therapists may suggest that group members exchange names and phone numbers, and that if they wish they may arrange for periodic reunions, with or without the leader. This suggestion typically leads to the group electing an informal secretary to take charge of arranging such reunions and clearing them with the leaders' schedules. If there is time, we may conclude the session with a final film. One that has been used with great success is *Going Down to Bimini*, available from Multi-Media Resources.

ILLUSTRATIVE CASES

The following four cases—representing a variety of ages, backgrounds, and presenting problems—are offered to provide a clearer picture of typical problems and cognitive/behavioral homeworks given during a six-session group.

CASE STUDY 1: PATRICIA

Session I

Key Issues

A 31-year-old teacher whose parents had told her she was so ugly she never would find anyone who could be attracted to her. Shy and un-self-confident, sees self as "asexual." Never orgasmed during masturbation, but thinks she once came with a partner. Little dating experience; no sexual contact in last two years.

Cognitive Assignments

Challenge belief that "because my parents think I'm a sexual washout, it must be true." Give self message that "I have a right to, and capacity for, sexual pleasure."

Behavioral Assignments

Session 1 homework (see pp. 237–240).

Session II

Key Issues

When discussing sexual history with two friends, found they did not know common sexual facts, and felt relief at discovery she was not as backward as she had thought. Felt freer to spend more time touching body than ever before (completed three sessions of self-exploration). Still feeling doubtful about orgasmic potential.

Cognitive Assignments

Reinforce beliefs that "I have a right to proceed at my own sexual pace" and "just because I'm having difficulty coming, doesn't mean I never will." Read *My Secret Garden* to help erotic focus.

Behavioral Assignments

Session 2 masturbation homework (see 242–243).

Session III

Key Issues

Reported "I still think I'm the only one who's not going to make it." Felt she was getting close to orgasm, but was scared she would "lose control, or lose consciousness—maybe even die."

Cognitive Assignments

Challenge beliefs that "I can't control my feelings/behavior" and "if something is fearsome, I must remain terribly upset about it."

Behavioral Assignments

Call another group member (who volunteered the suggestion) before beginning each masturbating session and ask her to phone 1½ hours later to check and see if she (Pat) is O.K.

Session IV

Key Issues

Felt much more relaxed during masturbation, so did not feel need to call group member "but was very reassured to know I had someone who could help if I was in trouble." Felt very close to orgasm; got scared but pushed self for another minute or two; then gave self permission to stop.

Cognitive Assignments

Anti-awfulize about not coming (or possibly coming!); plug in erotic imagery to distract self from "spectatoring." Read *Hite Report* for additional masturbation ideas/experiences.

Behavioral Assignments

Focus on erotic sensations; try two new masturbation techniques suggested by group or *Hite* respondents.

Session V

Key Issues

When feeling discouraged, decided to cheer self on with "Yeah, cunt, do your stunt!" (group applauds). Felt legs tensing, followed by relaxed, mellow feeling, but not sure it was an orgasm. (Group members assured her it almost certainly was, and probably would get more and more clearly punctuated, the more she "practiced.") Brought up fears of meeting men and being rejected by them.

Cognitive Assignments

Remind self to focus on good sensations and anti-awfulize about its "taking so long." Challenge idea that it is awful to be rejected, to be uncomfortable in social situations.

Behavioral Assignments

Continue to masturbate; try using vibrator in a "teasing" fashion; continue to use favorite fantasies. Go to one social event (of several suggested by group) and approach and converse with two new males.

Session VI

Key Issues

More clearly articulated orgasms; feels ready to approach partner sex. Role-played discussing with potential partner her sexual wants (also saying "no" if she didn't feel ready). Says through group she has "gone from being asexual to actually being horny—I think about sex at work and can't wait to get home and try it!"

Cognitive Assignments

(To prepare her for nonsexual and sexual risk-taking): Reinforce belief that it's O.K. to be imperfect, and that rejection is neither awful nor proof of her inadequacy. Read *Intelligent Woman's Guide to Dating and Mating.*

Behavioral Assignments

Increase assertive behavior, including giving and accepting compliments, asking for favors, making more spontaneous comments at work and in social situations.

CASE STUDY 2: AUDREY

Session I

Key Issues

A 44-year-old lawyer, married 12 years. Had orgasm once, in 20s, while necking, through manual stimulation. Little sexual enjoyment with husband, who criticizes her for weight. Anxious, guilty, and somewhat depressed: about money, lack of friends. Works 80 hours per week. Describes husband as sexy, self as frigid, parents as "first class Protestant-Ethickers." Husband verbally abuses, she withdraws.

Cognitive Assignments

Reinforce self-messages that "I am not a hopeless sexual dud" and "my current lack of sexual feelings doesn't make me a 'frigid person'." Read chapters in *New Guide to Rational Living* on self-downing.

Behavioral Assignments

Session 1 homework (see pp. 237–240).

Session II

Key Issues

Asked two close female acquaintances to do the sharing-of-sexual-histories portion of homework; felt depressed when they refused at realization she has no close friends (a group member volunteered to do it with her next week.) Spent only 20 minutes doing self-exploration, complaining "no time, too fatigued."

Cognitive Assignments

Give self message, "Work for money is important, but work for pleasure is, too; I have a right to take time for my pleasure."

Behavioral Assignments

Complete self-exploration section of homework one time, plus 2 sessions of Session 2 homework (beginning masturbation). Take 2 one-hour breaks from work this week.

Session III

Key Issues

Arrived looking unusually glowing and well-groomed, drawing warm compliments from group at which she appeared quite moved. Took long walk for one of breaks and bought self new dress; feeling much less depressed but still fearful of starving if she does not keep working. Completed all but one masturbation session and felt "first tingle in years."

Cognitive Assignments

Do realistic assessment of work/financial prospects and look for evidence she will starve in gutter. Examine "payoffs" of starving self emotionally, sexually, and economically.

Behavioral Assignments

Three masturbation sessions with husband out of house. Minimum three nonsexual self-pleasuring activities every week, henceforth. (E.g., take space for self by going for walk, visiting a gallery; pleasure senses by getting a massage, sitting in sun, rolling in grass, taking long bubble bath.

Session IV

Key Issues

Feeling "more and more sexy," though still masturbated one fewer time than assignment; completed three self-pleasuring activities and less anxious about taking time for self. Husband somewhat sabotaging of efforts, attacking her for weight and unsexiness shortly after she reported feeling pleased at masturbatory progress. Feeling a bit depressed and self-downing, fearful of losing husband if she doesn't "shape up."

Cognitive Assignments

Remind self that there are many problems, but there are specific things I can do to work on them. "I can survive and be happy even if my husband does reject me; I still can find others who will care for me."

Behavioral Assignments

Same as above and initiate contact with a possible new woman friend. Investigate places where she can enjoy an interest and meet new support network.

Session V

Key Issues

Completed all masturbation sessions, with increasingly pleasurable feelings (felt closer than ever to orgasm, but giving self time). Strengthening faith in eventually being able to enjoy sex and orgasms. Husband pressuring for partner sex, despite her indications she would prefer not to have genitally involved sex with him until further along. Role played how to communicate this more assertively.

Cognitive Assignments

Challenge ideas that if husband says she is unsexy, it must be true; and that it is awful if he keeps pressuring her.

Behavioral Assignments

Respond assertively to husband's attacks and pressuring, after role playing several more times with another group member.

Session VI

Key Issues

Fallen back on frequency of masturbatory practice, though still experiencing increasingly pleasurable feelings when she does. Somewhat anxious and depressed about husband's non-cooperation. Considering individual therapy for self after group ends to carry on some of the good progress she feels she's made. Still taking time for self-pleasuring and has had dinner with two good friendship prospects.

Cognitive Assignments

Read "Conquering Anxiety" and "How to Feel Undepressed Though Frustrated" chapters in *New Guide to Rational Living*.

Behavioral Assignments

Purchase relaxation tape and train self in relaxation procedures. Continue regular masturbatory practice, experimenting with reading erotic materials, more rapid and sustained rubbing of clitoral shaft. Recommend possible couples' counseling to husband.

CASE STUDY 3: MADELEINE

Session I

Key Issues

A 24-year-old computer programmer. Massively self-downing and self-conscious. Heavily tied to parents, who still have key to her apartment; and lots of guilt about sex. On-and-off relationship for two years with an "inconsiderate, domineering man." Regular sex but no orgasms (she fakes, he does not ask) and lots of anger and discontent with relationship.

Cognitive Assignments

Read at least half of assertiveness book (*Your Perfect Right*) and give self message that "I have the right and capacity for sexual pleasure."

Behavioral Assignments

Session 1 homework (see pp. 237–240).

Session II

Key Issues

Began report by comparing self negatively to all other members, announcing self as "the group failure." When reminded that she was not supposed to be "going for orgasm" this week, it emerged she had felt some very good feelings during self-exploration but did not "count" them.

Cognitive Assignments

Write down at least three positive things about self (traits or performances) each day. Reinforce belief that there is no "one right way to have sex, orgasms; there's my way."

Behavioral Assignments

Session 2 masturbation homework (see pp. 242–243). When anxiety/self-downing level gets too high, take break to calm self down.

Session III

Key Issues

Had orgasm via manual masturbation, but more involved in upsetness over urinating when she came. Angry at man friend and ready to break things off. Father arrived for unannounced visit and she insisted man friend hide in closet. Role played how to express feelings more assertively with father and boyfriend.

Had her re-do, in a more self-crediting way, announcement to group that she had had her first orgasm.

Cognitive Assignments

Tell self, "It's O.K. if I urinate when I come—I'm not a horrible freak." Give self assertion messages: "I am an adult with a right to my own apartment, to express my feelings and preferences," "My friend is not a condemnable louse for acting inconsiderately."

Behavioral Assignments

Urinate before having sex/masturbating; if necessary, put towel or rubber sheet over mattress. Experiment with Kegel exercises to see if greater sphincter control can be achieved. Request that parents never visit without first calling; speak up to friend about nonsexual things she is upset about. (Role play first with another friend.)

Session IV

Key Issues

Three more orgasms, better sphincter control. Told parents about wish for more adult relationship. Spoke to man friend about being neater when he used her bathroom and showed him clitoris (he had not been clear where it was) by putting his hand on it. Downing self because not immediately coming in partner sex.

Cognitive Assignments

"It's not awful when things don't go my way, right away." "I am not an inadequate person even if I never orgasm in intercourse."

Behavioral Assignments

Continue to give feedback (nonimpatiently) to man friend about the kind of sex play and clitoral stimulation she likes. Continue to assert self with parents and man friend in nonsexual areas. Do shame-attacking exercise.

Session V

Key Issues

Still tending to start each report with self-downing; asked each time to give self credit for positives and talk about negatives without attacking self. Asked for and got cunnilingus from friend; let self enjoy it even though she did not come.

Cognitive Assignments

Read half of *New Guide To Rational Living* and challenge idea that when she fails at something, she is a total failure.

Behavioral Assignments

Masturbate in front of man friend to model the kind of stimulation she likes. "Brag" about self once each day to someone (about something she has done).

Session VI

Key Issues

Reported in enthusiastic, positive terms first orgasm with partner manual stimulation; also came close during oral sex. Told friend she "sometimes just liked to cuddle and hug—without going for orgasms," and he responded well, without griping. "He's really changing . . . listens more." She attributes this to having tried to express self calmly, without blaming. Would like to try to have orgasms in intercourse.

Cognitive Assignments

Continue to remind self "I have the right to express my nonsexual (and sexual) feelings and preferences," "I am an adult."

Behavioral Assignments

Continue above assertiveness work; speak to boss about job advancement. Try stimulating self while partner is penetrating her, experimenting with the best positions.

Case Study 4: Miriam

Session I

Key Issues

A 53-year-old homemaker, married second time, for 12 years; orgasms only occasionally, via vibrator; downing self for slow progress despite all the reading she has done. Angry at husband for showing little interest in her sexually; feels her life "boring."

Cognitive Assignments

Give self messages: "Being frustrated is highly inconvenient, but not awful; just because I'm not enjoying sex much now, doesn't mean I never will."

Behavioral Assignments

Session 1 homework (see pp. 237–240).

Session II

Key Issues

Masturbated for one session; but grew so resentful at thought of husband's sexual withdrawal turned self off and gave up for the week. Impatiently interrupted group members' suggestions with "You don't understand." Leader offered support while pointing out the various ways her low frustration tolerance was getting her into trouble.

Cognitive Assignments

Give self messages: "My husband has a right to act badly; I don't like it, but I can stand it."

Behavioral Assignments

Session 2 homework (see pp. 242–243). When anxiety level starts shooting up (or other thoughts/feelings interfere), take a break from self-stimulation and do relaxation procedures (demonstrated in group).

Session III

Key Issues

Completed three masturbation sessions. Feeling far less hopeless and frustrated. Close to orgasm twice, but afraid to "let go, lose control." Desires part-time job, but afraid of "making a fool of herself" in job interview as she had not been in job market for 15 years.

Cognitive Assignments

Challenge belief that something awful will happen if I orgasm, and that I *must* always have perfect control. Anti-awfulize about fudging job interview.

Behavioral Assignments

Role play a cataclysmic orgasm, making crazy noises and thrashing around. Do a "shame-attacking exercise" to desensitize self to fear of appearing crazy, out of control.

Session IV

Key Issues

Experienced first orgasm in manual masturbation. Did shame-attacking exercise and one job interview and exhilarated at having taken risks and moved off dead-center as to a job. Told husband somewhat aggressively that it was clearly he who had a sex problem and he had better shape up, and he withdrew further. Group pointed out that anger is sexual turn-off and made several suggestions for new things they might try.

Cognitive Assignments

Challenge idea that "my husband must be perfectly sexually cooperative, right away" and "It's awful/he's awful for behaving this way."

Behavioral Assignments

Make a sensual "exchange contract" with husband for a (nongenitally-involved) "treat" each could give the other and execute contract. Do not make orgasm the goal.

Session V

Key Issues

Husband agreed to do sensual exchange, then did not initiate it on agreed-upon night. Miriam withdrew and sulked and depressed self over possibility of never having good sex with him. Group pointed out her demandingness that he change instantly and how anger on her part tends to elicit further passivity from him.

Cognitive Assignments

Challenge anger cognitions: "When I assert myself, he must respond positively the first time." Read *Increasing Sexual Pleasure with a Partner* handout with husband and get his reactions without attacking.

Behavioral Assignments

Reinitiate sensual exchange contract and follow through even if husband does not initiate it. Express feelings to husband in nonsexual areas without attacking. Do not go for orgasm.

Session VI

Key Issues

Husband cooperated beautifully in sensual exchange (he nibbled ears and breasts; she massaged back and buttocks). She initiated sex another time; both enjoyed it and though she did not come, feels confident she will in time. Reported improved marital communication, with less attacking by her and more active participation by him.

Cognitive Assignments

Keep anti-awfulizing about not always getting desired response from husband. Accept fact that she always may initiate and even prefer sex more than husband without concluding she must have miserable marriage.

Behavioral Assignments

Continue nonresentfully to initiate sensual/sexual encounters. Positively reinforce husband for assertive behavior and sexual initiation. Join assertiveness group to improve personal and vocational communication skills.

CONCLUSION

In a society where a good deal of female sexuality has been based on externally defined criteria (largely by males), all-women's sexuality groups are seen as a powerful way of helping women redefine their own sexuality and determine the form of their sexual expression. In an important position paper on women's sexuality (Childs, Sachnoff, & Stocker, 1975), written in collaboration with the Association for Women in Psychology, the characteristics of the sexually self-affirmed woman were summarized. The self-affirmed woman "is a woman who: (1) can enjoy her own body apart from others ('I have a primary sexual relationship with myself'); (2) can have sexual experiences for her own reasons; (3) can experiment and experience; (4) has her own standards and uses herself as the measure of her own experience. The self-affirmed woman understands the interpersonal issues found frequently in relationships that are sexual. She knows ways to negotiate, to fight, to settle, and to forgive. She knows when to leave relationships that are too costly."

Although these goals are rarely perfectly accomplished, it is our observation (Wolfe, 1976) that cognitive/behaviorally oriented sexual enhancement groups provide a corrective emotional experience and accomplish an impressive range of results in a relatively short time period. Sexual re-education, a climate of openness and support, and skills teaching (e.g., assertiveness training) are important ingredients in this process. It is the cognitive focus, however—the teaching of general anxiety-, anger-, and depression-combatting philosophies—that is seen as being particularly responsible for helping the women develop an expanded set of skills for more clearly defining and pursuing their sexual preferences.

REFERENCES

Alberti, R. E., & Emmons, M. L. *Your perfect right: A guide to assertive behavior.* San Luis Obispo, Calif.: Impact, 1978.

Barbach, L. G. Group treatment of preorgasmic women. *Journal of Sex and Marital Therapy,* 1974, *1,* 139–145.

Barbach, L. G. *For yourself: The fulfillment of female sexuality.* New York: Doubleday, 1975.

Barbach, L. G. *Women discover orgasm: A therapist's guide to a new treatment approach.* New York: Free Press/Macmillan, 1980.

Boston Women's Health Collective. *Our bodies ourselves: A book by and for women.* New York: Simon & Schuster, 1973.

Brady, J. P. Brevital relaxation treatment of frigidity. *Behavior Research and Therapy,* 1966, *4,* 71–77.

Chapman, J. D. Frigidity: Rapid treatment by reciprocal inhibition. *Journal of the American Osteopathic Association,* 1968, *67,* 871–878.

Childs, E., Sachnoff, E., & Stocker, E., in interaction with a Committee of the Whole of Association for Women in Psychology. Women's sexuality: a feminist view. *AWP Newsletter,* March–April, 1975, 1–4.

Dodson, B. *Liberating masturbation.* New York: Bodysex Designs, 1974.

Ellis, A. *The intelligent woman's guide to dating and mating.* Secaucus, N.J.: Lyle Stuart, 1979.

Ellis, A., & Harper, R. A. *The new guide to rational living.* North Hollywood, Calif.: Wilshire, 1975.

Friday, N. *My secret garden.* New York: Pocket Books, 1975.

Heiman, J., LoPiccolo, L., & LoPiccolo, J. *Becoming orgasmic.* Englewood Cliffs, N.J.: Prentice-Hall, 1976.

Heinrich, A. The effect of group and self-directed behavioral-educational treatment on primary orgasmic dysfunction in females treated without their partners. Ph.D. Dissertation, University of Minnesota, 1976.

Hite, S. *The Hite report.* New York: Macmillan, 1976.

Hunt, M. *Sexual behavior in the 1970s.* Chicago, Ill.: Playboy Press, 1974.

Kaplan, H. S. *The new sex therapy.* New York: Brunner/Mazel, 1974.

Kellogg, P. Personal communication, 1973.

Kinsey, A. C., Pomeroy, W. B., Martin, C. E., & Gebhard, P. H. *Sexual behavior in the human female.* New York: Simon & Schuster, Pocket Books, 1953.

Kuriansky, J., Sharpe, L., & O'Connor, D. Group treatment for women: The quest for orgasm. Paper presented at the American Public Health Association of Washington, D.C., October 1976.

Lazarus, A. The treatment of chronic frigidity by systematic desensitization. *Journal of Nervous and Mental Disease,* 1963, *136* (3), 272–278.

Lieblum, S., & Eisner-Hershfield, R. Sexual enhancement groups for dysfunctional women: An evaluation. *Journal of Sex and Marital Therapy,* 1977, *3*(2), 139–152.

Lobitz, W., & LoPiccolo, J. The role of masturbation in the treatment of orgasmic dysfunction. *Archives of Sexual Behavior,* 1972, *2*(2), 163–171.

LoPiccolo, L., & Heiman, J. *Becoming orgasmic: A sexual growth program for women.* New York: Focus International, 1976. (Film)

Madsen, C., & Ullman, L. Innovations in the desensitization of frigidity. *Behavior Research and Therapy,* 1967, *5* (1), 67–68.

Masters, W., & Johnson, V. *Human sexual inadequacy.* Boston: Little Brown, 1970.

Meador, B., Solomon, E., & Bowen, M. Encounter groups for women only. In N. Solomon

& B. Berzon (Eds.), *New perspectives on encounter groups*. San Francisco, Calif.: Jossey-Bass, 1972, 335–348.

Muench, G. The comparative effectiveness of long-term, short-term, and interrupted psychotherapy. Paper presented at Western Psychological Association, Portland, Ore., April 1964.

Multi media resources catalog. San Francisco, Calif.: Multi Media Resource Center, 1979.

O'Connor, J., & Stern, L. Results of treatment in functional sexual disorders. *New York State Journal of Medicine*, 1972, 72 (15), 1927–1934.

Paul, G. *Insight vs. desensitization in psychotherapy*. Stanford, Calif.: Stanford University Press, 1966.

SAR guide for a better sex life. San Francisco, Calif.: National Sex Forum, 1975.

Schneidman, B., & McGuire, L., Group therapy for nonorgasmic women: Two age levels. *Archives of Sexual Behavior*, 1976, 5, 239–247.

Walen, S. Our common sexual vocabulary. Unpublished manuscript, 1978.

Walen, S., Hauserman, N., & Lavin, P., *A clinical guide to behavior therapy*. New York: Oxford, 1977.

Wolfe, J. A cognitive behavioral approach to female sexuality and sexual expression. Paper presented at the annual convention of the American Psychological Association, Washington, D.C., September 1976.

Wolfe, J. How to be sexually assertive. New York: Institute for Rational Living, 1976.

Wolpe, J. *The practice of behavior therapy*. New York: Pergamon, 1969.

Yalom, I. D. *The theory and practice of group psychotherapy*. New York: Basic Books, 1970.

12

One's Company; Two's a Crowd
Skills in Living Alone Groups

Laura Primakoff

Introduction

> In our culture it is permissible to say you are lonely, for that is a way of
> admitting that it is not good to be alone . . . and it is permissible to want to
> be alone temporarily to "get away from it all." But if one mentioned that he
> (she) liked to be alone, not for a rest or an escape, but for its own joys, people
> would think that something was vaguely wrong with him (her)—that some
> parriah aura of untouchability or sickness hovered around him (her). And if a
> person is alone very much of the time, people tend to think of him (her) as a
> failure, for it is inconceivable to them that he (she) would choose to be alone.
> (May, 1953, p. 26)

Singleness and living alone are rapidly growing phenomena in our society (Stein, 1976). This is reflective of changes in life-style and values taking place on a societal level in the United States. Our society is beginning to experience some dramatic structural changes in the nature of people's social relationships and living arrangements that entail more and more people living outside the traditional context of marriage and romantic love; 1 of every 5 American households consists of just one person (*Going it Alone*, September 4, 1978, p. 76). (This figure does not include the sizeable number of single-parent households.) This may represent a type of sociological evolution in the latter part of the twentieth century, when for a variety of social, cultural, and economic rea-

LAURA PRIMAKOFF • Center for Cognitive Therapy, Department of Psychiatry, 133 South 36th Street, University of Pennsylvania, Philadelphia, Pennsylvania 19104.

sons, for a growing minority of the population, the individual constitutes the social unit, rather than the family or the couple.

There are a number of diverse populations for which the issue of living alone clearly has relevance. The young never-married, the divorced, the widowed, the elderly, and various types of formerly institutionalized individuals, including ex-mental patients.

The present chapter will present a cognitively focused, multimodal treatment approach to living alone. The program is based on a treatment manual developed in conjunction with an empirical exploration (Primakoff, 1981) of what constitutes the functional cognitive schemas (Beck, 1976) as well as behaviors of those people who are able to live alone contentedly versus the dysfunctional cognitive schemas and behaviors of those people who experience chronic loneliness and dissatisfaction when living alone.

There is virtually no theoretical or empirical work with regard to contented aloneness in the psychological literature. Existing descriptions of such a state are found in anecdotal and biographical accounts, case histories, novels, and poetry. However, the growing importance of aloneness and singleness from both the psychological and sociological viewpoint is beginning to be realized. As a result, psychological investigation of those individuals who either choose or find themselves single or living alone has begun (Kangas, 1977; Kanter, 1977; Kelly, 1977; Parmelee & Werner, 1978; Shaver & Rubinstein, 1979).

There are, however, a number of psychologists (Altman, 1975; Ittelson, Proshansky, Rivlin, & Winkel, 1974; Lilly, 1977) who have suggested that humans may have a need for privacy and that experiences of solitude can provide a variety of important benefits ranging from relaxation and emotional release to profound personal, philosophical, and creative insights. Lilly (1977) and Suedfeld (1981) have described the use of isolation as a treatment intervention for a variety of clinical problems.

Several areas of literature provide material suggestive of what might constitute contented aloneness. First, experimental and anecdotal accounts of sensory deprivation and extreme isolation experiences (Brownfield, 1972; Deaton, Berg, Richlin, & Litrownik, 1977; Zuckerman, 1964) suggest that individuals who are able to engage in various forms of cognitive, affective, and behavioral self-stimulation cope better in such circumstances. Second, several theorists (Ellis, 1962; Maslow, 1968) have proposed that those individuals whose self-esteem and basic life satisfaction are not contingent upon love and intimacy, but rather upon their own cognitive, behavioral, and affective resources, are more developed emotionally.

Central to an "alone-contented" cognitive schema is the belief that romantic love and intimacy are not required for happiness, satisfaction, or meaning (Primakoff, 1981). Individuals with such a schema are likely to have a more balanced and accurate view of the advantages and disadvantages of both intimacy and aloneness. When such individuals find themselves living alone, they are more able to focus on the advantages of that situation, thereby deriving satisfaction from it, even though their ideal preference might be to be involved in an intimate, love relationship.

When living alone, the alone-contented group has the ability to create for themselves a pleasurable and satisfying internal and external world. Such individuals have a range of activities and experiences engaged in alone and with others that may provide them as much or more satisfaction and involvement as does romantic/conjugal intimacy and commitment. In the absence of intimate love relationships, these important alternate sources of gratification very well may serve as sources of positive feeling in order to remain generally satisfied with the life-style of living alone and as powerful buffers against severe loneliness.

Cognitive-behavioral clinical work (Beck, 1976; Beck, Rush, Shaw, & Emery, 1979; Ellis & Harper, 1975; Lazarus, 1976; Meichenbaum, 1977) has demonstrated that it is possible to replace dysfunctional thinking and behaving with more adaptive cognitive and behavioral coping strategies. The goals of the current treatment program are to help individuals living alone systematically to develop an alone-contented cognitive schema as well as behavioral "solitude" skills for living alone.

The program has been conducted both as a therapy program and as an educational–enrichment program. Certain of the techniques, strategies, and homework assignments would need to be adapted to the specific clinical and/or socioeconomic needs of the particular group members. However, the basic principles are relevant for all individuals living alone. Thus far, the program has been successful in helping individuals of varying psychiatric diagnoses, socioeconomic status (SES), ages, past and current marital status, sexual orientation, with or without children living at home, and so forth. In addition, there have been a number of married individuals who have benefited from learning how to spend higher quality time separately from their spouses.

The cognitive and behavioral skills involved in tolerating and enjoying experiences alone are central to issues of autonomy versus social dependency in general. Thus, the treatment program addresses concerns that very well may be relevant to syndromes as seemingly disparate as agoraphobia, depression, and marital distress.

The program consists of 10 sessions conducted on a weekly basis; each session lasting 2½ hours. The remainder of the chapter will be a session-by-session description of the group program.

Session 1: Introduction and Rationale

The group experience begins by the leader or leaders introducing themselves in terms of basic demographic information: their own aloneness history, their own romantic/marital relationship history, and their reasons for being interested in leading the group.

I have found that this type of self-disclosure serves to model self-disclosure by group members and to begin to present the leader(s) as successful role model(s) in terms of living alone. My experience has been that in order to be able to lead such a group it is important for the leader(s) to have had some previous successful experience at living alone and to value that experience in its own right.

Group members then are requested to turn to the person sitting next to them and interview him or her for 10 minutes regarding the same kinds of information presented by the leader(s), that is, aloneness and relationship history, and why he or she came to the group. The process is then reversed and the interviewee now interviews his or her partner.

Then each person introduces the partner and presents the most relevant information with regard to him or her to the group. This is a fairly open-ended structure in that the person being described is free to add any comments and the leaders can ask additional questions in order to better understand and clarify the presentation.

The leaders then explain how inherent in the content and goals of the program is a questioning of both societal and members' personal assumptions concerning what life goals, values, types of social relationships, and living arrangements constitute normality and optimal psychological functioning. An increasing number of individuals find themselves living alone for the first time in their lives. However, many of them never have learned the requisite psychological and/or practical skills to live alone in a competent and satisfying manner. Traditionally, the assumption has been that living alone is an inherently undesirable, lonely, and temporary state to be escaped by the forming of relationships with other people, in particular, a romantic love relationship. However, the unique focus of this program is on one's relationship with oneself, and the development of one's own resources which can serve as supplements and alternatives to external relationships.

The "paradigmatic shift" being suggested is that singleness is a legitimate, alternative life-style, and that short- and long-term experiences of solitude provide unique benefits. It is suggested that one of the purposes of a *group* for those living alone is to bring singles together "out of the closet" in order to affirm that they constitute a significant demographic proportion of the American adult population, in terms of numbers, as well as economic and cultural influence. Such an affirmation helps in countering the self-concept of being freakish, marginal, and alone in one's life-style, as well as the notion that "everyone else" is married and coupled.

The following points constitute the rationale for the program:

1. The major goal of the program is for members to develop an intimate, loving, and accepting relationship with themselves; such a relationship involving the same kind of active process as developing an intimate relationship with another person, for example, the adoption of certain caring attitudes and behaviors, having a variety of meaningful and pleasurable experiences, and so forth.

2. In order to try to shift the attitudes and behaviors that one has practiced and had strongly culturally reinforced for 20 years or more, as powerful and systematic a change process as possible will need to be implemented.

3. A multimodal approach to change is introduced (Lazarus, 1976). The central notion of this approach is that clients experience dysfunction and dysphoria in their solitary and/or social behaviors, emotions, sensations, visual images, thoughts, and attitudes. In order to solve global and diffuse presenting problems effectively, a comprehensive and thorough assessment must be made within each of these modalities so as to be able to isolate the precise maladaptive habits and/or response deficits that are interfering with adaptive functioning. One then proceeds to teach the necessary competencies and coping skills within each of the modalities.

4. In order to change the overall quality of one's time alone and the experience of aloneness, one needs to change a variety of areas of functioning. However, since this is a cognitively focused multimodal program, the cognitive model of emotional distress and change is particularly emphasized. The basic notion is that one's internal world, that is, one's thoughts and images about aloneness and singleness, influence one's feelings and behavior to a great extent. The focus of much of the program will be the identification, questioning, and changing of dysfunctional thoughts about being alone.

5. The following list of the 10 sessions of the program is distributed and discussed.

Session 1:   Introduction and rationale
Session 2:   Aloneness and loneliness

Session 3: Love, sex, and approval "needs"
Session 4: Daily domestic living
Session 5: Being at home with yourself
Session 6: Going out with yourself
Session 7: Relationships with others
Session 8: Open session
Session 9: Developing a physical, sensual relationship with yourself
Session 10: Unique advantages and opportunities of the single lifestyle

6. Lastly, the various methods for systematic skills training and problem solving are presented, for example, aloneness journal and record keeping, cognitive and behavioral homework assignments, bibliotherapy, environmental interventions, and behavioral contracts. It is explained that as leaders we offer a number of resources, such as, discussion of ideas, sharing of experiences between group members, bibliotherapy, and various cognitive and behavioral change techniques. In terms of the actual change, however, it is a function of the extent to which group members implement and practice the various techniques that are presented.

Homework

The didactic portion of the session is followed by a relaxation exercise that is done in order to model a self-instructional, self-control procedure that group members can use to counter anxiety, fears of loneliness, and so forth. Relaxation instructions (Lazarus, 1971, pp. 273–275) are distributed so that participants can practice relaxing at home.

The first homework assignment for this session is to keep an aloneness record (Table 1), which consists of daily recording of the start and end of time alone, where one was, what one was doing, what one's mood was (put the first letter of mood word), and what one was thinking at the time, the actual sentences or images.

The second assignment is to formulate two cognitive or behavioral goals to be worked on during the therapy program. These are to be as realistic and specific as possible. Examples are:

1. I want to be able to go to the movies alone on a Saturday night.
2. I want to be able to have a dinner party in my home.
3. I want to believe that I can provide myself with some of my own happiness and meaning.

TABLE 1
Aloneness Record[a]

Name _____

Day and date _____

Time
_____

Start	End	Place	Activity	Mood[b]	Self-talk
6–12					
12–5					
5–9					
9–12					

[a]Adapted from Hawkins, Setty, and Baldwin (1977).
[b]Neutral, Content, Lonely, Angry, Depressed, Happy, Bored, Tired, or Unfocused.

4. I want to change the attitude that friends are worth less than lovers.

SESSION 2: ALONENESS AND LONELINESS

All of the sessions in the program are structured similarly. First, the leaders ask if there were any reactions to the previous session and these are discussed. Secondly, the homework assignments are handed in and any reactions or questions regarding them are discussed. The leaders are to read assignments between sessions in order to gain an understanding of members' aloneness and to provide any useful feedback to them. Thirdly, either written materials, verbal didactic material, or experiential exercises are used to generate discussion of participants' thoughts, feelings, and experiences with regard to the various topics addressed in the program. When a particularly illustrative or problematic personal issue is raised, the leaders use a variety of cognitive restructuring techniques, such as suggesting more plausible explanations for an event or contradictory evidence that questions a particular belief, in order to model how one can begin to change one's thinking. It often can be very effective for the leaders to elicit material from group members so that they offer each other the above kinds of alternatives, rather than their always being suggested by the leaders.

A questionnaire about loneliness is then distributed. Group members spend 10 to 15 minutes writing their answers to the following questions, which are then used as the basis for discussion:

1. What is the difference between aloneness and loneliness?
2. What kinds of situations make you feel lonely?
3. Are there certain times of the day, week, or year when you feel particularly lonely?
4. What exactly are your thoughts, visual images, and feelings when you're lonely?
5. What are your worst fears and fantasies about being alone?
6. What do you do when you feel lonely? How successful are your attempts to reduce loneliness?

In the discussion that follows, the following distinctions have proved useful:

1. "Aloneness" involves being with oneself, physically separate from others. (a) It is a neutral or potentially positive experience. (b) Some of the potential, positive aspects of solitude involve contented relaxation, self-awareness, and enjoyable absorption in activity and creativity.

2. "Lonesomeness" involves times when one is alone, but would *prefer* to be with others (Johnson, 1977).

3. "Loneliness" involves focusing on the *discrepancy* between the social relationships that one has and those that one believes one "should" or "must" have (Perlman & Peplau, 1981; Young, 1982). Such a focus then creates the following types of distorted and distressing thinking:

- A negative distortion of the relationships that one has: (a) Magnification of the discrepancy—"I feel *totally* alone in the world." "*Everyone* has deserted and abandoned me." (b) Discounting the number or quality of current relationships: "*No one* cares about me or is *really* interested in my life." (c) Dichotomizing relationships into romance versus "nothing": "My friends are okay, but I *need* a lover." Without a lover, I'm *completely alone.*"
- Extending the discrepancy into the past and future: "I've *never* really been loved." "I'm afraid I'll *always* be alone." "I'll *never* find anybody as good as X again." (e.g., hopelessness).
- Low frustration tolerance, for example, demanding that things be the way one wants them to be: "I *can't stand* being alone." "I *shouldn't have to* be alone." "I *can't stand* not having someone who loves me."
- Self-downing: "It's my *own fault* that I'm alone." "I'm *worthless* and *unlovable.*"

There is then a "secondary"loneliness that involves the following kinds of dysfunctional thinking in reaction to experiences of loneliness:

- Anxiety and low frustration tolerance about the loneliness: "I'm *afraid* these feelings are never going to go away." "I *can't stand* these feelings."
    In discussing this type of anxiety, the point is made that it is not being alone that people are afraid of, because there is nothing "dangerous" about being alone; rather, people are afraid of their own painful thoughts and feelings when alone.
- Further self-downing and shame for being lonely: "There must be something *wrong with me* feeling so lonely." "The only people out there are *rejects like me.*" "Hardly anyone is as lonely as I am." "I am *neurotic and screwed up* for being lonely." This latter self-deprecating thinking causes even further feelings of isolation and alienation, and so the lonely feelings continue to escalate.

Homework

The first homework assignment for this session involves focusing on feelings of loneliness in the aloneness journal. The purpose is to identify: When do I begin feeling lonely? What triggers it? How long does it last? Was I with a particular person? What was I thinking about? What helped to reduce it?

The second assignment involves attempting to identify the most distressing or frequent dysfunctional lonely thought and beginning to question its validity. In addition, participants design behavioral experiments to test some of their secondary loneliness reactions, for example, to increase tolerance of loneliness, force oneself to be alone and lonely for a certain period of time; to decrease shame about being lonely, *not;* to obtain information by asking other people about their loneliness, and so forth.

Some time is spent individually tailoring the second assignment. Homework sheets describing the assignments and respective behavioral contracts are distributed. (This is the format for homework for the remainder of the sessions.) The contract states, "If I do homework assignment Number 1, I will give myself _____." "If I do not do homework assignment Number 1, I will either deprive myself of _____ or make myself do _____."

Lastly, in order to further understanding of the cognitive model of emotional disturbance, two pamphlets are distributed, *Thinking and Depression* (Beck, undated) and *Coping with Depression* (Beck & Greenberg, 1974).

SESSION 3: LOVE, SEX, AND APPROVAL "NEEDS"

After discussing the kinds of maladaptive lonely self-talk that group members recorded during the week, the concept is presented that these kinds of distorted thoughts proceed from certain underlying dysfunctional assumptions regarding love, sex, and approval that are both personally and culturally based.

Obviously, there are a variety of types of human love relationships. In our culture, however, there is a societal/media overvaluing and preoccupation with one particular form of love; that is, the romantic, sexual form that culminates in marriage. The unfortunate consequence for many individuals of this cultural obsession is that romantic and conjugal relationships are overburdened with many functions and meanings that they cannot possibly fulfill. Many individuals have the unrealistic expectation that social relationships in general, but in particular romantic love relationships, can and should be the providers of their worth, self-esteem, identity, meaning, happiness, excitement, and intimacy. When love becomes the sole source of gratification in such a pervasive and profound way, one literally *needs* the external loved one to maintain one's emotional equilibrium. *Love and Addiction* (1976) by Stanton Peele is recommended reading for a vivid description of the parallels between this type of needy love and substance addictions.

At this juncture, the "alone–deficit" paradigm is described explicitly. Central to such a paradigm is the need for external others to provide love, stimulation, and meaning in one's life. Because of the demand for others to fulfill these functions, substitutes are not possible. The underlying theme in the alone–deficit schema is that the benefits of romantic intimacy in particular are overfocused on, exaggerated, overvalued, and demanded. In turn, the potentially gratifying aspects of objective reality both in terms of actual social relationships and experiences alone are to varying degrees ignored, minimized, devalued, and experienced as inherently incomplete, deficient, and unsatisfying. Clearly, this pattern of living alone results in extreme vulnerability to experiences of loneliness. Another negative consequence of this exaggerated emphasis on the necessity and desirability of romantic love and sex is that individuals living alone often conclude that they *should* want love and sex and that if they do not, for whatever length of time, there is something wrong with them.

The alternative "alone–contented" paradigm is then presented again, that is, the belief that one can be happy and satisfied living alone without romantic love and intimacy. In order to concretize and strengthen the alone–contented assumptions, an excerpt from the chapter "Tackling Dire Needs for Approval" (pp. 92–98), from *A New Guide to Rational Living* (Ellis & Harper, 1975), is distributed. The entire book is recommended reading as is *Feeling Good* (Burns, 1980). The selected excerpt questions philosophically and logically the idea that one's self-esteem and happiness are contingent on others' love and approval and suggests some more adaptive assumptions and behaviors. In order to provide additional specific suggestions, the following materials are given to participants and discussed with regard to the homework.

Cognitive and Behavioral Strategies for Reducing Loneliness; Love and Sex "Needs"

Behavioral Strategies

The guiding principle is to *plan ahead*. Have a list of activities that you know you enjoy doing and that help to reduce your loneliness.

1. Plan ahead for evenings, weekends, trips, and holidays so that there are enough activities and people for you.

2. Help someone else or something else; focus on loving rather than on being loved, for example, volunteer work, friends, or pets.
3. Write letters, visit friends, call local or long-distance friends.
4. Go out and do something pleasurable by yourself; for example, go to the movies, go shopping, go for a drive, take a walk.
5. Engage in some kind of physical recreation by yourself, for example, work with your hands, dance, engage in sports, or exercise.
6. Do some kind of physical or mental work by yourself, for example, clean up your home, study, do personal or job-related work.
7. Engage in some form of creative self-expression, for example, write in a journal, talk to yourself, sing, play music, draw or paint.
8. Keep a scrapbook of poems and advice; engage in spiritual activities, or religious or philosophical thinking that is comforting and meaningful to you.

Self-Talk Responses

1. Think about possible benefits of your experience of loneliness, such as telling yourself that you are learning to be self-sufficient or that you will grow from the experience.
2. People have survived for years by themselves.
3. I would rather be with someone tonight, but being here alone is okay.
4. Just because I'm alone now doesn't mean I'll always be alone.
5. I care about myself.
6. There are people who care about me (list them in your mind: family, friends, and so forth).
7. There are activities that I enjoy alone and things that are meaningful and important to me (list them in your mind).
8. Everybody gets lonely at times, even married people.
9. Just because this man or woman has rejected me does not mean they all will.
10. I won't die if I don't have sex tonight; I'll just be frustrated.
11. Remind yourself that you actually do have, or again will have, good relationships with people.
12. It is not so important to be liked by everyone.
13. It's all right at this point in my life not to be romantically involved.

14. Think about things that you are good at doing and qualities that make you attractive to others.

Attitudinal Alternatives

1. Focus on the advantages of living alone and not being involved in a romantic love relationship: (a) Living alone I have more time and emotional energy for myself. (b) Living alone I can feel freely and express my emotions. (c) There are many interests and pleasures that I engage in alone that are meaningful to me. (d) Living alone I can be involved with many different people in many different ways. (e) Living alone I can decide when I do and do not spend time with others. (f) There are some unique, exciting experiences that one can have living alone. (g) Living alone I can discover and develop my own values, beliefs, and interests. (h) I still can love; the less I *have* to be loved, the more energy I have to love others. (i) I can use this opportunity to increase my frustration tolerance for not getting what I want, that is, love.
2. Remind yourself of the disadvantages of being with people and/or involved in a romantic relationship. List in your mind the specific reasons that your last major relationship ended; remind yourself of all of the problems and heartaches.
3. Dispute the belief that only love gives meaning and happiness to your life: (a) Focus on the fact that you are living alone and functioning quite well. (b) The source of your enjoyment of life is *in you,* not in other people. (c) I have a commitment to my own growth and development. (d) I can be happy, even if for a long period of time I am not involved in an intimate love relationship.

In order to do the homework, the following example is handed out to help demonstrate how to answer one's lonely self-talk or automatic thoughts with more reasonable and realistic responses.

Homework

The first homework assignment for this session involves focusing on feelings of "needing" others' love and approval in the aloneness journal. The purpose is to identify: Who or what triggers these feelings? With which people or in what kinds of situations am I particularly needy? What are my thoughts? How can I begin to answer them more reasonably?

TABLE 2
Daily Record of Negative Automatic Thoughts[a]

Date	Situation	Emotion(s)	Automatic thought(s)
5/23	At home, reading–waiting for Bob to call—it's now 10 P.M.–he hasn't called	Sad; miserable; abandoned; lonely	Why didn't he call? Why is he rejecting me? I feel so miserable, I don't know what to do—why does this always happen to me—I just *can't* go on like this—what did I do wrong?

Questioning the evidence Reasonable/adaptive response	*Alternative therapy* Reasonable/adaptive response
Just because he didn't call doesn't mean he is rejecting me–I already saw him twice this week–if he didn't like me he would not have spent that much time with me–I *shouldn't* jump to crazy conclusions like that—and it's *not* true that "this" *always* happens to me. With John, *I* was the one who didn't want to keep up the *relationship*!!	There could be many reasons why he didn't call—besides rejection! He could be tied up with his clients, he could be trying to set bail for someone—it may have skipped his mind—he could be with friends—he may have had something to do. But even if he *is* having second thoughts about me—we could talk about it—it doesn't automatically mean that I can't hold on to him.

Re-attribution Reasonable/adaptive response	*De-catastrophizing* Reasonable/adaptive response
Why should I assume that his not calling has to do with *me*?? He may have a lot of reasons for doing what he does—things that may have *nothing* to do with me. It doesn't make sense to think that everything happens because of *me*–that I did something wrong. He must have his *own* feelings, ideas, and fears just like I. If things don't work out the way I'd like them–it could be because of his *own* things–it doesn't make sense to believe that I am *solely* responsible for what happens between the TWO OF US!!	Here I go *again*! Thinking that I am rejected!!–But even if I am (which I don't really know for sure) even if he doesn't want to see me—it's *not true* that I can't go on!! It's just a feeling I have. I have survived before even if this doesn't work–the worst that can happen is that I'll be sad, unhappy but it's *not* the end of the world— there are other men out there, and I have my friends, my job–I *can* go on.

[a]From Kovacs. Copies available from The Center for Cognitive Therapy, Room 602, 133 South 36th Street, Philadelphia, Pennsylvania 19104.

The second assignment involves identifying a central dysfunctional assumption and spending 10 to 15 minutes per day questioning its usefulness and/or validity in writing. Examples of such core beliefs would be "Love gives me worth." "Love gives meaning to my life." "I must have love."

Lastly, the following kinds of suggestions are made for cognitive and/or behavioral practice. These serve to generate experiential evidence directly counter to the unreasonable thinking.

1. Take interpersonal risks, e.g., act in ways *you* want to act with someone whose approval you want; try to get a person who might reject you interested in you—see if you survive.
2. Date several people at once.
3. Focus on others, rather than being obsessed with how they are reacting to you.
4. Practice thinking about being rejected or about a relationship that you're involved in ending, and see if you can alter your automatic thoughts and feelings; try to calmly imagine your lover being with other people.

SESSION 4: DAILY DOMESTIC LIVING

Group members fill out the following questionnaire and give it to the leaders. Usually, the two or three topics of majority concern are chosen to be discussed.

Circle the topics that you would find the most useful to discuss today:

1. Home:
   a) choice of place to live
   b) housekeeping: cleaning, laundry
   c) decorating and furnishing
   d) cooking for yourself
   e) entertaining at home
   f) physical safety
2. Maintenance:
   a) car maintenance
   b) house maintenance
   c) self-grooming, personal hygiene, physical health care
3. Problematic habits:
   a) overeating
   b) excessive drinking

    c) excessive "recreational"/self-medication drug use
    d) financial mismanagement
    e) time mismanagement, for example, overextending oneself;
       procrastination; wasting time
  4. Other daily domestic life issues that have not been listed

In this session it is suggested that in order to create a self-sufficient and autonomous life-style for oneself it is important to develop a variety of "solitude skills." The most fundamental and critical ones, upon which all others are contingent, involve creating a daily life for oneself that is as high quality and enjoyable as possible, in which one takes care of basic domestic and maintenance needs.

The following question calls attention to the kind of "alone–deprived" existence that many individuals living alone create for themselves: How long would you live with someone when all you had was bad meals, for example, tuna from out of the can, TV dinners; the place was always a mess; most of your spare time was spent watching TV and listening to the radio; when you hardly ever went out or did anything at home that was fun or interesting? (One group member "jokingly" answered, "Would you believe ten years?")

The following general principles provide an overall framework for the discussion of specific domestic topics: One's goal with regard to domestic, daily maintenance of one's life is mastery and self-sufficiency. In order to achieve such a goal, it is necessary to do a systematic task analysis of each problem so as to decide which combination of the following possibilities will solve the problem most effectively and efficiently:

  1. If one wants to solve the problem oneself: (a) learn the necessary skills and information through a variety of methods: self-help books, courses, friends, service people.
  2. If one cannot or does not want to solve the problem oneself: (a) learn how to find and enlist the necessary resources to do so; (b) be more assertive with service people and friends by asking for help and learning from them.

When one has been part of a couple there often has been a sex-role based division of skills and knowledge. Thus, one's partner may have possessed certain skills that now have to be found elsewhere. However, it is important to realize that even as a couple you both lacked many skills for which you had to depend on others. As a result, once one develops the attitude and capability of *finding* help, being alone constitutes much less of a realistic deficit of skills than ordinarily is thought. What is very apparent, however, is that whatever tendencies involving lack of confidence, assertiveness, self-caring, or self-control one had while living with another often can become intensified when living alone. There is none of the daily support and structure that often is provided by a conjugal relationship. You must create this for yourself.

It is beyond the scope of this session as well as the current chapter to discuss all of the domestic topics. However, some of the highlights of "alone–contented" domestic attitudes and behaviors will be presented here. Group members often will offer each other very ingenious suggestions and solutions to problems.

Home

Creating a high quality home life for oneself involves self-caring and self-expressive attitudes. The kinds of dysfunctional thinking that interfere with creating a nurturant and expressive home are: "Why bother, it's only me." "Why set up house when I don't want to be living alone?" "I have terrible taste anyway." "What will other people think if they see my place?"

One should do whatever is needed to create a *home* for oneself, physically and emotionally, so that it is a place to which you look forward to spending time with yourself as well as entertaining others. It is important for your home to be as comfortable and personally expressive as you would like it to be. This is one of the luxuries of living alone; you do not have to have anything that you do not like in your home. As your tastes change, you can change the decor. Inherent in decorating and taking care of one's place of residence is that one is making an expressive statement as to one's tastes and who one is, as well as at least some minimal commitment to being single. (Some individuals will choose to spend years living alone in an undecorated home because of the attitude that their situation is only a "temporary" one.)

In terms of comfort and pleasure, you can give yourself extravagances selectively, for example, flowers, a nice bed with decorated sheets, a full length mirror, or a good stereo. You can surround yourself with possessions that are meaningful and comforting to you, such as, pets, plants, your own or friends' paintings, or photographs.

Eating

Cooking for oneself and eating alone present difficulties for many individuals living alone. Often it is a lack of self-caring as well as an avoidance of feelings of loneliness that cause many people to either avoid eating by themselves or to make it a "quick and dirty" affair if they do. People often believe that one *should* not eat alone because eating is a social activity. However, eating alone has many of the same advantages as engaging in other activities alone, for example, flexibility and experimentation (time, choice of food), and increased intensity and focus on the experience itself.

There are numerous methods for making eating alone as pleasant as possible, such as being physically comfortable when you eat; having comforting and favorite foods and some good knives and wine glasses. For special occasions, one can indulge in candlelight, a glass of wine, breakfast in bed, or order in food. Cognitive/attentional strategies to counter loneliness and feeling the need for someone to eat with include listening to good music or reading while you eat; giving yourself time to relax and think about the day; appreciating the fact that you have made yourself a nice meal; really focusing on the taste of the food, rather than having your attention divided between talking to someone and eating.

Problematic Habits

Group members sometimes are reluctant to disclose that they may have a particular problem, such as excessive drinking or binge eating. There are several approaches that I have found to be helpful in defusing the shame associated with such problems. First, one provides a compassionate acknowledgement that those living alone are understandably at particular risk for having some of these problems, but that it is important to remember that many of those who are married also suffer from such difficulties. Second, a matter-of-fact problem-solving approach is suggested, wherein one's task is to employ the appropriate combination of cognitive, behavioral, and environmental interventions to solve the difficulty.

If one first examines the kinds of events, thoughts, and feelings that trigger the behavior, one can begin to see patterns of functions that the behavior may serve. A frequent function is that of "self-medication," in terms of reducing or avoiding the experiencing of unpleasant emotions such as anxiety, depression, and loneliness. The problem behaviors can range from excessive drinking to oversleeping to "workaholism." Another function is that of providing maladaptive forms of "pleasure," for example, overeating, drinking, or "interest," such as, shopping (overspending) or watching television.

There are several kinds of dysfunctional thinking that maintain

such behaviors. First, there are varying degrees of denial as to the consequences of one's actions, for example, "It doesn't matter, it's only me
(how fat I am, how chaotic my life is)." One can more easily think of
oneself as being invisible and no one else knowing or caring how one
looks or acts. A second problem is low frustration tolerance, for example, "I can't stand eating less, having a schedule, cleaning up." Third,
there may be shame as well as hopelessness about changing: "This is the
way I am." "I can't control myself." "I'd be too lonely and unhappy if I
didn't." Lack of knowledge regarding self-help methods and groups
contributes to the feelings of isolation and hopelessness.

Homework

The homework assignment for this session involves choosing one
aspect of daily living that one would like to begin changing. Individually
tailored assignments involve whatever techniques are appropriate, for
example, record keeping, information gathering about services, and so
forth. Group members are informed of numerous self-help books regarding domestic tasks and problems, some of which are written ex-
pressly for those living alone, for example, *The I Hate to Housekeep Book*
(Bracken, 1962); *Cooking for One is Fun* (Creel, 1976); *Living in One Room*
(Narr & Siple, 1976); *The Reader's Digest Complete Do-It-Yourself Manual*
(1981).

SESSION 5: BEING AT HOME WITH YOURSELF

In order to encourage interaction between group members in this
session, groups of three or four are formed in order to discuss their
responses to the following questions:

1. What kinds of things did your mother or father do for you that
   were especially comforting (e.g., chicken soup, warm baths.)?
2. What kinds of things did you enjoy doing alone when you were
   growing up?
3. Think of the friends and lovers you have had who have been
   really interesting and enjoyable to be with. What kinds of things
   did they do that were interesting and exciting to you? What
   things did you do together that you enjoyed? What made the
   relationship of high quality?
4. What are some interests and/or pleasures that you would like to
   pursue alone?

The conceptualization that is introduced in this session is that when living alone one can construct as high a quality relationship and life-style with oneself as with a spouse or cohabitant. The development of a relationship with yourself involves making a serious commitment to yourself and to your own self-development. This is achieved largely by providing for yourself the functions that other people ordinarily serve. Friends, family, and romantic partners provide nurturance, caring, interest, love, excitement, and fun; teachers, religious counselors, and therapists facilitate personal and spiritual growth. It is inherent in creating a primary, intimate relationship of this kind with oneself that one takes on a dual emotional and behavioral role involving being a companion *to* oneself, that is, the caretaker and the cared for.

The next question to be addressed is: What constitutes any high quality relationship and life-style? There are at least three necessary components: (1) everyday quality, that is, the kinds of domestic and maintenance issues discussed in the previous session, (2) ongoing interests and activities, and (3) special times. One's relationship with oneself is no different from a romantic/conjugal relationship in that it is vulnerable to boredom and stagnation in the absence of sufficient stimulation. People sometimes have a tendency to allow their relationships to "slip." They start taking each other for granted; their time together deteriorates into low-quality time. The same process all too easily can happen with yourself.

The idea being suggested is that you give the same commitment and caring to yourself that you would to a loved one on a daily basis. In order to develop ongoing interests and activities, as well as have special times, it becomes necessary to set aside regular times during the week for yourself, for example, "Monday and Wednesday nights are for me," the way you would for a lover. In order to do this, one has to be willing to risk other peoples' negative reactions to your wanting to spend time with yourself.

The remainder of the session is a discussion of the advantages and positive attitudes involved in choosing to spend time at home with yourself.

Initially, group members are encouraged to recall "forbidden" or "discouraged" activities engaged in when parents, roommates, or spouses were not home, in order to remind themselves of the playful, illicit, liberating experiences that aloneness potentially can offer.

Because of the total privacy involved in living alone, one has freedom to do as one pleases. The freedom exists on many levels. Since you are the only one physically and psychologically present, there are none of the usual explicit or implicit boundaries, constraints, and distractions inherent in living with another. You have the opportunity to be as bizarre and outrageous as you choose, for example, eat, wear, do whatever you want; listen to the kind of music you like; sing; dance; and so forth. You can push your experience to the limits. You have total flexibility and spontaneity in terms of the time and content of your activities. You have sufficient time and psychological space to engage in reflection, introspection, fantasy, and creativity.

This pursuit and development of your own values, beliefs, talents, interests, and pleasures provides you with the rare opportunity to discover and construct who you are independent of the desires, expectations, and demands of others. This is one of the most powerful aspects of self-development to be gained by living alone. No compromise is necessary. Inherent in this process you reduce your need and dependence on other people for meaning, involvement, and stimulation.

The goal is to shift one's attention from the fact that one is alone and "deprived" of someone to share activities with to the activity itself and one's enjoyment of it. When such shifts are made successfully, there can be a level of intensity and involvement in whatever one is doing that would be very difficult, if not impossible, to achieve with another person present.

The point is emphasized that relationships with others come and go for a variety of reasons: emotional, geographical, and so forth. However, your relationship with yourself remains constant and ongoing, whether you are in or out of a love relationship. A good relationship with yourself consistently can provide you with a unique sense of continuity, stability, familiarity, comfort, acceptance, and total intimacy, for example, you know everything about yourself.

An added motivation that can be given for developing an interesting life alone is to ask oneself, If I'm bored and unhappy with myself, what do I have to offer anyone else? What would I like to be able to offer others? How can I make a genuine commitment to someone else if I haven't made one to myself?

The following list of possibilities is then distributed:

Being at Home With Yourself

- Give yourself a manicure.
- Take a long, warm bath (try turning the lights off in the bathroom).
- Explore a particular subject in depth: history, art, rock music.
- Explore an old, undeveloped interest, or talent, for example, playing a musical instrument.
- Use your hands: painting, matting pictures, antiquing or building furniture, needlepoint, potting.
- Be creative: write, sing, dance, cook, photograph.

- Self-development: keep a journal, meditate, do reading related to personal growth.
- Listen to particular kind of music that you really enjoy.
- Study language on records or study about a foreign culture.
- Have a party for yourself.
- Play solitary games.
- Physical activities: yoga, self-massage, exercise program.
- Plant a garden—food or flowers.
- Set aside an afternoon, evening, or weekend to be with yourself and have a really good time.
- Indulge yourself: Act out a fantasy; put on make-up, a costume.
- Be *bizarre:* spend the day naked, eat chocolate ice cream all day.
- Just remember, *no one* is there to say or even to think "You are so *Weird!*"

Homework

The first homework assignment for this session involves recording thoughts, behavior, and feelings when home alone in the aloneness journal. Group members are asked to rate on a scale of 0 to 10 the quality of their time home alone in terms of both interest and pleasure. The second assignment involves setting aside some time during the week to do something at home alone that one has never done before. The third assignment involves working on one of the cognitive or behavioral goals that each member set for him or herself at the beginning of the program.

SESSION 6: GOING OUT WITH YOURSELF

As in the previous session, smaller groups are formed for discussion of the following questions:

1. Describe what would be a fantastic time for you with a friend or lover (day or evening).
2. What kinds of things do you do with friends or dates?
3. What kinds of things do you go out and do alone now?
4. What kinds of things would you like to be able to do alone that you aren't?
5. What prevents you from doing these things?

Within the context of members' answers to the last two questions, the following summary is presented regarding the kinds of dysfunctional attitudes that discourage people from going out alone: (1) fears of other people seeing you and viewing you as lonely and rejected because you are alone, (2) fears of being rejected at social events such as parties or dances, (3) fears of being disappointed by not meeting a romantic possibility at such an event, (4) fears of feeling lonely and of putting yourself down for being lonely and alone, (5) women's fears of being harassed or attacked by men, (6) passive, unrealistic attitudes that someone will call you and, therefore, you do not iniate social plans.

At this point, the following kinds of questions and strategies are posed in order to challenge the validity of the previously identified maladaptive thinking:

1. Are other people really looking? Even if they are, and have a negative view of you, does that have to influence how you feel about yourself? What other people think can have no direct impact on you. Remember that many of them are not enjoying who they are with, or wish they were single like you. Notice other people who are alone.
2. Will you survive rejection and disappointment? Is it not worth the risk?
3. Can you "stand" feeling lonely? What are you telling yourself that is making you feel lonely and down on yourself?
4. Women can learn to be more assertive with men who hassle them.

The remainder of the session is a discussion of the advantages and positive attitudes involved in choosing to go out with yourself. Virtually all of the advantages involved in spending time at home with yourself apply, with the added dimension of being out in the world and potentially interacting with others.

When going out alone one has tremendous freedom and flexibility. You can be totally spontaneous; you do not have to make plans ahead of time or coordinate logistics with another person. You are in control of where and when you want to go, as well as when to leave. On the one hand, you are not accountable to anyone at home, and on the other, you do not have to compromise with anyone that you are with.

Being able to go out alone is inherently liberating in that you are not allowing yourself to be controlled by your own or other people's negative attitudes about being alone, or by others' problematic behavior, for example, potential rejection or harassment.

If you are able to become absorbed in the situation and the activity itself, rather than in the fact that you are alone, other people's views of your being alone, or your *having* to meet a romantic possibility, it becomes possible to have experiences approximating the excitement and intensity of traveling alone.

When traveling alone, one is less constrained by the usual implicit or explicit personal or cultural frames of reference and so is freer to think and act in ways that one might not ordinarily. One is more likely under such circumstances to have direct encounters with people, since an intimate other is not present to serve as a buffer between oneself and external events. In addition, in the absence of conversational demands, one has a greater opportunity to observe, reflect on, and fantasize with regard to the ongoing stream of experience that one is having.

To the extent that one acquires a history of interesting and meaningful experiences with oneself, one is more likely to continue to seek out and to value such experiences in their own right. The realization that on any given night you can go anywhere and do anything alone and enjoy it, with the added excitement of the possibility of meeting someone new while you are doing it, serves to reduce your dependence on others for going out. Taking yourself out can be experienced as an opportunity to cultivate and practice an adventurous, risk-taking style. You then can begin to view it as *your* choice, as your *first* choice, not second best. You are making a commitment to spend an evening with yourself. The usual assumption is that of course you would prefer to be with someone else and could not find anyone (always forgetting that that someone else could be boring and/or unpleasant), and that is why you are alone, rather than the alternative possibility that you deliberately might have chosen and preferred your own company.

The following suggestion list is then distributed:

Taking Yourself Out

Basic Premise: Almost anything you can do with another person you can do alone; alone, you have the added possibility of meeting a new person.

- Drive in the country (car or public transportation)
- Local sightseeing
- Festivals, fairs
- Take a walk
- Have a picnic
- Do something outdoors, for example, hiking, swimming, camping
- Museum
- Zoo
- Singles' bars, discos
- Folk dancing
- Shopping
- Parties, dances

- Pursue an interest, develop a skill on your own, or take classes in gardening, photography, or another area
- Eat out
- Plays, concerts, movies
- Sporting events
- Participate in sports: bicycling, jogging, kite flying, ice skating
- Long distance traveling to wherever; for a day, a week, a month, a year
- Plan a whole day or weekend for yourself of special things to do and places to go
- Live out a fantasy with yourself: check into a fancy hotel; go to gourmet restaurants; or, a less expensive fantasy, spend all day at the movies

Homework

The first homework assignment for this session involves recording thoughts, behavior, and feelings when out alone in public in the aloneness journal. The purpose is to identify: What do you think other people are thinking about your being alone? What are you telling yourself that is making you feel lonely, embarrassed, and so forth?

The second assignment involves your spending some time taking yourself out and doing something that you ordinarily would not do alone. You might reward yourself by telling someone about it, or you might practice not telling anyone in order to keep the experience private.

Participants are particularly encouraged to risk going to places where they ordinarily would be ashamed or embarrassed to be seen, for example, places where couples or at least two people go together. Examples would be, going to a restaurant where there is a chance that they will be seen alone by people that they know, or going to a Friday night movie by themselves.

Session 7: Relationships with Others

The following suggestion list is distributed in order to stimulate discussion:

Ways of Meeting Friends and Acquaintances:

1. Entertain, have parties
2. Join any group, course, or organization in which you are interested

3. Start your own group, if one doesn't exist
4. Take a temporary, interesting job that puts you in contact with a lot of interesting people
5. Jobs in general

Ways of Initiating Potential Romance:

1. All of above methods, *plus*
2. Singles' bars and singles' clubs
3. Parties and dances
4. Tell friends that you're looking for people to go out with
5. Newspaper ads
6. Computer and dating services
7. The fine art of "the pickup"

Ways of Making Physical Contact:

1. Activities such as folk dancing, team sports
2. Set up massage group or reciprocal massage with friend
3. Spend time with children
4. Be physically affectionate with same-sex and other-sex friends
5. Sex

Additional Ways of Obtaining Intimacy and Emotional Support:

1. Co-counseling—get together with friend once a week and do mutual therapy
2. Women's, men's or mixed support group
3. Therapy—individual or group

Miscellaneous Ways of Having Contact with People:

1. Spend time in public at events where there are people present
2. Be part of a recreational, political, professional, or spiritual organization that interests you
3. Maintain contact with people who live in other places by writing, calling, and visiting
4. Travel—locally or further away
5. Do volunteer work, tutor, babysit . . .
6. Get to know neighbors
7. Keep in touch with family
   For more ideas, see: *Sex and the Liberated Man* (Ellis, 1976), *The Intelligent Woman's Guide to Dating and Mating* (Ellis, 1979), and *First Person Singular* (Johnson, 1977)

The following general principles for building a social network are suggested:

1. One should be active in establishing a social life for oneself in any and all ways that one can, for example, creating one's own groups and initiating contacts with people in many different circumstances.
2. One should be persistent in creating a social life, both in terms of repeatedly initiating with people who are not as responsive as one would like and in continuing to seek out new people with whom one wants relationships.
3. One can get involved in the *process* of meeting people rather than being overfocused on the *outcome*, for example, whether or not the other person likes you, whether or not the relationship will be romantic and sexual. One can begin to view meeting people as a game, as fun, as experimental and adventurous. If you persist enough you become desensitized to the fear and "shame" of rejection and begin to realize that in fact you have nothing to lose and everything to gain by extending yourself to others.
4. Friendship and a wide variety of social contacts is crucial to enjoying single life and is a unique opportunity when one is single.

Friendship

In *First Person Singular* Stephen Johnson points out a number of dysfunctional assumptions that may interfere with single people forming satisfying friendships:

1. Lovers are better than friends. This belief results in putting much more time and energy into the pursuit and maintenance of romantic relationships than into friendships.
2. Friendships should just happen. "People *should* be beating down my door." This is a corollary of "lovers are better than friends." It involves the idea that one does not have to pursue or work on friendships in the same way as one does romantic relationships.
3. Deliberately and openly looking for companionship is shameful and embarrassing, that is, "This proves that I'm a loser."
4. There are a number of rigid and excessive expectations that one can have about friends:

    a) Single people should have friendships only with others who are single.

  b) Good friends should be of the same sex.
  c) "Best" friends are the only worthwhile friends.
  d) Friends should always be there for you.

At this point, some basic concepts regarding the value of friendship when one is single are presented. When single, friends can become one's "family" and personal community. They sometimes provide as much or more emotional and practical support as mates or family members would. When single, it is important to have some single friends because they will be more likely to have as much investment and commitment to the relationship as you do. In addition, they can encourage and accompany you in looking for romance and can serve as powerful role models. Friendships generally tend to be more stable and enduring than dating relationships.

There are a number of unique opportunities and advantages in establishing friendships when one is single. You have the time, energy, and freedom to devote to high quality intimacy with friends as well as to a whole variety of types of friends. In fact, in terms of amount and quality of intimacy, one has the potential of being *less* lonely in certain respects than those who are isolated in couples.

One can have friendships with single and married individuals, couples, families with children, same-sex and other-sex individuals, people of all ages, interests, and walks of life. As with engaging in activities alone in general, one does not have a mate influencing or restricting one's choices either explicitly or implicitly.

One type of friendship from which one can derive particular benefits when single is platonic friendship with members of the opposite sex. Such relationships provide the freedom to act in ways other than traditional sex-role dating behavior. One has the opportunity to experiment with different and more satisfying behaviors with the opposite sex; to become aware of and experience the potential friendship aspects of romance. At the same time, there usually is some degree of flirtation and sexuality in cross-sex relationships. Thus, another purpose served is to receive sexual and emotional confirmation from a member of the opposite sex. This helps to defuse the "desperate" search for romance. Opposite-sex friends also can provide information as to the other sex's point of view and experiences, as well as serve the practical function of being an escort to various social events, if needed.

Inherent in having social relationships with a variety of different people is the experience of having others react to one's personality both positively and negatively. This multiplicity of reactions and feedback from others can be very liberating; it becomes increasingly difficult to attribute all negative reactions from others as being due to something wrong with you in the face of constant contradictory evidence that there are other people who seem to like and enjoy you.

Romance

With regard to romance, there are several myths that interfere with seeking out potential romantic others. First, there is the notion that finding a lover should happen spontaneously and that one should not have to work to find a desirable woman or man. Second, even if individuals acknowledge that there is a need to look actively for partners, they often regard legitimate ways of meeting the opposite sex as cheap, superficial, or degrading, for example, singles' bars, newspaper ads, and so forth. Attitudes such as 'Nice women don't approach strange men" or "What would my (mother, friends, ex-lover) think if they knew I was doing this?" prevent people from seeking out romantic relationships. Additional inhibitory factors involve women's fears of being hassled by men and both sexes' fears of being rejected.

Several concepts regarding seeking out romance are presented. Group members are asked to consider the importance and value that they place on a romantic love relationship in comparison with other central aspects of their lives, for example, job, place of residence, and so forth. People usually acknowledge that such relationships are of at least equal if not greater importance to them than any other aspect of their lives. They then are encouraged to ask themselves why it is that they would systematically, persistently, and openly look for a job or a place to live and not for a lover. An alternate conceptualization is offered, namely, viewing finding a relationship as an important second job in that it is a high priority goal in one's life. One then needs to employ whatever systematic, time and energy-saving techniques are required in order to attain this goal. These include any and all methods such as singles' bars, ads, parties, and initiating contact with strangers.

Ellis (1979) and Johnson (1977) eloquently describe the advantages in being able to encounter strangers who appear potentially desirable. It is clearly the quickest and most efficient (time, energy, and in terms of numbers) method for meeting members of the opposite sex. One can do it any time and anywhere, opening up an ever present possibility of meeting someone. This ability can help tremendously in reducing feelings of desperation and hopelessness about romance. Such encounters really provide one with the opportunity to focus on what each person has to offer rather than on finding the "one and only," and to view such experiences as learning and practice, and valuable in their own right, regardless of the outcome.

If time permits, at this point in the session, the group can break into pairs and practice initiating conversations, being rejected by others, and being assertive by saying, "No," if not interested.

A final perspective is suggested with regard to developing satisfying relationships when one is single, involving an objective analysis of what social relationships *in fact* provide.

The first category of experiences involves what others have to offer us. They offer us themselves as people, as well as any skills and interests that they may possess. In addition, many elicit certain ways of being in us, and in that sense they "offer" us particular experiences of ourselves, such as being witty, sexy, and so forth. Often we believe that we need a *particular* other person in order to express or experience a particular aspect of ourselves.

When single, one has the potential of multiple people to choose from both in terms of getting to know them and in getting to express different parts of oneself. The additional possibility that one has is to develop some skills, interests, and modes of self-expression for oneself.

A second category of experiences involves your experience of being loving and giving. Thus, rather than focusing on what you *get* or need from others, you can focus on what you have to *offer* and *give to* them. This involves shifting from a needy, deficit, powerless stance to an active, loving, giving one. You are in fact offering the other person both an opportunity to experience you and particular experiences of themselves that you can elicit.

When the focus of interpersonal gratification begins to shift to oneself in terms of one's *capacity* to love and one's experience of *being loving*, one realizes that there are many potential people who can receive one's love and giving. Other people then can be experienced as providing the opportunity for you to give and to love.

In summary, when single, one has the time, energy, and freedom to push one's interpersonal experience to its limits, for example, to engage in different types of relationships with a variety of different types of people, such as, simultaneous romances; to be experimental and live out one's fantasies in terms of certain kinds of people and/or activities. Thus, in this crucial area of one's life, one again has the luxury of exploring, indulging, and developing one's own tastes, desires, and rhythms, both emotionally and sexually.

Homework

The first homework assignment for this session involves doing an analysis of one's current friendship and romantic situations and their future possibilities in terms of quantity and quality. (See Johnson's *First Person Singular*, 1977, pp. 149–155, for details of analysis.) A second assignment is to initiate some new action with a friend or stranger, for example, hug a friend or practice starting a conversation with an other-sex stranger. A third possible assignment is to attempt to correct dysfunctional thinking about initiating contact with others, for example, "I couldn't stand it if she wasn't interested in going out with me." "He'll think I'm desperate if I just start talking to him out of the blue."

Group members are given *Skills for Friendship and Romance* (see below) to help them better identify what deficits they may have, so as to design appropriate homework assignments for themselves.

In addition, group members are asked to bring some of their favorite food to the next session, but are informed that the leaders also will have food available for them.

Skills for Friendship and Romance

1. Social attributes and skills for friendship maintenance
   - Making and keeping same-sex friends
   - Making and keeping other-sex friends
   - Developing depth of friendships
   - Ability to communicate with friends
   - Being with friends regularly
   - Initiating outside activities with friends
   - Entertaining friends at home
   - Finding ways to meet new friends
2. Social attributes and skills for dating, sex, and amative relationships
   - Initiating conversation with other sex
   - Finding ways to meet other sex
   - Ability to attract members of other sex
   - Ease in asking for dates
   - Ease in refusing dates
   - Dating regularly or often
   - Knowledge of and comfort with dating etiquette
   - Ease in communicating with other sex in early contacts or dating
   - General ease in dating
   - Ease in being affectionate
   - Ease in receiving and reciprocating affection
   - Ease in rejecting affection
   - Ease in making sexual advances
   - Ease in receiving and reciprocating sexual advances
   - Ease in rejecting sexual advances
   - General sexual ability
   - Ease in sexual interaction
   - Ability to communicate about affectional and sexual behavior
   - Ability to communicate in love-sex relationships
   - Quality of love-sex relationships
   (Johnson, 1977, pp. 80–81)

Session 8: Open Session

This session is designed to give group members an opportunity to discuss issues that are not included in the program or to further discuss issues that have been raised in the program.

The following kinds of topics have been suggested by group members:

1. Social pressure from peers and family to enter into a romantic relationship and get married and not remain single.
2. All aspects of intimate, romantic relationships, for example, initiating them, sexuality, ways to maintain one's individuality and identity.
3. How to become more personally, aesthetically, or intellectually creative when living alone.
4. How to develop a resource network for various kinds of practical and personal help.

The homework assignment for this session involves working on one of the cognitive or behavioral goals that each member set for him or herself at the beginning of the program. An alternate assignment is for the individual to work on one of the areas that has been raised during the course of the group that he or she would like to pursue further.

Session 9: Developing a Physical, Sensual Relationship with Yourself

This session begins with a relaxation exercise that facilitates group members feeling more comfortable with the subsequent experiential exercises.

This session focuses on one's ability to have direct encounters with the external, physical world, as well as to provide pleasure to oneself through tuning into and focusing on one's own ongoing bodily experiences. The appreciation of one's daily physical experience provides a type of direct confirmation that one is alive and exists, which sometimes can be weakened when living alone and out of physical touch with others.

Downing's ideas in *The Massage Book* (1972) form the basis of the discussion of body self-awareness. He states,

> Our body, its possibilities of movements, and its relation to gravity and the earth are the background from which everything else must emerge. To come

to terms with this on a real emotional level is perhaps the most important
kind of self-encounter a person can have. (p. 134)

Downing points out that the sense of touch is as crucial a contact
with reality as the sense of sight. However, in our culture the sense of
sight dominates. In order to tune into one's tactile experience, one can
become aware of one's body during the day. One can focus on such
sensations as weight, texture, and pressure, when picking up or handling objects or when making contact with the external environment,
such as sitting in a chair or walking. The notion of one's body as a field
of energy is introduced and the point is made that the goal of becoming
more aware of the body is to experience directly one's internal energy.

Self-massage

In *The Massage Book*, Downing has a section on self-massage. He
suggests that one can do self-massage when one is feeling tired and
numb, in order to "wake up" one's body. Learning to touch and nurture
one's body in this way is a good beginning at accepting and loving it. At
this point, the group does some yoga and stretching exercises in order to
loosen up physically so as to do some self-massage. The leaders then
demonstrate and instruct the group in a series of self-massage exercises.
(See *The Massage Book*, pp. 122–125 for details.) The goal is to experiment
and explore as much as possible different areas of one's body and different methods of massage.

Group members are given the self-massage instructions so as to be
able to continue practicing at home if so desired.

Sensory Awareness of Eating

The next exercise helps group members to focus on their physical
gratification in the *present* moment in their daily lives, by heightening
their awareness of the sensual, pleasurable aspects of eating. The exercise is excerpted from the *Weight Control Treatment Manual* (Hawkins,
Setty, & Baldwin, 1977).

Each group member eats a small portion of his or her favorite food
that they have brought to the session or the leaders can provide food.
The following instructions are then given:

First notice the sight of the food as you slowly raise it toward your mouth.
Hold it in front of your mouth and take in its smells. Notice how good it

smells as you slowly, slowly touch it to your lips . . . be aware of the sensation of the food touching your lips . . . now touch it to the tip of your tongue
and notice the food's texture . . . let it touch the rest of your tongue, noticing
texture and smell and now . . . bite down slowly, slowly on the food and
chew it slowly . . . continue slowly chewing being fully aware of the taste,
smell, temperature, and texture of the food . . . enjoy the pleasure of the
chewing . . . now swallow slowly and experience the pleasurable aftertaste
and concentrate on it for a moment as you put your utensils down . . . just
enjoy the food's aftertaste.

Now take the second bite in the same manner as the first. Enhance the
sensory pleasures as before, but this time as you swallow suggest to yourself
that the taste is still pleasant but now you're beginning to become aware of a
slight increase in comfort, fullness, and satisfaction. Pause to enjoy these
feelings.

With your third bite, continue to enjoy the pleasure of eating as feelings
of fullness, comfort, satisfaction, and relaxation grow stronger. Pause again
to enjoy these feelings.

As you continue to slowly eat and enjoy, your feelings of fullness, comfort, and satisfaction will become complete. Continue eating until you finish
the food you've chosen to eat, or stop earlier when you feel satisfied. (pp.
52–53)

Masturbation

At this point, both in terms of its being the ninth session of the
program, and having done relaxation and self-massage in this session, I
have found it fairly easy to straightforwardly raise the issue of masturbation when living alone.

Dodson's manifesto on masturbation, *Liberating Masturbation: A
Meditation in Self-Love,* (1974) and some ideas presented in *The Challenge
of Being Single* (Edwards & Hoover, 1974) form the basis of the discussion. Several myths about masturbation are presented. First, there is the
notion that only teenagers, lonely people, and masturbators do it. Masturbation has strong, negative connotations of childishness, perversion,
and loneliness. Second, there is the belief that if you masturbate at all,
and certainly if you do it too often, there is something wrong with you
and your sex life. It is generally considered to be a second-rate sexual
activity.

The facts, however, are contrary to these notions. Humans masturbate throughout their life cycle; married people masturbate regularly. It
would seem more accurate to view masturbation as *another* form of sexual activity, rather than as an inferior one. It is analogous to people
having a need for time alone when involved in a marital relationship.

The most important fact within the living alone context is that masturbation is the major consistent, dependable sexual outlet for unmarried adults. In fact, it can be as satisfying, or more so, both physically and emotionally, than sexual contact with someone else. It depends on how one chooses to view it. There are several distinct advantages that masturbation has over sex with another. It is always available. There are none of the performance, social, pregnancy, or venereal disease anxieties associated with sexual contact. One generally is guaranteed of attaining orgasm. One can gain sexual knowledge of oneself, practice being uninhibited, and engage in unlimited erotic fantasy. These latter experiences have the potential to be as arousing and exciting, or more so, than an actual sexual encounter.

Dodson describes how many individuals have self-loathing and shame about their bodies, appearance, and natural functions. Loving masturbation can help to counteract some of these self-destructive attitudes. Dodson takes a fairly radical position in stating that masturbation is our "primary sex life"; our first natural sexual activity and the way we originally discover our eroticism and learn to love ourselves. Everything beyond that is simply how we choose to "socialize" our sex life. Conceptually, this is a useful notion in that it provides a powerful metaphor for the primacy of achieving self-love when living alone and then extending one's love to others. Alternate terms such as *self-pleasure* or *sex with yourself* may better express the spirit of masturbation within this context.

On a practical level, the basic principle suggested for high-quality masturbation is to create an erotic environment in the same way as one would for a sexual experience with another; books and stores specializing in auto-erotica are mentioned.

A greater ability to truly appreciate and provide oneself with physically pleasurable and sensual experiences in one's daily life helps one to keep a more reasonable perspective with regard to sexual relations with others. Sexual contacts with others are extremely pleasurable physical experiences, but not the *only* ones, and not *always* the preferred ones.

The following suggestion list is then distributed:

Developing a Physical and Sensual Relationship with Yourself

- Relaxation exercises
- Meditation
- Yoga
- Various body awareness techniques
- Self-massage
- Burn incense
- Sports: bicycling, swimming, jogging

- Lying in sun
- Long, warm baths and showers, using your favorite lotions, soaps, and perfumes
- Listening to your favorite music
- Having a touchable pet
- Dancing at home
- Mirrors (looking at yourself doing whatever)
- Wearing clothes and having home furnishings that are pleasurable to touch and beautiful to look at
- Auto-eroticism: candles, colors you like in your home, "sex toys"
- Working with your hands to make things; building furniture, baking bread
- Pottery
- Painting
- Sculpting
- Spending time in nature—walking, hiking, swimming . . .
- Flowers
- Cooking good food
- Playing your own music—piano, guitar, singing

Homework

The first homework assignment for this session involves doing something physical or sensual with oneself that one has never done before, or changing the environment in some physically pleasurable way. The second assignment is to try to anticipate any reactions one might have to the termination of the group the following week and to attempt to generate cognitive and behavioral strategies for continuing work on unresolved problems in living alone.

SESSION 10: UNIQUE ADVANTAGES AND OPPORTUNITIES OF SINGLE LIFE-STYLE

This session is a discussion of the longer-term advantages and opportunities of living alone and being single. When single, one can grow and change at an accelerated rate because of the freedom, variety, and unpredictability of one's experience. Being single affords one the opportunity to channel the type of emotional energy that ordinarily would be directed toward a lover, spouse, and family into self-nurturance, various forms of artistic or intellectual creativity, or commitment to larger vocational or social causes.

The lack of obligations to a spouse and/or children results in certain types of freedom. One has financial independence and freedom; one can spend one's money on oneself and as one chooses. One can have a great deal of geographical mobility in terms of working, living, and traveling where one wants. These kinds of freedom provide the possibility of more adventure, novelty, and excitement, both in one's daily life and in a longer time frame, for example, spending a year living in a foreign country.

One can have social relationships of all kinds and experience different roles and ways of being while in them. One is free to make a primary commitment to different types of people, for example, a sibling or a close friend, or to a larger group of people, such as, friends or a communal group. One can participate in "alternate" life-styles such as communal living or living with a platonic other-sex friend. Living outside the structure of marriage opens up the possibility of questioning the traditional nuclear family, sex roles, and so forth. One can develop more personal and original life goals, perspectives, and values, without having to accommodate or compromise because of a marital relationship. One is freer to engage in more playful, creative, and imaginative ways of living, involving greater degrees of experimentation and risk taking.

Because of the greater availability of time and emotional energy when single, there is an increased potential to make substantial commitment to social causes involving large groups of people or communities. The fact that a greater possibility exists of being committed to people and goals outside of oneself when single is directly counter to the derogatory stereotypes of "selfishness" and "self-indulgent narcissism" that often are associated with choosing to live alone or be single. The reality is that single individuals have the necessary resources, in terms of time and energy, to devote to many people and the larger community, rather than being more restricted to the confines of the nuclear family.

A fundamental shift that can begin to occur for individuals who are committed to living alone and are successful at doing so is from content-oriented experiencing to process-oriented experiencing. When living alone for substantial lengths of time, one may develop a heightened awareness of the relativity, multiplicity, and changeability of the external circumstances of one's life. One's external reality shifts in terms of people, places, and activities. It becomes apparent that it is oneself who is constant in the face of such external changes and who gives the meaning, structure, and continuity to the events and experiences of one's life.

As a result of such realizations, one becomes more psychologically self-sufficient, as well as focused on one's internal experience and self-development; one's attachments, commitments, and values may change accordingly. Instead of the traditional commitment to long-term, exclusive, conjugal intimacy, or to any other particular external content, for example, financial or career achievement, commitments to modes or qualities of experience involving certain aesthetic, ethical, or spiritual dimensions, regardless of the specific content per se, may begin to take precedence. Such a shift in both the content and structure of an individual's consciousness may involve the ability to achieve transcendent states of consciousness in which there is a heightened sense of merging self with the external world of humankind and nature as a whole.

TERMINATION

A general approach to living alone that transcends the particular content areas *per se,* has been suggested in the program. The approach consists of: (1) making a commitment to a relationship and a life with oneself analogous to a commitment to a love relationship, (2) seeking out the unique opportunities and life experiences that only living alone has to offer, and (3) identifying the actual emotional and practical deprivations and deficits involved in living alone and systematically attempting to substitute or replace them.

It is emphasized that obviously 10 weeks is not sufficient time to relearn basic ways of living alone. An attempt is made to give group members a realistic anticipation of difficulties that they may encounter as they continue to live alone. The suggestion is made that one's relationship with oneself goes through the same kinds of fluctuations and phases as an intimate relationship with another; such cycles being a function of the relationship itself, as well as a multitude of life events and circumstances. It is during the problematic phases that members are encouraged to implement self-care, self-management, and problem-solving techniques. These involve first doing a careful assessment of precisely what the problem is and then either learning to solve it oneself or finding the necessary resources to do so.

The following specific suggestions for following through on the program are made: (1) For emotional support, one can set up a "co-counseling" arrangement with someone, getting together an hour each week to express feelings and exchange suggestions, support, and advice. Another possibility is to form one's own singles' support group. (2) For cognitive support, one can continue to respond in writing and behavior to one's own dysfunctional thinking. One can make audio tapes of oneself talking more reasonably and play these when alone to remind oneself of people who do care, the advantages in being alone, the disadvantages of being in a love relationship, and so forth. One can continue to do reading that reinforces the ideas discussed in the group. Two books that are highly recommended for this purpose are: *Single Blessedness* (Adams, 1976) and *The Challenge of Being Single* (Edwards & Hoover, 1974), as well as several biographical books, *Gift from the Sea* (Lindbergh, 1955), *Journal of a Solitude* (Sarton, 1973), and *Walden and Other Writings* (Thoreau, 1937) that provide affirming and inspiring role

Lastly, group members are encouraged to continue to structure weekly goals into their lives either on their own or through the help of a singles' support group, employing any and all methods, such as specific homework assignments, rewards for themselves, and so forth. Group members often exchange phone numbers so as to continue either individual or group contact.

There are several goals that the program strives to achieve. A primary one is to offer a vision and a taste of a discovery and self-construction process in which one has the unique luxury of engaging when living alone and single. Strengthening group participants' ability to spend pleasurable, involving time, alone and with a variety of others, helps them to reduce their *need* for a romantic relationship. Paradoxically, in fact, such a discovery/construction process of who one is and what one wants and values is likely to enhance one's ability to seek out, obtain, and maintain a long-term intimate relationship, if one is desired. Regardless of one's long-term goals, however, the óbjectives of the program are to improve the quality of one's ongoing experience alone so that the single life-style, for whatever duration, becomes an enjoyable and meaningful way to live.

REFERENCES

Adams, M. *Single blessedness*. New York: Basic Books, 1976.

Altman, I. *The environment and social behavior*. Monterey, Calif.: Brooks/Cole, 1975.

Beck, A. T. *Thinking and depression*. New York: The Institute for Rational Living, undated. (Reprinted from *Archives of General Psychiatry*, 1963, *9*, 324–333. Copies available from the Institute for Rational Living, Inc., 45 East 65th St., New York, N.Y., 10021.)

Beck, A. T. *Cognitive therapy and the emotional disorders*. New York: International Universities Press, 1976.

Beck, A. T., & Greenberg, R. L. *Coping with depression*. New York: The Institute for Rational Living, 1974. (Copies available from the Institute for Rational Living, Inc., 45 East 65th St., New York, N.Y., 10021.)

Beck, A. T., Rush, A. J., Shaw, B. F., & Emery, G. *Cognitive therapy of depression*. New York: Guilford, 1979.

Bracken, P. *The I hate to housekeep book.* New York: Fawcett, 1962.
Brownfield, C. A. *The brain benders.* New York: Exposition, 1972.
Burns, D. *Feeling good.* New York: Morrow, 1980.
Creel, H. L. *Cooking for one is fun.* New York: Quadrangle, 1976.
Deaton, J. E., Berg, S. W., Richlin, M., & Litrownik, A. J. Coping activities in solitary confinement of U.S. Navy POW's in Vietnam. *Journal of Applied Social Psychology,* 1977, *7,* 239–257.
Dodson, B. *Liberating masturbation: A meditation of self-love.* New York: Author, 1974.
Downing, G. *The massage book.* New York: Random House, 1972.
Edwards, M., & Hoover, E. *The challenge of being single.* New York: New American Library, 1974.
Ellis, A. *Reason and emotion in psychotherapy.* New York: Lyle Stuart, 1962.
Ellis, A. *Sex and the liberated man.* Secaucus, N.J.: Lyle Stuart, 1976.
Ellis, A. *The intelligent woman's guide to dating and mating.* Secaucus, N.J.: Lyle Stuart, 1979.
Ellis, A., & Harper, R. A. *A new guide to rational living.* Hollywood, Calif.: Wilshire, 1975.
Going it alone: The new status of singleness. *Newsweek,* September 4, 1978.
Hawkins, R., Setty, R. & Baldwin, B. *Weight control treatment manual.* Unpublished manuscript, University of Texas at Austin, 1977.
Ittelson, W. H., Proshansky, H. M., Rivlin, L. G., & Winkel, G. H. *An introduction to environmental psychology.* New York: Holt, Rinehart & Winston, 1974.
Johnson, S. M. *First person singular.* New York: Signet, 1977.
Kangas, P. E. *The single professional woman: A phenomenological study.* Unpublished doctoral dissertation, California School of Professional Psychology, 1977.
Kanter, M. K. *Psychological implications of never-married women who live alone.* Unpublished doctoral dissertation, California School of Professional Psychology, 1977.
Kelly, K. L. *Lifestyles of unmarried adults.* Unpublished doctoral dissertation, The University of Nebraska-Lincoln, 1977.
Kovacs, M. *Cognitive therapy of depression: Maladaptive structures.* Unpublished manuscript, Center for Cognitive Therapy, Philadelphia, Pa.
Lazarus, A. A. *Behavior therapy and beyond.* New York: McGraw-Hill, 1971.
Lazarus, A. A. *Multimodal behavior therapy.* New York: Springer, 1976.
Lilly, J. C. *The deep self.* New York: Warner, 1977.
Lindbergh, A. M. *Gift from the sea.* New York: Random House, 1955.
Maslow, A. H. *Toward a psychology of being.* New York: D. VanNostrand, 1968.
May, R. *Man's search for himself.* New York: Norton, 1953.
Meichenbaum, D. *Cognitive-behavior modification.* New York: Plenum, 1977.
Naar, J., & Siple, M. *Living in one room.* St. Paul, Minn.: Vintage, 1976.
Parmalee, P., & Werner, C. Lonely losers: Stereotypes of single dwellers. *Personality and Social Psychology Bulletin,* 1978, *4,* 292–295.
Peele, S. *Love and addiction.* New York: Signet, 1976.
Perlman, D., & Peplau, L. A. Toward a social psychology of loneliness. In R. Gilmour & S. Duck (Eds.), *Personal relationships in disorder.* London: Academic Press, 1981.
Primakoff, L. *Patterns of living alone and loneliness: A cognitive-behavioral analysis.* Unpublished doctoral dissertation, University of Texas at Austin, 1981.
The Reader's Digest complete do-it-yourself manual. New York: Norton, 1981.
Sarton, M. *Journal of a solitude.* New York: Norton, 1973.
Shaver, P., & Rubinstein, C. *Living alone, loneliness and health.* Paper presented at the annual convention of the American Psychological Association, New York, September 1979.
Stein, P. J. *Single.* Englewood Cliffs, N.J.: Prentice-Hall, 1976.

Suedfeld, P. Aloneness as a healing experience. In L. A. Peplau & D. Perlman (Eds.), *Loneliness: A sourcebook of current theory, research and therapy*. New York: Wiley-Interscience, 1982.

Thoreau, H. D. *Walden and other writings*. Ed. by Brooks Atkinson. New York: Random House, 1937.

Young, J. Loneliness, depression and cognitive therapy: Theory and application. In L. A. Peplau & D. Perlman (Eds.), *Loneliness: A sourcebook of current theory, research and therapy*. New York: Wiley-Interscience, 1982.

Zuckerman, M. Perceptual isolation as a stress situation. *Archives of General Psychiatry*, 1964, *11*, 255–276.

13

The Apprenticeship Model
Training in Cognitive Therapy by Participation

STIRLING MOOREY AND DAVID D. BURNS

INTRODUCTION AND HISTORY OF CO-THERAPY

Psychotherapy traditionally has been a meeting of two individuals; whether the therapist has seen him or herself as counselor or analyst, the assumption has been that the one-to-one relationship is an essential factor in the solution of the patient's problems. In the relatively brief history of psychotherapy, there have been those who have noted the value of a therapeutic ratio greater than one-to-one, both as a treatment and training method. In the 1920s Adler remarked on the usefulness of bringing in another counselor when sessions with children became difficult and emotional blocking occurred. Reeve (1939) used a combination of social worker and psychiatrist to teach the former interviewing skills and found the "joint interview" surprisingly effective as both a therapeutic and a training device. It was only in the 1950s that "multiple therapy" was explored in any systematic manner. Whitaker, Warkentin, and Johnson (1950) found it more effective than individual therapy with virtually all patients. They felt that this approach required therapists of "equal capacity" and therapeutic experience. Dreikurs (1950) in contrast claimed that multiple therapy could be used with therapists in training. His description of the techniques and dynamics involved in this type of theory contains the clearest and most practical advice of all the papers in this field. Haigh and Kell (1950) also saw the potential of this method.

STIRLING MOOREY • The Maudsley Hospital, Denmark Hill, London SE5, England.
DAVID D. BURNS • Department of Psychiatry, School of Medicine, University of Pennsylvania, Philadelphia, Pennsylvania 19104.

They emphasized that the student gains far more if he or she is a participant in the session than if the role is restricted to that of passive observer, which is the more common form of teaching (Strauss, 1950). Lott (1952) used "multiple therapy" as a means of training nonmedical psychotherapists, while Adams (1958) described his use of a model where supervisor and trainee worked directly and actively with the patient.

More recently, Rosenberg, Rubin, and Finizi (1968) recorded the thoughts of supervisor and student on the experience of "participant–supervisor" in the teaching of psychotherapy. They found the opportunity for direct observation of the trainee valuable and felt the setting allowed the trainee to try out new kinds of interventions in a safe atmosphere, as well as providing against the therapist getting on the wrong track. Treppa (1971) and Watterson and Collinson (1974) have provided reviews of the development of multiple therapy in all its forms. These reports all have been from a broadly psychodynamic viewpoint. Although there are scattered reports of participant training in behavior therapy (e.g., Matefy, Solanch, & Humphrey, 1975) there is no detailed discussion of this method; yet it is a method widely employed in training behavior therapists. Similarly, there have been no accounts of the use of co-therapy in a cognitive setting.

Before moving on to discuss our own experience of this method as a training device it may be useful to clarify some of the nomenclature in this area. An enormous number of names have been applied to the three-way approach, including: co-therapy, multiple therapy, role-divided therapy, three-cornered therapy, joint interview, cooperative psychotherapy, and dual leadership. Multiple therapy seems to be the most widely used, but is ambiguous. We prefer the term *co-therapy*, which is short and clearly conveys the cooperative nature of the enterprise. In addition, we see the process of learning by participating as a form of learning by apprenticeship, and for this reason refer to the use of co-therapy for training as the *apprenticeship model*.

THE APPRENTICESHIP MODEL OF COGNITIVE CO-THERAPY

The apprenticeship model was born in the summer of 1979 when Beck suggested that the student therapist Moorey spend some time sitting in on therapy sessions with the senior therapist, Burns. We both found this an interesting and useful way of training. Our experience was built up during two one-month stays when we worked together intensively and developed some of the techniques described below.

THE PROCESS OF COGNITIVE CO-THERAPY

Our method of co-therapy evolved over a number of sessions as the student therapist became more confident and capable of increasingly sophisticated interventions. The co-therapy differed from individual therapy on two major counts: the structure of the session and the type of techniques used.

Structure of the Therapy Session

With any patient the preparation for this form of therapy begins outside the therapy session. The patient is asked if he or she objects to the apprentice sitting in on one or more sessions (only one patient declined out of approximately 30 who were approached). A brief description is given of the student's qualifications, experience as a therapist, and personality, and it is emphasized that the apprentice will participate fully and equally in the session as a co-therapist. Surprisingly, most patients find the prospect of another active therapist much less threatening than the idea of a passive observer. Patients are reassured that although it may seem awkward at first to have a stranger join the session, the majority of patients have become quite comfortable with the co-therapist's presence and have benefited from the additional feedback. It is further emphasized that if at any time during the first or subsequent sessions the patient wishes the apprentice to leave this is totally acceptable.

At the beginning of the first co-therapy session the therapist summarizes the patient's history. This summary includes a brief personal history, the current focus of therapy and the strengths and weaknesses of the therapy so far. The patient is then asked if he or she feels the summary was accurate.

The initial summary serves several important functions. The apprentice gets an overview of the patient's difficulties and hears how an experienced therapist has conceptualized the problem and devised methods for change. Once the apprentice has been presented with the weaknesses of the present approach he or she immediately can begin to think of alternative strategies. Thus the slightly different outlook of the apprentice immediately is brought to bear on the area where he or she can be most useful.

The summary also provides a unique opportunity for the patient to see how the therapist approaches the problem. The therapist can benefit from the patient's feedback and further input. It is useful to provide further summaries at the start of each interview, particularly if the apprentice is not able to attend every session.

> Example—Mr. Jones has been in treatment with numerous therapists for over 25 years because of mild depression and severe tension and anxiety which he experiences at work. In particular, he is plagued by headaches and neck tension which persist all day, every day, and has had no relief despite continuous psychotherapeutic efforts. He holds a top executive position in a prominent corporation but feels intensely inadequate—he experiences himself as a "fraud"—in spite of an illustrious career.
>
> We are currently focussing on his fear of disapproval. This causes him to experience great apprehension in group discussions with peers. Although he sees intellectually that this fear of disapproval is somewhat irrational, he continues to believe emotionally that a catastrophe would occur if he tried to offer some ideas of his own and appeared foolish in front of his associates. Consequently, he feels inhibited and anxious and says very little during group meetings. The therapy has been characterized by excellent rapport and substantial learning, but Mr. Jones is disillusioned because his five months of once weekly sessions have failed to produce any significant emotional change or relief from neck tension. He is beginning to feel pessimistic about the chances that cognitive therapy will work.
>
> We have recently been using role playing to teach him how to talk back to the negative thoughts that tend to upset him when he is in a group meeting. He attacks me with negative thoughts and I model rational ways of responding. Then we reverse roles so he can learn how to change his thinking. He finds this exciting, so much so that he has recently been playing tapes of the sessions several times between sessions.

Mr. Jones then is asked to add his impressions. Following this the agenda is set for the day's session and a therapeutic strategy is adopted that allows the patient and the two therapists to work as a three-member team. Specific techniques employed in cognitive cotherapy will be described in the next section.

Toward the end of the session the therapist asks for specific negative and positive feedback regarding the presence of the apprentice. Once these reactions have been noted the patient is asked if he or she would like the apprentice to participate in further sessions. In our experience, patients usually responded with a strong affirmative. In such cases it is crucial to spell out precisely when the apprentice will or will not be present, because the unexpected absence of the apprentice at a future session may be quite upsetting to the patient. For example, when the apprentice was not present for the second session with a 45-year-old depressed accountant, the patient burst into tears. His cognitions were: "I wasn't interesting enough for Stirling (Moorey) to want to come back. This shows what a dull person I really am." The patient reported he believed these thoughts "over 99%." When the senior therapist pointed out that, in fact, Stirling was in Boston that day to meet his parents who had flown in from London, the patient was able to see just how wide of the mark his interpretation had been. Although this evolved into an excellent learning experience for this patient, the potential for hurt feelings can be minimized if the patient knows beforehand whether or not the apprentice will be present.

THERAPEUTIC TECHNIQUES

All the interventions of the individual therapy sessions are, of course, used in the three-way session (See Beck, Rush, Shaw, & Emery, 1979; Burns, 1980). At certain points one therapist will sit back while the other pursues a certain line of inquiry, using techniques such as the Socratic method, asking for evidence regarding certain irrational beliefs, and so forth. At these moments the session is in effect a conventional psychotherapeutic interview. There is always the danger of allowing the three-way approach to become two two-way approaches and for this reason it is best to combine the use of individual techniques with the use of three-way techniques in as harmonious a way as possible.

From the apprentice's point of view these short two-way interactions within the co-therapy session may be very valuable. When the supervisor is talking to the patient the student has the opportunity to watch an experienced therapist at close quarters. Audio- and videotapes cannot capture the immediacy and involvement of this experience. The apprentice watches the therapist tackling the same cognitive fallacies that he or she at any moment may be called on to work with. In addition to the proximity of a model, the trainee also has the opportunity to make interventions. For the novice therapist these first interventions can be set up very carefully by the supervisor. The three-way session provides a nonthreatening environment in which the apprentice can try out the techniques learned from books and seminars. If anything goes wrong the supervisor always can sort out the problems. Haigh and Kell (1950) have emphasized the value of this setting in giving the novice confidence in his therapeutic ability.

Three-Way Techniques (See Table 1.)

1. *Externalization of Voices.* In our experience this has proved one of the most exciting and powerful therapeutic tools of co-therapy. It is an extension of the written automatic thoughts/rational response technique

used in cognitive therapy. Instead of writing down his or her automatic thoughts the patient is encouraged to speak them out loud and the therapist responds with a more adaptive statement. The patient can give feedback on whether or not the response was meaningful. The situation then is reversed, with the therapist verbalizing the negative thoughts and the patient providing rational responses. This technique lends itself very well to the three-way model because of the number of possible dyadic interactions. These can be arranged in a hierarchy of difficulty and potential threat to the patient.

	Automatic thoughts	Rational responses
Option 1	First therapist	Second therapist
Option 2	Patient	Either therapist
Option 3	Either therapist	Patient

In the least threatening interaction (Option 1) the patient watches while the two therapists play his or her internal dialogue. By listening and observing he or she quickly is able to learn the method. In the most threatening (Option 3), the patient has to provide rational responses to his or her own very convincing negative thoughts which are verbalized by the therapists. This is not only difficult but also arouses anxiety over possible failure. As the role playing passes down the hierarchy from Option 1 to Option 3 the patient gains confidence in answering his or her automatic thoughts.

Here is an example of Option 2. The patient is again Mr. Jones. We are dealing with his automatic thoughts about disapproval in social situations and his fears about role playing in particular.

JONES: (*Playing the role of the Automatic thoughts*): This kind of back and forth conversation and discussion in small groups is what makes you get uptight so you feel you don't even have a single thought in your mind.

STIRLING: (*In the role of the Rational responses*): It's not true that I don't have a single thought in my mind because I can usually bring something out. The more exposure that I have to a situation that brings about tension the more likely I am to be able to cope with it.

JONES: (*As Automatic thoughts*): Well, that may be so but you know how embarrassed you get if you open your mouth and don't have a real classic gem of an opinion to present. So therefore it's better to keep your mouth shut and be quiet.

STIRLING: (*As Rational responses*): It seems safer to keep quiet but that is really a distortion. Keeping quiet is going to increase my tension, increase my fear of saying something. If I say something, anything at all, then I'm going to break out of this cycle of tension. So the more times I can say something, even if it is totally ridiculous, the more likely I am to solve this problem.

Now the roles are reversed with Stirling and Dave as the automatic thoughts and Mr. Jones providing the rational responses, as in Option 3.

STIRLING: (*In the role of the Automatic thoughts*): If you say anything at all at one of these meetings you're going to make a fool of yourself and that's going to be the end of everything. You'll lose all the praise and esteem you've had from your colleagues.

JONES: (*In the role of the Rational responses*): Well, I don't think there's any evidence really to support that, because over the last 30 years I have performed in a responsible way or I wouldn't be where I am, and I'm not going to lose that overnight.

DAVID: (*Also playing the role of the Automatic thoughts*): Yeah, but if you've got a beaker filled with clear water and we've been talking about one drop of black ink, it can discolor the whole beaker.

JONES: (*As Rational responses*): Well, I think that's all-or-nothing thinking and I don't think that one little drop of black ink is going to have much effect on the color of the whole glass of water.

STIRLING: (*As Automatic thoughts*): It's going to change the way your peers think of you. You better not take a chance of making a fool of yourself.

JONES: (*As Rational responses*): Well, my peers have known me now for 30 years and even if I advance an opinion which doesn't merit the support of the majority, that doesn't mean I'm no good or worthless.

DAVID: (*As Automatic thoughts*): Yes, but you'd be so humiliated you couldn't stand it.

JONES: (*As Rational responses*): It might be a little embarrassing to say something foolish, but I could survive and I could give myself credit for finally speaking up and trying something new.

The use of externalization of voices has been developed by David Burns in his work with patients on a one-to-one basis, and has grown out of his personal interest and ability in the art of role playing. The technique is equally well suited to the co-therapy setting. It is interesting to note that Dreikurs (1950) described something very similar 30 years ago:

> A special type of situation is one in which the therapist actively interprets to the patient the meaning of his actions while the other therapist 'argues from the point of view of the patient's private logic.' . . . In such a situation the patient often recognizes his faulty perception as he sees the therapist using his own mechanisms. (pp. 223–224)

Role playing may prove to be one of the best forms of intervention in multiple therapy for both apprentice and patient.

2. *Communication Training Using Role Playing.* Role playing also can be used to help the patient with his or her interpersonal problems. Real life situations can be re-created and adaptive reactions modeled. The

presence of two therapists allows for a variety of interactions. For instance, the patient initially might take the role of a hostile critic and the therapist can model adaptive responses. Then the roles might be reversed. Finally, both therapists together can play critics and allow the patient to defend himself.

Examples of situations we have dealt with in this way include:

1. Coping with criticism from a spouse, or at work.
2. Handling a difficult teenager who misbehaves and refuses to talk.
3. Facing a job interview.
4. Initiating and maintaining a conversation with a stranger you might wish to date.
5. Responding to a stranger without embarrassment.

3. *Reformulation.* Another valuable technique open to two therapists is "reformulation," using different words to convey the same message. If the patient does not understand an explanation or suggestion given by one therapist the co-therapist can repeat it in his own words. The alternative phraseology is often very helpful to the patient. The same method of reformulating the other therapist's message is also worthwhile when a particularly important point is being put across.

4. *Two-Way and Three-Way Dialogue.* The presence of two therapists often means that there are times when they discuss the progress of the session or theoretical points about what is happening. This may slow down the session or digress from the main point; if used judiciously, however, it can be of great value for the patient and the apprentice. Actually observing two other people talking about his or her problem can help the patient to distance him or herself from it. The therapist and apprentice can gain by discussing their ideas at the moment of conception in the session, and the patient can give feedback on their appropriateness. When this works well the initial two-way dialogue becomes a three-way interaction in which patient, therapist, and apprentice generate ideas and work toward a clearer understanding of the problems involved and the patient's own view of them.

Here is an example of how discussion between the two therapists in the session actually can help the patient. The therapists have just been giving rational responses to the patient's fears about speaking in groups:

STIRLING: I am wondering if we were presenting too much of a mastery model. If we were to present more of a coping model in our rational responses . . . by talking about how embarrassed we feel, but how we're managing to overcome it. Do you think that would be more useful?

DAVID: What we are doing is like a karate model.

STIRLING: Yes.

DAVID: You know when you take karate classes they get up and hit you in the face. They don't actually make contact. As you learn by practicing certain maneuvers to deflect your opponent's most vicious blows you overcome your fear of people attacking you because you have ways to handle it. You become calm in the face of battle. I think that's very much the way we are working. What are you suggesting . . . that might raise perfectionistic expectations?

STIRLING: Yes, but also there is experimental evidence that the more effective model is the one who has difficulties but can be seen to be coping with them. This may get better results than if you model the thinking process of someone who seems to have complete mastery of the threatening situation. It may seem more realistic to the patient who is feeling overwhelmed or hopeless.

This dialogue brought out the possibility of a different strategy for dealing with this man's problems with embarrassment in groups, that is, demonstrating how to cope with anxiety. The patient was next asked if the mastery model really did induce perfectionistic tendencies in him. The therapist then demonstrated two types of rational responses and the patient indicated which of the two approaches he found most helpful. The patient was in this way drawn into the planning of his own therapy and allowed to give his reactions to the methods being used.

PATIENTS' REACTIONS TO CO-THERAPY

Since the viability of apprenticeship as a training model depends on the willingness of patients to participate in a time-limited co-therapeutic experience, we studied their reactions to these sessions. Twenty-two of the patients seen were given a therapy session feedback form containing questions similar to those in Table 2. The majority of responses were positive ones. Seventy-two percent of patients said that they found the experiment very useful and 100% agreed that this type of training would be useful for other trainees and patients. Some patients found the presence of an additional therapist embarrassing, but most (86%) were not embarrassed at all. Only two of the patients felt there were issues that they could not discuss in the trainee's presence.

The general consensus was that the two therapists worked well together. Twenty-eight percent said that the presence of another therapist slowed down the session and 23% felt that the smoothness of therapy was interrupted but the rest of the patients (72%, 77%, respectively), did not notice any disruption of the flow of therapy.

TABLE 1

Interventions Suited for the Two Therapist Model

Method	Description of method	Why this is suited to the two-therapist model
1. Externalization of Voices	1. Using a role-playing format the patient and therapist act out the patient's self-defeating automatic thoughts and rational responses. For example, the patient, in the role of Automatic Thoughts might say: "Because you didn't get that promotion it shows you're a total failure." The therapist, in the role of the Rational Responses, might replay: "That's all-or-nothing thinking, I've succeeded at many things in my life so I can't be a *total failure.* Let's find out why I didn't get the promotion and work on how to improve my performance in the future." This verbal exchange continues with frequent role reversals.	1. A) If one therapist's rational responses are not proving helpful the other therapist immediately can take over using a different strategy, thus preventing an impasse. B) One therapist can play the role of the patient and model what the patient is expected to do. This can greatly cut down the time necessary to train the patient in the use of the method. By observing one therapist play his role while the other therapist administers treatment, the patient can attain an objective frame of reference and more readily observe how illogical and self-defeating his (or her) negative thoughts are.
2. Communication Training Using Role Playing	2. The patient and therapist act out situations that are difficult to the patient, such as dealing with hostility, criticism, or rejection. By using frequent role	2. A) If the patient does not find one therapist's verbal style acceptable the other therapist can suggest an alternative approach.

reversals the therapist can model self-expression and listening skills and then give the patient the opportunity to master these while "under fire." This provides insight as well as mastery.

3. Reformulation

One therapist repeats what the other therapist has said using his own words and his own personal examples. The patient is more likely to challenge his distortions if he finds both therapists agree. The second therapist repeating the message adds emphasis and may get closer to what is personally meaningful to the patient.

4. Dialogue

The two therapists discuss the progress of therapy and possible direction. The patient can sit back and find out how the therapists perceive his problems. He may gain a useful perspective but if he disagrees he can give the therapists feedback on where they have misunderstood him.

B) If the patient feels shy about the role playing, the two therapists can demonstrate the method with one of them playing the patient's role. This allows the patient to learn by watching and to become more comfortable with the role-playing method.

3. This utilizes the experience and personal style of both therapists. If only one therapist is present the effect cannot be achieved.

4. The patient can be drawn into a three-way interaction when he collaborates in planning his own therapy.

The results of the questionnaire (Table 2) are on the whole encouraging. In addition the patients came up with some interesting observations. The most frequently cited benefit from this method came from the presence of a different perspective, for example, "It has been very useful to have a second point of view. Sometimes someone who is not as 'intensively' involved as the primary therapist, but who has some knowledge and training as a therapist can be more objective and often has 'insightful' remarks or ideas. In this way the sessions were faster moving, more 'intense' and, to my mind, that is extremely positive." Other patients found the role playing helpful, while some found listening to the dialogue between the two therapists of use.

"A new perspective was added. It was interesting to hear the two therapists talk together about the therapy and share possible interventions and suggest new approaches." One patient found the apprentice's input helpful in overcoming a block in therapy.

Since the work described in this chapter took place, the senior therapist has had the opportunity to carry out co-therapy on a more limited basis with two other participants. The first was an untrained observer (a journalist) who just sat in sessions and the second was an untrained participant (also a journalist) who did participate in the therapeutic role playing under the therapist's supervision. A comparison of some of the patient's responses is given in Table 3. Although the number of patients involved in the two most recent collaborations are smaller than the first, some interesting comparisons are suggested. The trainee therapist consistently is given the most favorable ratings while the observer is given the least favorable. The untrained participant comes somewhere between the two throughout. This suggests that there are in fact benefits for the patient from the apprenticeship model and that an active trainee is less embarrassing than a passive one. The fact that the untrained participant received ratings that were nearly as good as the apprentice therapist's would seem to support Dreikurs's claim that co-therapy is suitable for therapist training and does not require therapists of equal capacity as proposed by Whitaker *et al.* (1950). These findings also have implications concerning the potential for training of lay counselors, such as nurses, clergymen, and others, in cognitive techniques and confirm the probable benefits of cognitive group therapy.

These preliminary investigations suggest that the apprenticeship model may be of positive benefit to patients as well as student therapists. Further research is needed to find out if this subjective effect is reflected by a speedier symptomatic improvement or better sustained recovery.

THE NATURE AND POWER OF CO-THERAPY

In our hands, the apprenticeship model appeared to be surprisingly effective. We observed patients who had been refractory to drug therapy and to individual psychotherapy over a period of years experience a change in mental outlook along with a substantial reduction of symptoms after a small number of sessions. The uniformly high ratings on the patients' evaluations of these sessions attest to their enthusiasm (See Table 2). There are two possible explanations of this phenomenon. First, although the apprentice in this experiment was a novice, he proved to be a highly talented therapist. The skill of two therapists working together as a team may have simple additive effect. Second, there may be

TABLE 2
Patient's Reactions to the Apprenticeship Model

	Not at All	A Little	A Moderate Amount	Very Much	Yes	No
1. Overall did you find this experience useful?	0[a]	5	23	72	—	—
2. Do you consider that the presence of another therapist added to the value of the session?	0	13	23	64	—	—
3. Would this type of training be helpful for other trainee therapists and patients?	—	—	—	—	100	0
4. Was the presence of an additional therapist embarrassing?	86	9	5	0	—	—
5. Were there any issues you could not discuss because of the two therapists?	—	—	—	—	10	90
6. Did the two therapists work well together?	—	—	—	—	100	0
7. Did you feel that the three-way approach:						
a) slowed down the session?	72	23	5	0	—	—
b) interfered with the smoothness of therapy?	77	23	0	—	—	—

[a]Scores are percentages of answers. Sample $N = 22$.

TABLE 3
Comparison of Patients' Respones to Three Participants

	Not at All	A Little	A Moderate Amount	Very Much
1. Overall value of experiment				
Trainee therapist[a]	0[d]	5	23	72
Untrained participant[b]	0	14	29	57
Untrained observer[c]	30	40	30	0
2. Value of therapists presence				
Trained therapist	0	13	23	64
Untrained participant	14	14	29	43
Untrained observer	50	30	20	0
3. Embarrassment due to participant				
Trained therapist	86	9	5	0
Untrained participant	71	29	0	0
Untrained observer	60	20	10	0

[a]$N = 22.$
[b]$N = 7.$
[c]$N = 10.$
[d]Scores are percentages of answers.

something specifically powerful about this two-on-one treatment model. This could be mediated by specific technical effects made possible by the two therapist model or by so-called nonspecific interpersonal factors that were activated by the presence of the apprentice.

There is probably some truth in both hypotheses. The apprentice made effective contributions because he combined two important qualities. First, he demonstrated warmth and empathy which fostered trust and allowed patients to open up readily in his presence. They found no difficulty in sharing their thoughts and feelings with him. He perceived patients' mind sets and value systems accurately and they sensed no hostility or judgmentalism. This created strong rapport which provided the fertile soil for technically meaningful interventions.

His second asset was that he utilized a "pure" cognitive methodology that was relatively uncontaminated by prior training in other schools of treatment. He made no "dynamic interpretations" but formed hypotheses based on the data—the patients' automatic thoughts. His therapeutic interventions primarily involved attempts at altering the patients' perceptions using straightforward cognitive techniques. Because he was effective in suggesting alternative and more objective ways for patients to interpret painful situations, he was able to facilitate rapid attitudinal change.

Was there also something specifically beneficial about the two-therapist model? According to cognitive theory, emotional and behavioral change ultimately is mediated by a change in perception. The process of attitude and perception modification can be speeded up considerably by the presence of two therapists working as a team, because if one therapist becomes bogged down the other therapist immediately can intervene and suggest a fresh and different approach.

For example, a depressed woman had been stuck for many years in the pattern of distortion called "personalization": She was excessively self-blaming and consistently assumed that any negative feeling or problem her husband or children might have indicated she was "a failure." Although the list of potentially helpful interventions for the personalization error is lengthy, this particular mind-set, like many others, can be quite refractory to modification. The therapeutic process can reach an impasse when the therapist begins to run out of creative ideas and experiences frustration. He then may view the patient as "stubborn" or "difficult" or "resisting treatment." At this point the patient is likely to sense the therapist's tension and may become increasingly self-critical. Because of the patient's tendency to personalize, she is likely to tell herself that she is also to blame for upsetting the therapist and conclude that she is a failure as a patient as well. The therapist, sensing the patient's worsening depression may in turn feel even more inadequate and frustrated. Essentially, the two become locked in a foil-a-deux.

This phenomenon rarely occurs with the two-therapist model, because the other therapist can intervene and suggest an alternative strategy that will infuse new life and vitality into the session. This raises the probability that each session will be productive for the patient. It is as if both therapists provide ongoing preception and feedback for each other, and the patient's self-defeating attitudes have only the slimmest chance for survival against what becomes a profusion of alternative frames of reference and ways of intervening. Each therapist helps the other avoid falling into mental traps and power struggles with the patient. Slow points and lulls in therapy are reduced and often entirely circumvented. Since the personal style and background of each therapist is likely to be different it seems quite easy for one to provide a meaningful direction when the other feels temporarily stymied.

The overall effect was that sessions progressed at a rate that appeared to be greater than either therapist could achieve alone. It may be that the two-therapist model, while more costly,[1] might prove beneficial

---

[1] The cost is not a factor when one therapist functions as an apprentice since there is no additional charge.

and actually cost-effective in treating refractory patients who commonly waste months and years in treatment with a single therapist without measurable results. This is the general consensus from the literature (Whitaker, Malone, & Warkentin, 1956; Watterson & Collinson, 1974; Treppa, 1971), but there has been little systematic research directed at the following questions: (1) Is the two-therapist method actually more effective in treating mood disorders? (2) Does the increased efficacy simply result from the enthusiasm that is generated by the presence of an additional therapist or are there other more specific effects occurring? (3) What are the most useful two-therapist methods and strategies? (4) What mechanisms for change can be mobilized more effectively when two therapists are present?

Finally, we might begin to consider how our experience of the apprenticeship model fits into the framework of multiple therapy as practiced by others. We have been struck by the importance of the relationship between the two therapists and what Treppa describes as the "therapists' spontaneous and reciprocal interaction." The achievement of what has been called "social democracy" seems to be one of the important nonspecific factors involved. However, our version of co-therapy would seem to be somewhere between the descriptions of "multiple therapy" and "co-therapy" given by Treppa (1971) and Mullan and Sanguiliano (1964). Cognitive therapy requires a structured, problem-solving approach allowing therapists to adopt particular fixed roles from time to time. He would seem to fit the description of co-therapy given by Treppa. Nevertheless cognitive co-therapy also requires a collaboration between patient and therapists and a free atmosphere where all the participants can work together. This would seem to fit the description of what the above authors see as the superior, more existential "multiple therapy": "Multiple therapy is a cooperative effort; the full therapeutic impact of this technique is realized only when the therapist–therapist relationship is characterized by trust, emotional harmony, and collaboration" (Treppa & Nunnelly, 1974, p. 71). It may be that the apprenticeship model falls somewhere between these two forms of directive and nondirective co-therapy. Again we await research to elicit what factors contribute to the effectiveness of this method.

APPRENTICESHIP AND PRECEPTION

The apprenticeship model presents a number of opportunities to the student that are not available in traditional supervision (Table 4). These arise in two main areas: observation of the senior therapist, and feedback from the senior therapist. The apprentice can watch his or her teacher at close quarters and absorb nonverbal as well as verbal style. The availability of the supervisor as a model may speed up the time taken in learning cognitive therapy. In any other form of psychotherapy training modeling has to take place at a distance through videotapes and audiotapes. Conversely, the therapist can observe the student more closely than in the conventional training format. The apprentice's first attempt can be observed sympathetically and modified, under direct supervision. If he or she gets stuck it is possible to ask for advice then and there without having to wait until after the session. There are, however, areas of therapeutic skill that this model cannot teach. In the apprenticeship model the senior therapist is in control, or the control is a joint effort. In conventional supervision the trainee has complete control of his individual therapy session. This allows for experience in planning long-term strategies, whereas in apprenticeship the strategies are short-term ones devised and tested within the session. The rewards in supervision are internal, coming from a feeling of mastery in holding a session on one's own, and from developing a close one-to-one relationship with the patient. The apprentice is externally rewarded by the senior therapist's approval. It can be argued that the three-way session can be optimally useful to someone who also has experience of psychotherapy, and it is certainly true that the broader considerations of where the therapy is going and when to terminate can be learned primarily in the traditional manner.

The apprenticeship model is not such a radical departure from conventional medical training in which the intern, resident, and attending physician work together as a team; but this is rarely done in the training of psychologists and psychiatrists who are supposed to figure things out on their own because the relationship between the therapist and patient is viewed as sacred. In fact the team approach nearly always works in the patients' interest and can protect the patient from certain errors of inexperience. These include:

1. Failure to inquire about suicidal impulses or to intervene effectively
2. Mistakes in diagnosis
3. Being trapped in a sexual or romantic relationship with a patient
4. Insensitivity about the patient's value system
5. Inability of the therapist to recognize his own distortions or self-defeating reactions to difficult patients
6. Inability to develop a focussed meaningful problem-solving agenda coupled with specific strategies for change such that the therapy moves forward instead of getting bogged down

TABLE 4
Comparison of Apprenticeship and Preception

Apprenticeship	Preception

Modelling supervisor's skills:
  1. Defining problems and
    devising strategies
  2. Establishing rapport
  3. Handling difficult patients
	Verbal guidance from supervisor

Guided use of techniques	Post hoc suggestions
Short term strategies	Experience in long-term strategies
Rapid, specific feedback	Delayed, general feedback
External reward: praise	Internal reward: mastery

A period of apprenticeship might well help the novice avoid these mistakes when he or she participates in individual psychotherapy. An integrated program in which the trainee receives both apprenticeship training and preception of individual therapy might be optimal.

The experience of others in their use of three-way therapy for training is gratifying (Dreikurs, Schulman, & Masak, 1952; Haigh & Kell, 1950; Rosenberg et al., 1968) but as yet the evidence is merely anecdotal. Because of our enthusiasm for what was admittedly a small trial, we would like to see the approach evaluated on a larger scale to see if the potential for training is as great as we believe it to be.

SUMMARY

We have found cognitive co-therapy an exciting and rewarding experience. Cognitive techniques easily can be applied to the three-way approach, and we have begun to develop some cognitive strategies specifically for this model. The apprenticeship model has much potential for training, but in addition can be a valuable experience for both the senior therapist and the patient: We have seen remarkable symptomatic improvement in our co-therapy sessions. Much of our experience has agreed with other writers on co-therapy although they have written from a psychodynamic viewpoint. Despite our encouraging results we have to stress that our research like all the previous literature is anecdotal and we await objective investigations of this method. We hope that others will try the apprenticeship model for themselves and discover its benefits for student and patient alike.

REFERENCES

Adams, W. R., Ham, T. H., Maward, B. H., Scali, H. A., & Weisman, R. A naturalistic study of teaching in a clinical clerkship. *Journal of Medical Education*, 1958, *33*, 211–220.

Beck, A. T., Rush, A. J., Shaw, B. F., & Emery, G. *Cognitive therapy of depression*. New York: Guilford, 1979.

Burns, D. D. *Feeling good: The new mood therapy*. New York: Morrow, 1980.

Dreikurs, R. Techniques and dynamics of multiple psychotherapy. *Psychiatric Quarterly*, 1950, *24*, 788.

Dreikurs, R., Schulman, B. H., & Masak, H. Patient–therapist relationship. I. Its advantages to the therapist. *Psychiatric Quarterly*, 1952, *26*, 219.

Haigh, G., & Kell, B. L. Multiple therapy as a method of training and research in psychotherapy. *Journal of Abnormal Social Psychology*, 1950, *45*, 659.

Lott, G. M. The training of non-medical cooperative psychotherapy by multiple psychotherapy. *American Journal of Psychotherapy*, 1952, *6*, 440.

Matefy, R. E., Solanch, L., & Humphrey, E. Behavior modification in the home with students as co-therapists. *American Journal of Psychotherapy*, 1975, *29*, 212.

Mullan, H., & Sanguiliano, I. *The therapist's contribution to the treatment process*. Springfield, Ill.: Charles C Thomas, 1964.

Reeve, G. H. Trends in therapy: V. A method of coordinated treatment. *American Journal of Orthopsychiatry*, 1939, *9*, 743.

Rosenberg, L., Rubin, S. S., & Finizi, H. Participant-supervision in the teaching of psychotherapy. *American Journal of Psychotherapy*, 1968, *22*, 280.

Strauss, B. V. Teaching psychotherapy to medical students. *Journal of the Association of American Medical Colleges*, July 1–6, 1950.

Treppa, J. A. Multiple therapy: Its growth and importance. *American Journal of Psychotherapy*, 1971, *25*, 447.

Treppa, J. A., & Nunnelly, K. G. Interpersonal dynamics related to the utilization of multiple therapy. *American Journal of Psychotherapy*, 1974, *28*, 71–86.

Watterson, D., & Collinson, S. Explorations in co-psychotherapy. *Canadian Psychiatric Association Journal*, 1974, *19*, 572.

Whitaker, C. A., Warkentin, J., & Johnson, N. L. The psychotherapeutic impasse. *American Journal of Orthopsychiatry*, 1950, *20*, 641.

Whitaker, C. A., Malone, T. P., & Warkentin, J. Multiple therapy and psychotherapy. In F. Fromm-Reichman & J. L. Moreno, (Eds.), *Progress in psychotherapy* (Vol. 1). New York: Grune & Stratton, 1956.

14

The Group Supervision Model in Cognitive Therapy Training

ANNA ROSE CHILDRESS AND DAVID D. BURNS

INTRODUCTION

In the spring of 1980, several beginning therapists—psychiatry residents and psychologists at the University of Pennsylvania—attended a series of introductory seminars in cognitive therapy presented by the second author. Because several of the novice therapists were excited by their initial exposure to cognitive therapy, ongoing group case supervision was arranged. The decision to meet as a group had pragmatic origins: Dr. Burns could not offer individual supervision to all those who wished it. In retrospect this limitation was fortunate. We rapidly discovered, to the delight of both students and supervisor, that group supervision and cognitive therapy techniques were natural complements for each other; the mode of supervision actually facilitated the teaching and learning process and produced an experience that was unexpectedly rich. In this chapter, we present the group supervision model we used, discussing its particular—and often unique—advantages for the therapist-in-training, the supervisor, and the patient.

FORMAT USED IN COGNITIVE THERAPY GROUP SUPERVISION

As a foundation for group supervision in cognitive therapy, trainees are given exposure through lectures, reading, or demonstrations to basic cognitive therapy techniques and interpersonal/communication skills

ANNA ROSE CHILDRESS AND DAVID D. BURNS • Department of Psychiatry, School of Medicine, University of Pennsylvania, Philadelphia, Pennsylvania 19104.

(see Appendix A for a description of basic techniques). As basic reading in the theory and techniques of cognitive therapy, trainees were encouraged to read Burns (1980) and Beck, Rush, Shaw, and Emery (1979). This foundation gives the trainees a common language and background, allowing the group supervision to proceed smoothly, without time lost in defining terms or basic concepts. Regular weekly sessions (1–1½ hours) of group supervision are arranged. The group size is limited—usually five to six members—to maximize individual involvement. For each session, the approach is problem-oriented, with attention focused upon generating specific therapeutic strategies. Typical topics might include how to set a specific agenda for a vague, unfocused patient; how to develop rapport and collaboration with an angry, suspicious, or oppositional patient; how to train patients to identify and talk back to distorted negative thoughts; how to manage suicidal patients; how to help patients pinpoint and restructure self-defeating belief systems; how to motivate apathetic patients to develop a schedule of satisfying activities, and so forth.

Each weekly session begins with the supervisor's request for case material. Volunteers are never in short demand, as trainees are not placed "on the hot seat": the atmosphere is one of group support and mutual teaching. The trainee will present a "problem case"—one in which progress has been slow or difficult. The initial case vignettes are brief, presented with necessary background information, but with emphasis on defining and solving therapeutic problems in the here and now.

SUPERVISOR: Who has some case material for us?

SAM (trainee): I have a case—an intelligent, articulate 35-year-old woman with a two-year history of chronic depression and anxiety attacks. The depression began following her resignation from a high prestige administrative job. She says she resigned because she was too anxious to work after her complaints about the performance of one of her staff resulted in his dismissal. She hasn't worked in two years, and now lives with her two children in her mother's home. She believes her usual activities offer no interest or pleasure. She complains of blue mood, panic attacks, difficulty sleeping, lack of appetite, and lack of energy. She spends most of her time as a virtual recluse in her mother's home. In our last session, we talked about her looking for some kind of work. Her automatic thoughts included themes of hopelessness ("I can't ever see things changing"); helplessness ("I can't control my life—I'm not strong enough for work"), and low self-esteem ("I am just a sham . . . and the interviewer would see it"). She also predicts, "I can't go out for a job interview—I would get an anxiety attack . . . and I wouldn't be able to hold the job anyway, the shape I'm in. . . ." Right now, I can't seem to get therapy off the ground with this patient. She has problems in so many areas it should be easy, I guess, but she seems to get so overinvolved in talking about her symptoms (her weight, her appetite, her insomnia, her anxiety, and so forth) that we never get anywhere. And she is very reluctant when I want her to write down her automatic thoughts and work out rational responses. What should I try?

(*At this point the supervisor may quickly solicit possible approaches from others in the group.*)

SUPERVISOR: There would seem to be a number of possible approaches. Let's hear some ideas. John?

JOHN (trainee): Well, you could start working with the patient in *other* ways to change her thoughts—such as using the *Pleasure Predicting* sheet to test her belief that nothing gives her pleasure anymore. It might give her some relief and encouragement to see that she can still experience some pleasure/satisfaction, and then she might be willing to work on writing down her thoughts.

JAMES (trainee): Along those lines, you might try *role playing* some of her automatic thoughts, verbally naming the cognitive distortions and working out rational responses. . . .

MARY (trainee): Maybe the idea of "going for a job interview" is too overwhelming for this patient right now—maybe you could instead talk about that area by breaking the task down into small parts that would seem more manageable, like looking for an ad or making one phone inquiry—essentially working out a *graded task assignment* that would elicit fewer anxiety producing thoughts.

JANE (trainee): I think it might be useful to start by finding out her thoughts *about* writing down her automatic thoughts/rational responses . . . we don't know why she is reluctant, but it could be for any number of reasons—that she thinks it is useless, that nothing will work; that she thinks you will judge her harshly if she doesn't perform well, and so forth. You might be able to get at this by using *externalization of voices*—having her voice her inner dialogue *about* writing down her thoughts, and then work together on some rational responses to those thoughts.

SUSAN (trainee): Maybe she's reluctant to work by writing down her thoughts because she feels you must appreciate her distress first; that this writing-down task seems cold and impersonal. If you've been strongly focused on the writing task and feel frustrated by the fact that she's not working, it might be time to use some *interpersonal/communication* skills . . . a good dose of *empathy* and *inquiry* might quickly dissolve her reluctance.

SUPERVISOR: We have a lot of good suggestions here . . . all of them may be useful at one point or another. I think right now a first step might be to find out about her reluctance, if possible. Maybe we can combine Jane's and Susan's suggestions, using initial empathy and inquiry, then leading the patient to voice/externalize her automatic thoughts *about* writing down her thoughts, and so on. John, why don't you play the patient, and I'll take on the role of therapist for the moment.

In this example, the supervisor encourages group members to contribute ideas spontaneously, in brainstorming fashion. He then reinforces the suggestion making and leads the work in a direction that might be most useful to the therapist and the patient at that point. In this case, sensing the therapist's frustration ("not getting anywhere") and apparent focus on the "writing-down" task, he leads the work in the direction of increased *rapport/empathy* with the patient, while still emphasizing cognitive techniques—eliciting the patient's thoughts about the writing-down task, and working on rational responses to these thoughts.

In a full session, the preceding exchange would constitute only a small initial segment. The subsequent work could take a multitude of directions, with the supervisor perhaps modeling empathy/inquiry; reassigning the therapist/patient roles to other group members; rapidly alternating patient/therapist roles; eliciting rational responses to the patient's negative automatic thoughts; and, finally, outlining an integrated strategy—or several possible strategies—for the trainee's next session with the patient. As the trainees become more practiced, group work proceeds rapidly, allowing discussion of more than one vignette per session. For each case, the approach remains two-fold, with emphasis upon the acquisition of technical and interpersonal skills.

ADVANTAGES FOR THE THERAPIST-IN-TRAINING

After only a few weeks of work, our trainee therapists began to recognize distinct advantages of group supervision in comparison with other modes. These advantages were apparent in areas of both technical growth and professional confidence/self-esteem factors.

Technical Advantages

One of the most obvious technical advantages is that a group supervision format gives each trainee exposure to a far greater number of "problem" cases than he or she would encounter if limited to his or her own personal case load. This broader exposure means the trainee will gain familiarity with the full gamut of cognitive–behavioral techniques stimulated by the larger number of cases. In group supervision the trainee not only learns from the cases he or she personally presents, but also from each case that others present as well. Each new case represents an opportunity to evolve therapeutic strategies rapidly and then to practice the cognitive-behavioral techniques required to implement these strategies. The result of this experience can be dramatic, rapid learning. This is perhaps understandable if we recognize that trainees are, in a sense, "treating" and learning from four to five patient pools in addition to their own.

The group context also facilitates the learning of interpersonal/communication skills. When a trainee assumes the therapist role in a case vignette, the supervisor and other group members can provide immediate feedback on the therapist's interpersonal handling of the "patient." The novice therapist immediately can find out how his or her approach is "heard" from several individual perspectives, and can practice altering that approach in accord with observations distilled from the group comments. The group context is supportive and nonjudgmental, making group comments welcome as opposed to dreaded.

In addition to providing exposure to multiple case sources of feedback on technical and interpersonal skills, group supervision gives the trainee therapist another advantage: the presence of multiple role modes for refining skills in both these areas. In individual supervision, the trainee often is left with the choice of adopting the technique/style of the supervisor (which may be limiting, uncomfortable, or inappropriate), or gradually developing his or her own working methods by trial—and very often, error. Group supervision largely eliminates this difficulty; the novice has multiple role models—peers and supervisor—for modeling cognitive techniques and interpersonal skills. The trainee can pick and choose freely among these models, adopting techniques and communication skills as he or she finds it useful. The greater availability of the role models increases the likelihood that the trainee will find techniques that are more comfortable, more natural, and thus probably more effective for him or her as a therapist.

Professional Confidence/Mood Factors

Although increased therapeutic effectiveness is an important bottom line, group supervision in cognitive therapy also yields personal and professional benefits for the beginning therapist. Most of these benefits have to do with reduced anxiety, increased confidence, and increased immunity to buying into the patient's feelings of hopelessness and frustration.

As beginners, novice therapists often are somewhat anxious and insecure about their therapeutic skills. Individual supervision with a seasoned clinician does little to allay these concerns, since the experienced therapist frequently appears to "know more" than the trainee. Group supervision, on the other hand, provides a more realistic reference group against which the beginner can assess his or her developing skills. In the group, he or she can observe that others—even skilled others—can have "problem" cases. This realization in itself often serves to reduce anxiety and insecurity about professional competence. Comparing skills within an appropriate reference groups, with a realistic appraisal of developing strengths and weaknesses, actually can increase confidence.

The group supervision process also proves an effective antidote to the frustration and hopelessness experienced by beginners in the face of a difficult case. The process of arming the therapist with a number of fresh approaches can help reduce the therapist's feelings of frustration and hopelessness. Trainees commonly report coming to the conference feeling overwhelmed by a particular patient and leaving the conference feeling much more confident and optimistic.

Finally, group supervision may be able to prevent the novice therapist from suffering embarrassment or other difficulty resulting from inappropriate handling of a case. Alert group members may be able to "troubleshoot" a difficult case *before* problems occur by anticipating possible crises (suicidal threats, sexual overtures, acting out, and so forth) and pre-planning a course of action with the training therapist.

It also can be helpful for group members to use cognitive techniques in coping with anxiety and other so-called countertransference reactions that develop in dealing with difficult patients (for a more detailed discussion of this approach, see Burns, 1980, pp. 349–360). Therapists are encouraged to write down their automatic thoughts and to develop rational responses to them. Other group members can be helpful in facilitating this. For example, a therapist felt angry and guilty when a patient persistently failed to do self-help assignments in spite of promises to the contrary. The therapist had these automatic thoughts: "My patient is being passive-aggressive. I'm trying my best, so he *should* do his part. Actually I *shouldn't* be reacting this way. A therapist *should* be more objective. A professional *shouldn't* get so angry. Other therapists would be handling this better." With the help of the group, these rational responses were generated: "It won't be helpful to blame him or to label him as passive–aggressive. It would be far better to find out *why* he has difficulty doing self-help assignments by asking about his automatic thoughts. It's a fairy tale that therapists never feel angry or frustrated. While it's not comfortable to feel this way, it shows that I'm quite human and I don't need to be ashamed of that. Over time, I will learn not to feel so upset when patients procrastinate since this is a common therapeutic problem." The therapist reported that looking at it this way helped him feel some relief. The group then helped him develop a list of strategies for breaking the therapeutic log-jam with this particular patient.

It can be noted that these benefits of the group supervision process are really more than pleasant incidentals; therapists who are anxious, insecure, underconfident, frustrated, and overwhelmed will have difficulty delivering the best patient care, however good their intentions or their technical skill. Increased control in these areas will lead to increased therapeutic effectiveness.

ADVANTAGES FOR THE SUPERVISING THERAPIST

The group supervision model of cognitive therapy training also has distinct advantages for the supervising therapist. Prominent among these is increased time efficiency. Using a group supervision model, a senior therapist can train six therapists in the same amount of time (one hour per week) usually alloted for one trainee in individual supervision. Training effectiveness is not sacrificed but actually may be enhanced. A four- to six-fold increase in time efficiency, with no apparent loss in teaching effectiveness, may endear this mode of training to supervisors pressed for time but eager to teach and maintain contact with students.

Another advantage for the supervising therapist is the vast number of "teaching tools" at his or her disposal. In individual supervision, the supervisor's teaching is limited by his or her own imagination and that of the single trainee. After a time, supervisor and trainee often evolve certain predictable approaches or interactions that can block fresh, innovative solutions. In group supervision, on the other hand, the training potential is tremendously expanded. The supervisor may use any group member or combination of group members to illustrate a strategy or work out a technique. Each trainee not only learns while participating in the exercise, but also functions as a tool so that others learn from him or her. As training proceeds and the supervisor becomes more familiar with the relative strengths and weaknesses of group members, he or she can orchestrate the supervision appropriately. If a student is particularly facile with rational responses, for example, the therapist may pair this trainee with one who is less skilled at rational responding and then encourage role playing of automatic thoughts/rational responses, with rapid and frequent role reversals.

The group supervision format also serves as a natural forum for discovery of new cognitive–behavioral techniques and refinement of familiar techniques. These sessions provide an opportunity to examine theoretical concepts underlying the techniques taught and to work on theoretical refinements suggested by the clinical data at hand. Group supervision sessions also may trigger research ideas and lead to experiments that further understanding of cognitive therapy processes. Several promising studies of the relationship between cognition and mood have been initiated by members of the preception group.

ADVANTAGES FOR THE PATIENT

Advantages for patient care may be apparent at this point, but are worth stating. Group supervision provides a training ground in which beginning therapists are given exposure to a wide range of cases and techniques, increasing the probability that they will adopt an effective approach for a given patient. This is especially important because of the high incidence of suicidal impulses among patients being treated for depression. Many research studies have documented that the patient's belief he or she never can improve is based on illogical thinking and has a high correlation with suicidal urges and attempts (Beck & Burns, 1978; Beck, Kovacs, & Weissman, 1975; Wetzel, 1976). Since some patients seem to have the capacity to persuade friends, associates, and even their therapist that they *are* hopeless, the novice therapist may feel threatened and be unable to pinpoint and reverse the distortions in the patient's persistently pessimistic thinking. The group can help the therapist develop effective strategies to reverse the patient's hopelessness and engage him or her in a collaborative therapeutic relationship. Some of the strategies developed by members of our group are now in press (Burns & Persons, 1982).

The therapist receives grounding in interpersonal skills that facilitate communication with the patient, allowing the patient to feel understood as well as "helped." The therapist himself is less anxious, more secure, and more confident—a better executor of the chosen therapeutic strategy. For a specific patient, multiple "case solutions" are generated and considered by the group. The final therapeutic choice(s) will reflect an optimal distillation of the supervisor's accumulated knowledge and the group members' varied perspectives, maximizing the probability of therapeutic success. A patient under the care of a group supervision trainee enjoys the benefits of a patient with several doctors constantly consulting and guiding treatment, but without the cost that actuality would entail.

TABLE 1

A Comparison of Apprenticeship, Individual Supervision, and Group
Supervision Cognitive Therapy

Apprenticeship	Individual supervision[a]	Group supervision
Modelling supervisor's skills	Verbal guidance from supervisor	Increased support/confidence for trainee
Guided use of techniques	Post hoc suggestions	Multiple sources of feedback for trainee
Short term strategies	Experience in long-term strategies	Exposure to larger number of cases/techniques
Rapid, specific feedback	Delayed, general feedback	Increased therapeutic effectiveness
External reward:praise	Internal reward:mastery	Increased time efficiency for supervisor
		Increased teaching effectiveness for supervisor

[a]Group supervision also supplies these benefits.

COMPARISON OF INDIVIDUAL PRECEPTION, APPRENTICESHIP AND GROUP SUPERVISION

In a recent article, Moorey and Burns (1982) compared several features of individual preception versus apprenticeship. As seen in Table 1, group supervision offers features characteristics of both these modalities. A group supervision session often will include replay, commentary, and *ad hoc* guidance characteristic of individual supervision, and then rapidly shift to an *in vivo* treatment situation with all the immediacy characteristic of an apprenticeship mode, but without the pressure of an actual treatment situation. For the trainee, group supervision allows exposure to a greater number of cases/techniques, provides increased moral support, encourages a realistic assessment of skills relative to a peer group, and offers multiple sources of feedback and ideas for the management of difficult patients. Advantages for the supervisor include increased time efficiency and increased teaching effectiveness.

SUMMARY

Group supervision has been used for training in other psychotherapies with varying success (Matarazzo, 1971; Traux & Carkhuff,

1967). At this point there are no studies that have determined empirically the relative effectiveness of different supervision modalities in either the teaching of cognitive therapy or in patient outcome measures. Probably an ideal teaching model would utilize all these modalities. It appears that group supervision is an outstanding teaching vehicle for cognitive therapy training which offers multiple advantages to the trainee, supervisor, and patient.

APPENDIX

Techniques Introduced in Group Supervision in Cognitive Therapy

A. Cognitive/behavioral techniques
   1. *Triple-Column technique:* Patient writes down negative automatic thoughts, the cognitive distortions they contain, and possible rational responses to the thoughts in a three-column format.
   2. *Daily record of dysfunctional thoughts:* An elaboration of the triple-column technique to include the situation giving rise to the automatic thoughts and feelings caused by the automatic thoughts. Degree of feeling and extent of belief in the automatic thoughts are initially rated and then re-rated following work on rational responses.
   3. *Externalization of voices:* The patient's inner dialogue—in the form of automatic thoughts/criticism, and so forth—is externalized, voiced, and acted out by the therapist and patient, with focus on developing rational responses to the negative automatic thoughts.
   4. *Role playing:* Therapist and patient "play out" situations that give the patient difficulty (such as job interviews or asking someone for a date) with emphasis upon developing the appropriate social skills.
   5. *Labeling of cognitive distortions:* Patient is given a list of common cognitive distortions or "thought traps" and learns to recognize the distortions inherent in his or her automatic thoughts, recognizing that these distortions are the trigger for negative feelings.
   6. *"Collecting evidence"—"Conducting experiments":* Patient is asked for confirming or disconfirming evidence to a given

belief—and may be asked to conduct a test of the belief, that is, to see if his or her spouse will reject him or her if they disagree.

7. *Pleasure predicting sheet:* A before and after sheet used in helping the patient to test his or her belief that nothing give him or her satisfaction or that he or she cannot find pleasure in doing things alone. The patient lists a variety of activities with a potential for growth or enjoyment and predicts ahead of time how satisfying each of them will be using a zero to one hundred rating scale. After the activity has been completed, he records how satisfying it actually was, using the same rating scale.

8. *Graded task assignment:* Large, seemingly overwhelming tasks are broken down into small, manageable components and then assigned to the patient.

9. *Stress innoculation:* The therapist assumes an attacking role, bombarding the patient with increasingly difficult criticisms that the patient in turn learns to counter, "innoculating" him or her to future stress from those thoughts.

10. *BIAS Test (Burns Interpersonal Attitude Scale):* A 93-item scale designed to pinpoint dysfunctional belief clusters that lead to interpersonal conflict.

11. *BDI (Beck Depression Inventory):* A 21-item scale measuring the severity of depression and useful in monitoring the patient's weekly progress.

B. Interpersonal/communication skills

These techniques are useful in management of the difficult, angry, or "resistant" patient. They are used to increase rapport and to decrease polarization/conflict. They also can be taught to patients for their use in managing conflict or responding more effectively to criticism.

1. *Empathy*

(a) *Thought empathy:* Paraphasing the other person's thoughts to let him or her know that you understand what he or she is thinking. For example, suppose the patient has not been doing self-help assignments. When the therapist asks about this the patient says "being told to do all this written homework is a pain in the neck. It's a waste of time. It's just like being in school again." The therapist can say, "I take it you think the written homework assignments wouldn't really help you and they remind you of being in school again. Is that how you see it?"

(b) *Feeling empathy:* Acknowledging the person's feelings behind his or her thoughts, for example, the therapist might
say, "I can see how you might be feeling frustrated or bossed
around if you're being forced to do something that you're not
convinced will help you. Is that how you feel?"

2. *Disarming:* Finding the "grain of truth" in the other person's
argument (however unreasonable it seems) and repeating it
actually will have the paradoxical effect of melting oppositional feelings. In the above dialogue, the therapist might
disarm the angry patient by saying, "It sounds like you need
more time to get your feelings off your chest and to receive
some feeling of support from me. Sometimes the therapy can
seem too preoccupied with techniques, and not sufficiently
warm and human. Is this how I've been coming across?"

3. *Inquiry:* Use of questions to find out more about the other's
thoughts and feelings, with the goal of turning negative criticisms into a concrete problem, "What in particular did I say
or do that turned you off?"

4. *Stroking:* Expressions of positive regard for the other person
(even in the heat of disagreement) will tend to cool his or her
angry feelings and and make the person more receptive to
your point.

5. *Tactful self-expression:* Expression of thoughts, needs, and feelings in a constructive, objective, noncoercive way.

6. *Problem solving and negotiation:* Define the problem in concrete
terms, developing options, and negotiating while taking into
account each person needs.

References

Beck, A. T., & Burns, D. Cognitive therapy of depressed suicidal outpatients. In J. O. Cole,
A. F. Schatzberg, & S. H. Frazier (Eds.), *Depression: Biology, psychodynamics and treatment.* New York: Plenum, 1978.

Beck, A. T., Kovacs, M., & Weissman, A. Hopelessness and suicidal behavior: An overview. *Journal of the American Medical Association,* 1975, *234,* 1146–1149.

Beck, A. T., Rush, A. J., Shaw, B. F., & Emery, J. *Cognitive therapy of depression.* New York:
Guilford, 1979.

Burns, D. D. *Feeling good: The new mood therapy.* New York: Morrow, 1980.

Burns, D. D., & Persons, J. B. Hope and hopelessness: A cognitive approach. In L. E. Abt
& I. R. Stuart (Eds.), *The new therapies: A sourcebook.* New York: Van Nostrand
Reinhold, 1982.

Matarazzo, R. Research on the teaching and learning of psychotherapeutic skills. In A.

Bergin & S. Garfield (Eds.), *Handbook of psychotherapy and behavioral change.* New York: Wiley, 1971.

Moorey, S., & Burns, D. D. The apprenticeship model of cognitive therapy training. Unpublished manuscript, in press.

Traux, C., & Carkhuff, R. *Toward effective counseling and psychotherapy: training and practice.* Chicago: Aldine, 1967.

Wetzel, R. D. Hopelessness, depression and suicidal intent. *Archives General* Psychiatry, 1976, *30*, 1069–1073.

Index